African Sacred Groves

D0732734

African Sacred Groves
Ecological Dynamics
& Social Change

EDITED BY
Michael J. Sheridan
& Celia Nyamweru

JAMES CURREY
OXFORD

OHIO UNIVERSITY PRESS
ATHENS, OH

UNISA PRESS
PRETORIA

James Currey Ltd
73 Botley Road
Oxford
OX2 0BS

Unisa Press
P.O. Box 392
Unisa
Muckleneuk 0003

Ohio University Press
19 Circle Drive
The Ridges
Athens OH 45701-2979

1 2 3 4 5 6 13 12 11 10 09 08

British Library Cataloguing in Publication Data
African sacred groves : ecological dynamics & social change
1. Sacred groves - Africa, Sub-Saharan 2. Forest
conservation - Social aspects - Africa, Sub-Saharan
I. Sheridan, Michael J. II. Nyamweru, Celia
306.6'0967

ISBN 978-1-84701-400-9 (James Currey paper)
ISBN 978-1-84701-401-6 (James Currey cloth)
ISBN 978-1-86888-494-0 (Unisa Press paper)

Library of Congress Cataloging-in-Publication Data
available on request

ISBN-10 0-8214-1788-6 (Ohio University Press Cloth)
ISBN-13 978-0-8214-1788-1 (Ohio University Press Cloth)
ISBN-10 0-8214-1789-4 (Ohio University Press Paper)
ISBN-13 978-0-8214-1789-8 (Ohio University Press Paper)

Typeset in 10.6/11.6 pt Bembo by Long House Publishing Services
Printed and bound in Malaysia

Contents

List of Figures, Tables & Photographs

Notes on Contributors

Liz Alden Wily, Ph.D., is a political scientist specializing in customary land tenure and natural resource management, and works as an independent consultant. Most of her work concerns land tenure and forest management reform in Africa, particularly as relating to common property rights.

Joseph Bahati is a senior lecturer in the Department of Biology and Ecosystems Management at Makerere University, Kampala, Uganda. He has research interests in silviculture and forest ecology, and is also a database manager for the Uganda Forestry Resources and Institutions Center.

Abwoli Y. Banana is an associate professor in the Department of Forest Products Engineering at Makerere University, Kampala, Uganda. He is co-leader of the Uganda Forestry Resources and Institutions Center, which is studying the relationship between local communities and their forests in Uganda. He also studies how institutions affect access, use and condition of forest resources.

Mohamed Berriane is Dean of the Faculty of Letters and Human Sciences at Mohammed V – Adgal University in Rabat, Morocco. His research concerns issues of tourism, migration and ecology and their roles in local and regional development in Morocco and North Africa.

Gérard Chouin received his M.Phil. in African history at the University of Paris-I, Panthéon-Sorbonne, and plans to receive his Ph.D. in anthropology from Syracuse University in 2007. He has taught at the University of Paris-I, the University of Ghana-Legon and the University of Cape Coast. His research agenda addresses the intersections of archaeology, history, environmental studies and development studies. He currently works for the French Ministry of Foreign Affairs as the director of a French language and cultural centre in eastern Nigeria.

John Cooke is Dean of the Faculty of Science and Agriculture at the University of KwaZulu-Natal, South Africa. He is a professor of environmental biology and his broad research interests in applied ecology include ethno-ecology, reclamation ecology and ecotoxicology.

Heike Culmsee is a lecturer in the Department of Vegetation and Phytodiversity Analysis of the Albrecht-von-Haller Institute for Plant Sciences at the

University of Goettingen, Germany. His research addresses human impacts on the spatial biodiversity of desert ecosystems in northwest Africa, tropical rain forests in Indonesia, and agrarian landscapes in Germany.

Ulrich Deil is a professor and director of the Department of Geobotany at the University of Freiburg, Germany. He specializes in the vegetation and ecology of Mediterranean and desert ecosystems; human impacts on biodiversity, landscape and vegetation structure; and the comparative analysis of traditional and modern managed landscapes. He has extensive research experience in the European Mediterranean, northwest Africa, and the Arabian Peninsula.

William Gombya-Ssembajjwe is an associate professor in the Department of Forest Management at Makerere University, Kampala, Uganda. He co-directs the Uganda Forestry Resources and Institutions Center, which coordinates research on social forestry in Uganda. His research interests include forest economics and management, policy and institutional analysis.

Alma Gottlieb is an Africanist cultural anthropologist working in the interpretive tradition. A past Guggenheim Fellow, she is the author most recently of *The Afterlife Is Where We Come from*. She is a professor of anthropology at the University of Illinois at Urbana-Champaign.

Nadia Rabesahala Horning teaches political science at Middlebury College. She was an international development consultant for Associates in Rural Development (ARD, Inc.) before beginning her doctoral studies at Cornell University. Her doctoral research concerned the institutional aspects of natural resource management in her native country of Madagascar, and her current work focuses on the comparative politics of nature conservation in Kenya, Madagascar and Uganda.

Staline Kibet is an ethnobotanist and plant ecologist at the National Museums of Kenya. Currently he coordinates the East African portion of the Survey of Economic Plants for Arid and Semi-Arid Lands Project (SEPASAL) in partnership with the Royal Botanic Gardens Kew, Great Britain.

Aiah Randolph Lebbie has a Ph.D. in forestry from the University of Wisconsin-Madison and is a Lecturer at Njala University College in Sierra Leone. He was born and raised in Sierra Leone and continues to teach, conduct research and consult there on issues of resource management and conservation of forests and wildlife, especially with respect to ethnobotany, conservation of sacred groves and endangered wildlife.

Celia Nyamweru teaches in the Department of Anthropology and the African Studies Program at St. Lawrence University in Canton, New York. She was born in England, where she earned her degrees in geography from Cambridge University. She first traveled to Kenya in 1965 and subsequently taught at Kenyan universities for 20 years. She has done research in Kenya and other parts of Africa on a wide array of topics including paleoclimatology, volcanology, Ugandan barkcloth and the conservation of natural sacred sites.

Mohamed Pakia was born in Kwale District, Kenya, and attended Egerton University and the University of Natal before receiving his Ph.D. in ethnobotany from the University of Bayreuth, Germany. He is currently an assistant professor at the University College of Education, Zanzibar, Tanzania.

Eric Ross is a cultural and urban geographer. Born in Turkey, he attended Montreal's English and French universities, earning a degree in Islamic Studies. Since 1998 he has been teaching geography at Al Akhawayn University in Ifrane, Morocco, where he is an associate professor. Ross has conducted research on Sufi institutions and Muslim towns in Senegal. He has also studied cultural heritage, tourism and urban planning in Morocco.

Michael J. Sheridan is an assistant professor of anthropology at Middlebury College. His research focuses on the intersections of material and symbolic processes in African resource management. His primary research site is in the North Pare mountains of northern Tanzania.

Ute Siebert received her Ph.D. in 2003 from the Department of Social Anthropology at the Free University Berlin, Germany. Before and after her Ph.D. studies, she worked in human rights and environmental NGOs such as Transparency International and the German Association for Environmental Protection (NABU). Currently she works as a freelance social anthropologist and artist (fine arts) in Berlin.

Tsehai Berhane-Selassie received her D.Phil in social anthropology from the University of Oxford. She has taught anthropology, development and gender studies in Britain, Ethiopia and the USA, and she currently lectures part-time at Mary Immaculate College, University of Limerick, Ireland. Her publications comprise anthropological studies of history, politics, gender and development in northeastern Africa.

Nathan Vogt, Ph.D., is an associate researcher at the Anthropological Center for Research and Training (ACT) and at the Center for the Study of Institutions, Population, and Environmental Change (CIPEC) at Indiana University in Bloomington, Indiana. His research interests include environmental science and remote sensing.

1
Introduction

CELIA NYAMWERU
& MICHAEL J. SHERIDAN

African sacred groves are often treated as the remains of primeval forests, ethnographic curiosities, and cultural relics from a static pre-colonial past. Their continuing importance in African societies, however, shows that this 'relic theory' is inadequate for understanding current social and ecological dynamics. This interdisciplinary book by an international group of scholars and conservation practitioners provides methodological frameworks for understanding these forests by examining their ecological characteristics and delineating how sacred groves relate to social dynamics and historical contexts. By exploring their political implications as power-laden landscape features, and analyzing their symbolic and ideological aspects, the authors also evaluate the groves' strengths and weaknesses as sites for community-based resource management and the conservation of cultural and biological diversity in Africa. Each chapter in this volume demonstrates that ecology, socio-political organization, and symbolism intersect in African sacred groves. The volume demonstrates that rather than privileging one form of analysis from a single disciplinary perspective, trans-disciplinary approaches that focus on intersecting dynamic processes offer deeper insight into the form, function, and meanings of sacred groves in Africa. Without such an appreciation of their complexity, conservation programs that seek to build upon the strengths of African sacred groves are likely to fall short.

Sheridan's review of the literature on sacred groves in Africa (and beyond) in Chapter 2 outlines the key themes explored in this book's case studies. A common assumption in the literature on sacred groves is that they are static forms of climax vegetation and peak cultural florescence. This 'relic theory' is based on outdated notions of tropical ecology and African societies. Recent work in both the natural and social sciences show that African ecosystems and social systems are dynamic at different temporal and spatial scales. Sheridan draws on the recent literature in non-equilibrium ecology to argue that African forests are dynamic processes that have long intersected with changing African societies. Similarly, he shows how the institutional forms and functions of African sacred groves relate to settlement patterns, migration, and land tenure processes. Sheridan reviews the meanings of trees in Africa and shows how these key symbols relate to both group identities and Africans' experiences of colonization and rapid social (and cognitive) change. Finally, he argues for a 'hybrid science' that gives equal weight to ecological, social, and symbolic factors, and which can contribute to the development of adaptive co-management systems at local, regional, and global levels.

The eleven case studies that make up this book are grouped into four parts. In Part 1, 'The Human Ecology of Sacred Groves,' examples from Sierra Leone, Kenya and Morocco are used to illustrate the impacts that different human activities have on the vegetation composition of sacred groves. In Chapter 3 Lebbie and Guries draw on fieldwork performed at 14 groves in Moyamba District of Sierra Leone to show that these groves, despite their small size (they range from one to six hectares in area) are floristically rich in terms of native woody plant species. This is so even though at the time of the survey (1994–1995) several of the groves were in relatively early stages of recovery from major disturbances. Most of these groves owe their protection to the secret *poro* and *sande* societies, who control access to them, allowing occasional access to harvest woody plants of medicinal value for personal use. Unlike the situations in Kenya and Uganda respectively described by Nyamweru *et al.* in Chapter 4 and Banana *et al.* in Chapter 12, there was no evidence of active timber harvesting from these groves at the time of Lebbie and Guries' survey. Lebbie and Guries conclude by stressing the importance of these small forested areas as sources of both cultural pride and biological diversity. However, they warn that the groves have probably been at risk of destruction or degradation during Sierra Leone's decade-long civil conflict (1991–2002) and stress the need to involve local communities in the management of the groves, as state claims to ownership and management are unenforceable and often serve to alienate local communities.

In Chapter 4 Nyamweru, Kibet, Pakia and Cooke describe the situation at three kaya forests, the sacred groves of the Mijikenda people of coastal Kenya. Here, despite the involvement of local communities in conservation initiatives, the extraction of woody plants (particularly to meet house building and firewood needs in local communities) continues. Similar to the Sierra Leone groves, the kaya forests cannot be considered 'pristine' vegetation communities; signs of disturbance are widespread and the environmental history of this region includes both physical and human processes that have kept the vegetation in a constant state of flux, responding to external forces. However, the indigenous belief systems have, as in Sierra Leone, served to limit intensive use of plant products from the kaya forests, though the power of these controls has weakened significantly over recent decades. Pakia's fieldwork at Kaya Mtswakara and Kaya Fungo showed that the harvesting of building poles was having a significant impact on forest composition, with a loss of canopy tree species, transformation of dense forest to wooded grassland and scrubland, and the entry of invasive species. At Kaya Mudzimuvya, Kibet's mapping identified several different plant communities, with closed forest dominating in all areas to which access was limited by taboos and the existence of supernatural powers, and more open vegetation in areas subject to less powerful sanctions. In Kenya, as in Sierra Leone, the full involvement of local communities in forest conservation is the key to the survival of these increasingly threatened sites.

The third case study in Part I is from a very different socio-cultural context, namely the Islamic region of the North African Maghreb. Deil, Culmsee and Berriane describe the conservation role played by Muslim saints' tombs in Chapter 5, with particular reference to two Moroccan sacred sites. The surroundings of these tombs are used today as burial grounds by local people and often shelter small patches of forest vegetation in otherwise intensively cultivated regions. The authors describe the results of vegetation analysis to show how these areas are characterized by fine-grained vegetation mosaics including evergreen sclerophyllous forests, thorny thickets and many annual flowering plants. These different vegetation types tend to be distributed in a repetitive spatial pattern which shows a zonation from the inner sacred area (surrounded by forest) to more open grassy vegetation at the outer fringes. This zonation can be related to the multiple forms and intensities of moderate use that continue at these sites today, including pasturing of small domestic livestock, small-scale burning and grave digging. The zonation at these Moroccan sites parallels the situation at Kaya Mudzimuvya in Kenya, where vegetation cover reflects the fact that the 'most sacred' areas tend to be more lightly used than the marginal and less sacred areas, subject to frequent extraction of woody plants. Deil *et al.* stress the importance of the social and symbolic context within which the vegetation at these Moroccan sacred sites is protected, but caution that modern socio-cultural trends including the conversion of 'traditional' pilgrimages into commercialized events for domestic tourism may put these small sites at risk of further degradation.

In Part 2, 'The Social Organization of Sacred Groves,' three contrasting case studies illustrate different socio-political contexts within which sacred groves are, or are not, protected. Tsehai Berhane-Selassie's account of Ethiopian sacred groves in Chapter 6 shows how religious beliefs inform the social construction of power, which then shapes ecological relationships. Most Ethiopians consider sacred groves to be mysterious and incomprehensible places, and rely on groups of specialists to link the social and cosmological worlds through social action. These specialists or ritual experts often belong to endogamous low status groups (sometimes referred to as 'artisans') with occupational specializations other than agriculture, and political events over the last 30 years have brought drastic changes in their status. Tsehai Berhane-Selassie shows how the Illubabor sacred forest in Dizi, western Ethiopia, was a symbol of the legitimate land tenure claims of Dizi farmers, who relied on the ritual experts to perform the sacrifices necessary to maintain regional fertility and well-being. Government intervention, in part to change the older socio-political system in which artisans were subordinate to farmers, has created a contradictory and ambiguous situation in which no sacrifices are carried out in the Illubabor sacred grove although this is desired by most local residents. At

Lake Abaya, forced relocation of the artisans (locally known as *Chinasa*) and their conversion from potters to farmers on land that once had a sacred grove has led to the degradation of the same forest where they had once conducted rituals for all of local society. Though the Ethiopian Orthodox Church occupies a very different position in society from the marginalized artisans, the situation of the several thousand church woodlands (surrounding churches, monasteries, nunneries and natural healing centres such as springs, wells and rivers) is also precarious, as over recent decades the church has lost the authority to enforce respect for its lands and forests. From these case studies Tsehai Berhane-Selassie shows that even though various hierarchical processes have tended to dissolve the linkages between Ethiopian sacred groves and community belief systems, the groves do not simply become irrelevant. Though the local socio-politics of sacred ecosystems is dynamic, most social actors treat the meanings, categories and values of sacred groves as fixed and static, and development planners and conservationists need to pay attention to these culture-specific ways of valuing landscapes.

In Chapter 7 Horning describes Analavelona sacred forest in southwestern Madagascar, which a comparison between aerial photographs taken in 1949 and satellite images from 1989 shows to be exceptionally well conserved, considering the degradation of much of this nation's forests. By comparing the socio-economic situations in two communities that border the forest, she shows that traditional community rules governing access to forest resources seek to maintain orderly ecological, social and moral relationships, and that each of the two communities has its own set of traditional rules about the sacred forest. Horning also discusses the fractious relationship between state and community rules controlling access to the forests, and shows how it is easier to avoid sanctions for breaking state rules than it is with community rules. Individuals have the option of paying fines or offering bribes if they break state rules; in contrast, when community rules are broken the spirits do not negotiate and harsh sanctions are perceived as imminent and inescapable. In conclusion, Horning suggests that the continued conservation of Analavelona sacred forest results from the fact that the local communities have by and large contained outsiders' intrusion into the management of community affairs, and that there is a broad convergence between state and community interests in forest conservation in this area.

Ross describes a very different example of sacred 'forests', in Chapter 8 focusing on the large, often solitary, individual trees found in many Senegalese settlements which go by the general name of 'palaver trees'. Baobab (*Adansonia digitata*) and kapok (*Ceiba pentandra*) are among the most common palaver trees, which may be 'foundation trees' that play important historical roles in the construction and maintenance of collective identities. Kings were crowned beneath certain trees, held court and administered justice beneath others, and were buried beneath yet others. In a region where public architecture tended to be neither monumental nor permanent, these great trees assumed the symbolic functions of monumentality and permanence, and many of them still stand today. Ross shows how these trees have become incorporated into contemporary Islamic practice, in particular in the settlements established by the

Sufi Mouride movement between the 1880s and the 1950s in previously sparsely inhabited areas of Senegal. As he points out, the modern Sufi movement in Senegal has organized space on older principles of settlement design, in which political and spiritual legitimacy were embedded in palaver trees. Despite the rapid urbanization currently in progress in Senegal, as in most other African countries, the palaver tree remains a potent embodiment of political and social concepts, and thirteen of them have been classified as historic monuments by the Senegalese Government.

Part 3, 'The Symbol of Forests,' draws on three West African case studies to further explore the meaning and symbolism of sacred forests. Gottlieb begins in Chapter 9 with an account of her visit to a forest in the Beng region of Ivory Coast, which to her was 'an organic, singular place whose massiveness seemed forever unknowable'. To her local guide the forest was powerful but certainly not undifferentiated. He demonstrated his ecological knowledge of plant and animal species, his social knowledge of the individual and community rights to forest space and resources, and finally his perception of an entire unseen cosmos – a cultural imaginary whose contours he charted as precisely as he did the more tangible components of the forest. Gottlieb goes on to describe the different forest-dwelling spirits and the religious practitioners who maintain ties with them on behalf of other individuals and the community at large. The spirits are said to live in human-like villages in the forest, located in specific sites that Beng adults can readily identify; they are gendered and have the same bodily desires as humans. While the Beng routinely try to accord the spirits respect, this is not true of all visitors to the region, and Gottlieb describes a situation in which loggers cut down several *iroko* (*Chlorophora excelsa*) trees without offering the resident spirits propitiatory sacrifices in advance. Several loggers were injured or even killed by the very trees they were endeavouring to fell, and this has been interpreted as the result of the forest spirits' revenge. At the time of writing, the security situation in this region was such that logging activity had been totally disrupted, in contrast to the situation in Sierra Leone described by Lebbie and Guries who fear that civil conflict may have increased the risk of forest destruction. However, Gottlieb is not optimistic about the long-term future of these forests, pointing out that nearly all of the iroko trees in the Beng region have already been cut down, and that the timber companies have focused entirely on short-term gain at the expense of sustainable yields or survival of the forest. As the trees they call home are destroyed, the forest spirits will move in search of new homes.

Loggers have also been at work in the Bassila region of northern Bénin where Siebert did fieldwork in 1999 and 2000. At Igbéré the loggers were keen to cut large trees growing in the circle of sacred forest that surrounded the village, and the forest priest asked the two forest gods for permission for this to be done. Both gods agreed in exchange for compensatory sacrifices, and the forest ring survives. At Kikélé the negotiations were between village elders and young men, who needed more land to cultivate and, as Muslims, started to interpret the old ceremonies and taboos around the forest god as pagan practices. A compromise was worked out; in exchange for a compensatory sacrifice, the young men were allowed to cut part of the forest circle if they left enough trees around the god's shrine to keep him hidden and shaded from the sun. Siebert's other case studies further support her point that these communities demonstrate a flexible attitude to protective norms, which may result in the diminution of forests or even in the substitution of a forest by a single tree. Sacred forests, as she demonstrates in Chapter 10, are not static institutions. Further, the powers and attractiveness of the forest gods do not seem to have decreased with the transformation of their abodes. However, Siebert also draws attention to the fact that while the historical and spiritual aspects of sacred forests may enhance the motivation for conservation, they do not present sufficient motivation by themselves. In communities where there are no alternative sources of future income, many informants pointed to the need to exploit their remaining forests.

Chouin's contribution (Chapter 11) examines sacred groves in the village of Nsadwer in coastal Ghana to make a distinction between the social processes that created sacred groves and the subsequent uses of those groves. This categorization is important because it allows him to demonstrate that the original reasons for having a sacred grove in pre-colonial Africa may be quite different from the trees' social purposes in the colonial period and in the present. As an archaeologist, Chouin is particularly interested in how these dissimilar processes can result in the same landscape features. He uses the concept of *lieux de mémoire* (places of memory) to discuss how sacred groves are key sites for African societies' reconceptualization of their pasts to suit their needs in the present. He provides a particularly interesting example of this process in his discussion of how 'urbanized' sacred groves in southern Ghana are being replaced by enclosures of concrete blocks with no loss of sacredness. As he says, sacred groves can erase history but recycle memory, and conservation policy-making itself reproduces African sacred groves as *lieux de mémoire*.

Finally in Part 4 of the book we look to 'The Future of African Sacred Groves.' Banana, Gombya-Ssembajjwe, Bahati and Vogt describe two sacred groves in southern Uganda, Magezigoomu and Mukasa, in Chapter 12. These small forests (16 and 4 hectares respectively) are located close to each other and controlled by the same ethnic group (the Baganda) and clan (the Kayozi clan), but are subject to different rules of access. At Magezigoomu community members are permitted to hunt wild game and gather wild fruits and firewood for subsistence use, while at Mukasa no such uses are permitted; it is a shrine to worship the god Mukasa for the provision of rain, good health and good luck. The question raised in this chapter is whether the difference in rules of access has any discernible impact on the vegetation status of these forests, now and for the foreseeable future. Are people more likely to conserve a forest from which they can harvest useful resources, or one whose value is seen as purely cultural or spiritual? Botanical surveys done in 1995 and 2000 showed that Magezigoomu was significantly more degraded than Mukasa; at Magezigoomu there was no evidence of self-policing or any other form of collective action by the community to protect this forest patch from degradation. Mukasa (despite being a smaller forest patch) showed no evidence at all of any form of degradation in 1995, and in only 20 per cent of the sample plots in 2000. Banana *et al.* conclude that the integrity of Mukasa forest is at present secure, though they go on to speculate that the reason for this may not be the presence of an effective monitoring and rule enforcement institution, but rather the fear by the community of snakes that are reported to be numerous in this forest patch. They stress the need to revitalize the indigenous systems for managing common pool resources such as sacred forests by appropriate legislation at the national level, in particular by registering them as Community Forests.

The question of legislation is extended to an Africa-wide focus in the concluding chapter (13) by Alden Wily, in which she examines the legal status of forests in sub-Saharan Africa. She stresses the dynamic nature of African forest policy and legislation; at least 40 of Africa's 56 mainland and island states have new national forest policies and/or laws to hand, and implementation is widespread. A review of thirteen cases of new forest laws provided mixed results, in terms of the recognition given to the socio-cultural uses and values of forests. Of these, only four countries (Lesotho, Mainland Tanzania, Mozambique and Kenya) make really concrete provision for sacred forests and socio-cultural values in general, in particular in terms of providing significant power to local communities to manage sacred forests. Alden Wily also points out that the legal status of forests cannot be considered in isolation from the broader issue of land tenure and in particular the relationship between customary and formally registered tenure regimes. In many African countries the trend (initiated during the colonial era but often continued under the new African governments) has been to devalue customary tenure regimes and replace them with European-derived forms of individual freehold or leasehold tenure. Such trends have not been favourable to communal property rights over areas of forest, pasture and wildlife rangeland, and have weakened community controls and led to open access tragedies in many places. Alden Wily cites a number of examples from different African countries to show that changing land tenure policies (in particular, the acceptance of customary land rights as statutorily protected) are dramatically improving the capacity of communities to legally hold on to their shared resources, sacred groves included. As in the Uganda case study, she stresses the new legal construct of Community Forests as being of especial importance in this context. However, she ends with a caution that the balance between socio-cultural and economic benefits from forest is not always easy to achieve, and communities are not always united in the value they place on different benefits to be gained from their forests. National legislation has to be implemented at the community level, where the real work of forest conservation goes on.

This survey of African sacred groves has demonstrated how these landscape features are simultaneously ecological, socio-political, and symbolic processes, and so require interdisciplinary analysis. Multiple levels of analysis form an analytical framework for understanding such forests, but this requires ecological analysis to include socio-political and symbolic systems as factors, and symbolic and socio-political analysis to pay close attention to ecology. This sort of 'hybrid science' can, we hope, encourage the sort of hybrid policy-making that can both conserve biodiversity and allow cultural self-determination. Such hybridized policy-making requires African governments to collaborate with local institutions to produce authentically decentralized co-management systems. As examples of local empowerment and institution-building, sacred groves can help to construct sustainable livelihoods in Africa, but only if their dynamism as ecological, social, political, and symbolic processes is fully acknowledged.

2

The Dynamics of African Sacred Groves
Ecological, Social & Symbolic Processes

MICHAEL J. SHERIDAN

Few images evoke the interdependence of nature and society like the term 'sacred grove.' These trees and forests demonstrate the linkages between biodiversity and cosmology and the intersections between the social and the natural sciences. Given current rates of tropical deforestation and the growth of environmentalism in societies at the world's industrialized core, sacred groves have a newfound salience in the twenty-first century. Throughout much of the twentieth century, scholarship on sacred groves depicted them as ethnographic curiosities, indicators of cultural and ecological continuity, and backdrops for social action (Castro 1990). In recent decades, however, the growth of transnational environmentalism (Guha 2000), its linkage with social and economic policy to form 'sustainable development' (WCED 1987), and the search for community participation in conservation efforts (Adams and Hulme 2001, Agrawal and Gibson 1999) has led scholars and policymakers to recognize sacred groves as resource management systems. In 2005, for example, UNESCO convened an international symposium in Tokyo to draft guidelines for the management of sacred natural sites. After reviewing case studies of sacred forests, mountains, and rivers, the participants issued a declaration calling for collaboration between government agencies, non-governmental organizations, and researchers in the social and natural sciences to safeguard 'the cultural and biological diversity embodied in sacred natural sites and cultural landscapes' (UNESCO 2005, see also Dudley *et al.* 2005). The notion that such diversity may be 'safeguarded' implies that conservation policy should keep these sacred natural sites (and, by extension, the ideologies that revere them) in an unchanged state. Given that two of the key factors shaping our planet in the twenty-first century are globalized capitalism and global climate change, however, any ecological and cultural equilibrium will be extraordinarily difficult to maintain. This book responds to these challenges by bringing together scholars and practitioners in the fields of anthropology, botany, forestry, geography, history, and political science to evaluate the status of and prospects for sacred groves in Africa. As will be discussed below, sacred groves have long been considered examples *par excellence* of ahistorical cultural and ecological equilibria, but closer scrutiny shows them to be sites where ecological, social, political, and symbolic dynamics intersect (and disconnect) over time. We therefore focus on Africa's sacred groves as complex dynamics ill-suited for simplifying conservation policies.

Forests make up about 21.8 per cent of Africa's land area, and these represent 24 per cent of the world's total moist tropical forests (Whitmore 1997) and a large proportion of the earth's total biodiversity. Africa's deforestation rate is increasing while other continents show static or decelerating rates (FAO 2005). The World Bank argues that Africa is mired in a Malthusian trap of rapid population growth, static food production, and hapless governments unable to cope with the crisis (Cleaver and Schreiber 1994), which suggests to some that conservation efforts will be trumped by Africans' land hunger (Musters *et al.* 2000). At the same time, forecasts on the effects of global climate change in Africa suggest that the continent is likely to experience extreme climatic variability (Houghton *et al.* 2001) – and this on a continent where a majority of the human population makes a living from the land. The sense of crisis is palpable.

Sacred groves emerged as an issue in African conservation in the 1990s. The failure of many state-led conservation efforts led researchers and policy-makers to look for ways to empower or create community-based institutions for natural resource management (Adams and Hulme 2001, Western *et al.* 1994). Scholars, activists, and policy analysts pressed conservation agencies and governments to decentralize natural resource management and to build upon existing local institutions (Little and Brokensha 1987, Veit *et al.* 1995). Sacred groves epitomize contemporary conservation policy's goals of grassroots participation, sociocultural legitimacy, and demonstrated ecological efficacy. Arguing that sacred groves constitute indigenous conservation areas protected by taboos (see Berkes *et al.* 1998, Colding and Folke 2001), conservationists and development practitioners investigated how to incorporate these forests into conservation policy (e.g., Dorm-Adzobu *et al.* 1991; Gerden and Mtallo 1990, and Robertson and Luke 1993). Agencies and organizations such as UNESCO, Friends of the Earth, the World Wide Fund for Nature (WWF), and the United Nations Development Programme funded community-based conservation projects organized around African sacred groves (respectively, Anane 1997, Schaaf 1998, Nyamweru 1996, and UNDP 2004). In recent years many authors have argued that governments and funding agencies must explore the conservation potential of sacred groves if they are to build effective institutions for conservation and development in Africa (e.g., Anyinam 1999, Madeweya *et al.* 2004, Ntiamoa-Baidu 2001, and Okeke 1999).[1]

African sacred groves interest conservationists for ecological values as well as

---

[1] For examples of the argument that sacred groves are indigenous conservation systems, see Gadgil and Chandran 1992, Apfell-Marglin and Mishra 1993, Basu 2000, Binggeli *et al.* 2003, Fargey 1992, Lebbie and Guries 1995, Mgumia and Oba 2003, Mwihomeke *et al.* 2000, Ntiamoa-Baidu 1993, and Zoundjihekpon and Dossou-Glehouenou 1999.

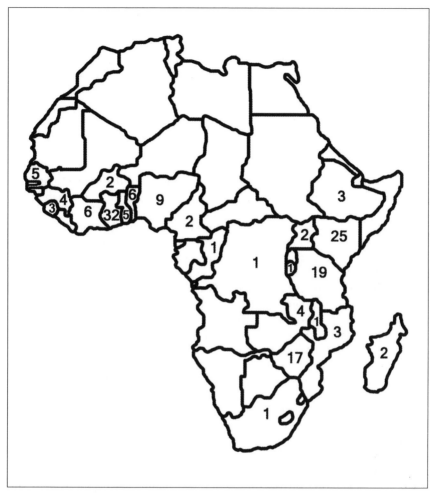

Figure 2.1 Map of the African sacred groves literature, 1913–2006, showing three major geographic zones of scholarship in West and East Africa. The numbers correspond to the amount of books, articles, and reports (of which the author is aware) describing sacred groves in each country. Gaps in coverage probably indicate lack of scholarship more than lack of sacred groves.

their assumed institutional stability. Although the literature features several studies from southeast Asia (Darlington 1998, McWilliam 2001, Sponsel *et al.* 1998, and Wadley and Colfer 2004) and China (Pei 1991), most studies focus on India and Africa. Indeed, environmental interest first emerged in the Indian academic literature, largely in response to Gadgil and Vartak's classic paper (1976) on sacred groves.[2] The literature on sacred groves in Africa reveals four

[2] The literature on sacred groves in India is too voluminous to be summarized here, but for representative works see Chandrakanath and Romm 1991, Chandran and Hughes 1997, Ramakrishnan *et al.* 1998, Freeman 1999, Roy Burham 1995 and Roy Burham 2003. On

dominant research areas: the Guinean-Congolian rainforests of West Africa, the Eastern Arc and Coastal forests of East Africa, and hill forests in both Madagascar and Zimbabwe. With the exception of Zimbabwe, these areas correspond with the 'hotspots' of biodiversity in Africa (Mittermeier et al. 1999). Ecological studies in these areas suggest that human agency is contributing to their rapid deforestation. Madagascar is losing about 100,000 hectares of forest annually (Kull 2004), while Newmark (2002:25) estimates a 76 per cent decline in the area of Kenya and Tanzania's Eastern Arc and Coastal forests over the twentieth century. The situation in West Africa may be even more dire. Current FAO estimates of annual deforestation in the region range from 0.5 per cent (Guinea) to 3.4 per cent (Togo) of these countries' forested areas (FAO 2005:134).[3] In addition to the incalculable value of lost biodiversity, this deforestation process undermines the sustainability of agrarian livelihoods across Africa by changing hydrology, pollination patterns, soil nutrient cycling, and other 'ecosystem services'. The declining availability of forest products – ranging from medicinal herbs to building materials – will also threaten livelihoods already made precarious by the inequalities of the global political and economic system. Sacred groves therefore represent opportunities to conserve both biological and cultural diversity while also enhancing the sustainability of rural livelihoods (Anyinam 1999).

Although many authors agree that African sacred groves have great potential as authentically participatory decentralized land management systems, most also confirm that these stands of socially significant trees face serious threats. Like the knots of a tapestry, multiple threads of social, political, and cosmological relationships met in the sacred groves of pre-colonial Africa, but the far-reaching changes of the colonial and postcolonial periods eroded their institutional legitimacy and cultural relevance. As this social fabric unraveled (and was re-woven) over the twentieth century, sacred groves became increasingly marginalized institutions, and therefore accessible for resource exploitation. Axes and chainsaws replaced sacrifices and initiation ceremonies. Descriptions of this process have coalesced into a standard narrative about sacred groves, in Africa and beyond.[4] This discourse has four components, and leads to the inevitable conclusion that robust conservation efforts are necessary, as soon as possible:

[2] (cont.) sacred trees in Britain, see Thomas 1983. Increasingly, groves and particular trees are being sacralized in the United States; see Hughes and Chandran 1998:78 for a description of the AIDS National Memorial Grove in San Francisco, and see Friend 2005 for a description of how the American funeral industry is promoting 'green funerals' by planting trees over non-embalmed corpses.

[3] Recent work by James Fairhead and Melissa Leach (1996, 1998) argues that these deforestation rates are greatly exaggerated.

[4] For elements of this narrative, see Amoako-Atta 1995, Anoliefo et al. 2003, Baffoe 2002, Guinko 1985, Sibanda 1997, Okeke 1999, Chidhakwa 2003, Mwihomeke et al. 1998, Oates et al. 1992, Tchamie 2000, Warren and Pinkston 1998, Wilson 1993, Ylhaisi 2000, Fisiy 1994, Matawonyika 1997, and Bagine 1998. For examples of this discourse in the South Asian literature, see Apfell-Marglin and Parajuli 2000, Gadgil, Berkes, and Folke 1993, Sharma, Rikhari, and Palni 1999, Pandey 1998, Khiewtam and Ramkrishnan 1989, Sinha 1995, and Tiwari, et al. 1998.

- The assertion that sacred groves, as remnants of pristine primeval forests, have vital ecological functions.
- The assertion that ideas about the groves' sacredness are relics of pre-colonial religious beliefs, now threatened by social change (especially the advent of Christianity).
- The assertion that sacred groves are the common property of the members of particular social categories, especially the ethno-linguistic groupings popularly known as 'tribes.'
- The assertion that because traditional spiritual values caused sacred groves to be conserved in the first place, the appropriate conservation policy is to empower local caretakers and validate traditional beliefs and practices.

Although this narrative is powerful and persuasive, it is based on a rather old-fashioned set of assumptions about tropical ecology, religious belief systems, and African societies. Recent work in ecology, social history, anthropology, and conservation policy shows that tropical forests are not simply relics of primeval forests (Willis *et al.* 2004), and that contemporary African religions are not simply relics of pre-colonial ideas and practices (Ranger 1988). The taken-for-granted notion that 'tribes' and ethnic groups have always been key units in African societies has been replaced by an appreciation for the historically contingent construction of such identities in various contexts (Bravman 1998). Finally, the assumption that community-based conservation is a simple matter of decentralizing authority to the appropriate local level has been re-evaluated for its political complexities and ambiguities (Walley 2004, Larson and Ribot 2005). For example, recent policy studies have shown that much of what passes for community-based natural resource management in Africa constitutes a deconcentration of conservation responsibilities without the concomitant decentralization of rights to resources and decision-making power that actually give communities incentives to conserve (Alden Wily and Mbaya 2001). Taken together, these shifting intellectual currents show a transformation from a focus on simple static systems to dynamic and historically contingent complexities.

The standard discourse about African sacred groves posits that these relics of ecological and cultural climax can contribute to tropical conservation efforts. In this volume, we wholeheartedly agree that sacred groves have great conservation potential – but we also find that the Relic Theory of sacred groves can prevent attention to important ecological, historical, social, political, and symbolic dynamics with serious implications for conservation policy. We therefore seek to redefine the topic by demonstrating the dynamic nature of sacred groves. Even the term 'sacred grove' deserves closer scrutiny. In his seminal discussion of sacredness, Emile Durkheim asserted that 'the sacred thing is *par excellence* that which the profane should not touch, and cannot touch with impunity' (1954:40). This distinction between sacred and profane is a European analytical construct dating from the mid-nineteenth century, and not all societies organize their worlds using these categories. It is all too easy to suppose that sacredness explains the existence of such stands of trees, which therefore removes political and economic factors from consideration. In Africa, sacred groves are simultaneously ecological, social, political, and religious phenomena.

The Appeal of Sacred Groves

Although sacred groves and sanctified trees feature in many of the classic texts of history, religion, and mythology (Hughes 1994), the foundational text is James Frazer's *The Golden Bough* (1951), a literary blockbuster which grew from a three-page essay on taboo in the 1888 *Encyclopaedia Britannica* to a monumental 13-volume set by 1936 (Ackerman 1987). Frazer begins (and ends) his speculative historical reconstruction of human cognitive evolution in the sacred grove of Diana of the Woods at Nemi, Italy. The 'grim figure' of a priest guarded a sprig of mistletoe and waited for a successor to kill and replace him (1951:1). The goddess Diana, her priest, and her worshippers are now gone – but the sacred grove remains as a relic of past religious and political institutions (ibid.:827).[5]

This nostalgic approach in writings about sacred groves is deeply embedded in classical literature. In one of the first written texts from ancient Mesopotamia, the *Epic of Gilgamesh*, King Gilgamesh and his friend Enkidu defeat the semi-divine giant Humbaba and cut down his sacred cedar grove (Anonymous 1990). Authors such as Seneca, Ovid, Pliny the Elder, and Virgil described the role of sacred groves in ancient Greece and Rome, while Julius Caesar and Tacitus documented groves throughout northwestern Europe (Hughes 1994:170, Hughes and Chandran 1998:76). As Christianity became the dominant political and religious system throughout Europe, missionaries, saints, and kings cut down the sacred groves maintained by autonomous peoples on the margins of empire. Charlemagne, for example, cut down the Saxon sacred grove of Irminsul in order to consolidate his power in what is now Germany, and a century later, AD 895, the Council of Nantes ordered all Christians to destroy trees used for demon worship in (Hughes and Chandran ibid.: 82).

Writing in the heyday of colonial expansion, Frazer picked up these pieces of decontextualized and disparate literary and ethnographic data on sacred plants, sacrifice, and taboo to delineate the contours of what he called 'primitive religion'. In doing so he established sacred groves as icons of integrated social, political, and ecological order, in opposition to the disorderly tumult and anomie of the early twentieth century. Sacred groves were there-

---

[5] Frazer is often ignored as a founding figure in anthropology, largely because his methods eschewed fieldwork. He was, however, one of the most influential figures in early 20th-century anthropology. *The Golden Bough* was required reading among Anglophone elites and shaped the way millions of people understood human history and institutions. Frazer was an avid supporter of the young Bronislaw Malinowski, and wrote the preface to his seminal *Argonauts of the Pacific* (1922). Malinowski often had his students read Frazer as a foil for his own critique (Ackerman 1987:269). See also Tylor 1874:215ff and Philpot 1897 for nineteenth century analyses of sacred groves, as well as Frazer's summary of 'the worship of trees' in his *Aftermath* (1966:126–49).

fore synonymous with 'tradition,' and by definition of little interest to modernizing elite policy-makers for much of the twentieth century. As the global environmental movement grew in the late twentieth century, however, interest in sacred groves boomed because they provided examples of nature–society relationships quite unlike the bureaucratic indifference, crass materialism, and hyper-consumption of industrialism (Altman 1994). Sacred groves fascinate precisely because they represent values-based models of environmental stewardship in contradistinction to rational science-based exploitation and conservation. The nostalgic Relic Theory of sacred groves' culture and ecology has, in sum, long been an appealing foil for the multiple contradictions and dissonances of modernity.

In African studies, from colonial-era ethnography and ecology (e.g., Chevalier 1933) to recent work on conservation and development (e.g., Omari 1990, Sibanda 1997), sacred groves often appear as vestiges of a lost precolonial social and ecological order.[6] In the 1930s, for example, Jomo Kenyatta described how initiation ceremonies conducted next to sacred trees functioned to integrate Kikuyu society (1965:134) but also noted that 'many of these trees were cut down when Europeans took possession of Gikuyu lands' (1965:235). Meyer Fortes described Tallensi sacred groves as material expressions of kin group solidarity and social equilibrium (1945:101), but insisted that this equilibrium had been distorted by colonial rule and economic change (ibid.:250). In his summary of the status of sacred groves in French West Africa, Chevalier (1933) lamented that 'since our contact the primitive has abandoned his creed, and the sacred groves are disappearing.' According to many authors, Africa's sacred groves are still disappearing today because of social and religious change, but community-based conservation promises to conserve these sites of bio- and cultural diversity (Bagine 1998, Fisiy 1994, Little and Brokensha 1987:204, Mgumia and Oba 2003, Ylhaisi 2000). The discourse is remarkably consistent: a cultural and ecological equilibrium was destabilized by external pressures, but carefully designed conservation of its relics may be able to restore stability.

The Relic Theory is powerful because it appeals to different constituencies. Conservation practitioners use it to press for better land management, academics use it to assert the validity and wisdom of indigenous practices as opposed to colonial and neo-colonial influences, and sacred grove caretakers use it to claim authority and legitimacy.[7] The notion of a functional and beneficial steady-state equilibrium between society and nature is, of course, the goal of 'sustainable development' – but examples of such a neo-traditional sustainability are notoriously difficult to find. Communities rarely achieve complete consensus (Agrawal and Gibson 1999), although they retain extraordinary abilities to find consensus when shared resources or interests are externally threatened. Ecosystems, in turn, are characterized more by the 'flux of nature' than its balance

---

[6] This theme is also widespread in the literature on sacred groves in South Asia. See Apfell-Marglin and Parajuli 2000, Gadgil and Vartak 1976, Malhotra 1998, Rajendaraprasad *et al.* 1998, Ramakrishnan 1996, and Roy Burnham 2003.

[7] For an analysis of ways that peripheral peoples adopt global environmental discourses to suit their own ends, see Dove *et al.* 2003. For a review of the ways that local sacred sites acquire global symbolic values through 'glocalization,' see Hay-Edie and Hadley 1998.

(Gillson *et al.* 2003, Pickett and Ostfeld 1995), although geophysical steady states and biological adaptation often form consistent patterns in time and space. The assumption of ecological, social, political, and symbolic equilibrium in the Relic Theory of sacred groves often hides more than it reveals, and can lead to inappropriate conservation policies. This volume redefines Africa's sacred groves as dynamic processes rather than relics of climax forests and peak cultural florescence. The remainder of this introduction therefore reviews the shift from static to dynamic approaches in the study of ecology, society, politics, and symbolism, surveys the existing literature on African sacred groves for evidence of this dynamism, and contextualizes the case studies which follow.

The Ecology of African Sacred Groves – from Balance to Flux

Notions of balance, order, and stability have long characterized Western ecological thought, but these assumptions have recently come into question (Egerton 1973). The ancient Greeks built their science, medicine, and philosophy on ideas of equilibrium, while medieval Christians perceived nature as a perfect and stable divine creation. Renaissance thinkers described an orderly cosmos as a Great Chain of Being, which ranked everything in existence on a scale of Christian morality and divine complexity (e.g., insects, mice, dogs, humans, angels, God). Mechanistic ideas about nature emerged as theology transmuted into science after Galileo and Newton, and machine metaphors (of, for example, gears and wheels) came to dominate Western models of natural phenomena during the Industrial Revolution (Botkin 1990, Glacken 1967, Pahl-Wostl 1995, and Worster 1993).

The science of ecology drew on these concepts in order to explain the form and function of natural phenomena. In 1864, for example, George Perkins Marsh stated that

> Nature, left undisturbed, so fashions her territory as to give it almost unchanging permanence of form, outline and proportion, except when shattered by geological convulsions; and in these comparatively rare cases of derangement, she sets herself at once to repair the superficial damage, and to restore, as nearly as practicable, the former aspect of her dominion.
>
> (Marsh 1965:12)

This long tradition of equilibrium thinking is still common in much popular environmentalist thought, as well as in the social sciences, and is often linked to evolutionary ideas about change from one steady state to another (e.g., structural functionalism in anthropology, tradition/modernity in sociology, etc.). As field and experimental ecologists developed the study of natural history into the science of ecology, they often took theoretical concepts and metaphors from mathematics and physics (about systemic stasis, homeostatic regulation, and stable equilibrium points) rather than developing ecological theory from their observations (Botkin 1990:33). Ecological research therefore focused on examples of classical static stability, such as the inevitable succession of vegetation toward its 'climatic climax' (Clements 1916) and Malthusian models of food supply and population growth toward an ecosystem's particular 'carrying capacity' (Odum 1953). The natural world was defined as sets of self-regulating systems with fixed pathways and feedback loops between cause and effect. These notions about the inherent stability of forests and wildlife populations became the logical foundations of conservation theory, the environmentalist social movement, and the pragmatic struggles against deforestation, desertification, and degradation – particularly in the peripheries of expanding colonial and post-colonial empires (Anderson and Grove 1987, Grove 1997, Guha 2000). Although assumptions about the 'balance of nature' drove theory-building in ecology, demonstrating its existence proved notoriously difficult in actual ecosystems (Connell and Sousa 1983:789; Elton 1930:15). By the 1970s the gap between ecological theory and empirical data was wide enough to spur a paradigm shift (Kuhn 1970) toward non-equilibrium theories about the 'flux of nature' (Gillson *et al.* 2003, Pickett and Ostfeld 1995).

This 'new ecology' avoids the assumption that ecosystems seek a stable equilibrium. Nonequilibrium ecological theory instead focuses on nonlinear dynamics, heterogeneity and variability in time and space, and complexity. In practice, this approach makes disturbance an integral feature of ecosystems rather than exceptions to their balanced functioning. For example, fire suppression has long been a standard conservation practice, but this ignored the ecological benefits of fire (e.g., some trees' dependence on fire for seed dispersal and growth). In recent years, for example, American environmental policy has promoted fire as a natural (even desirable) force on forest landscapes – which led to public debate about the meaning of conservation after the Yellowstone National Park fire of 1988. The terminology that has emerged to describe ecosystems as ongoing mosaics of processes (rather than endpoints) within the new paradigm includes resistance (the degree to which an ecosystem absorbs disturbance without change), resilience (the rate of recovery to a former state), persistence (the period over which a given state exists), variability (the degree of change over time), sensitivity (the relative vulnerability of particular variables to change), and surprise (unexpected, stochastic, and nonlinear causation) (Harrison 1979, Pickett *et al.* 1992, Pimm 1991). This new ecological paradigm does not stipulate that ecological equilibria cannot exist; it insists, however, that equilibrium is but one possible state among many. Research inspired by the new ecology has investigated complexity and chaos in population dynamics and variation and patterning across different temporal and spatial scales (Scoones 1999:483). These new ideas from the natural sciences have tremendous potential for elucidating African landscapes and livelihoods. All too often, however, analyses in the social sciences take the 'balance of nature' as an unmoving backdrop for social action, politics, and hermeneutics.

For research on African sacred groves to have explanatory power, it is particularly important to take the 'flux of nature' seriously. Recent work in archaeology and the emerging fields of historical ecology and paleoecology (Crumley 1994) has questioned the persistence and resilience of tropical forests and the role of humans in their dynamics. The extent and composition of tropical forests changed dramatically as recently as the onset of the Holocene

14,000 years ago (Maley 2001). New research shows that the forests that we often perceive as 'wilderness' are in fact at least partly anthropogenic (Willis *et al.* 2004, Gillson and Willis 2004). The Upper Xingu region of Brazil, for example, is the largest contiguous tract of 'virgin' rainforest in the southern Amazon – yet archaeologists have shown that the area's pre-Columbian population was dense enough to transform the area into a 'cultural parkland' (Heckenberger *et al.* 2003). The forest cover of New Georgia in the Solomon Islands appears to be as young as 150 years old, the resilient ecological by-product of a human population crash and outmigration (Bayliss-Smith *et al.* 2003). In many ways, therefore, current forest ecosystems in many areas are best seen as products of human influence and disturbance throughout the Holocene. This suggests that most tropical forests are, to some degree, products of human social interaction. The same lesson applies at the regional scale as well, as the groundbreaking work by James Fairhead and Melissa Leach on the human origins of 'forest islands' in West Africa's savanna-forest transition zone demonstrated (1996, 1998, see also Neumann and Müller-Haude 1999). The principle of uniformitarianism – that past processes were not radically different from those observed in the present – therefore demands that we consider the possibility that sacred groves are not 'natural' forests. As Leach and Fairhead have emphasized, institutional analysis offers far more insight into African forests than the assumption of climax vegetation (2000). The Relic Theory of sacred groves would preclude historical investigation of the role of people in their formation and management, which would make a poor foundation for conservation policy.[8]

Recent work on ecological fragmentation and the formation of vegetation mosaics is particularly appropriate for understanding African sacred groves. Indeed, many groves in Africa are by definition fragments or patches of vegetation in largely agricultural landscapes. One ecological model well-suited to evaluating African sacred groves at different scales in space and time is the hierarchical patch dynamics paradigm (HPDP). This approach centers on the intersections of pattern, process, and scale to explore the nonequilibrium dynamics of plant communities (Watt 1947, Whittaker *et al.* 2001, Wu and Loucks 1995). Each patch, defined as 'a spatial unit differing from its surroundings in nature or appearance' (Wu and Loucks 1995:446), interacts with adjacent patches through physical and biological interactions (ranging from storms and fire to predation and parasitism, for example). A patch can be an ocean, a region, a forest, or a single tree – so the paradigm allows us to envision ecosystems as nested hierarchies of relationships from global levels to the microscopic. Adding temporal scales (from millions of years to milliseconds) to these spatial hierarchies provides a robust framework for investigating ecological dynamics (Willis and Whittaker 2002, Gillson 2004).

The HPDP model lies firmly within the domain of the positivistic and predictive natural sciences, and has great potential for explaining vegetation dynamics through mathematical modelling. Conspicuously lacking in this

---

[8] On the need to incorporate non-equilibrium ecology into conservation policy, see Knapp 2003. For a foundational text on the notion of 'forest islands' in the African savannah, see Aubreville 1939.

paradigm, however, is human agency.[9] African sacred groves only exist as such alongside people, so the use of patch dynamics for understanding the ecology of sacred groves requires the insertion of humans into the model's temporal and spatial scales. Yet humans do not fit neatly into these scales, and the variability of human motivation and action would play havoc with the equations developed to describe plant behavior.

One solution to this epistemological dilemma is to examine the interplay between the capacities of individual actors and the limits imposed by social institutions. This view of social structure and human agency is mostly associated with the work of sociologist Anthony Giddens (1984), who coined the term 'structuration' to describe the dynamics through which social actors shape, and are shaped by, social institutions. Recent work by environmental anthropologists has sought to bring such a perspective to bear on human ecology (Leach *et al.* 1999, Scoones 1999:493). Structuration is a useful concept for understanding African sacred groves because these groves usually correspond with particular forms of social organization, and many of the challenges facing these groves stem from their misfit with the secular and religious institutions of the nation-state. African sacred groves are typically community institutions in which power and authority are local in space and temporally tied into the life-cycle of kin groups. They often represent legitimate resource ownership, which explains much of their persistence compared to other forested areas in Africa during a period of rapid social change. The dynamic structuration inherent in the social organization of African societies is therefore a factor shaping the ecological dynamics of sacred groves. This amendment to the hierarchical patch dynamics paradigm allows us to link social history with vegetation dynamics and to avoid the Relic Theory of untouched primeval forests in equilibrium.[10]

The interdisciplinary work of integrating New Ecology into analyses of African sacred groves is just beginning.[11] Some of these patches may indeed be relics of once-larger forests, but the assumption that sacred groves are relics of a balance of nature and culture should not guide policy (Guyer and Richards 1996). A more dynamic view of ecology and its connections to social organization, politics, and symbolism shows that many sacred groves are the historically

---

[9] The hierarchical patch dynamics paradigm is a botanical model, and its content reflects these disciplinary boundaries. The study of land use is, however, an intrinsically interdisciplinary project that requires methodological and theoretical hybridization to bridge 'the gap between social science, natural science, and the humanities' (Haberl *et al.* 2001, see also Batterbury *et al.* 1997 and Gillson *et al.* 2003).

[10] See, for example, Berkes and Folke 1998 for a systems approach to human ecology that links institutional analysis with non-equilibrium ecological theory. For an African example of the integration of the hierarchical patch dynamics paradigm into a social scientific analysis, see Elliott and Campbell 2002.

[11] For examples of the Africanist biogeographical literature on sacred groves, see Beier *et al.* 2002, Decher 1997a, 1997b, Decher and Bahian 1999, Lukumbuzya 2000, Schmidt 1991, Tyynela and Mudavanhu 2000, Mussanhane *et al.* 2000, Okafor and Ladipo 1995, and Bossart *et al.* 2006. For examples of the corresponding literature from South Asia, see Boraiah *et al.* 2003, Deb *et al.* 1997, Mishra *et al.* 2004, Rathakette *et al.* 1984, Ramanujam and Praveen Kumar Cyril 2003, and Upadhaya *et al.* 2003.

contingent results of vegetation change following shifting social values and functions. Many of Africa's sacred groves now grow over former settlement sites, although current forest caretakers may insist that the trees are relics of a primeval forest (Chouin 2002b, Fairhead and Leach 1997:12, Guillot 1980, Lebbie and Guries, this volume, Nyamweru et al., this volume). Many sacred sites in Africa only acquired these cultural values within the context of – and possibly in reaction to – the dislocations and insecurities of colonial rule (Campbell 2004:227, 2005:158, Ranger 1999). The sacredness of groves is not the result of cultural values abstracted from their contexts in human lives. It is not in the trees, plants, vines, springs, pools, rivers, and rocks. Sacredness is embedded in the social institutions that sacred groves manifest in African landscapes, which means that the ecological status of these patches follows from the shifting social organization of African societies and the flux of historical change on the continent.

The Social Life of African Sacred Groves

This dynamic view of African sacred groves as institutions demands a review of African social organization. African societies are breaktakingly diverse, complex, and rarely fit into neat analytical categories. Indeed, much of the discipline of anthropology has revolved around the construction and revision of general models of social organization derived from the rapidly shifting African context (Moore 1994). In the classical period of Africanist social science (roughly 1935–1960), the analytical keywords were the structural units of household, lineage, and tribe (Fortes and Evans-Pritchard 1987, Guyer 1981). The rapid social changes that followed decolonization and various experiments with socialism and neoliberalism eroded the utility of these terms and spurred analysts to refocus on specific processes rather than abstract structural regularities. Much of the recent scholarship in both history and the social sciences agrees that African societies are better characterized by mobility, flexibility, and change than by structural continuity (e.g., Berry 1993, Kuper 1996). Nonetheless, the notion and construct of 'the African community' is remarkably consistent in both policy and practice, despite its shifting composition. As the case studies in this collection illustrate, African sacred groves exist at the intersection of multiple social processes, ranging from the localized division of social labor by gender, age, and kinship to regional politics and global economics. Explaining how sacred groves can be both fundamental social institutions and threatened ecological patches requires an approach that can account for their existence throughout Africa and their shifting social significance.

Although there are numerous regional variations, African sacred groves typically serve as historical markers and sites for initiation, burial, and sacrifice in societies based on horticulture and agriculture.[12] These social functions

---

[12] Many authors emphasize that sacred groves correspond with a horticultural mode of production; for examples from South Asia, see Chandran 1998, Chandran and Hughes 1997, Gadgil and Guha 1992, and Gokhale et al. 1998; from Africa, see van Binsbergen 1981,

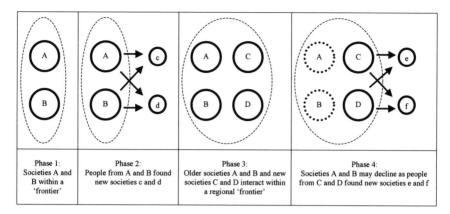

Phase 1: Societies A and B within a 'frontier'	Phase 2: People from A and B found new societies c and d	Phase 3: Older societies A and B and new societies C and D interact within a regional 'frontier'	Phase 4: Societies A and B may decline as people from C and D found new societies e and f

Figure 2.2 Simplified schematic representation of Kopytoff's 'internal African frontier' hypothesis. Note that the left-to-right representation here does not correspond to the west–east diffusion of the Bantu expansion. There have been many frontiers in African history, in many directions.

embed the present in the past by asserting and legitimizing the continuity of a particular organization of society, so sacred groves often have a socially conservative character. A theoretical model of African cultural history that can account for the striking continuities and similarities of sacred groves from Senegal to Madagascar is the 'internal African frontier' hypothesis presented by Igor Kopytoff (1988). Kopytoff argues that because Africa has historically been so under-populated that labor was the scarce factor of production (rather than land, as in Eurasia), African societies developed mechanisms to organize rights in people along a moving frontier of demographic expansion.[13] The model posits the following growth cycle of African societies: some people leave a mature 'core' society due to various pressures or opportunities, and move to its periphery. Given the institutional vacuum in this frontier, they construct a new society based on the conceptual toolkit of older cultural and ideological resources (ibid.:10). After devising ways to attract and bind new settlers into their new community, demographic growth allows emergent elites to shift the organization of the new society from a focus on kin group solidarity to a more organic solidarity of interdependent rulers and subjects. Some people leave this mature society, and the process begins anew, with minor structural variations (see fig. 2.2). Kopytoff argues that this model can account for the 'ceaseless flux' (ibid.:7) of African cultural features, such as the organization of social hierarchies by gender, age, and kinship, the notion that political relationships can be expressed via the idiom of kinship, the use of initiation rituals to

[12] (cont.) Colson 1997, and Kull 2004:149. The relatively scarce literature on sacred groves among African pastoralists describes how territoriality and group identity are expressed in sacred sites. See Fitz-Henry and Olol-Dapash 2002, Legesse 1986, Niamir 1990, and Schlee 1992.

[13] The notion of wealth in people, and particularly wealth in relationships, is a useful tool for linking historical demography and social history. See Iliffe 1995 and Guyer 1995 for examples.

establish social roles and sacrificial shrines to define political territories, and the legitimization of contemporary authority by reference to the order of ancestral settlement of an area. This reconceptualization of African societies as unfolding historical processes generates a vision of dynamic patterns at different scales in time and space; 'instead of being a patchwork of classic tribes, it was through the centuries more like a shimmering beadwork of repetitive patterns – hamlets, little and large chieftaincies, kingdoms, and empires – each of which was in constant structural motion as it changed its shape from one pattern to another' (ibid.:77). Sacred groves were one of the key mechanisms for recreating social and ecological order on the frontier, and this explains their presence across Africa in societies with quite different degrees of political centralization.

Examples of this process can be found throughout sub-Saharan Africa. In south-central Africa, immigrant Nyakyusa kings planted trees in rituals to mark their authority over indigenous commoners. The resulting thickets became their gravesites, and developed into sacrificial groves where subsequent leaders legitimized their authority (Wilson 1959:70). The kaya forests of the East African coast were once fortified villages on forested hilltops, but became sacred groves when the Mijikenda peoples adopted a more dispersed settlement pattern in the nineteenth century (Mutoro 1994, Nyamweru *et al.* this volume, Willis 1996). Social organization in the kaya villages had been mediated by age-set initiation ceremonies re-enacting the migration of the Mijikenda ancestors and the founding of the settlement. These rituals focused on the unity of kin groups precisely because they were the idiom for assimilating unrelated groups into the polity (Spear 1978:51). In much of West Africa, planting trees (especially *Dracaena arborea* or *Milicia excelsa*) is the founding act of village settlement. These sites become focal points for institutions ranging from initiation ceremonies to land tenure arrangements, and the density of both vegetation and symbolic value increases apace within a few generations (Juhé-Beaulaton 1999, Juhé-Beaulaton and Roussel 2002, Michaloud and Dury 1998:136). These forests can outlast the institutions that generated them. Although the caretakers of many West African sacred groves insist that these sites are relics of primary forest, for example, even cursory archaeological analysis of surface features shows them to be abandoned settlements (Chouin 2002a, 2002b, see also Schmidt 1997). Sacred groves are therefore embedded in particular local histories of migration, settlement, demographic growth, and institution-building, but as a regional phenomenon they show a rhythmic pattern. Sacred groves were key sites in the 'shimmering beadwork' of institutional dynamics on the pre-colonial African frontier, and therefore remain part of the warp and woof of Africa's social fabric today.[14]

The reasons for this striking continuity relate to the ongoing usefulness of sacred groves as locations for important institutions (and places for creating new ones) rather than any inherent traditionalism in African societies. The

[14] Institutional aspects of sacred groves in precolonial Africa are also reviewed in Castro 1995, Chretien 1978, Lebbie and Freudenberger 1996, Niangoran-Bouah 1983, Riley and Brokensha 1988:197, Schloss 1988, and Sanogo 1983. For an interesting example of the use of sacred grove discourse to establish tenurial rights in contemporary Haiti, see Beckett 2004.

livelihoods of African farmers depend on their access to land and their control of labor, and sacred groves remain socially and ecologically relevant where the institutions embedded in them link these critical factors of production. In Uganda and Congo-Brazzaville, as in many other parts of Africa, sacred groves represent the moral authority of patrilineal land tenure systems (Gombya-Ssembajjwe 1995, Guillot 1980). Sacred groves are thus material expressions of the organization of society through kinship relations (Fortes 1945:101). The patterns of kinship, the division of labor, and the dynamics of tenure systems were in flux throughout Africa over the long twentieth century of colonial and neocolonial rule, so sacred groves should not be conceptualized as part of a static normative structure. African land tenure is better seen as an ongoing process of negotiation and innovation (Berry 1993, Juul and Lund 2002), and in many areas sacred groves have served as arenas in which terms of land access and control are asserted and legitimized in particular historical junctures. In northern Tanzania, for example, some socially marginal kin groups hide the existence of their sacred groves (by deliberately not planting *Dracaena usambarensis*, a common marker of clan property) in order to avoid challenges by dominant groups over the validity of their rights to land during colonial and post-colonial land reform efforts (Sheridan 2001). Land use in Africa is a process that is both material and metaphysical (Shipton 1994), and it is in sacred groves that many of these intersections of agricultural production and social reproduction occur.[15]

African sacred groves are therefore 'places of power' (Colson 1997) not because of any inherent sacredness, but rather because they represent social order.[16] This makes them focal points for cooperation and conflict rather than icons of static tradition (Schoffeleers 1992:10). Maintaining any form of social order is the essence of politics, and sacred groves are thus sites where political power may be contested and reinforced. The political aspects of sacred groves are particularly pronounced in frontier societies characterized by a division of rights and labor between autochthonous first settlers and later immigrants. Typically, the immigrant group creates its own sacred groves as touchstones for its legitimacy as rulers of people and owners of land, yet also relies on rituals in the subordinate firstcomers' groves to maintain the well-being of the land (e.g., Fortes 1987:59, Mitchell 1961, van Binsbergen 1981:115, and Wilson 1959). Because the political status quo is constantly shifting and subject to renegotiation, however, the political roles of sacred groves in Africa have also been dynamic. In southern Senegal, for example, the Atlantic slave trade created new elite classes that built new multi-ethnic shrines focusing on the wealth of individuals rather than relying on more communal rituals in sacred groves for

[15] Recent work to establish an interdisciplinary focus on the intersections between religion, culture, and nature focuses on this imbrication of metaphysics and ecology. 'Spiritual ecology' is rooted in a basic lesson of cultural ecology: that some abstract symbolic systems (about, for example, sacred or taboo sites or species) can have material ecological consequences (Sponsel 2001).

[16] Being a 'place of power' does not necessarily cause sacred groves to be protected by political elites. In postwar Mozambique, many groves were damaged or destroyed by bush fires that had been set to create tenurial rights by clearing the land. There were no efforts to apprehend those who started the fires because many people believed that the groves would exact their own vengeance by crop failure or madness (Schafer and Black 2003).

the general prosperity of entire groups or regions (Baum 1999). This example shows the interdependence of local and regional ideological systems and the global political economy, which is quite unlike the sort of static continuity often ascribed to African religions.

Although both the forms and functions of political legitimacy and authority were dismantled, transformed, and innovatively remade in colonial and post-colonial Africa, sacred groves remain arenas for strategic and instrumental political action that establishes, defends, or transforms rights in people and in land. As Hughes and Chandran note, 'sacred groves serve as examples of local ownership and autonomy, and may serve as rallying points for local people when these are threatened' (1998:70). As icons of social and cultural distinctiveness that often contain or legitimize core social institutions, sacred groves can become sites of protest and resistance. In colonial North Pare, Tanzania, a former ruling clan organized and justified its resistance to a chief from a rival clan by appealing to the United Nations for control of its sacred groves (Sheridan 2000).[17] The sacred groves of southern Senegal (described above) were initiation sites for secret societies throughout the colonial period. Although the postcolonial government had suppressed these rituals from 1962 until 1994, in 1982 the groves became sites for antigovernment protesters to press for regional autonomy (Geschiere and van der Klei 1988). Uninitiated and non-local policemen entered a sacred grove in December 1983 to break up a political gathering, which triggered a cycle of protest and violent repression. These political dynamics reshaped the institutional basis of the sacred groves in southern Senegal – what had been parochial kin group institutions became a global political phenomenon of ethnic identity construction in 1994. Migrants returned from Holland and France for the initiation ceremonies and engaged in competitive displays of wealth to compete for the status of authentic 'sons of the soil' (de Jong 1999, 2002). In Bénin, on the other hand, the government has co-opted the discourse of sacred groves (and, in some cases, the pragmatics of management) in order to assert and legitimize nationalism (Juhé-Beaulaton 2003). These examples demonstrate how sacred sites in Africa can function as political arenas for both conflict and cooperation in different historical contexts (Ellis and ter Haar 2004, Mukamuri 1995, Ranger 1999).[18]

The Symbol of Forests

Sacred groves were symbols of power, locality, ownership, and authenticity on the 'internal African frontier,' but the far-reaching changes of European colo-

17 These struggles did not, however, contribute to the drive for nationalism because they were by definition local matters. In fact, the groves became liabilities when the postcolonial socialist government made it clear that common property systems managed by clans were politically incorrect (Sheridan 2004).

18 See also McCaskie 1990 and Grove 1997:149 for discussions of a conflict over a sacred grove in Ghana in 1849. In this example, an educated Christian elite hungry for timber and fertile soil challenged the local political and religious elites for control of sacred woodlands. For an example of sacred groves becoming sites of resistance against state elites in South Asia, see Roy Burman 1995.

nization and the construction of postcolonial nation-states shifted the locus of power in Africa into new institutions. Even with their social salience diminished, sacred groves can continue to symbolize the group autonomy lost to a new political order. As Cohen reminds us, 'the greater the pressure on communities to modify their structural forms to comply more with those elsewhere, the more are they inclined to reassert their boundaries symbolically by imbuing these modified forms with meaning and significance... In other words, as the structural bases of boundary become blurred, so the symbolic bases are strengthened' (1985:44). In postcolonial Africa, however, clear-cut 'communities' are notoriously difficult to identify analytically (Guyer 1981), so symbolic bases are usually contested and boundaries remain ambiguous. This leads to vibrant identity politics that usually revolve around the distinctions between 'strangers' and autochthonous 'people who belong' to particular places. In the wake of the neoliberal reforms imposed on African governments by international institutions in the 1980s and 1990s, 'belonging,' exclusion, and ethnic citizenship have become increasingly important (Geschiere and Nyamnjoh 2000).

As icons of autochthony, sacred groves often lie squarely at the center of such struggles over categories and meanings, and are thus concentrated forms of symbolic capital. Discourses about 'threatened' sacred groves being the relics of larger forests are often environmental narratives that connect global conservation agendas with local negotiations of group identity, legitimate land tenure, and relations with the state (e.g., Ceuppens and Geschiere 2005, Fairhead and Leach 1997:16, Juhé-Beaulaton and Roussel 1998:368). In such fluid contexts, sacred groves' meaning and symbolism often reflects thoroughly modern issues despite their ostensible embodiment of 'tradition' (e.g., Mukamuri 1995, Probst 2004, Wamue 2001). Parkin, for example, argues that the sacred groves (kaya) of the Giriama people of coastal Kenya are 'spatial texts' on which various meanings have been written, erased, and edited (1991:9). The sacredness of these former settlements, he asserts, increased under colonial rule as an idealized static foil against which the Giriama experienced sweeping social change. Sacred groves are, much like 'customary law,' 'traditional African religion,' and 'African communities,' inventions and constructions that are constantly adapting to new conditions while still appearing timeless and changeless (Greene 2002, Moore 1986, Ranger 1994, Spear 2003). Popular discourses on the static ecological, social, and symbolic continuity of African sacred groves is ultimately an essential part of their dynamic character.

These multiple levels of dynamism make it rather surprising that centrifugal forces do not cause the meanings of sacred groves to scatter like leaves in the wind. The centripetal forces that keep these meanings together surely involve the multiple economic, social, and political institutions embedded in African sacred groves, but what is it that makes trees such compelling sites of significance and memory, rather than stones or soil? Maurice Bloch (1998) argues that trees are 'good to think with' because they are alive yet immobile – and therefore ideal vehicles for symbolizing the 'rootedness' of social groupings. Trees are natural symbols (Douglas 1970) in which social institutions and political projects may be built, so that trees may 'become the social agents through which modernity, progress, the erasure of the colonial past, and the close partnership between the state and the community are articulated' (Rival 1998:13). Much like machines serve as pervasive metaphors and 'key symbols' of social processes in industrial societies (Ortner 1973), the growth and fixedness of trees offers metaphors and symbols for the dynamics of agrarian societies in which rights to land and the organization of labor are paramount concerns.[19] The shifting status of African sacred groves is therefore not just a matter of older social institutions becoming eclipsed by newer ones. The process also indicates the way that African webs of meaning are being rewoven by the continent's fractious engagement with colonialism and the current hegemony of neoliberal capitalism.

These meanings are far from static; they are as subject to historical process as are ecological systems and social institutions. Vitally important symbolic systems such as African ethnic identities were taken for granted by generations of scholars. Customs, traditions, agricultural practices, and religious ideologies were aspects of the integrated wholes that anthropologists called 'cultures' or 'societies.' A more critical view of these bundles of traditions emerged in the postcolonial historical scholarship on ethnicity in Africa (Ranger 1983, Vail 1989). The consensus is that precolonial ethnic identities were often quite flexible, but that governments imposed rigid categories, such as 'tribes,' indexed to the emerging political economy of colonial Africa (Southall 1997). These hybrid symbolic systems became so deeply essentialized and embedded in African societies, that 'ethnicity, though a colonial invention, could rapidly appear natural, even immemorial' (Ranger 1994:13). Studies of African ethnicity, custom, and tradition therefore tend to focus on how social actors rely upon forms of 'strategic essentialism' (Igoe 2005:383) while they simultaneously reconstruct the form and content of these ideas themselves and assert the timelessness of those 'neo-traditional' reconstructions (Spear 2003). Just as essentializing analyses are inappropriate for examining shifting identities and practices, African sacred groves are also neither culturally essential nor traditional, although they usually appear as icons of these conditions. As many chapters in this book demonstrate, they are both discursive and material relational phenomena, in which ecological conditions interact with social organization and ideological systems in shifting historical conjuctures (Sivaramakrishan 1999, Fairhead and Leach 1996, Ranger 1999).[20]

The recent scholarship on African witchcraft has great potential for illuminating the murky question of why African sacred groves have become such important focal points for conservationists, politicians, neo-traditionalists, and

[19] Economies in rural Africa have long been marked by divisions of social labor by gender, age, and kinship, so sacred groves often serve as (in Ortner's terms) 'summarizing symbols' that condense meanings about these divisions. See Lan 1985, Schmidt 1994, and Weiss 2003 for examples of sacred sites that summarize these principles of social organization.

[20] For an example of an essentializing account of African sacred groves, see Daneel 2001. For analyses focusing on the instrumental uses of sacred groves by local elites, see De Jong 2002 and Probst 2004. For an example of a constructivist approach showing both instrumental action and the invocation of essentialized cultural materials in an Asian ecology movement, see Darlington 1998.

academics. Witchcraft accusations and occult beliefs were long considered to be quintessential examples of African traditionalism, but are now increasingly viewed as modern phenomena (Geschiere 1997, Comaroff and Comaroff 1999). The new scholarship shows that witches, zombies, vampires, and monsters provide compelling ways for Africans to think and talk about the frustration, anxiety, and fear fostered by ongoing political and economic disorder in their societies (Ellis and Ter Haar 2004).[21] Sacred groves are equally compelling, and quite opposite, ways to talk about ecological, social, political, and moral order during a period of rapid change. Orderly relationships become particularly salient when conditions of disorder prevail. Various social actors, from international conservationists to Ghanaian farmers, therefore symbolically reconstruct and discursively redeploy the notion of sacred groves, usually through the Relic Theory described above, both in pursuit of strategic interests and as a foil for the contradictions of modernity. Ultimately, therefore, African sacred groves have no single unifying meaning because of the great diversity of African notions of orderly ecosystems, societies, politics, and morality.

Conclusions

The complex and overlapping forms of ecological, socio-political, and symbolic dynamism in African sacred groves should make us cautiously optimistic about their conservation potential. The biodiversity and cultural diversity that sacred groves exemplify are indeed precious things and hallmarks of resilient ecological and social dynamics. Conservation, on the other hand, tends to define and preserve a relatively static set of conditions, and to value cultural diversity when it suits these environmental goals. In practice, this has meant that rationalizing, generalizing, and bureaucratic scientific institutions acquire socio-economic and political power (as well as the power to assign meanings) over the cultural diversity in which the biodiversity they seek to enhance is embedded. Like many international institutions promoting socio-economic change, conservation agencies seek reliable funding and predictable results (Robertson 1984, Scott 1998). Local socio-cultural distinctiveness can lead to unacceptably diverse and less predictable outcomes, so conservation organizations (and governments) simplify that diversity and mitigate that risk with blueprint approaches that seek to replicate success stories in very different circumstances. This often leads to tensions between conservation agencies and the people whose lands and resources they seek to conserve (Chapin 2004). Were African sacred groves to fall under the control of centralized conservation agencies, as has been the policy for sacred groves in South Asia (Gadgil and Vartak 1976), it is likely that their very dynamism and diversity would often lead to contradiction and conflict rather than preservation.[22]

---

21 This literature is too voluminous to review here, but for recent examples see Sanders 2003, Ashforth 2005, and West 2005.

22 In India, for example, state management of sacred groves has led to increased forest exploitation by social elites (Roy Burham 1994). The assumption that these groves constitute community resources ignores the evidence that Indian sacred groves have different meanings for

In the last decades of the twentieth century, the dismal record of top-down efforts spurred development practitioners and conservationists to embrace a more bottom-up approach. In their efforts to avoid entanglements with inefficient and often corrupt African states, many conservation agencies have focused their efforts on community-based conservation (CBC, also known as community-based natural resource management or CBNRM) (Adams and Hulme 2001). This sort of decentralized conservation has great potential to enhance both biodiversity and sustainable livelihoods. Sacred groves are, in many ways, ideal for community-based conservation – they clearly have ecological functions, they already have institutional legitimacy, and they embody community values. Sacred groves are, however, not simply culture-specific forms of the ecosystem concept (Berkes *et al.* 1998). As this volume shows, the assumption that sacred groves equal conservation tends to rely on notions of equilibrium that the empirical evidence on sacred grove ecology, social organization, and meaning contradict. Forest patches are usually in a state of flux, the African communities posited by CBC are not characterized by homogeneous social structures and shared norms, and the meanings of sacred groves are often multiple, overlapping, or ambiguous. Social flexibility and shifting, historically contingent ideologies and practices are basic to the dynamism and resilience that African sacred groves exemplify.

Efforts to decentralize and democratize resource management are often rife with contradictions such as these. Government authorities and non-governmental organizations often remain unaccountable to local authorities in Africa, and local political institutions often have very limited downward accountability to their constituents. Populist efforts to increase local democratic institutions are therefore having the perverse effect of increasing conflict and ambiguity (Byers 2004, Larson and Ribot 2005, Manor 2005). Outsiders' efforts to enhance local government and their uncritical acceptance of all that is local, indigenous, and traditional can produce institutional conflict rather than social synthesis, especially because such efforts introduce new ways to accumulate status and wealth. The administrative need to identify communities with clear boundaries and membership can therefore encourage divisive local political processes in which formerly flexible social groupings harden into blocs of 'stakeholders' and 'outsiders' (Byers *et al.* 2001, Geschiere 2004, Meynen and Doornbos 2005). African sacred groves' multiple meanings and institutional functions suggest that any effort to rationalize that diversity in the name of conservation would likely create more problems than it solves.[23] Policies that make sacred groves' legitimacy dependent on their conservation status can undermine the legitimacy and the 'moral ecological framework' (Cleaver

---

[22] (cont.) different caste groups, and that they have complex and variable implications for resource access and control for different social groups (Rival 1999, Bharucha 1999, Kalam 1998). Indian forest policy tends to be rationalizing and utilitarian, which leads to ecological classifications that are often at odds with the religious and social classifications of Indian sacred groves. Hybrid secular and religious policies could mitigate some of these problems (Chandra-kanath and Romm 1991).

[23] For examples of calls to rationalize African sacred groves, see Okafor and Ladipo 1995, Mgumia and Oba 2003 and Dorm-Adzobu *et al.* 1991.

2000) of the local institutions embedded in the groves. Sacredness is unquestionable, dangerous, often shrouded in secrecy, and usually emerges (and is reconstructed) in ritual contexts (Rappaport 1999). This is a poor match for the institutional transparency, democratic accountability, and critical evaluation of biophysical indicators that most conservation bureaucracies demand.

With challenges such as these, Africa's sacred groves are unlikely to become successful conservation areas without drastic alteration of their social relationships and cultural meanings (Nummelin and Virtanen 2000). Conservation policy should not, however, admit defeat in the face of complexity. Recent work on the emerging interdisciplinary topic of political ecology offers some clues for a form of African conservation that can avoid the anti-humanistic stance of the 'authoritarian biologist' (Guha 1997), the political contradictions of community-based conservation, and the intellectual morass of uncritical populism. Political ecology merges political economy with cultural ecology to produce analyses of resource access and control, and comprises both the political structure of struggles for resource control and the symbolic contestations that constitute those struggles (Moore 1993, Paulson *et al.* 2004, and Walker 2005). The power of discourse, such as that embedded in the Relic Theory used so often to discuss Africa's sacred groves, has emerged as a key theme in political ecology (Vayda and Walters 1999, Watts and Peet 2004). Political ecology therefore offers a rich intellectual framework for analyzing the multiple forms of power, modes of contestation, matters of scale, and complex relationships between Nature and Society. Incorporating non-equilibrium ecological theory, such as the hierarchical patch dynamics paradigm described above, into the more sociocentric methods of political ecology constructs a meeting place for the natural and social sciences.

Understanding Africa's sacred groves (and planning for their future) requires such a hybridized, synthetic natural/social science because these areas' ecological dynamics are so thoroughly interwoven with their social and ideological processes.[24] A hybrid form of science can encourage a sort of hybrid policy-making that, we hope, can lead to enhanced biological and cultural diversity, mutually beneficial relationships between state and local levels of society, and more sustainable livelihoods in Africa. Despite the lessons of non-equilibrium ecology and social science, however, much resource management policy is still based on assumptions about the 'balance of nature,' the feasibility of rigid social and ecological boundaries, and the homogeneity of communities (Zimmerer 2000, Agrawal and Gibson 1999). Greater policy diversity can help to move the elusive search for sustainability beyond reductive and rationalizing legal frameworks toward a more organic paradigm based on the co-management of culturally diverse global, regional, and local institutions (Botkin 1990:156, Beltrán 2000). This mosaic of adaptive co-management systems and hybrid science analyses would synthesize social, cultural, and natural capital and provide greater flexibility and resilience for the co-evolution of socio-ecological systems in Africa under conditions of rapid population growth, economic globalization, and global climate change (Berkes and Folke 1998). As icons and examples of

---

[24] The call for hybrid scientific research can be found in Batterbury *et al.* 1997, Zimmerer and Bassett 2003, and Zimmerer and Young 1998.

local empowerment and institution-building, African sacred groves can anchor policies to reduce the chronic tenurial insecurity of the poor (see Alden Wily 2006 for a thorough discussion of insecurity in African land matters). Such an approach to localized diversity of resource management policy could also check the increasing tendency in African conservation to reproduce the political dependencies of colonial indirect rule (Ribot 1999, 2003, 2004). The key question, therefore, is not how best to incorporate sacred groves into African conservation efforts, but rather how to transform conservation in Africa through its engagement with the multiple levels and forms of ecological, social, and symbolic processes embedded in African sacred groves.

References

Anonymous, 1990, *The Epic of Gilgamesh*. Stanford, CA: Stanford University Press.

Ackerman, Robert, 1987, *J.G. Frazer: His Life and Work*. Cambridge: Cambridge University Press.

Adams, William, and David Hulme, 2001, 'Conservation and community: Changing narratives, policies and practices in African conservation'. In *African Wildlife and Livelihoods*. David Hulme and Marshall Murphree, eds, pp. 9–23. Cape Town: David Philip.

Agrawal, Arun, and Clark Gibson, 1999, 'Enchantment and disenchantment: The role of community in natural resource conservation'. *World Development* 27(4):629–49.

Alden Wily, Liz, 2006, 'Land rights reform and governance in Africa: How to make it work in the 21st century?' UNDP Discussion Paper. New York: UNDP.

Alden Wily, L. and S. Mbaya, 2001, *Land, People, and Forests in Eastern and Southern Africa at the Beginning of the 21st Century*. Nairobi: IUCN.

Altman, Nathaniel, 1994, *Sacred Trees*. San Francisco: Sierra Club Books.

Amoako-Atta, Boakye, 1995, 'Sacred Groves in Ghana'. In *Cultural Landscapes of Universal Value*. B. von Droste, Harald Plachter, and Mechtild Rössler, eds, pp. 80–95. Stuttgart: Gustav Fischer Verlag and UNESCO.

Anane, Mike, 1997, *Religion and Conservation in Ghana*. New York: United Nations Non-Governmental Liaison Services.

Anderson, David, and Richard Grove, eds, 1987, *Conservation in Africa: People, Policies, and Practice*. Cambridge: Cambridge University Press.

Anoliefo, G. O., O. S. Isikhuemhen, and N. R. Ochije, 2003, 'Environmental implications of the erosion of cultural taboo practices in Awka-South Local Government Area of Anambra State, Nigeria: 1. Forests, trees, and water resource preservation'. *Journal of Agricultural and Environmental Ethics* 16:281–96.

Anyinam, Charles, 1999, 'Ethnomedicine, sacred spaces, ecosystem preservation and conservation in Africa'. In *Sacred Spaces and Public Quarrels: African Cultural and Economic Landscapes*. Paul Zeleza and Ezekiel Kalipeni, eds, pp. 127–46. Trenton, NJ: Africa World Press.

Apfel-Marglin, Frédérique, and P. C. Mishra, 1993, 'Sacred groves: Regenerating the body, the land, the community'. In *Global Ecology: A New Arena of Political Conflict*. W. Sachs, ed. pp. 197–207. London: Zed Books.

Apfel-Marglin, Frédérique, and Pramod Parajuli, 2000, 'Sacred grove and ecology: Ritual and science'. In *Hinduism and Ecology: The Intersection of Earth, Sky, and Water*. C. Chapple and M. Tucker, eds, pp. 291-316. Cambridge, MA: Harvard University Press.

Ashforth, Adam, 2005, *Witchcraft, Violence, and Democracy in South Africa*. Chicago: University of Chicago Press.

Aubreville, A., 1939, 'Forêts reliques en Afrique Occidentale Française' (Relic Forests in French Western Africa). *Revue de botanique appliquée et d'agriculture tropicale* 19:479–84.

Baffoe, Abraham, 2002, 'Ghana: Ancient tradition in community forest management'. *World Rainforest Movement Bulletin* 60. http://www.wrm.org.uy/bulletin/60/AF/html.

Bagine, R. K. N., 1998, 'Biodiversity in Ramogi Hill, Kenya, and its evolutionary significance'. *African Journal of Ecology* 36(3):251–63.

Basu, Ramsankar, 2000, 'Studies on sacred groves and taboos in Purulia district of West Bengal'. *Indian Forester* 126:1309–18.

Batterbury, S., T. Forsyth, and K. Thomson, 1997, 'Environmental transformations in developing countries: Hybrid research and democratic policy.' *The Geographical Journal* 163(2): 126–32.

Baum, Robert, 1999, *Shrines of the Slave Trade*. New York: Oxford University Press.

Bayliss-Smith, Tim, Edvard Hvidling, and Tim Whitmore, 2003, 'Rainforest composition and histories of human disturbance in Solomon Islands'. *Ambio* 32(5):346–52.

Beckett, Greg, 2004, 'Master of the wood: Moral authority and political imaginaries in Haiti'. *Political and Legal Anthropology Review* 27(2):1–19.

Beier, P., M. van Drielen, and B. O. Kankam, 2002, 'Avifaunal collapse in West African forest fragments'. *Conservation Biology* 164:1097–111.

Beltrán, Javier, ed., 2000, *Indigenous and Traditional Peoples and Protected Areas: Principles, Guidelines and Case Studies*. Gland, Switzerland: IUCN.

Berkes, Fikret, and Carl Folke, 1998, 'Linking social and ecological systems for resilience and sustainability'. In *Linking Social and Ecological Systems: Management Practices and Social Mechanisms for Building Resilience*. F. Berkes and Carl Folkes, eds, pp. 1-25. Cambridge: Cambridge University Press.

Berkes, Fikret, Mina Kislalioglu, Carl Folke, and Madhav Gadgil, 1998, 'Exploring the basic ecological unit: Ecosystem-like concepts in traditional societies'. *Ecosystems* 1:409–15.

Berry, Sara, 1993, *No Condition is Permanent*. Madison, WI: University of Wisconsin Press.

Bharucha, E., 1999, 'Cultural and spiritual values related to the conservation of biodiversity in the sacred groves of the Western Ghats in Maharashtra'. In *Cultural and Spiritual Values of Biodiversity. A Complementary Contribution to the Global*. D. Posey, ed. pp. 382–5. London: Intermediate Technology Publications and UNEP.

Binggeli, Pierre, Desalegn Desissa, John Healey, Matt Painton, John Smith and Zewge Teklehaimanot, 2003, 'Conservation of Ethiopian sacred groves'. *European Tropical Forest Research Network (ETFRN) News* 38:37–8.

Bloch, Maurice, 1998, 'Why trees, too, are good to think with: Towards an anthropology of the meaning of life'. In *The Social Life of Trees: Anthropological Perspectives on Tree Symbolism*. L. Rival, ed. pp. 39–55. Oxford and New York: Berg Publishers Ltd.

Boraiah, K. T., R. Vasudeva, S. Bhagwat, and C. G. Kushalappa, 2003, 'Do informally managed sacred groves have higher richness and regeneration of medicinal plants than state-managed reserve forests?' *Current Science* 84 (6):804–8.

Bossart, J. L., E. Opuni-Frimpong, S. Kuudaar, and E. Nkrumah, 2006, 'Richness, abundance, and complementarity of fruit-feeding butterfly species in relict sacred forests and forest reserves of Ghana'. *Biodiversity and Conservation* 15(1):333–59.

Botkin, D., 1990, *Discordant Harmonies*. New York: Oxford University Press.

Bravman, William, 1998, *Making Ethnic Ways: Communities and their Transformations in Taita, Kenya 1800–1950*. Portsmouth, NH: Heinemann.

Byers, Bruce, 2004, 'Mhondoro: Spirit lions and sacred forests.' In *This Sacred Earth*. Roger S. Gottlieb, ed. pp. 651–60. New York: Routledge.

Byers, Bruce A., Robert N. Cunliffe, and Andrew T. Hudak, 2001, 'Linking the conservation of culture and nature: A case study of sacred forests in Zimbabwe'. *Human Ecology* 29(2): 187–218.

Campbell, Michael O'Neal, 2004, 'Traditional forest protection and woodlots in the coastal savannah of Ghana'. *Environmental Conservation* 31(3):225–32.

—— 2005, 'Sacred groves for forest conservation in Ghana's coastal savannas: Assessing ecological and social dimensions'. *Singapore Journal of Tropical Geography* 26(2):151–69.

Castro, Peter, 1990, 'Sacred groves and social change in Kirinyaga, Kenya'. In *Social Change and Applied Anthropology*. M. Chaiken and Anne K. Fleuret, eds, pp. 277–89. Boulder, CO: Westview Press.

—— 1995, *Facing Kirinyaga: A Social History of Forest Commons in Southern Mount Kenya*. London: Intermediate Technology Publications.

Ceuppens, Bambi, and Peter Geschiere, 2005, 'Autochthony: Local or Global? New Modes in the Struggle over Citizenship and Belonging in Africa and Europe'. *Annual Review of Anthropology* 34(1):385–407.

Chandrakanth, M. G. and Jeff Romm, 1991, 'Sacred forests, secular forest policy and people's actions'. *Natural Resources Journal* 31(4):741-756.

Chandran, M. D. S., 1998, 'Shifting cultivation, sacred groves, and conflicts in the colonial forest policy'. In *Nature and the Orient*. Vinita Damodaran, Richard Grove and Satpal Sangwang, eds pp. 674–707. Oxford and New Dehli: Oxford University Press.

Chandran, M. D. S. and J. Donald Hughes, 1997, 'The sacred groves of South India: Traditional communities and religious change'. *Social Compass* 44(3):413–27.

Chapin, Mac, 2004, 'A challenge to conservationists'. *World Watch Magazine* Nov./Dec.:17–31.

Chevalier, A., 1933, 'Les bois sacrés des noirs, sanctuaires de la nature'. *Compte rendue de la Société de Biogéographie*: 37.

Chidhakwa, Zvidzai, 2003, 'Traditional institutions manage their Nyakwaa and Chizire forests in Chimanimani, Zimbabwe'. *Policy Matters* 12:132–40.

Chouin, Gérard, 2002a, 'Sacred groves as historical and archaeological markers in southern Ghana'. *Ghana Studies* 5:177–196.

—— 2002b, 'Sacred groves in history'. *IDS Bulletin* 33(2):39-46.

Chretien, J., 1978, 'Les arbres et les rois, sites historiques du Burundi'. *Culture et société* (1):35-47.

Cleaver, Frances, 2000, 'Moral ecological rationality, institutions and the management of common property resources'. *Development and Change* 31:361–83.

Cleaver, Kevin, and Götz Schreiber, 1994, *Reversing the Spiral: The Population, Agriculture, and Environment Nexus in Sub-Saharan Africa*. Washington, DC: World Bank.

Clements, F., 1916, *Plant Succession: An Analysis of the Development of Vegetation*. Washington, DC: Carnegie Institution of Washington.

Cohen, A. P., 1985, *The Symbolic Construction of Community*. London: Routledge.

Colding, J., and C. Folke, 2001, 'Social taboos: "Invisible" systems of local resource management and biological conservation'. *Ecological Applications* 11(2):584–600.

Colson, Elizabeth, 1997, 'Places of power and shrines of the land'. *Paideuma: Mitteilungen zur Kulturkunde*, 43:47–57.

Comaroff, Jean and John L. Comaroff, 1999, 'Occult economies and the violence of abstraction: Notes from the South African postcolony'. *American Ethnologist* 26(2):279–303.

Connell, J., and W. Sousa, 1983, 'On the evidence needed to judge ecological stability or persistence'. *American Naturalist*, 121:789–824.

Crumley, Carole, ed., 1994, *Historical Ecology: Cultural Knowledge and Changing Landscapes*. Santa Fe, NM: School of American Research Press.

Daneel, Marthinus, 2001, *African Earthkeepers*. Maryknoll, NY: Orbis Books.

Darlington, Susan, 1998, 'The ordination of a tree: The Buddhist ecology movement in Thailand'. *American Ethnologist* 37(1):1-15.

Deb, D., K. Deuti, and K. C. Malhotra, 1997, 'Sacred grove relics as bird refugia'. *Current Science* 73(10):815–17.

Decher, J., 1997a, 'Bat community patterns on the Accra Plains of Ghana, West Africa'. *Zeitschrift für Säugetierkunde* 62(3):129–42.

—— 1997b, 'Conservation, small mammals, and the future of sacred groves in West Africa'. *Biodiversity and Conservation* 6:1007–26.

Decher, Jan, and L. K. Bahian, 1999, 'Diversity and structure of terrestrial small mammal communities in different vegetation types on the Accra Plains of Ghana'. *Journal of Zoology* (London) 247:395–408.

De Jong, Ferdinand, 1999, 'The production of translocality: Initiation in the sacred grove in southern Senegal'. In *Modernity on a Shoestring*. R. Fardon, ed., pp. 315–40. Leiden: EIDOS.

—— 2002, 'Politicans of the sacred grove: Citizenship and ethnicity in southern Senegal'. *Africa* 72(2):203–21.

Dorm-Adzobu, C., O. Ampadu-Agyei, and P. G. Veit, 1991, *Religious Beliefs and Environmental Protection: The Malshegu Grove in Northern Ghana.* Nairobi: African Centre for Technology Studies (ACTS) and WRI Center for International Development and Environment.

Douglas, Mary, 1970, *Natural Symbols: Explorations in Cosmology.* New York: Vintage Books.

Dove, Michael, R., Marina T. Campos, Andrew Salvador Matthews, Laura J. Meitzner Yoder, Anne Rademacher, Suk Bae Rhee and Daniel Somers-Smith, 2003, 'The global mobilization of environmental concepts: Re-thinking the Western/Non-Western divide'. In *Nature Across Cultures.* H. Selin, ed., pp. 19–46. Dordrecht, The Netherlands: Kluwer Academic Publishers.

Dudley, Nigel, Liza Higgins-Zogib, and Stephanie Mansourian, 2005, *Beyond Belief: Linking Faiths and Protected Areas to Support Biodiversity Conservation.* Gland, Switzerland: World Wide Fund for Nature.

Durkheim, Emile, 1954, *The Elementary Forms of the Religious Life.* Glencoe, IL: The Free Press.

Egerton, F. N., 1973, Changing Concepts of the Balance of Nature'. *Quarterly Review of Biology* 48:322–50.

Elliott, Jennifer A. and Michael O'Neal Campbell, 2002, 'The environmental imprints and complexes of social dynamics in rural Africa: Cases from Zimbabwe and Ghana'. *Geoforum* 33:221–37.

Ellis, Stephen, and Gerrie ter Haar, 2004, *Worlds of Power: Religious Thought and Political Practice in Africa.* Oxford: Oxford University Press.

Elton, C. 1930, *Animal Ecology and Evolution.* Oxford: Oxford University Press.

Fairhead, James, and Melissa Leach, 1996, *Misreading the African Landscape: Society and Ecology in a Forest-Savanna Mosaic.* Cambridge: Cambridge University Press.

—— 1997, 'Culturing trees: Socialized knowledge in the political ecology of Kissia and Kuranko forest islands of Guinea'. In *Nature is Culture: Indigenous Knowledge and Socio-Cultural Aspects of Trees and Forests in Non-European Cultures.* K. Seeland, ed. pp. 7–18. London: Intermediate Technology Development Group Publishing.

—— 1998, *Reframing Deforestation: Global Analysis and Local Realities – Studies in West Africa.* London: Routledge.

Food and Agriculture Organization (FAO), 2005, *State of the World's Forests 2005.* Rome: Food and Agriculture Organization.

Fargey, Patrick, 1992, 'Boabeng-Fiema Monkey Sanctuary'. *Oryx* 26(3):151–6.

Fisiy, C. F., 1994, 'The Death of a Myth System: Land colonization on the slopes of Mount Oku, Cameroon'. In *Land Tenure and Sustainable Land Use.* R. J. Bakema, ed. pp. 12–20. *Kit Bulletin* No. 332. Amsterdam: Royal Tropical Institute.

Fitz-Henry, Erin, and Meitamei Olol-Dapash, 2002, 'Sacred site under threat'. *Cultural Survival Quarterly* 26:78–9.

Fortes, Meyer, 1945, *The Dynamics of Clanship among the Tallensi.* London: Oxford University Press.

—— 1987, *Religion, Morality, and the Person.* Cambridge: Cambridge University Press.

Fortes, Meyer, and E. E. Evans-Pritchard, eds, 1987 [1940], *African Political Systems.* London: KPI Limited.

Frazer, James, 1951, *The Golden Bough* (abridged edn). New York: Macmillan and Company.

—— 1966, *Aftermath.* London: Macmillan and Company.

Freeman, J. R. 1999, 'Gods, groves, and the culture of nature in Kerala'. *Modern Asian Studies* 33(2):257–302.

Friend, Tad, 2005, 'The shroud of Marin'. *New Yorker.* August 29, 2005.

Gadgil, Madhav, Fikret Berkes, and Carl Folke, 1993, 'Indigenous knowledge for biodiversity conservation'. *Ambio* 22(2–3):151–6.

Gadgil, Madhav, and Ramachandra Guha, 1992, *This Fissured Land.* Berkeley, CA: University of California Press.

Gadgil, Madhav, and V. D. Vartak, 1976, 'The sacred groves of Western Ghats in India'. *Economic Botany* 30:152–60.

Gadgil, Madhav, and M. D. S. Chandran, 1992, 'Sacred groves'. In *Indigenous Vision: Peoples of India Attitudes to the Environment.* G. Sen, ed., pp. 183–7. New Delhi: Sage.

Gerden, C. A., and S. Mtallo, 1990, 'Traditional forest reserves in Babati District, Tanzania'. Swedish University of Agricultural Sciences, International Rural Development Centre, working paper #128.

Geschiere, Peter, 1997, *The Modernity of Witchcraft: Politics and the Occult in Postcolonial Africa*. Charlottesville, VA: University Press of Virginia.

—— 2004, 'Ecology, belonging and xenophobia: The 1994 forest law in Cameroon and the issue of "community"'. In *Rights and the Politics of Recognition in Africa*. H. Englund and Francis Nyamnjoh, eds, pp. 237–59. London: Zed Books.

Geschiere, Peter, and Francis Nyamnjoh, 2000, 'Capitalism and autochthony: The seesaw of mobility and belonging'. *Public Culture* 12(2):423–52.

Geschiere, Peter, and Jos van der Klei, 1988, 'Popular protest; the Diola of south Senegal'. In *Religion and Development: Towards an Integrated Approach*. P. Quarles van Ufford and M. Schoffeleers, eds, pp. 209–30. Amsterdam: Free University Press.

Giddens, Anthony, 1984, *The Constitution of Society: The Outline of a Theory of Structuration*. Cambridge: Polity Press.

Gillson, Lindsey, 2004, 'Evidence of hierarchical patch dynamics in an East African savanna?' *Landscape Ecology* 19:883–94.

Gillson, Lindsey, Michael Sheridan, and Dan Brockington, 2003, 'Representing environments in flux: Case studies from East Africa'. *Area* 35(4):371–89.

Gillson, Lindsey, and Kathy Willis, 2004, 'As earth's testimonies tell: Wilderness conservation in a changing world'. *Ecology Letters* 7:990–8.

Glacken, Clarence, 1967, *Traces on the Rhodian Shore*. Berkeley, CA: University of California Press.

Gokhale, Y., R. Velankar, M. D. S. Chandran, and M. Gadgil, 1998, 'Sacred woods, grasslands, and waterbodies as self-organized systems of conservation'. In *Conserving the Sacred for Biodiversity Management*. P. S. Ramakrishnan, K. G. Saxena and U. M. Chandrashekara, eds, pp. 365–96. New Delhi: Oxford & IBH Publishing.

Gombya-Ssembajjwe, William S., 1995, 'Sacred forests in modern Ganda society'. *Uganda Journal* 42:32–44.

Greene, Sandra, 2002, *Sacred Sites and the Colonial Encounter*. Bloomington, IN: Indiana University Press.

Grove, Richard, 1997, *Ecology, Climate, and Empire: Colonialism and Global Environmental History, 1400–1940*. Cambridge: White Horse Press.

Guha, Ramachandra, 1997, 'The authoritarian biologist and the arrogance of anti-humanism: Wildlife conservation in the Third World'. *The Ecologist* 27:14–20.

—— 2000, *Environmentalism: A Global History*. New York: Longman.

Guillot, Bernard, 1980, 'La création et la destruction des bosquets Koukouya, symboles d'une civilisation et de son declin'. *Cahiers O.R.S.T.O.M. Serie Sciences Humaines* 17:177–89.

Guinko, Sita, 1985, 'Contribution à l'étude de la végétation et la flore de la région du Burkina-Faso. Les reliques bois sacrés'. *Bois et Forêts des Tropiques* 208:29–36.

Guyer, Jane, 1981, 'Household and community in African studies'. *African Studies Review* 24(2/3):87–137.

—— 1995, 'Wealth in people, wealth in things: introduction'. *Journal of African History* 36:83–90.

Guyer, Jane, and Paul Richards, 1996, 'The invention of biodiversity: Social perspectives on the management of biological variety in Africa'. *Africa* 66(1):1–13.

Haberl, H., S. Batterbury, and E. Moran, 2001, 'Using and shaping the land: A long-term perspective'. *Land Use Policy* 18:1–18.

Harrison, G., 1979, 'Stability under environmental stress: Resistance, resilience, persistence, and variability'. *American Naturalist* 1135:659–64.

Hay-Edie, T. and M. Hadley, 1998, 'Natural sacred sites: A comparative approach to their cultural and biological significance'. In *Conserving the Sacred for Biodiversity Management*. P. S. Ramakrishnan, K. G. Saxena and U. M. Chandrashekara, eds, pp. 47-67. New Delhi: Oxford & IBH Publishing.

Heckenberger, Michael, *et al.*, 2003, 'Amazonia 1492: Pristine forest or cultural parkland?' *Science* 301:1710–14.

Houghton, J. T., *et al.*, 2001, *Climate Change 2001: The Scientific Basis*. Cambridge: Cambridge University Press.

Hughes, J. D., 1994, *Groves and Gardens, Parks and Paradises*. Baltimore, MD: Johns Hopkins University Press.

Hughes, J. D., and M. D. S. Chandran, 1998, 'Sacred groves around the Earth: An overview'. In *Conserving the Sacred for Biodiversity Management*. P. S. Ramakrishnan, K. G. Saxena and U. M. Chandrashekara, eds, pp. 69–86. New Delhi: Oxford & IBH Publishing.

Igoe, Jim, 2005, 'Global indigenism and spaceship earth: convergence, space, and re-entry friction'. *Globalizations* 2(3):377–90.

Iliffe, John, 1995, *Africans: The History of a Continent*. Cambridge: Cambridge University Press.

Juhé-Beaulaton, Dominique, 1999, 'Arbres et bois sacrés: lieux de mémoire de l'ancienne Côte des Esclaves'. In *Histoire d'Afrique. Enjeux de mémoire*. J. P. Chrétien and J. L. Triaud, eds, pp. 101–18. Paris: Karthala.

—— 2003, 'Processus de réactivation de sites sacrés dans le Sud du Bénin'. In *Lieux de culture, culture de lieux. Production(s) culturelle(s) locale(s) et émergence des lieux: dynamiques, acteurs, enjeux*. M. Gravari-Barbas and P. Violier, eds, pp. 67–79. Rennes: Presses Universitaires de Rennes.

Juhé-Beaulaton, Dominique, and Bernard Roussel, 1998, 'A propos de l'historicité des forêts sacrées de l'ancienne Côte des Esclaves'. In *Plantes et paysages d'Afrique, une histoire à explorer*. M. Chastanet, ed. pp. 353–82. Paris: Karthala and CRA.

—— 2002, 'Les sites religieux vodou: des patrimoines en permanente évolution'. In *Patrimonialiser la nature tropicale. Dynamiques locales, enjeux internationaux*. M. C. Cormier-Salem, D. Juhé-Beaulaton, J. Boutrais, and B. Roussel, eds, pp. 415–38. Paris: IRD Editions.

Juul, Kristine and Christian Lund, 2002, *Negotiating Property in Africa*. Portsmouth, NH: Heinemann.

Kalam, M. A., 1998, 'Sacred groves in Coorg, Karnataka'. In *The Social Construction of Indian Forests*. R. Jeffery, ed., pp. 39–54. New Delhi: Manohar.

Kenyatta, Jomo, 1965, *Facing Mt. Kenya*. New York: Vintage Books.

Khiewtam, Ramesh S., and P. S. Ramkrishnan, 1989, 'Socio-cultural studies of the sacred groves at Cherrapunji and adjioning areas in northeastern India'. *Man in India* 69(1):64–71.

Knapp, Sandra, 2003, 'Dynamic diversity'. *Nature* 422:475.

Kopytoff, Igor, 1988, 'The internal African frontier: The making of African political culture'. In *The African Frontier*. I. Kopytoff, ed., pp. 3-85. Bloomington, IN: Indiana University Press.

Kuhn, Thomas, 1970, *The Structure of Scientific Revolutions*. 2nd edn. Chicago: University of Chicago Press.

Kull, Christian, 2004, *Isle of Fire*. Chicago: University of Chicago Press.

Kuper, Adam, 1996, *Anthropology and Anthropologists: The Modern British School,* 3rd edn. London: Routledge.

Lan, David, 1985, *Guns and Rain*. London: James Currey.

Larson, Anne, and Jesse Ribot, 2005, 'Democratic decentralization through a natural resource lens: An introduction'. In *Democratic Decentralisation through a Natural Resource Lens*. J. Ribot and A. Larson, eds, pp. 1-25. London: Routledge.

Leach, Melissa, and James Fairhead, 2000, 'Fashioned forest paths, occluded histories? International environmental analysis in West African locales'. *Development and Change* 31:35-59.

Leach, Melissa, Robin Mearns, and Ian Scoones, 1999, 'Environmental entitlements: Dynamics and institutions in CBRNM'. *World Development* 27(2):225–47.

Lebbie, A. R., and M. S. Freudenberger, 1996, 'Sacred groves in Africa: Forest patches in transition'. In *Forest Patches in Tropical Landscapes*. J. G. Schelhas and Russell Greenberg, eds, pp. 300–24. Washington, DC: Island Press.

Lebbie, A. R. and R. Guries, 1995, 'Ethnobotanical value and conservation of sacred groves of the Kpaa Mende in Sierra Leone'. *Economic Botany* 49(3):297–308.

Legesse, A, 1986, 'Boran-Gabra pastoralism in historical perspective'. In *Rangelands, a Resource under Siege: Proceedings of 2nd International Rangeland Congress*. P. J. Ross, P. W. Lynch and O. B. Williams, eds, pp. 481–2. Cambridge: Cambridge University Press.

Little, Peter and David W. Brokensha, 1987, 'Local institutions, tenure, and resource management in East Africa'. In *Conservation in Africa*. D. Anderson and Richard Grove, eds, pp. 193–210. Cambridge: Cambridge University Press.

Lukumbuzya, Kahana, 2000, 'The effects of different management regimes on the diversity and regeneration of woody vegetation under a joint forest management model, in Tabora, western Tanzania'. *Silva Carelica* 34:159–77.

Madeweya, K. H., H. Oka, and M. Matsumoto, 2004, 'Sustainable management of sacred forests and their potential for eco-tourism in Zanzibar'. *Shinrin Sogo Kenkyujo kenkyu hokoku* (Bulletin of the Forestry and Forest Products Research Institute) 3(1):33–48.

Maley, Jean, 2001, 'The impact of arid phases on the African rain forest through geological history'. In *African Rain Forest Ecology and Conservation*. L.W. William Weber, Amy Vedder, and Lisa Naughton-Treves, eds, pp. 68–87. New Haven, CT: Yale University Press.

Malhotra, K. C., 1998, 'Anthropological Dimensions of Sacred Groves in India: An Overview'. In *Conserving the Sacred for Biodiversity Management*. P. S. Ramakrishnan, K. G. Saxena and U. M. Chandrashekara, eds, pp. 423–38. New Delhi: Oxford & IBH Publishing.

Malinowski, Bronislaw, 1922, *Argonauts of the Western Pacific*. New York: E. P. Dutton & Co., Inc.

Manor, James, 2005, 'User committees: A potentially damaging second wave of decentralisation?' In *Democratic Decentralisation through a Natural Resource Lens*. J. Ribot and A. Larson, eds, pp. 192–231. London: Routledge.

Matawonyika, Joseph, 1997, 'Resource management and the Shona people in rural Zimbabwe'. In *Indigenous Peoples and Sustainability*. pp. 257–66. Utrecht, the Netherlands: IUCN Intercommision task force on indigenous peoples.

McCaskie, T. C., 1990, 'Nananom Mpow of Mankessim: An Essay in Fante History'. In *West African Economic and Social History: Studies in Memory of Marion Johnson*. David Henige and T. C. McCaskie, eds, pp. 133-150. Madison, WI: University of Wisconsin African Studies Program.

McWilliam, Andrew, 2001, 'Prospects for the sacred grove: Valuing lulic forests on Timor'. *Asia Pacific Journal of Anthropology* 2(2):89–113.

Meynen, Wicky, and Martin Doornbos, 2005, 'Decentralising natural resource management: A recipe for sustainability and equity?' In *Democratic Decentralisation through a Natural Resource Lens*. J. Ribot and A. Larson, eds, pp. 235–54. London: Routledge.

Mgumia, F. H. and G. Oba, 2003, 'Potential role of sacred groves in biodiversity conservation in Tanzania'. *Environmental Conservation* 30(3):259–65.

Michaloud, G. and S. Dury, 1998, 'Sacred trees, groves, landscapes and related cultural situations may contribute to conservation and management in Africa'. In *Conserving the Sacred for Biodiversity Management*. P. S. Ramakrishnan, K. G. Saxena and U. M. Chandrashekara, eds, pp. 129–43. New Delhi: Oxford & IBH Publishing.

Mishra, B. P., O. P. Tripathi, R. S. Tripathi, and H. N. Pandey, 2004, 'Effects of anthropogenic disturbance on plant diversity and community structure of a sacred grove in Meghalaya, northeast India'. *Biodiversity and Conservation* 13:421–36.

Mitchell, J. Clyde, 1961, 'Chizere's Tree: A note on a Shona land-shrine and its significance'. *NADA: The Southern Rhodesia Native Affairs Department Annual* 38:28–35.

Mittermeier, Russell A., *et al.*, eds, 1999, *Hotspots: Earth's Biologically Richest and Most Endangered Terrestrial Ecoregions*. Mexico City: CEMEX / Conservation International.

Moore, Donald, 1993, 'Contesting terrain in Zimbabwe's eastern highlands: Political ecology, ethnography, and peasant resource struggles'. *Economic Geography* 69(4):380–401.

Moore, Sally Falk, 1986, *Social Facts and Fabrications: 'Customary' Law on Kilimanjaro, 1880–1980*. Cambridge: Cambridge University Press.

—— 1994, *Anthropology and Africa: Changing Perspectives on a Changing Scene*. Charlottesville, VA: The University Press of Virginia.

Mussanhane, Jaime, Luis Nhamuco, and Pekka Virtanen, 2000, 'A traditionally protected forest as a conservation area: A case study from Mozambique'. *Silva Carelica* 34:89–115.

Musters, C. J. M, H. J. de Graaf, and W. J. ter Keurs, 2000, 'Can protected areas be expanded in Africa?' *Science* 287:1759–60.

Mukamuri, B. B., 1995, 'Local environmental conservation strategies: Karanga religion, politics and environmental control'. *Environment and History* 1:297–311.

Mutoro, H. W., 1994, 'The Mijikenda Kaya as a sacred site'. In *Sacred Sites, Sacred Places*. Jane Hubert, David Carmichael, Brian Reeves and Audhild Schanche, eds, pp. 132–9. London: Routledge.

Mwikomeke, S. T., Charles Mabula, and Matti Nummelin, 2000, 'Plant species richness in the traditionally protected forests of the Zigua, Handeni District, Tanzania'. *Silva Carelica* 34:178–93.

Mwihomeke, S. T., T. H. Msangi, C. K. Mabula, J. Ylhaisi, and K. Mndeme, 1998, 'Traditionally protected forests and nature conservation in the North Pare mountains and Handeni District, Tanzania'. *Journal of East African Natural History* 87:279–90.

Neumann, K., and P. Müller-Haude, 1999, 'Forêts sèches au sud-ouest du Burkina Faso: végétation - sols - action de l'homme'. *Phytocoenologia* 29(1):53–85.

Newmark, W. D., 2002, *Conserving Biodiversity in East African Forests: A Study of the Eastern Arc Mountains*. Berlin: Springer-Verlag.

Niamir, Maryann, 1990, 'Traditional woodland management techniques of African pastoralists'. *Unasylva* 41(160):49–58.

Niangoran-Bouah, G., 1983, 'Le silence dans les traditions de culture Africaine'. *Revue Ivoirienne d'Anthropologie et de Sociologie* 3:6–11.

Ntiamoa-Baidu, Yaa, 1993, 'Indigenous protected area systems in Ghana'. In *African Biodiversity: Foundation for the Future*. pp. 66–7. Washington, DC: USAID Biodiversity Support Program.

——, 2001, 'Indigenous versus introduced biodiversity conservation strategies: The case of protected area systems in Ghana'. In *African Rain Forest Ecology and Conservation*. L.W. W. Weber, A. Vedder, and L. Naughton-Treves, eds, pp. 385–94. New Haven, CT: Yale University Press.

Nummelin, Matti, and Pekka Virtanen, 2000, 'Local forest management by traditional and introduced means in southern Africa – A synthesis and recommendations'. *Silva Carelica* 34: 220–29.

Nyamweru, Celia, 1996, 'Sacred groves threatened by development: The Kaya forests of Kenya'. *Cultural Survival Quarterly* 20(3):19–21.

Oates, John, Pius Anadu, Elizabeth Gadsby, and J. Lodewijk Were, 1992, 'Sclater's guienon – A rare Nigerian monkey threatened by deforestation'. *National Geographic Research and Exploration* 8(4):476–91.

Odum, E., 1953, *Fundamentals of Ecology*. Philadelphia: Saunders.

Okafor, J. C. and D. O. Ladipo, 1995, 'Fetish groves in the conservation of threatened flora in southern Nigeria'. In *Conservation of Biodiversity in Africa*. L. A. Bennun, R. A. Aman, and S. A. Craftes, eds, pp. 167–79. Nairobi: National Museums of Kenya.

Okeke, S. E., 1999, 'The vanishing sacred groves in Igboland: A case for immediate action'. *Nigerian Heritage* 8:130–41.

Omari, Cuthbert, 1990, 'Traditional African land ethics'. In *Ethics of Environment and Development: Global Challenge, International Response*. J. R. Engel, and Joan Gibb Engel, eds, pp. 167–75. Tuscon, AZ: University of Arizona Press.

Ortner, Sherry, 1973, 'On key symbols'. *American Anthropologist* 75(5):1338–46.

Pahl-Wostl, Claudia, 1995, *The Dynamic Nature of Ecosystems: Chaos and Order Entwined*. Chichester, NY: Wiley.

Pandey, Deep Narayan, 1998, *Ethnoforestry: Local Knowledge for Sustainable Forestry and Livelihood Security*. Udaipur and New Delhi: Himanshu Publications.

Parkin, David, 1991, *Sacred Void: Spatial Images of Work and Ritual among the Giriama of Kenya*. Cambridge: Cambridge University Press.

Paulson, Susan, Lisa Gezon, and Michael Watts, 2004, 'Politics, ecologies, genealogies'. In *Political Ecology across Spaces, Scales, and Social Groups*. S. Paulson, and Lisa Gezon, eds, pp. 17–37. New Brunswick, NJ: Rutgers University Press.

Pei, Shengji, 1991, 'Conservation of biological diversity'. *Ethnobotany* 3:27–35.

Philpot, J. H., 1897, *The Sacred Tree, or The Tree in Religion and Myth*. New York: Macmillan and

Company.

Pickett, Steward, and Richard Ostfeld, 1995, 'The shifting paradigm in ecology'. In *A New Century for Natural Resources Management*. Richard Knight and Sarah Bates, eds, pp. 261–78. Washington DC: Island Press.

Pickett, Steward, Thomas Parker, and Peggy Fiedler, 1992, 'The new paradigm in ecology: implications for conservation biology above the species level'. In *Conservation Biology*, Peggy Fiedler and Subodh Jain, eds, pp. 66–88. New York: Chapman and Hill.

Pimm, S., 1991, *The Balance of Nature? Ecological Issues in the Conservation of Species and Communities*. Chicago: University of Chicago Press.

Probst, Peter, 2004, 'Keeping the goddess alive: performing culture and remembering the past in Osogbo, Nigeria'. *Social Analysis* 48(1):33–54.

Rajendraprasad, M., P. N. Krishnan, and P. Pushpangadan, 1998, 'The life form spectrum of sacred groves-a functional tool to analyze the vegetation'. *Tropical Ecology* 39(2):211–17.

Ramakrishnan, P. S., 1996, 'Conserving the sacred: Ecological and policy implications'. *Nature and Resources* 32(1):11–19.

Ramakrishnan, P. S., K. G. Saxena and U. M. Chandrashekara, eds, 1998, *Conserving the Sacred for Biodiversity Management*. New Delhi: Oxford & IBH Publishing.

Ramanujam, M. P., and K. Praveen Kumar Cyril, 2003, 'Woody species diversity of four sacred groves in the Pondicherry region of South India'. *Biodiversity and Conservation* 12:289–99.

Ranger, Terence, 1983, 'The invention of tradition in colonial Africa'. In *The Invention of Tradition*. E. Hobsbawm and Terence Ranger, eds, Cambridge: Cambridge University Press.

—— 1988, 'African traditional religion'. In *The Study of Religion, Traditional and New Religions*. Peter Clarke and Stewart Sutherland, eds pp. 106–114. London: Routledge.

—— 1994, 'The invention of tradition revisited: The case of colonial Africa'. In *Inventions and Boundaries*. P. Kaarsholm and Jan Hultin, eds, pp. 9–50. Roskilde Univ. Occasional paper #11. Roskilde, Denmark.

——, 1999, *Voices from the Rocks: Nature, Culture and History in the Matopos Hills of Zimbabwe*. Harare: Baobab, Bloomington, IN: Indiana University Press, and Oxford: James Currey.

Rappaport, Roy, 1999, *Ritual and Religion in the Making of Humanity*. Cambridge: Cambridge University Press.

Rathakette, Pagarat, *et al.*, 1984, 'Taboos and traditions: Their influence on the conservation and exploitation of trees in social forestry projects in northeastern Thailand'. In *Community Forestry: Socio-Economic Aspects*. Y. S. Rao, N. T. Vergara, and G. Lovelace, eds, pp. 363–70. Bangkok: FAO – Regional Office for Asia and the Pacific (ROAP).

Ribot, Jesse, 1999, 'Decentralization, participation, and accountability in Sahelian forestry: Legal instruments of political-administrative control'. *Africa* 69(1):23–65.

—— 2003, 'Democratic decentralization of natural resources: Institutional choice and discretionary power transfers in sub-Saharan Africa'. *Public Administration and Development* 23:53–65.

—— 2004, *Waiting for Democracy: The Politics of Choice in Natural Resource Decentralization*. Washington, DC: World Resources Institute.

Riley, Bernard, and David Brokensha, 1988, *The Mbeere in Kenya*. Lanham, MD: University Press of America.

Rival, Laura, 1998, 'Trees, from symbols of life and regeneration to political artefacts'. In *The Social Life of Trees: Anthropological Perspectives on Tree Symbolism*. L. Rival, ed., pp. 1–36. Oxford and New York: Berg Publishers Ltd.

—— 1999, 'Trees and the symbolism of life in indigenous cosmologies'. In *Cultural and Spiritual Values of Biodiversity*. D. Posey, ed., pp. 358–63. London: Intermediate Technology Publications and UNEP.

Robertson, A. F., 1984, *People and the State: An Anthropology of Planned Development*. Cambridge: Cambridge University Press.

Robertson, S. A. and W. R. Q. Luke, 1993, *The Vegetation and Conservation Status of Kaya Coastal Forests in Kenya: A report to WWF*. Nairobi: National Museums of Kenya.

Roy Burham, J., 1994, 'Sacred groves and the modern political economy'. *Lokayan Bulletin* 10:41–52.

—— 1995, 'The dynamics of sacred groves'. *Journal of Human Ecology* 6:245–54.

—— 2003, *Sacred Groves and Communities*. New Delhi: Mittal Publications.

Sanders, Todd, 2003, 'Reconsidering witchcraft: Postcolonial Africa and analytic (un)certainties', *American Anthropologist*, 105(2):338–52.

Sanogo, D., 1983, 'Bois sacré: temple ou école?' *Revue Ivoirienne d'Anthropologie et de Sociologie* 3:59–62.

Schaaf, T., 1998, 'Sacred groves in Ghana: Experiences from an integrated study project'. In *Conserving the Sacred for Biodiversity Management*. P. S. Ramakrishnan, K. G. Saxena and U. M. Chandrashekara, eds, pp. 145–50. New Delhi: Oxford & IBH Publishing.

Schafer, Jessica, and Richard Black, 2003, 'Conflict, peace and the history of natural resource management in Sussundenga District, Mozambique'. *African Studies Review* 46(3):55–81.

Schlee, Gunter, 1992, 'Ritual topography and ecological use: The Gabbra of the Kenyan/Ethiopian borderlands'. In *Bush Base: Forest Farm*. E. Croll and D. Parkin, eds, pp. 110–28. London: Routledge.

Schloss, Marc, 1988, *The Hatchet's Blood: Separation, Power and Gender in Ehing Social Life*. Tuscon, AZ: University of Arizona Press.

Schmidt, Peter, 1994, 'Historical ecology and landscape transformation in eastern equatorial Africa'. In *Historical Ecology: Cultural Knowledge and Changing Landscapes*. C. Crumley, ed., pp. 99-125. Santa Fe, NM: School of American Research Press.

—— 1997, 'Archaeological views on a history of landscape change in East Africa'. *Journal of African History* 38:393-421.

Schmidt, Robert, 1991, 'Kenias Kayas'. *Naturwissenschaftliche Rundschau* 44(11):421–4.

Schoffeleers, M., 1992, *River of Blood*. Madison, WI: University of Wisconsin Press.

Scoones, Ian, 1999, 'New ecology and the social sciences'. *Annual Review of Anthropology* 28:479–507.

Scott, James, 1998, *Seeing Like a State: How Certain Schemes to Improve the Human Condition have Failed*. New Haven, CT: Yale University Press.

Sharma, Subrat, Hem Rikhari, and Lok Man Palni, 1999, 'Conservation of natural resources through religion: A case study from Central Himalaya'. *Society & Natural Resources* 12(6):599–612.

Sheridan, Michael J., 2001, 'Cooling the land: The political ecology of the North Pare mountains, Tanzania', Ph.D. dissertation, Boston University.

—— 2000, 'The sacred forests of North Pare, Tanzania'. African Studies Center Working paper #224. Boston, MA: Boston University African Studies Center.

—— 2004, 'The environmental consequences of independence and socialism in North Pare, Tanzania, 1961-88'. *Journal of African History* 45(1):81–102.

Shipton, Parker, 1994, 'Land and culture in tropical Africa: Soils, symbols, and the metaphysics of the mundane'. *Annual Review of Anthropology* 23:347–77.

Sibanda, Backson, 1997, 'Governance and the environment: The role of African religion in sustainable utilization of natural resources in Zimbabwe'. *Forests, Trees and People Newsletter* (34).

Sinha, R. K., 1995, 'Biodiversity conservation through faith and tradition in India: Some case studies'. *International Journal of Sustainable Development and World Ecology* (2):278–84.

Sivaramakrishnan, K., 1999, *Modern Forests*. Stanford, CA: Stanford University Press.

Southall, Aidan, 1997, 'The illusion of tribe'. In *Perspectives on Africa*. R. G. Grinker and C. Steiner, eds, pp. 38–51. Oxford: Blackwell.

Spear, Thomas, 1978, *The Kaya Complex*. Nairobi: Kenya Literature Bureau.

—— 2003, 'Neo-traditionalism and the limits of invention in British colonial Africa'. *Journal of African History* 44(1):3–27.

Sponsel, Leslie, 2001, 'Do anthropologists need religion, and vice versa? Adventures and dangers in spiritual ecology'. In *New Directions in Anthropology and Environment*. Carole L. Crumley, ed., pp. 177-200. Walnut Creek, CA: Altamira Press.

Sponsel, Leslie, Poranee Natadecha-Sponsel, Nukul Ruttanadakul, and Somporn Juntadach, 1998, 'Sacred and/or secular approaches to biodiversity conservation in Thailand Worldviews'. *Environment, Culture, Religion* 2:155–67.

Tchamie, Thiou, 2000, 'Évolution de la flore et de la végétation des bois sacrés des Massifs Kabyè et des régions environnantes (Togo)'. *Lejeunia* 164:1–36.

Thomas, Keith, 1983, *Man and the Natural World*. New York: Pantheon Books.

Tiwari, B. K., S. K. Barik, and R. S. Tripathi, 1998, 'Biodiversity value, status, and strategies for conservation of sacred groves of Meghalaya, India'. *Ecosystem Health* 4(1):20–32.

Tylor, Edward, 1874, *Primitive Culture, 2e*. Volume 2. New York: Henry Holt and Company.

Tyynela, Tapani, and Happyson Mudavanhu, 2000, 'Management and species diversity of a sacred forest in a deforested area: The case of Dzete Mountain, north-east Zimbabwe'. *Silva Carelica* 34:55–64.

United Nations Development Programme (UNDP), 2004, *Jachie and Kagyasi Sacred Grove Conservation Project*. New York: UNDP Small Grants Program.

United Nations Educational, Cultural, and Social Organization (UNESCO), 2005, *Conserving Cultural and Biological Diversity: The role of sacred natural sites and cultural landscapes (symposium)*. Paris: UNESCO.

Upadhaya, K., H. N. Pandey, P. S. Law, and R. S. Tripathi , 2003, 'Tree diversity in sacred groves of the Jaintia Hills in Meghalaya, northeast India'. *Biodiversity and Conservation* 12:583–97.

Vail, Leroy, ed., 1989, *The Creation of Tribalism in Southern Africa*. London: James Currey.

van Binsbergen, Wim M. J., 1981, *Religious Change in Zambia: Exploratory Studies*. London: Kegan Paul International.

Vayda, Andrew, and Bradley Walters, 1999, 'Against political ecology'. *Human Ecology* 27(1):167–79.

Veit, Peter, Adolfo Mascarenhas, and Okyeame Ampadu-Agyei, 1995, *Lessons from the Ground Up: African Development that Works*. Washington, DC: World Resouces Institute.

Wadley, Reed, and Carol J. Pierce Colfer, 2004, 'Sacred forest, hunting, and conservation in West Kalimantan, Indonesia'. *Human Ecology* 32(3):313–38.

Walker, Peter, 2005, 'Political ecology: Where is the ecology?' *Progress in Human Geography* 29(1):73–82.

Walley, Christine J., 2004, *Rough Waters: Nature and Development in an East African Marine Park*. Princeton, NJ: Princeton University Press.

Wamue, Grace Nyatugah, 2001, 'Revisiting our indigenous shrines through Mungiki'. *African Affairs* 100:453–67.

Warren, D. Michael, and Jennifer Pinkston, 1998, 'Indigenous African resource management of a tropical rainforest ecosystem: A case study of the Yoruba of Ara, Nigeria'. In *Linking Social and Ecological Systems: Management Practices and Social Mechanisms for Building Resilience*. F. Berkes and Carl Folkes, eds, pp. 158–89. Cambridge: Cambridge University Press.

Watt, A. S., 1947, 'Pattern and process in the plant community'. *Journal of Ecology* 35:1–22.

Watts, Michael, and Richard Peet, 2004, 'Liberating political ecology'. In *Liberation Ecologies,* 2nd edn. M. Watts, and Richard Peet, eds, pp. 3–47. London: Routledge.

Weiss, Brad, 2003, *Sacred Trees, Bitter Harvest: Globalizing Coffee in Northwest Tanzania*. Portsmouth, NH: Heinemann.

West, Harry G., 2005, *Kupilikula: Governance and the Invisible Realm in Mozambique*. Chicago: University of Chicago Press.

Western, David, R. Michael Wright, and Shirley C. Strum, eds, 1994, *Natural Connections: Perspectives in Community-based Conservation*. Washington, DC: Island Press.

Whitmore, T.C., 1997, 'Tropical forest disturbance, disappearance, and species loss'. In *Tropical Forest Remnants: Ecology, Management, and Conservation of Fragmented Communities*. W. F. Lawrence, and R. O. Bierregaard, Jr., eds, pp. 3–12. Chicago: University of Chicago Press.

Whittaker, R. J., K. J. Willis, and R. Field, 2001, 'Scale and species richness: towards a general, hierarchical theory of species diversity'. *Journal of Biogeography* 28: 453–70.

Willis, Justin, 1996, 'The northern kayas of the Mijikenda: A gazetteer, and an historical reassessment'. *Azania* 31:75–98.

Willis, K., L. Gillson, and T. Brncic, 2004, 'How virgin is virgin rainforest?' *Science* 304:402–03.

Willis, Katherine J. and Robert J. Whittaker, 2002, 'Species diversity – Scale matters'. *Science* 295: 1245–8.

Wilson, A., 1993, 'Sacred forests and the elders'. In *The Law of the Mother: Protecting Indigenous Peoples in Protected Areas*. E. Kemf, ed., pp. 244-248. San Francisco, CA: Sierra Club Books.

Wilson, Monica, 1959, *Communal Rituals of the Nyakyusa*. London: Oxford University Press.

World Commission on Environment and Development (WCED), 1987, *Our Common Future*. Oxford: Oxford University Press.

Worster, Donald, 1993, *The Wealth of Nature: Environmental History and the Ecological Imagination*. Oxford: Oxford University Press.

Wu, Jianguo, and Orie Loucks, 1995, 'From balance of nature to hierarchical patch dynamics: A paradigm shift in ecology'. *Quarterly Review of Biology* 70(4):439–66.

Ylhaisi, Jussi, 2000, 'The significance of the traditional forests and rituals in Tanzania: A case study of Zigua, Gweno, and Nyamwezi ethnic groups'. *Silva Carelica* 34:194–219.

Zimmerer, Karl, 2000, 'The reworking of conservation geographies: Nonequilibrium landscapes and nature-society hybrids'. *Annals of the Association of American Geographers* 90(2):356–69.

Zimmerer, Karl, and Kenneth Young, 1998, 'Introduction: The geographical nature of landscape change'. In *Nature's Geography*. K. Zimmerer, and Kenneth Young, eds, pp. 3–34. Madison, WI: University of Wisconsin Press.

Zimmerer, Karl, and Thomas Bassett, 2003, *Political Ecology: An Integrative Approach to Geography and Environment-Development Studies*. New York: Guilford Press.

Zoundjihekpon, Jeanne, and Bernadette Dossou-Glehouenou, 1999, 'Cultural and spiritual values of biodiversity in West Africa: the case of Benin and Cote d'Ivoire'. In *Cultural and Spiritual Values of Biodiversity*. D. Posey, ed., pp. 370–71. London: Intermediate Technology Publications and UNEP.

PART ONE
The Human Ecology of Sacred Groves

3

The Role of Sacred Groves
in Biodiversity Conservation in Sierra Leone

AIAH LEBBIE
& RAYMOND P. GURIES

Deforestation is widely regarded as a global problem with estimates of forest losses often paralleling trends in poverty, population pressures, agricultural expansion and other social phenomena (Moran and Ostrom 2005, Vajpeyi 2001). Given the graphic accounts and images placed before the public, estimates of the scale of deforestation and concomitant losses of soil, biodiversity and other resources make any objective discussion of causes and solutions difficult. In this environment, however, a few authors have concluded that historic deforestation in West Africa may have been exaggerated for political, economic and social reasons (arguments summarized in Fairhead and Leach 1996, 1998). The ebb and flow of forests across large expanses of Africa has been the subject of debate for at least several decades (see Richards, 1952) and what may appear to be a relatively untouched forest today may have been heavily exploited in the past. Forest clearing, especially for timber extraction and agriculture, marked periods of human population expansion, while forest recovery followed periods of disease, war or social upheaval (Fairhead and Leach 1998, Nyerges 1996). Favorable climates, fluctuating population sizes, reforestation programs and local actions all have contributed to forest loss and recovery at different times and places.

Estimates of the original and current extent of the Upper Guinean coastal rainforest (Cole 1968, Sayer *et al.* 1992), including Sierra Leone, are uncertain but such uncertainty is a common situation in much of West Africa (Van Rompaey 2002). Accounts of forest vegetation in Sierra Leone during the eighteenth and nineteenth century probably report derived conditions (e.g., Blyden 1872), while early twentieth century narratives followed a century of colonial timber exploitation and several centuries of warfare and slave raiding (Fyfe 1962, Migeod 1926). Timber exploitation was common in nineteenth century Sierra Leone, and as Unwin (1920) noted '... very little revenue has been received for timber-felling fees, which means really that in the past the forests have been destroyed .... it does indeed make one pause and think what immense forests must have existed in the days of 1827, when so many loads of timber were exported...'. Much colonial timber exploitation paralleled the major rivers in Sierra Leone, yet forest fragments that exist today often occur as narrow strips along rivers, or as sacred groves protected by rural communities for religious and cultural reasons (Lebbie and Freudenberger 1996).

Sacred groves, well known in Africa and Asia (Laird 1999, Chouin 2002), are typically small forested areas that mark sites of historical, cultural or religious significance. These groves usually serve several social purposes, including sites for induction of young men and women to puberty, cultural indoctrination, burial grounds and other religious rituals. Access to and use of such groves is restricted by various taboos and customs with control vested in specific members of a community, often elders, but also 'secret societies.' Sacred groves are now viewed as having a conservation value that parallels other cultural or religious values (e.g. Campbell 2004, Githitho 2003, Schaaf 2003), but the issue of whether conservation is a deliberate purpose of such groves or only a fortuitous coincidence, and whether traditional beliefs and values associated with sacred forests can aid conservation purposes, remains the subject of debate (Githitho 2003, Sarfo-Mensah 2002, Siebert, this volume).

Large forest reserves generally are preferred for maintaining intact floras and faunas (e.g., Riitters *et al.* 2000, Terborgh 1992), as small, fragmented forests can experience a rapid loss of species, especially vertebrates (Daily and Ehrlich 1995, Laurance *et al.* 1997). Plant species also may experience diversity declines in fragmented landscapes, but evidence from Singapore (Turner *et al.* 1994, 1996) and Hong Kong (Corlett and Turner 1997) suggests that woody plants are somewhat less vulnerable than mammals to rapid local extinction. However, the levels of diversity remaining in secondary forests and forest fragments (Guindon 1996, Lugo 1995, Nkongmeneck *et al.* 2002, Turner 1996) still make their conservation important as they may become the sole sources of native species for future restoration efforts.

Forest remnants in Sierra Leone clearly have experienced substantial human disturbance, especially those around villages, and virtually all have been disturbed a number of times. Despite the large size attained by some trees, very few remnant forests here could be called 'ancient' and virtually all are in the process of recovery from recent or earlier disturbances. Oftentimes, small sacred groves are the only forests that exist as islands in an otherwise agricultural landscape, but whether such islands are relics of a once larger forest, or represent man-made islands surrounding villages can be difficult to determine (Fairhead and Leach 1998). Given their long history of disturbance and exploitation, our focus was on assessing the biological diversity still contained in sacred groves in Moyamba District of Sierra Leone and why its continued existence in the face of human and natural disturbance regimes has important conservation value even if conservation was not their intended purpose. This paper summarizes information on the cultural and biodiversity value of 14 sacred groves in Moyamba District of Sierra Leone and the challenges facing conservation efforts, together with recommendations that would give sacred groves a more prominent position in conservation efforts by local, national and international communities.

Sacred Groves and Secret Societies

Many villages in Sierra Leone are associated with at least one sacred grove maintained by secret societies (e.g., *poro* and *sande*) having authority to enforce sanctions and limit exploitation of such sites (Lebbie and Freudenberger 1996). Brown (1937) describes the *poro* society 'as a religious institution, remarkable for the peculiar character of the initiation ceremony imposed for entry upon members', as well as 'an institution for instructing boys and girls in social duties, sexual responsibilities and industrial crafts.' In a male-only association, '...*poro* members have a strong sense of identity and cohesiveness due in part to sharing circumcision rituals and the associated training in the traditions and proper comportment of the culture' (Lebbie and Freudenberger 1996).

The secret society for women known as *sande* is also associated with sacred groves, and is primarily concerned with female circumcision rites and socio-cultural education. In particular, new initiates are taught 'appropriate behavior toward their future husbands and the wider community' (ibid.).

Sacred groves are central to the spiritual, political and cultural needs of a diverse collection of village organizations like the secret societies that also serve a governance function as arbiter of village social and political debates. For both males and females, sacred groves have served to foster group solidarity through initiation rites and rituals. As Castro (1990) noted for the numerous sacred groves in the Kirinyaga region of Kenya, 'the extent of local or neighborhood identity was almost defined by shared worship at a particular grove.' In this region of Kenya, sacred groves were frequently located on hilltops and ridges and contained huge trees exceeding 30 meters in height. They were virtually inviolable and any infringement was considered 'sacrilege and treated as a serious anti-social act requiring expiation' (Lambert 1950).

Cultural Assessments of Sacred Groves in Moyamba District

Moyamba District of southwestern Sierra Leone is divided into 14 chiefdoms with a total land area of approximately 6,900 square kilometres. During 1994–95, we were able to survey 14 sacred groves distributed among the Dasse, Kori, and Kowa chiefdoms (Table 3.1) based on accessibility and personal security at the time the assessments were conducted. These groves, ranging from one to six hectares in size, occupy lowland or riparian sites and are embedded in 'farm bush' vegetation, grasslands and cocoa/coffee/kola plantations. The predominant 'farm bush' vegetation is one of dense thickets of woody plants that colonize recently fallowed agricultural lands. As fallow periods decline, the frequent use of fire favors the succession of farm bush to grassland dominated by cogon grass (*Imperata cylindrical*), an invasive species native to southeast Asia. Some sacred groves surveyed here appear to have arisen out of former

Table 3.1 Name, size, landscape position and cultural association of 14 sacred groves in the Moyamba District, Sierra Leone.

Sacred Grove (Chiefdom)	Size (ha)	Landscape Position	Cultural Association
Njama (Kowa)	4.5	Riparian zone; embedded in oil-palm area; one of several groves on Taia River near Njama	*poro* society; *njayei, sande* and *wunde* society groves exist nearby; MIC[1]
Njayahun (Dasse)	1.6	Riparian zone adjacent to village near ephemeral stream	*sande* society; female prayer site
Mogbwama (Dasse)	2	Lowland grove near village edge; embedded in coffee/kola nut grove	*poro* society; MIC
Kamato (Kori)	4	Taia River fragment; embedded in grassland	*poro* society; former village & burial ground; MIC
Kwoehun (Kori)	3.2	Riparian zone; embedded in farm bush adjacent to a second grove	*poro* society; MIC
Waiima (Kori)	4	Riparian zone along Taia River; embedded in coffee/kola nut grove	*poro* society; MIC
Bagbema (Kori)	4.5	Lowland grove embedded in farmbush/grassland; frequent fires evident	*poro* society; MIC
Boamahun (Kori)	1	Lowland grove embedded in farmbush; *Enantia polycarpa* collection area	*poro* society; MIC
Foinda (Kori)	5.5	Lowland grove near coffee grove; embedded in grassland	*poro* society; site of former village & first chiefdom; MIC
Konda 1 (Kori)	5	Lowland grove; embedded in coffee grove; 200m. from Konda 2 site	*poro* society; site of former village; MIC
Konda 2 (Kori)	6	Lowland grove sited at small stream; *Enantia polycarpa* collection area	site of oracles & former village; community grove
Mosenge (Kori)	2.5	Lowland grove near village edge; embedded in oil palm/kola nut groves	*poro* society; MIC
Pendembu (Kori)	3	Lowland grove at village edge; embedded in farm bush/cash crop fields	*poro* society; MIC
Taninihun (Kori)	2	Lowland grove near village; embedded in coffee/kola nut groves	*poro* society; MIC

[1] MIC: site of Male Initiation Ceremonies.

settlement sites, but other groves located in riparian zones carried a large complement of plant species characteristic of relict forests. It seems unlikely that a large number of native trees, lianas and herbs would have been maintained unless forest recovery was based in large part on natural regeneration from wild sources. The presence of semi-domesticated species (e.g. *Mangifera indica, Gmelina arborea, and Cola nitida*) indicates that periodic cycles of disturbance and recovery involving plantation crops in agricultural settings have been important throughout the region. No sacred grove surveyed here represents 'pristine' forest conditions and all show evidence of substantial natural and anthropogenic disturbance.

The occurrence of earthworks and other artifacts in some of these groves indicates human use that predates the colonial era. The intense slave raiding that took place throughout West Africa for hundreds of years (Miers and Kopytoff 1977) led to coordinated village resistance and the construction of many earthen and stone fortifications still in evidence today (Siddle 1969, MacEachern 2001, Hawthorne 2003). According to Siddle (1969), each village was surrounded by 'a layer of high forest, between a quarter and half a mile wide, which acted as a camouflage mechanism' with defense as one of the principal functions of these settlements. Siebert (this volume) describes a similar situation in northern Benin. Forests along rivers and marshy coastal regions were easier to defend against slave raiders and became the sites for fortified villages. Hawthorne (2003) recounts a seventeenth century description of a coastal settlement 'surrounded by a stockade formed of pointed stakes with sharp tips, fastened together with cross bars, and it has two gates which are closed at night.' That such walls may have initiated high forest that persists today is one line of argument used to account for forest groves in a savanna landscape (Fairhead and Leach 1998). Three of the four groves in Moyamba District were located on steep slopes or adjacent to a river and bordered with trenches, both features offering additional security. Following the decline of slavery, such groves continued to serve similar functions in minimizing contact with colonial authorities (Siebert, this volume). Some sacred groves today serve as a poignant reminder of resistance to enslavement or colonial rule.

In four of the sacred groves we visited (Njama, Kamato, Tanninahun and Konda), informants reported that digging of trenches was a common strategy to ensure the protection of entire communities. In one of the Konda groves, we found two concentric rings of trenches now partially filled with earth. The sacred grove at Kamato, located by the Taia River, also incorporates a relic trench reported to have been dug during the era of the slave trade. According to local legend, the ancestors of this settlement were forced to abandon the entrenchment under intense attacks from slavers and drowned themselves rather than surrender. Custodians indicated that these groves were prior settlement sites, but with the end of the slave trade in the early twentieth century (Oates 1999) new settlements were built within short distances of the pre-war settlement sites. The former settlements were transformed into sacred groves.

Despite numerous recent social, political and ecological changes that have occurred in Sierra Leone, the strong cultural and religious values associated with sacred groves and the authority of secret societies such as *poro* and *sande* have contributed to their survival. There are indications, however, that groves are being disturbed and their cultural and ecological significance is gradually being eroded.

Biodiversity Value of African Sacred Groves

Only a few studies have surveyed the biotic diversity of African sacred groves, but all indicated that groves harbored endemic or rare species. The Malshegu sacred grove in northern Ghana harbors an important assemblage of trees and seed dispersers, and serves both ethnobotanical and religious functions (Dorm-Adzobu *et al.* 1991). On the Accra Plains of Ghana, Decher (1997, 1999) found that several small mammals occurred only in sacred groves. In southern Ghana, the Anweam sacred grove provides important ethnobotanical resources to local communities working with managers charged with protecting the larger Esukawkaw Forest Reserve (Amoako-Atta 1998). The sacred Mijikenda kaya forests of coastal Kenya contain a very high proportion of endemic plant and animal species (Burgess *et al.* 1998, Githitho 2003). Surveys of sacred groves in The Gambia, Ghana, Nigeria and Tanzania all provide evidence for conservation of wildlife, insects and plants (Hall and Swaine 1981, Ellenberg *et al.* 1988, Mgumia and Oba 2003).

Woody Plant Resources of Sacred Groves in Moyamba District

Assessments of woody plant diversity and forest condition were made using forty-seven 0.1 hectare plots (50m x 20m) sited in the 14 groves (Table 3.1). All trees and lianas ≥10 cm diameter breast height (dbh) were measured and identified in plots using informants and local field manuals (Deighton 1957, Savill and Fox 1967). Voucher specimens, and unidentified plants collected for subsequent identification, were deposited at the Njala University College Herbarium.

Interviews with informants affiliated with sacred groves were conducted for 6 of the 14 groves. Gender restrictions prevented us from gaining access to female (*sande*) sacred groves (with the exception of the grove at Njayahun), but we were allowed access to groves of the men's *poro* society. Interviews regarding *poro* society groves were always conducted inside the groves and focused on the reasons for the grove's existence, rules and regulations governing access, exploitation of forest resources and cultural taboos associated with the grove. For the *sande* groves, female herbalists and informants collected plants of medicinal value from each forest and brought them for identification and similar discussions on the role of these groves.

Almost every woody plant in forest and farm bush is exploited, usually for more than one use, with medicinal uses being most common (Lebbie and Guries 1995, Nyamweru *et al.* this volume). Bark, leaves and/or roots are harvested for use in traditional folk medicines, but harvesting also occurs for

Table 3.2 Ethnobotanical uses of woody plants found in three or more of the 14 sacred groves in the Moyamba District, Sierra Leone

Species	Sacred Grove[1]	Uses
Acioa scabrifolia	1,2,3,4,5,6,7,8,9,11,12, 13,14	medicinal, charcoal
Afzelia africana	1,3,6,7,10,12	fish poison, furniture, medicinal, red dye
Albizia adianthifolia	1,2,4,6,7,9,10,11,13	medicinal, fetishes
Albizia ferruginea	5,7,11	medicinal, timbers, utensils
Albizia zygia	1,2,3,4,5,6,7,9,10,12,13,14	medicinal
Allophylus africanus	2,3,13,14	medicinal, poles, utensils
Anisophyllea laurina	3,6,7,8,13	edible fruit, medicinal, lumber and poles
Annickia polycarpa	2,4,5,7,9	medicinal
Anthonotha macrophylla	3,4,6,7,8,9,12,13, 14	medicinal, tool handles and hooks
Berlinia confusa	1,7,8	mortars, lumber, soap making
Bersama abyssinica	3,4,12	medicinal, rodent poison
Blighia welwitschii	3,7,8,11	fish poison, poles, utensils
Bombax buonopozens	2,3,4,5,6,7,12,13	medicinal, utensils, pillow filler, games
Bridelia micrantha	1,3,4,5,6,7,12,13	latex, medicinal, crafts, poles
Carapa procera	3,7,8,10	bark twine, pottery glaze, tools/crafts
Ceiba pentandra	2,3,4,5,6,7,8,11,13,14	pillow filler, canoes, tools/crafts, fetishes
Cleistopholis patens	3,4,5,6,7,8,9,12	bark twine, medicinal
Cola lateritia	3,4,5,6,7,8,9,11,12,14	edible husk
Cola nitida	1,3,4,5,6,7,8,9,12,14	kola nuts, medicinals, fetishes
Dialium guineensis	1,2,4,5,10,13	charcoal, edible fruit, medicinal, tools
Diospyros heudelotii	2,5,6,7,8,12,13	tools
Elaeias guineensis	1,2,3,4,6,7,8,11,12	palm wine, medicinal, fibers, poles, fetishes
Ficus mucuso	3,4,6,7,8,9	medicinal, tools, fetishes
Funtumia africana	2,3,4,5,6,7,8,9,12,13,14	latex, pillow filler, utensils
Hannoa klaineana	1,4,5,6,7,8,10,14	crafts, lumber, medicinal
Holarrhena floribunda	2,3,4,5,6,7,8	pillow filler, tools and utensils
Homalium letestui	1,2,3,4,5,6,7,11,13,14	medicinal, poles
Hunteria elliotii	4,5,7,12	medicinal, tool handles and utensils
Hymenocardia lyrata	1,5,10,11	charcoal
Landolphia owariensis	2,4,6,7,8,9,10,11,12,13,14	edible fruit, latex, medicinal, tools
Lannea nigritana	2,3,13	edible fruit, soap making
Macaranga barteri	1,3,4,6,7,9,12	medicinal, poles
Mammea africana	2,4,7,10,12	edible fruit, latex, medicinal, furniture
Mareya micrantha	3,4,6,7,9,12,13	medicinal, poles
Milicia regia	1,2,3,4,5,6,7,9,12,13	latex, lumber, medicinal, tools, fetishes

Table 3.2 cont.

Species	Sacred Grove[1]	Uses
Millettia rhodantha	1,3,4,7,8,10,13,14	cough medicine, small poles
Nauclea diderrichii	3,10,12,13	medicinal, mortars
Paramacrolobium coeruleum	4,9,11,14	tools, games
Parinari excelsa	1,2,9,10,12	edible fruit, medicinal, charcoal
Phyllanthus discoideus	3,8,11,12,14	charcoal, furniture, medicinal
Phyllocosmus africanus	1,2,3,5,7,9,12,13	charcoal, traps
Piptadeniastrum africanum	6,7,8,10,11	medicinal, fish and rodent poison, lumber
Pterocarpus santalinoides	3,4,10,11	edible fruit, medicinal
Pycnanthus angolensis	1,2,4,5,6,7,8,9,11,12,14	medicinal, oilseed
Ricinodendron heudelotii	3,4,5,6,7,11,14	crafts, oilseed, soap making, utensils
Santiria trimeria	7,8,10,11,14	crafts, tools
Smeathmannia pubescence	1,2,6,7,12,13	edible fruit, medicinal
Spondias mombin	3,4,6,7,13,14	edible fruit, medicinal, soap
Sterculia tragacantha	1,3,4,6,7,8,11	bark rope, edible fruit, medicinal, soap
Strephonema pseudocola	1,4,5,7,12,14	construction, medicinal
Terminalia ivorensis	2,3,6,8,9,13	timbers and joinery, antiseptic, yellow dye, drums, boat parts
Trema guineensis	6,8,12	bark twine, medicinal, poles
Tricalysia deigthonii	3,4,5,6,7,9,13	medicinal
Trichilia heudelotii	1,2,3,4,5,6,7,8,9,12,13	edible fruit, medicinal, red dye, tools
Uapaca guineensis	1,3,5,6,7,9,10,12	charcoal, edible fruit, medicinal, red dye
Vitex micrantha	1,3,5,7,9,11,12,14	poles
Xylopia aethiopica	1,11,12,	medicinal, poles

[1] Sacred groves in which selected tree species were found: 1) Bagbema, 2) Boamahun, 3) Foinda, 4) Kamato, 5) Kwoehun, 6) Konda 1, 7) Konda 2, 8) Mogbwama, 9) Mosenge, 10) Njama, 11) Njayahun, 12) Pendembu, 13) Taninihun, 14) Waiima.
(In the interest of space, species used exclusively for timber/lumber (e.g., *Brachystegia, Lophira, Entandophragma*), or rare trees found in only one or two groves, are not included.)

other uses, including edible fruit and seeds, poisons, dyes, household utensils, hunting and farm implements, fetishes and local games (Table 3.2). Restrictions on the exploitation of plant resources in sacred groves are usually enforced by *poro* and *sande* societies, although access to the groves is occasionally granted. When such access is granted, harvested plants or plant parts are meant only for personal use, not for commercial trade. These restrictions appear to be effective in some groves at certain times, but limited exploitation of woody plants in sacred groves is not uncommon. A few herbalists noted that certain plants can now be found only in sacred groves as farm bush populations have disappeared due to over-exploitation.

The most recent comprehensive guide to the woody plants of Sierra Leone (Savill and Fox 1976) provides descriptions for 477 species from 242 genera and 53 families. Our limited sampling of these 14 groves in Moyamba District contained a total of 2,495 individual trees and lianas ≥10 cm dbh representing 147 species (including 9 unidentified species) from 104 genera and 35 families. Thus, despite our very limited sampling in a single district in southwestern Sierra Leone, approximately 31 percent of the tree species and most of the woody plant families known in Sierra Leone were identified from one or more groves.

A few widespread species were present in all groves (e.g., *Funtumia africana*, *Elaeis guineensis*, *Cola lateritia*), while other species were encountered only one or a few times, e.g., *Erythrococa anomali*, *Guibourtia copaillifera* and *Irvingia gabonensis*. Many of the woody plants encountered in these groves have multiple ethnobotanical uses (Table 3.2) but most groves are not heavily exploited for these products; similar inventories have been produced for other regions (see Nyamweru *et al.* this volume). Timber species of merchantable size such as *Ceiba pentandra*, *Terminalia ivorensis* and *Parkia bicolor* occasionally provide timbers for community projects such as village schools. Local authorities at Pendembu and Konda expressed an interest in timber extraction from sacred groves because farm bush simply did not produce trees with diameters appropriate for lumber. However, a consensus in the community is usually sought prior to any logging activities in sacred groves. During the time of these inventories, we saw no active timber harvesting in any grove.

Wildlife Resources in Sacred Groves in Moyamba District

Wildlife resources recorded in the sacred groves mostly represent species that are adapted to forests disturbed by human use. Two prosimians, the dwarf galago (*Galago demidovii*) and the potto (*Perodicticus potto*), were recorded in nearly all sacred forests, while the spot-nosed monkey (*Cercopithecus petaurista*) and Campbell's monkey (*C. campbelli*) were also common in several groves. The black and white colobus monkey (*Colobus polykomos*) was recorded in the Njama sacred grove. Informants also reported chimpanzees (*Pan troglodytes*) frequenting the grove at Njama, mostly to raid wild pineapples growing in the vicinity. The hoof prints of the African buffalo (*Syncerus caffer*) were noted at the Foinda and Bagbema groves, and their presence was further confirmed by two hunters who claimed to have killed several in the past. Fecal remains and sightings of Maxwell's duiker (*Cephalophus maxwelli*) were confirmed for several groves, and on a few occasions, bushbucks (*Tragelaphus scriptus)* were observed in the farm bush adjoining most groves. Three carnivores including the African civet (*Viverra civetta*) and the slender mongoose (*Herpestes sanguineus*) were confirmed in nearly all sacred groves, with the exception of those at Boamahun, Njayahun and Taninihun.

We recorded more than 50 species of birds in the sacred groves and immediate vicinity, including birds common in farm bush and other agricultural landscapes. A few birds known to frequent high forests, including the allied hornbill (*Tockus fasciatus*), piping hornbill (*Bycanites fistulator*), blue plantain eater (*Corythaeola cristata*), Fraser's rusty thrush (*Stizorhina fraseri*) and the black winged oriole (*Oriolus nigripennis*) were observed at least once. Groves adjacent to riparian habitats frequently attracted species such as the grey heron (*Ardea cinerea*), crocodile bird (*Pluvianus aegyptius*), reef heron (*Egretta gularis*), long tail shag (*Phalacrocorax africanus*) and the palm nut vulture (*Gypohierax angolenis*).

Patterns of Tree Species Diversity in Moyamba District

The larger groves at Foinda, Kamato, Kondo 2, Kwoehun and Pendumbu had a somewhat greater diversity of tree species than other groves, even correcting for different numbers of plots, but even the smallest groves were surprisingly rich in woody species diversity (Table 3.3). Each additional plot inventoried added previously uncounted species, so a complete inventory at each grove undoubtedly would reveal more species. Only the two smallest groves at Boamahun and Njayahun did not contain at least one species unique to those groves and most groves contained several unique species (Table 3.3).

Data on individual woody plants ≥10cm at breast height were collected to describe the structural differences among groves and estimate Species Importance Values (SIV), a general measure of the extent to which a species dominates a forest (Table 3.3). SIV is calculated as the sum of the *relative frequency* (number of plots in which a species occurs), *relative density* (number of individuals in a plot) and *relative dominance* (a measure of tree size) of woody plants in each grove (Keel *et al.* 1993). All species values are 'relative' because the combined sum for all the trees in the plot must sum to 100 percent. Combining all three components creates the Species Importance Value with a total potential value of 300, with 100 points possible for each of the three components.

The sacred groves at Foinda, Kwoehun, Konda 2, Mogbwama, Pendembu and Taninihun, all in relatively early stages of recovery from major disturbances, were dominated by *Anthonotha, Elaeias,* and *Funtumia* trees that are common in 'farm bush' and other highly disturbed landscapes. Such young and highly disturbed groves tended to have moderate to large Species Importance Values (SIV) with the five most important species typically accounting for 33-53 percent of the total SIV score (Table 3.3). With the exception of the small grove at Taininihun, these groves were among the most species rich (Table 3.3). The grove near Mogbwama is an interesting exception in that a few *Piptadeniastrum* trees dominate an otherwise young grove that probably regenerated after a fire. In general, groves in which species characteristic of farm bush achieved the highest SIV and dominance scores are subject to frequent disturbance and dominated by large numbers of relatively small trees that regenerate quickly but are usually short-lived. A few exotic species such as *Mangifera indica* and *Gmelina arborea* were also recorded in some of these groves. The absence of trees with large diameters, together with other evidence of disturbance (e.g., fire scars, cut stumps), all suggest that these groves represent relatively early phases of secondary forest succession.

Table 3.3 Ecological characteristics for 14 sacred groves of the Moyamba District, Sierra Leone*

Sacred Grove	No. of Species (Unique Species)	Dominant Tree Species	SIV Value[1]	Successional Position[2]
Young/Disturbed Groves				
Foinda	51 (3)	Ceiba pentandra, Macaranga barteri, Funtumia africana, Anthonotha macrophylla, Cola lateritia	102.97	E
Konda 2	47 (3)	Elaeis guineensis, Funtumia africana, Trichilia heudelotii, Ceiba pentandra, Ricinodendron heudelotii	160.75	E
Kwoehun	44 (2)	Cola lateritia, Funtumia africana, Ricinodendron heudelotii, Hannoa klaineana, Trichilia heudelotii	117.74	E
Mogbwama	40 (3)	Piptadeniastrum africanum, Cola lateritia, Elaeis guineensis, Funtumia africana, Myrianthus arboreus	118.87	M
Pendembu	49 (3)	Funtumia africana, Parinari excelsa, Elaeis guineensis, Chlorophora regia, Chrysophyllum albidum	141.53	E-M
Taninihun	30 (1)	Trichilia heudelotii, Ochthocosmus africanus, Albizia zygia, Anthonotha macrophylla, Funtumia africana	137.02	E-M
Maturing Groves				
Boamahun	27 (0)	Funtumia africana, Dialium guineense, Parinari excelsa, Ceiba pentandra, Terminalia ivorensis	119.19	M
Kamato	53 (5)	Elaeis guineensis, Cola lateritia, Cynometra leonensis, Funtumia africana, Ricinodendron heudelotii	107.39	M
Konda 1	29 (3)	Funtumia africana, Uapaca guineensis, Hannoa klaineana, Afzelia africana, Elaeis guineensis	107.56	M
Mosenge	38 (3)	Terminalia ivorensis, Cola lateritia, Funtumia africana, Acioa scabrifolia, Ochthocosmus africanus	118.95	M
Waiima	43 (10)	Cynometra leonensis, Pycnanthus angolensis, Paramacrolobium coeruleum, Funtumia africana, Cola lateritia	99.08	M
Mature Groves				
Bagbema	32 (4)	Parinari excelsa, Afzelia africana, Elaeis guineensis, Berlinia confusa, Millettia rhodantha	154.76	M-L

Table 3.3 cont.

Sacred Grove	No. of Species (Unique Species)	Dominant Tree Species	SIV Value[1]	Successional Position[2]
Njama	26 (1)	*Piptadeniastrum africanum, Mammea africana, Afzelia africana, Plagiosiphon emaginatus, Pterocarpus santalinoides*	140.02	M-L
Njayahun	29 (0)	*Santiria trimera, Piptadeniastrum africanum, Elaeis guineensis, Afzelia bracteata, Pentaclethra macrophylla*	148.25	M-L

* Groves are grouped by stage of successional development (young, maturing, mature) based upon field assessments and information provided in Savill and Fox (1967). Species Importance Value (SIV) here is the proportion accounted for by the five most 'important' species (from a base of 300).

[1] Species Importance Value is a joint measure to account for the Relative Frequency, Relative Abundance and Relative Dominance of each species; each component has a score of 100. The three components combine to create a single index that totals 300 points. Values shown here are the sum of the five 'most important' species.

[2] Successional position (E = early successional, M = mid successional, L = late successional) based on information contained in SIV values and additional information regarding canopy position and biological features related to size and age.

Maturing groves at Boamahun, Kamato, Konda 1, Mosenge and Waiima contain complements of both early and mid-to-late successional species with *Elaeias guineensis* and *Funtumia africana* being present but having lower importance (Table 3.3). Species such as *Piptadeniastrum africanum, Terminalia ivorensis* and *Cynometra leonensis* and others characteristic of mature forests were also present as larger canopy dominants. Some of these canopy dominants are recognized as 'Class A' timber species, trees that dominated timber exploitation in West Africa for decades but are increasingly uncommon (Savill and Fox, 1969). SIV scores tended to be relatively low for these groves, with the five 'most important' species accounting for 33–39 per cent of the total SIV score. Modest SIV scores indicate that many different species were present, that no single group of species dominated the forest, and that no canopy emergents had yet over-topped the forest as happened at Njama and the few 'mature' groves (Table 3.3). Mid-successional forests that contain species characteristic of both early successional and mature forests are often the most species rich, as evidenced by the relatively large numbers of species identified in these groves (Table 3.3).

Finally, the groves at Bagbema, Njama and Njayahun were dominated by large mature forest trees such as *Berlinia confusa, Parinari excelsa, Mammea africana* and *Piptadeniastrum africanum*. These groves had relatively large SIV scores contributed by the top five species (always greater than 47 per cent), as expected if a few older trees dominate the canopy. The groves at Njama and Bagbema contained several large *Piptadeniastrum africanum* and *Parinari excelsa* trees, both canopy emergents. Their relatively low species richness is due to the absence of many of those species associated with early stages of recovery following disturbance.

Our failure to record some species for some groves does not necessarily mean they are absent, but only indicates that they are probably not abundant. Some of these trees may have been extirpated locally, the result of past over-exploitation or regeneration failures. Loss of tree species from small forest fragments has been documented in Singapore and Hong Kong (Corlett and Turner 1997), but we lack the historic records to document site-specific losses in Sierra Leone.

We conclude that the sacred groves studied here are floristically rich in terms of native woody plant species despite their relatively small size and history of disturbance. The criticism against protecting small forest fragments, that is, that each simply duplicates species found in other fragments (Blake 1991) appears not to be true for the woody plants of sacred groves in Moyamba District. While some informants indicated that these groves have been in existence for as long as they can remember, it is obvious from their structure and composition that they have experienced substantial change during recent decades. No grove could be considered 'pristine' and several bore signs of recent and/or frequent disturbance. While some sacred groves are often viewed as ancient, the reality in Moyamba District is that sacred groves may be almost any age and all have experienced some disturbance.

The ability of the village societies to protect these groves has eroded over time and at least some non-sanctioned uses have occurred. Periodic disturbance is both natural and desirable in order to maintain mixtures of species and age classes, and to provide opportunities for regeneration, but excessive disturbance from exploitation, grazing or fire clearly poses problems to their continued existence. Given the evidence of frequent anthropogenic disturbance observed here, we believe that these sacred groves do not represent traditional conservation areas although they still provide conservation functions (see Siebert, this volume).

Recommendations

This survey of sacred groves in Moyamba District of Sierra Leone expands our knowledge regarding their potential in biodiversity conservation. However, the existence of such groves is tenuous and most could easily be lost to over-exploitation or disturbance, especially during times of civil turmoil or war (Lebbie and Freudenberger 1996, McNeely 2003). In a few countries (e.g., Ghana and India, see Laird 1999), efforts to protect sacred groves are underway as information on their cultural and biological significance becomes available. The small size of most sacred groves has led some planners to exclude these forests from national conservation networks (Wilcox and Murphy 1985). Pessimistic generalizations concerning the likelihood of local extinctions, the lack of biological inventories, and continuing agricultural pressure from rural populations, all undermine efforts to protect sacred groves and other forest fragments scattered across many tropical landscapes.

We believe that sacred groves have much to offer local communities as well as international conservation interests, but their value and potential role in conservation programs needs to be understood in the context of local history and culture as well as ecology. Given the lack of strong national or international incentives for conservation in Sierra Leone today, local communities pose both the greatest threat to, and the greatest opportunity for, conservation. The historical, social, cultural and political elements that have afforded some protection to sacred groves in the past probably will not be sufficient in the future given a growing population and the attendant pressures for food and income. Four issues regarding sacred groves in Sierra Leone seem particularly important, but our recommendations below may also pertain to groves elsewhere.

Size and Fragmentation Issues

The small size (most are less than five hectares) and continued isolation of most sacred groves in Sierra Leone make them vulnerable to loss from a variety of biophysical and anthropogenic forces. Small fragments may fall below the minimum size needed to maintain viable populations of many animals that are important pollinators and seed dispersers. Minimum viable population sizes are unknown for many forest species as we lack even the most basic information on breeding systems, demography and genetic composition needed to ensure the production of viable progeny (Bawa and Ashton 1991, Cascante *et al.* 2002). At a minimum, an assessment of viable seed production could be completed by sampling ripe fruit or pods and conducting germination tests. The inability of some species to set fruit or produce sound seed could identify populations that may have fallen below minimum viable population sizes that could lead to local extinction. This would provide a powerful biological argument in support of expanding the size of present groves in order to maintain or restore natural regeneration processes.

One problem related to expanding grove size is a fear that groves will start harboring 'dangerous' animals such as leopards, elephants and the African buffalo. Wild animals and the crop damage they cause make them unpopular in rural areas dependent upon subsistence agriculture. However, animist belief systems favor protection of rare (but not 'dangerous') wild animals. For example, in the Gola Forest region, people protect the nesting sites of the rare yellow-headed rock fowl (*Picathartes gymnocephalus*) in sacred groves because they consider the bird to be the embodiment of their ancestral spirits (Leach 1994). Carefully planned around a strong educational component, expanding the size of existing sacred groves could be accomplished as demonstrated by a successful program we undertook with the sacred groves at Konda (Lebbie and Freudenberger 1996). However, we believe that combining an economic function such as propagation of medicinal plants or other increasingly uncommon resources with a conservation function is more likely to be successful than conservation alone.

Sierra Leone's decade-long civil conflict (1991–2002) affected large parts of the country, and some sacred groves were targeted for destruction by the military. Civil strife is often correlated with increased levels of deforestation

(FAO 2005) for many reasons including the loss of agency or civilian control, financing war, opportunities for plundering by military leaders, and high concentrations of desperate refugees in need of forest products, especially fuel (McNeely 2003, Plumptre 2003). Sacred groves were often the only forested patch of land located close to human settlements and afforded insurgents the opportunity to launch attacks against military and village inhabitants. Attacks during the 1990s led to suggestions that forested patches, including sacred groves, adjacent to villages in the south and east of the country be cleared to eliminate hiding places, but it is not clear how many sacred groves were destroyed in Moyamba district. No post-conflict assessments have been made to determine whether they have reverted back to their original status as sacred groves or remained desecrated, but we are in the process of determining their fate. Civil strife poses a clear danger to the continued existence of sacred groves but solutions to such losses clearly cannot be based on their conservation value.

Land Tenure and Resource Access Issues

Efforts should be made to prevent the decline or loss of groves due to unregulated exploitation. Differential access to cropland, fuel wood and other resources makes land tenure issues locally volatile and threatens the integrity of isolated groves. We believe that issues of land and resource tenure and access to important forest resources could be addressed through the *poro, sande* and *wunde* societies, the historic mainstays of the village governance structure (Lebbie and Freudenberger 1996). Although the influence of these societies has declined in recent decades, often in the face of state claims of ownership, a surprisingly large proportion of rural people still respect these institutions (Oates 1999: 91). Their respect relates to the historic or cultural traditions that led to their creation, not any conservation tradition, so expanding or elaborating the role and values of the groves should necessarily also change.

Diminished governance during periods of conflict often results in 'open access' resource tenure and reverses decades of conservation and protection efforts. Refugee migrations confound this problem by creating locally intense pressure on natural resources. Large pools of cheap (and desperate) labor, combined with refugees working outside their traditional communities, exacerbate tenure and access problems. Given the value of the medicinal plant resources still contained within the groves, and the potential for economic as well as cultural benefits, we believe that rural communities and especially traditional societies like the *poro* and *sande*, could play a renewed role in managing tenure regimes but government ministries would need to agree to share power (see for example, Besong 1997, Mupada 1997). State claims to ownership and management of forests and sacred groves are, practically speaking, unenforceable and often serve to alienate rural communities who could (but usually won't) support state claims. Legal protections and the visibility that such recognition could bring to these forests could be useful as Sierra Leone rebuilds from a decade of civil strife. However, they cannot ensure that groves will continue unless educational, cultural and economic interests are also considered, as noted for the Kaya sacred forests of Kenya (Githotho 2003). The local societies offer the government an alternative to deferring control to communities because the *poro* and *sande* societies historically provided for community interests. Sharing power today merely returns some control to a traditional village institution rather than to the village at large.

Maintaining Cultural Resources

The fact that sacred groves were once sites of human habitation prior to colonial rule provides an additional reason to protect these landscape features for their heritage value (DeCorse 2001, Siebert, this volume). Although western conservation interests do not necessarily connect sacred forests to part of a larger existing cultural landscape, we see little likelihood that rural villages will assign high conservation values to sacred groves without other benefits. The economic potential of nature tourism has been cited as an important conservation tool (e.g. Brandon 1996, Cater 1995) but tourism is essentially non-existent in Sierra Leone today. Cultural or historical resources are hardly protected at the national level in Sierra Leone, and many have been lost to mining and agricultural development (Abraham and Fyle 1976, Conteh 1979). Informants confirmed that besides being former settlement sites, many sacred groves in Moyamba District were sites of tribal battles fought for territorial expansion and the taking of slaves. Several groves showed either single or double concentric rings of earth works dug to protect villages during times of warfare. Although partly eroded by natural processes, these features together with the graves of ancestors are still prominent in the sacred groves at Konda, Foinda and Kamato. Renewed cultural pride, in addition to economic interests in conserving medicinal and other useful plants, could provide the needed incentives to conserve and expand biotic diversity in Sierra Leone's sacred groves, but the institutions and incentives to accomplish this are mostly lacking (Barrett *et al.* 2001).

Biological Inventories

It will remain difficult to assign 'threatened or endangered' status to species now considered merely 'uncommon' without more comprehensive surveys of native flora and fauna. We emphasize that incomplete information should not be viewed as grounds for complacency as many of the species which currently occur in sacred groves may exist in few other places. Some species such as insect pollinators important to agricultural crops, or birds and bats that provide biological services appear to be resident in some groves (Power 1996). Many herbalists, 'tree spotters' and hunters provided anecdotal evidence that species with medicinal, timber or other uses are exploited to the point of extirpation outside sacred groves. Important medicinal plant resources, over-exploited or extinct in the surrounding landscape, should be completely inventoried in the groves, and efforts put in place for their protection. Eventually, sacred groves could serve as sources for seeds and propagation materials for semi-domestication efforts as local industries, or to restore important and useful species to other forests and groves.

It seems obvious that biodiversity conservation actions should be based on accurate knowledge of a country's biological resources (Burgess *et al.* 1998, Burley and Gauld 1995, Gauld 1997). Past investments in biological surveys in Sierra Leone remain under-utilized, with many botanical and zoological specimens in danger of being lost due to recurring civil conflicts. For example, Njala University College (Sierra Leone), originally a colonial agricultural training center, invested heavily in documenting the country's invertebrate fauna. A large entomological collection, especially butterflies, was assembled over more than 50 years (c. 1920–1970) but many specimens have never been vouchered and are unknown outside Sierra Leone. When programs at Njala University College were moved to Freetown during the civil war (1991–2002), the collection remained in Moyamba District where it still survives today. This and similar collections represent important links to Sierra Leone's 'biological legacy', and provide a historic baseline against which current and future inventories can be compared and losses enumerated. Inventory and monitoring activities can only succeed with the support of international organizations and resources and expertise from developed countries, but the participation of local communities in such actions is also critical (Davies and Ndam 1997, Lengeler 1997). Developing a biodiversity monitoring system in Sierra Leone against which future threats to biodiversity could be measured should be an important and continuing activity.

References

Abraham, A., and C. M. Fyle, 1976, 'Report on Bunce Island Rehabilitation Camp', 6–10 December, 1976. *African Research Bulletin* 7(1):71–8.

Amoako-Atta, B., 1998, 'Preservation of sacred groves in Ghana: Esukawkaw Forest Reserve and its Anweam sacred grove'. Paris: UNESCO Working Paper # 26, South-south Cooperation Programme for Environmentally Sound Socio-economic Development in the Humid Tropics.

Barrett, C. B., K. Brandon, C. Gibson, and H. Gjertsen, 2001, 'Conserving tropical biodiversity amid weak institutions'. *BioScience* 51(6):497–502.

Bawa, K. S., and P. S. Ashton, 1991, 'Conservation of rare trees in tropical rain forests: A genetic perspective'. In *Genetics and Conservation of Rare Plants*, D. A. Falk and K. E. Holsinger, eds, pp. 62–71. Oxford: Oxford University Press.

Besong, J. B., 1997, 'Best options for securing the future of the African rainforest'. In *African Rainforests and the Conservation of Biodiversity, Proceedings of the Limbe Conference*. S. Doolan, ed., pp. 39–42. Oxford: Earthwatch Europe.

Blake, J. G., 1991, 'Nested subplots and the distribution of birds on isolated woodlots'. *Conservation Biology* 5:58–66.

Blyden, E. W., 1872, 'Report on the expedition to Falaba'. *Journal of the Royal Geographical Society* 17 (2).

Brandon, K., 1996, 'Ecotourism and conservation: A review of key issues'. Environment Department Paper #33. Washington, DC: World Bank,

Brown, G. W., 1937, 'The poro in modern business: A preliminary report of field work'. *Man*

3:8–9.

Burgess, N. D., G. P. Clarke, and W. A. Rogers, 1998, 'Coastal forests of eastern Africa: Status, endemism patterns and their potential causes'. *Biological Journal of the Linnaean Society* 64:337–67.

Burley, J., and I. Gauld, 1995, 'Measuring and monitoring forest biodiversity'. In *Measuring and Monitoring Biodiversity in Tropical and Temperate Forests*, J. B. Boyle and B. Boontawee, eds, pp.19–46. Kuala Lumpur: CIFOR.

Campbell, M., 2004, 'Traditional forest protection and woodlots in the coastal savannah of Ghana'. *Environmental Conservation* 31:225–32.

Cascante, A., M. Quesada, and J. L. E. Fuchs, 2002, 'Effects of dry tropical forest fragmentation on the reproductive success and genetic structure of the tree, *Samanea saman*'. *Conservation Biology* 16:137–47.

Castro. P., 1990, 'Sacred groves and social change in Kirinyaga, Kenya'. In *Social Change and Applied Anthropology: Essays in Honor of David W. Brokensha*. M. S. Chaiken and A. K. Fleuret, eds, pp. 277–89. Boulder, CO: Westview Press.

Cater, E., 1995, 'Ecotourism in the Third World – Problems and prospects for sustainability'. In *Ecotourism: A Sustainable Option?* E. Cater and G. Lowman, eds, pp 68–87. Chichester, UK: John Wiley & Sons.

Chouin, G., 2002, 'Sacred groves in history: Pathways to the social shaping of forest landscapes in coastal Ghana'. *IDS Bulletin* 33(1):39–46.

Cole, N. H. A., 1968, *The Vegetation of Sierra Leone*. Freetown: Njala University Press.

Conteh, J. S., 1979, 'Diamond Mining and Kono Religious Institutions: A Study in Social Change'. Unpubl. Ph.D. dissertation, Bloomington, IN: Indiana University.

Corlett, R. T. and I. M. Turner, 1997, 'Long-term survival in tropical forest remnants in Singapore and Hong Kong'. In *Tropical Forest Remnants: Ecology, Management and Conservation of Fragmented Communities*, W. F. Laurance, R. O. Bierregaard, and C. Moritz, eds, pp. 333–45. Chicago: University of Chicago Press.

Daily, G. C., and P. R. Ehrlich, 1995, 'Preservation of biodiversity in small rainforest patches: Rapid evaluations using butterfly trappings'. *Biodiversity and Conservation* 4:35–55.

Davies, G. and N. Ndam, 1997, 'Limbe Botanic Garden: How botanic gardens can support forest conservation, and approaches to long-term financing for conservation centres in Africa'. In *African Rainforests and the Conservation of Biodiversity, Proceedings of the Limbe Conference*. S. Doolan, ed., pp. 88–97. Oxford: Earthwatch Europe.

Decher, J., 1997, 'Conservation, small mammals, and the future of sacred groves in West Africa'. *Biodiversity and Conservation* 6:1007–26.

——— 1999, 'Diversity and structure of terrestrial small mammal communities in different vegetation types on the Accra Plains of Ghana'. *Journal of Zoology* (London) 247: 395–408.

DeCorse, C. R., ed., 2001, *West Africa during the Atlantic Slave Trade: Archaeological Perspectives*. London: Leicester University Press.

Deighton, F. C., 1957, *Vernacular Botanical Vocabulary for Sierra Leone*. Norwich, UK: Jarrold and Sons Ltd.

Dorm-Adzobu, C., O. Ampadu-Agyei, and P. G. Veit, 1991, *Religious Beliefs and Environmental Protection: The Malshegu Sacred Grove in Northern Ghana*. Washington, DC: World Resources Institute, Center for International Development and Environment. From the Ground Up Case Study No.4.

Ellenberg, H., A. Galat-Luong, H-J von Maydell, M. Mühlenberg, K. F. Panzer, R. Schmidt-Lorenz, M. Sumser and T. W. Szolnoki, 1988, *Pirang: Ecological Investigations in a Forest Island in the Gambia*. Hamburg. Stiftung Walderhaltung in Africa.

Fairhead, J. and M. Leach, 1996, *Misreading the African Landscape: Society and Ecology in a Forest-Savanna Mosaic*. Cambridge: Cambridge University Press.

——— 1998, *Reframing Deforestation: Global Analysis and Local Realities – Studies in West Africa*. London: Routledge.

FAO, 2005 *State of the World's Forests*. Rome: FAO.

Fyfe, C., 1962, *A History of Sierra Leone*. Oxford: Oxford University Press.

Gauld, I. D., 1997, 'Inventorying and monitoring biodiversity: a taxonomist's perspective'. In *African Rainforests and the Conservation of Biodiversity, Proceedings of the Limbe Conference*. S. Doolan, ed., pp. 1–9. Oxford: Earthwatch Europe.

Githitho, A. N., 2003, 'The sacred Mijikenda Kaya forests of coastal Kenya and biodiversity conservation'. In *UNESCO Proceedings of the International Workshop on the Importance of Sacred Natural Sites for Biodiversity Conservation*, C. Lee and T. Schaaf, eds, pp. 27–35. Paris: UNESCO.

Guindon, C. F., 1996, 'The importance of forest fragments to the maintenance of regional biodiversity in Costa Rica'. In *Forest Patches in Tropical Landscapes*, J. Schelhas and R. Greenberg, eds, pp. 168–86. Washington, DC: Island Press.

Hall, J. B. and M. D. Swaine, 1981, *Distribution and Ecology of Vascular Plants in a Tropical Rain Forest: Forest Vegetation in Ghana*. The Hague, Netherlands: Dr. W. Junk Publishers.

Hawthorne, W., 2003, 'Strategies of the decentralized: Defending communities from slave raiders in coastal Guinea–Bissau, 1450–1815'. In *Fighting the Slave Trade: West African Strategies*. S. A. Diouf, ed., pp.152–69. Athens, OH: Ohio University Press.

Keel, S., A. H. Gentry and L. Spinzi, 1993, 'Using vegetation analysis to facilitate the selection of conservation sites in Eastern Paraguay'. *Conservation Biology* 7:66–75.

Nyamweru, C., S. Kibet, M. Pakia, and J. A. Cooke, 2007, 'The kaya forests of coastal Kenya: "Remnant patches" or dynamic entities?' This volume.

Laird, S., 1999, 'Forests, culture and conservation'. In *Cultural and Spiritual Values of Biodiversity*, D. A. Posey, ed., pp. 347–58. Nairobi: UNEP.

Lambert, H. E., 1950, *The Systems of Land Tenure in the Kikuyu Land Unit*. Cape Town: School of African Studies, Communication No.22.

Laurance, W. F., R. O. Bierregaard, and C. Moritz, 1997, *Tropical Forest Remnants: Ecology, Management and Conservation of Fragmented Communities*. Chicago: University of Chicago Press.

Leach, M., 1994, *Rainforest Relations: Gender and Resource Use Among the Mende of Gola, Sierra Leone*. Washington, DC: Smithsonian Institution Press.

Lebbie, A. R. and M. S. Freudenberger, 1996, 'The sacred groves of Africa: A case study of forest patches in transition in Sierra Leone'. In *Forest Patches in Tropical Landscapes*, J. Schelhas and R. Greenberg, eds, pp. 300–24. Washington, DC: Island Press.

Lebbie, A. R. and R. P. Guries, 1995, 'Ethnobotanical value and conservation of sacred groves of the Kpaa Mende of Sierra Leone'. *Economic Botany* 49:294–308.

Lengeler, J., 1997, 'Local people's participation in forest resource assessment: A review of field experience.' In *African Forests and the Conservation of Biodiversity, Proceedings of the Limbe Conference*. S. Doolan, ed. Oxford: Earthwatch Europe.

Lugo, A. E., 1995, 'Management of tropical biodiversity'. *Ecological Applications* 5:956–61.

McNeeley, J., 2003, 'Biodiversity, war and tropical forests'. *Journal of Sustainable Forestry* 16:1–20.

MacEachern, S., 2001, 'State formation and enslavement in the southern Lake Chad basin'. In *West Africa during the Atlantic Slave Trade*. C. R. DeCorse, ed., pp. 131–51. London: Leicester University Press.

Mgumia, F. H. and G. Oba, 2003, 'Potential role of sacred groves in biodiversity conservation in Tanzania'. *Environmental Conservation* 30: 259–65.

Miers, S. and I. Kopytoff, 1977, *Slavery in Africa: Historical and Anthropological Approaches*. Madison, WI: University of Wisconsin Press.

Migeod, F. W. H., 1926, *A View of Sierra Leone*. London: Kegan, Paul, Trench and Trubner.

Moran, Emilio F. and Elinor Ostrom, 2005, *Seeing the Forest and the Trees: Human-environment Interactions in Forest Ecosystems*. Cambridge, MA: MIT Press.

Mupada, E. 1997, 'Towards collaborative forest management in the conservation of Uganda's rain forests'. In *African Rainforests and the Conservation of Biodiversity. Proceedings of the Limbe Conference*. S. Doolan, ed., pp. 68–76. Oxford: Earthwatch Europe.

Nkongmeneck, B. A., M. D. Lowman and J. T. Atwood, 2002, 'Epiphyte diversity in primary and fragmented forests of Cameroon, Central Africa: A preliminary survey'. *Selbyana* 23(1): 121–30.

Nyerges, A. E., 1996, 'Ethnography in the reconstruction of African land use histories: A Sierra Leone example'. *Africa* 66: 122–43.

Oates, John F., 1999, *Myth and Reality in the Rain Forest*. Berkeley, CA: University of California Press.

Plumptre, A. J., 2003, 'Lessons learned from on-the-ground conservation in Rwanda and the Democratic Republic of the Congo'. *Journal of Sustainable Forestry* 16:71–92.

Power, A., 1996, 'Arthropod diversity in forest patches and agroecosystems of tropical landscapes'. In *Forest Patches in Tropical Landscapes*, J. Schelhas and R. Greenberg, eds, pp. 91–110. Washington, DC: Island Press.

Richards, P. W., 1952, *The Tropical Rainforest: An Ecological Study*. Cambridge: Cambridge University Press.

Riitters, K., J. Wickham, R. O'Neill, B. Jones and E. Smith, 2000, 'Global scale patterns of forest fragmentation'. *Conservation Ecology* 4:1–29.

Sarfo-Mensah, P., 2002, 'Is "Tumi" in the sacred grove really gone? Local interpretations of changes in the landscape of the forest-savanna transition in Ghana'. *IDS Bulletin* 33(1):47–54.

Savill, P. S. and J. E. D. Fox, 1967, *Trees of Sierra Leone*. Freetown: Sierra Leone Government Press.

Sayer, J. A., C. S. Harcourt, and N. M. Collins, eds, 1992, *The Conservation Atlas of Tropical Forests: Africa*. London: Macmillan.

Schaaf, T., 2003, 'UNESCO's experience with the protection of sacred natural sites for bio-diversity conservation'. In *International Symposium on 'Natural' Sacred Sites – Cultural Diversity and Biological Diversity* organized by UNESCO, the Centre National de la Recherche Scientifique and the Musée National d'Histoire Naturélle, pp. 13–20.

Siddle, D. J., 1969, 'The evolution of rural settlement forms in Sierra Leone circa 1400 to 1968'. *Sierra Leone Geographical Journal* 13:33–44.

Siebert, U., 2007, 'Are sacred forests in northern Bénin "traditional conservation areas"?: Examples from Bassila Region'. This volume.

Terborgh, J., 1992, 'Maintenance of diversity in tropical forests'. *Biotropica* 24:283–292.

Turner, I. M., H. T. W. Tan, Y. C. Wee, A. B. Ibrahim, P. T. Chew, and R. T. Corlett, 1994, 'A study of plant species extinction in Singapore: lessons for the conservation of tropical biodiversity'. *Conservation Biology*, 8:705-12.

Turner, I. M., 1996, 'Species loss in fragments of tropical rain forest: a review of the evidence'. *Journal of Applied Ecology* 33:200–9.

Turner, I. M. and R. T. Corlett, 1996, 'The conservation value of small, isolated fragments of lowland tropical rain forest'. *Trends in Ecology and Evolution* 11:330–33.

Turner, I. M., K. S. Chua, J. S. Y. Ong, B. C. Soong, and H. T. W. Tan, 1996, 'A century of plant species loss from an isolated fragment of lowland tropical rain forest'. *Conservation Biology* 10:1229–35.

Unwin, A. H., 1920, *West African Forests and Forestry*. New York: Dutton and Co.

Vajpeyi, Dhirendra K., ed., 2001, *Deforestation, Environment, and Sustainable Development: A Comparative Analysis*. Westport, CT: Praeger.

Van Rompaey, R., 2002, 'New perspectives on tropical rain forest vegetation ecology in West Africa: typology, gradients and disturbance regime'. *IDS Bulletin* 33(1):33–8.

Wilcox, B. A. and D. D. Murphy, 1985, 'Conservation strategy: The effects of fragmentation on extinction'. *American Naturalist* 125: 879–87.

4

The Kaya Forests of Coastal Kenya
'Remnant Patches' or Dynamic Entities?

CELIA NYAMWERU, STALINE KIBET,
MOHAMMED PAKIA & JOHN A. COOKE

The kaya forests of coastal Kenya have been interpreted as historical sites of the Bantu-speaking Mijikenda peoples. The word kaya means a settlement in the languages of the nine closely related Mijikenda groups, whose oral histories tell of migration from a northern homeland several centuries ago to settle in fortified villages within thick belts of forest (Spear 1978). The results of linguistic and more recent archaeological research have cast doubt on this version of Mijikenda history (Helm 2004, Morton 1972, 1977, Walsh 1992) but the kaya forests still retain powerful cultural significance to many Mijikenda today. Though attitudes to and knowledge of the kaya forests differ according to criteria that include age, gender and degree of exposure to formal education as well as to Islam and Christianity, there is a general consensus among the Mijikenda that the kaya forests are central to their cultural identity and indeed to their community well-being (Nyamweru 1997, 1998, 2003).

The forest vegetation of coastal Kenya has been identified as part of the Zanzibar-Inhambane lowland moist forest ecosystem, an important and highly threatened centre of endemism containing plants that are 'representatives of lineages which evolved millions of years ago and have become relict in the coastal forests as the available lowland forest habitat in eastern Africa has shrunk' (Burgess et al. 1998:362). The approximately 60 kaya forest patches that have been identified in Kwale, Kilifi and Malindi districts are believed to be some of the last fragments of the Zanzibar-Inhambane moist forest, 'remnant patches of the once extensive and diverse coastal tropical lowland forests of the East African coast' (WWF 1998:20). They vary in size (ranging from about five to 250 hectares); some are on flat land close to sea level, others on the low ridges overlooking the coastal lowlands or further inland, on the plateau. Being on sites that differ in terms of terrain, geology and distance from the sea (thus also in the annual rainfall they receive), the plant communities of the kaya forests vary considerably. Most of the larger, better preserved kaya

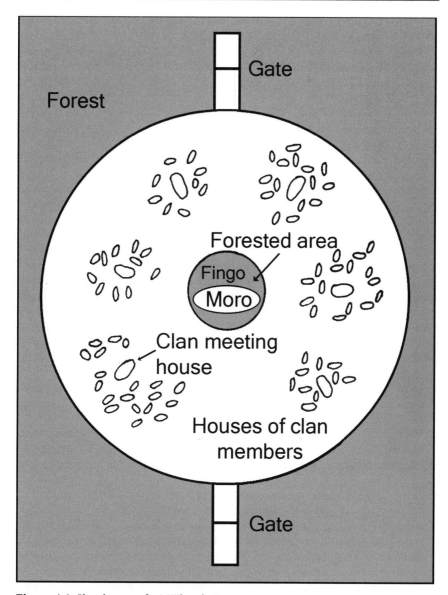

Figure 4.1 Sketch map of a Mijikenda Kaya
Source: T.T. Spear, *The Kaya Complex*, 1978, fig. 1, p. 47 (Nairobi: Kenya Literature Bureau)

forests retain a central clearing that the Mijikenda identify as the former settlement site and the site where rituals such as community prayers for rain are still carried out. A few paths lead from the forest margins through the forest belt to the central clearing, and according to Mijikenda tradition each clan of the local community had its own path, through which the clan elders would approach the central clearing. Spear (1978:47) illustrates the 'original' ground plan of the kaya (Fig. 4.1) at the time when it was a densely populated settlement. Today very few elders live permanently in clearings in the kaya forests, but in some of them, elders have built small shelters of sticks and grass where they occasionally pass the night. The fig and baobab trees that Spear described as the sites under which elders held their meetings can also be found in several of the central clearings.

Many Mijikenda, as well as Kenyan and foreign ecologists and conservationists, recognize how vulnerable these small forest patches are to degradation or outright destruction. Land-hungry Mijikenda clear the forest to obtain farmland, while land speculators and property developers take advantage of endemic corruption to obtain private title to community land in the kaya forests for housing developments and tourist resorts (Wilson 1993, Nyamweru 1996). Mining of iron ore, lead and most recently titanium-rich sands threatens some of the forests. Trees are extracted for timber, wood carvings and sale to local or outside consumers. Local uses include the extraction of firewood (largely by women) and of building poles (by both men and women). Medicinal plants are harvested both for personal and commercial uses. Local use may be more sustainable, but as the surrounding populations have increased and the level of poverty remains high, the demand for forest products risks exceeding sustainable levels. Over the last few decades some kaya forests have been totally destroyed, many have been drastically reduced in area, and virtually all have suffered significant ecological change through the selective extraction of certain plant species. However, we believe that it is too simplistic to assume that before these currently observable drastic changes were set in motion (probably within the last century or so), the kaya settlements were surrounded by a stable plant community, the 'primeval' forest, that is described as the Zanzibar–Inhambane lowland moist forest ecosystem.

What we hope to do in this chapter is first to show that even when the first European missionaries and explorers arrived at the Kenya coast in the mid-nineteenth century, it is highly unlikely that the forest patches surrounding the kaya settlements were in any sense 'natural' or stable plant communities; numerous physical and anthropogenic forces had been at work for preceding millennia to create highly dynamic vegetation patterns in this region. We then focus on the results of two recent field studies within some of the kaya forests to show the ways in which human activities today are impacting the forest vegetation, and the extent to which the indigenous institutions still control access to the forest. Finally we suggest possible lines for future research that might help us to understand more of the environmental history of this region.

Physical Influences on Kenyan Coastal Forests Through Time

The most important physical influence on vegetation over time is climate. Climatic variations and trends set in motion changes in the composition of vegetation communities, which may constantly be adjusting to climatic change. The presence of large wild herbivores (in Africa most notably elephants) can also have a significant effect on vegetation, as has been demonstrated by the work of Dublin *et al.* (1990), among others. Håkansson summarizes it well: 'Except for humans, no other mammals have as profound an impact on their environment as elephants' (2004:571). Elephants tend to create or maintain grassland at the expense of woody plants; they destroy trees in several ways, by defoliating them, stripping their bark and (in the case of young males) pushing them down out of sheer aggression. Dublin suggests that following the great rinderpest epidemic of the 1890s (which killed many wild herbivores as well as domestic livestock, leading to the starvation deaths of pastoral nomads) East African woodlands expanded at the expense of grassland. She goes on to speculate that 'savannah woodlands may be characterised by even-aged stands, appear and disappear in pulses, and can switch back and forth between vegetation states when viewed over a few centuries' (1990:1158). It is reasonable to assume that similar behaviour would characterise the woodland-grassland interface on the low plateaux where some of the interior kaya forests (for example Kaya Fungo and Kaya Duruma) are located. However, it is impossible, on available data, to be more specific about how coastal vegetation may have responded to changes in wildlife and domestic livestock populations over the last 150 years. We have no data on how the rinderpest epidemic affected coastal Kenya, though we can be fairly sure that the human impact on elephants has been much more intense at the coast than for example in the Serengeti-Mara ecosystem where Dublin and her co-workers did their study.[1] Thus we can only recognize the probability of significant changes in animal populations over the last few hundred years, which are likely to have influenced the distribution and composition of coastal vegetation communities.

There is a large body of published research on African palaeoclimates, and the broad picture of swings between cool/dry and warm/moist periods over the last few million years is relatively well established (Goudie 1996, Battarbee *et al.* 2004).[2] However, relatively few data are available from the East African coastlands. Most of this research has been done in lake basins and river valleys in areas that are now arid to semi-arid, supporting vegetation communities ranging from desert to savannah bushland and scrubland. Palaeoenvironmental data have been obtained from the lake basins of the African Rift System (lakes Malawi, Rukwa, Natron, Magadi, Naivasha, Turkana and the Ethiopian rift lakes among them), from the Lake Chad, Lake Bosumtwi and Lake Victoria basins, and from a variety of sites in the semi-arid regions of Southern Africa. Data have also been obtained from sediment cores collected from high altitude lakes including those on Mount Kenya, Mount Elgon and Ruwenzori, as well as from ice cores from the shrinking glaciers of Kilimanjaro (Thompson *et al.* 2002). Much less research of this kind has been done along Africa's equatorial coastal belt; a rare example is Cole and Dunbar's 2000 report on 194 years of sea surface temperature data based on oxygen isotopes in corals at Malindi. In

---

[1] Håkansson's maps show elephants exterminated from the Kenya coastal strip south of the R.Sabaki before 1840, but still 'common' between the Sabaki and Tana rivers in 1840; exterminated or rare for the whole Kenya coast except the Tana delta by 1890 (2004:567, 569).

[2] The several relevant chapters in this volume contain up-to-date lists of references; the interested reader is referred to these, in particular to the chapters by Barker *et al.* 2004 and Verschuren 2004, listed in the References for this chapter.

general, however, our understanding of climatic change at the Kenya coast has to be based on inferences drawn from neighboring regions which today have different climates, or from distant regions such as the Lake Bosumtwi basin in Ghana. Among the several climatic events for which there is relatively solid evidence from a variety of sites and different climatic proxies are the following:

- **Between 140 and 90 kyr (thousand years ago):** high water levels of Rift Valley lakes at several periods, including Lake Naivasha at 135, 110 and 90 kyr, and a lake over 47 metres deep in the presently very arid Magadi-Natron basin at 130 to 140 kyr.
- **Between 15.9 and 14.2 kyr:** Lake Victoria dried out briefly, and possibly also slightly earlier, between 18 and 17 kyr (Stager et al. 2002).
- **Approximately 15 kyr:** A spectacular, substantial rise in lake levels, for example of Lakes Magadi, Manyara and Tanganyika; the onset of what has been called the 'African humid period' (Barker *et al.* 2004:125). Lake Victoria also rose substantially at about this time, presumably following the drying out episode referred to above.
- **13.5 kyr:** Evidence of a major discharge pulse in the River Congo from sediments of the offshore 'Congo Fan.' Sediments in the Niger Delta indicate an abrupt decline in salinity at about the same time, which is interpreted as the result of a dramatic increase in freshwater outflow of the River Niger.
- **12.5 to 11.5 kyr:** Many lakes show substantial regressions for this interval, followed by a re-establishment of the African humid period.
- **8.4 to 8 kyr:** Major dry period of the Ethiopian lakes (Lake Abhé, Lakes Ziway and Shala) and of Lake Bosumtwi.
- **5.5 kyr:** Abrupt end of the African humid period, with a widespread regression of lakes centred on 4.2 to 4.0 kyr.[3]

Though much of the evidence for these climatic changes is composed of sedimentary, geochemical and isotopic data, pollen analysis provides direct information about vegetation changes. Contemporary with the high Congo river discharge of the 13.5 kyr event there is said to have been a '… rise in lowland rainforest taxa, which continues into the Holocene, [and] begins at this period, coincident with a decline in dry grassland taxa,' while the 4.2 to 4.0 kyr arid event is reflected in East Africa by a 'decline in moist rainforest and its replacement by dry forest types' (Barker *et al.* 2004:123, 129).

Coming closer to the present day, there is evidence of continued climatic fluctuations; according to Verschuren 'the last 2000 years of Africa's climatic history were punctuated by major, century-scale climatic anomalies of possibly continent-wide extent' (2004:140). Verschuren suggests that between about AD 900 and 1270 (broadly coeval with the Medieval Warm Period in mid-latitude Europe) most areas of inter-tropical Africa were drier than today (*ibid*.:152). Relatively moist conditions (interrupted at least twice by decade-scale episodes of severe aridity dated to around AD 1400 and the late 1500s)

---

[3]   This information (key climatic events) is extracted from Barker *et al.* 2004.

may have prevailed in equatorial East Africa between about AD 1270 and the mid-1700s, coincident with the Little Ice Age in mid-latitude Europe. Widespread drought appears to have returned to much of Africa during the late 1700s and early 1800s, with maximum aridity possibly occurring during the 1790s.

While the broadest trends over millennia were probably continent-wide, there is no guarantee that such parallelism was replicated on a local level and for shorter-term events.[4] Recent evidence shows that not all of Africa experienced relatively dry conditions during the Medieval Warm Period; for example, analysis of a core from Lake Edward in the western Rift Valley showed droughts (with intervening moister periods) at approximately AD 1600, 1100 and 500 (as well as earlier) (Russell *et al.* 2003: 678). Conditions during the Little Ice Age may not have been moist across all of Africa either; Lake Bosumtwi in central Ghana may have been at a low level between about AD 1500 and 1000 (Brooks *et al.* 2005, Talbot *et al.* 1984). A core from the sediments underlying Lake Masoko in south-western Tanzania indicates relatively dry conditions between about AD 800 to 1500, covering at least part of the Little Ice Age (Vincens *et al.* 2003). Citing evidence from a number of sources, Vincens *et al.* point out that 'In south tropical East Africa, late Holocene forest and woodland changes have been registered in numerous pollen records ... However, the timing of these changes appears to be asynchronous from site to site, and their interpretation, mainly concerning declines, in terms of ecological change and/or human interference is not clear' (2003: 329).

Whatever the actual history of climatic fluctuations may have been, it seems clear that climatic variations of a sufficient order to influence the relative areas of wooded and grassland vegetation have occurred over recent millennia and centuries along the Kenya coast. At these equatorial latitudes it can be assumed that tree growth is drought-limited rather than temperature-limited, so climatic changes involving a reduction in net moisture availability for natural ecosystems would favour the expansion of grassland at the expense of woody vegetation. Reduction in net moisture availability (and variations in seasonal distribution of rainfall) might also increase the role of fire as an ecological agent, encouraging the spread of fire-tolerant species at the expense of fire-vulnerable species. Though lack of localized historical and ecological data prevents a more detailed analysis of how climatic change has affected the vegetation of coastal Kenya over recent millennia, we have to accept that such change has taken place, and that, independently of anthropogenic influences, the vegetation of the kaya forests may still be responding to climatic changes dating to the Little Ice Age or earlier.[5]

---

[4]   The experience of modern day El Niño-Southern Oscillation events shows how climatic anomalies can move in opposite directions between relatively nearby regions; equatorial East Africa tends to experience above-average rainfall while much of southern Africa is in the grip of drought (World Meteorological Organization 1999:59-61).

[5]   At some sites closest to the sea, sea-level changes may also have influenced vegetation; as Burgess *et al.* comment 'Forests of the lowest ground closest to the sea ... cannot have existed on those sites for more than ten thousand years as such features have developed mainly since the end of the last Ice Age' (1998:362).

Anthropogenic Influences on Kenyan Coastal Forests Through Time

According to Mutoro:

> The fauna and flora of this region [the Kenya coast] have been adversely affected by human activities. These include charcoal burning, cutting of mangroves for exports, hunting of wild game for trophies, etc. As a result, what we see today is not a true picture of conditions in earlier centuries. Evidence from documentary sources attest to the existence of thick moist forests and savanna vegetation teeming with different types of fauna and flora. One eye-witness in 1860, for instance, observed that the flora of this region was not only an extensive one, but also contained some of the finest timber in the world.
>
> (Mutoro 1987:15)

Mutoro goes on to quote from Charles New's description of the variety of large hardwood trees, medicinal herbs and roots that existed in the coastal forests at the time of his visit to the region in the 1860s. The implication is that in the mid-nineteenth century the vegetation of coastal Kenya was in a relatively undisturbed state, and that the bulk of human impacts have occurred since then. However a closer look at the settlement and land use history of this region may lead us to a different conclusion.

Kusimba and Kusimba provide an outline of human subsistence economies over the last 2000 years in the Taita-Tsavo region, about 150 km inland from the Kenya coast. Among the activities they provide evidence for at sites such as Bungule and Kirongwe (radiocarbon dated to between 170 and 380 years BP) are pottery making, iron smelting and forging, the keeping of domestic livestock, and the creation of dry stonework terraces and irrigation canals (Kusimba and Kusimba 2005:407-409). Mutoro cites evidence of iron working and pottery at Kwale (on the coast) dating back to the second century AD, and probably earlier (1987:25). Overall we can put together a picture of human activities over several thousand years that would have had a considerable effect on vegetation. The harvesting of woody plants to yield fuel for both pottery firing and iron smelting must have had an impact on the woodland/grassland balance, at least on a local level, as has been well demonstrated by Schmidt (1997), who carried out detailed field and ethnographic studies in the Kagera region of north-western Tanzania. Schmidt's conclusion that the remaining swamp forests of this region 'are not pristine remnants of a prehistoric era but are artifacts of centuries of forest exploitation by humans' (Schmidt 1997:420) may well be applied to the kaya forests of coastal Kenya.

Debate continues over the origin of the Mijikenda, and the length of their occupation of coastal Kenya. Their oral narratives of their own origins, collected and interpreted by Spear (1978), tell of migration from a northern homeland of 'Singwaya' or 'Shungwaya'; this migration has been dated at about 1550-1600 AD (Mutoro 1987:32–33). Mijikenda elders today still tell versions of this narrative, which is taught to primary school children at schools in coastal Kenya[6] and has also become an integral part of the current forest

---

[6] 'Singwaya is part of the GHC [Geography-History-Civics] package for pupils below standard 3 in the Coast province … other provinces similarly have different packages due to different ethnic set-up' (A. Githitho and L.Chiro, pers. comm., 9 May 2006).

conservation discourse, for example through its inclusion in a documentary film produced for and by the Coastal Forest Conservation Unit in the late 1990s (Makaya: the sacred forests). The earliest challenges to this narrative were based largely on linguistic and textual evidence (Morton 1972, 1977, Walsh 1992) but more recently archaeological evidence has added greatly to our understanding of coastal settlement history. Mutoro accepts the physical reality of Singwaya/Shungwaya, but points out that there is evidence for 'a continuity of Mijikenda presence [in coastal Kenya] extending well back before the Singwaya developments could have affected the region' (1987:34). Helm goes further, positing that 'Shungwaya never was a single settlement or town' but rather 'a region made up of several settlement localities, the extent of which must have incorporated a multiplicity of ethno-linguistic communities' (2004:67). Based on the results of his own fieldwork, Helm questions not only 'the existence of an actual migration event, but also the previous perception of restricted and centralised Kaya habitation' (*ibid*.:71). His evidence supports the picture of 'a continuous and evolving cultural sequence of iron working and farming societies spanning the early first to late second millennium AD' (*ibid*.:73) and he distinguishes four phases of settlement pattern (2004:74-75). During Phases 1 and 2 (which he dates from c. 100 BC to 1000 AD) there was a gradual increase in settlement size, followed by a decrease in settlement size towards a growing number of smaller-scale family based units in Phase 4, from 1650 AD onwards. The physical evidence shows that these were settlements of mixed farmers who carried out iron-working and pottery making, testifying to a long history of intensive use of vegetation resources along the coastal strip and in its immediate hinterland.

There is thus ample evidence that the subsistence activities of settled communities have affected vegetation in this region for at least 2000 years. We can no longer accept the picture of Mijikenda pioneers moving into forests occupied only by nomadic bands of hunter-gatherers during the sixteenth and seventeenth centuries AD. Given the reality of farming and livestock keeping habitation over many centuries, the impact on vegetation in the areas surrounding the original settlements must have been considerable. If fortified settlements were indeed set up in forested areas, as the kaya forest villages are supposed to have originated, these were not 'pristine' forests at the time, and these forests would not have remained untouched by the presence of humans and livestock within such villages, even with local restrictions on the use of forest resources.

Population estimates for the nine Mijikenda groups cited by Mutoro (1987: 36–8) range from about 40,000 in the late seventeenth century to 60,000 or more by the mid-nineteenth century. Such populations, clustered in communities of 1000 to 1500 people, must have had a significant influence on the surrounding flora and fauna. During the nineteenth century, the Mijikenda cultivated a variety of annual crops, among them sorghum, millet, cowpeas and exotic cultigens such as rice and maize. Several exotic tree crops became very important, in particular the coconut palm but also mango and cashew. The Mijikenda also kept livestock (cattle, sheep and goats) and hunted wild game including elephant and buffalo. Both of these activities involved burning of the natural vegetation; according to Charles New (who visited Kayas Kambe, Jibana, Chonyi and Kauma in 1865) 'The Wanika[7] set fire to the grass in order to facilitate their hunting. To the same cause may be attributed the stunted growth of many of the trees' (1971:70). New goes on to describe the vegetation of the hinterland as 'a vast uncultivated tract of prairie, jungle, wood and forest', pointing out that 'dense jungles are rendered impossible by the yearly burnings which take place over these tracts' (1971:75).

Evidence of commercial extraction of forest products during the nineteenth century is provided by Mutoro, who states that:

> The forest provided them [the Mijikenda] with very useful woods that were cut into planks and boards to be sold to the Waswahili on the coast for *dhow* construction, doors, and the like. Copal, a kind of gum, was collected in large quantities and sold in the market in Mombasa and Zanzibar. On the whole the Mijikenda people valued their forests and protected them jealously.
>
> (Mutoro 1987:39)

He goes on to quote from Krapf to the effect that 'At one stage, for instance, they had to fine their chief heavily for allowing the sheikh of Mombasa to cut more trees for ship-building than had been permitted by the elders (Krapf 1860:302)'. While this testifies to the existence of limits on forest use controlled by the elders (and raises the question of who this 'chief' may have been, if not an elder himself), it also shows that even in the mid-nineteenth century, commercial pressures were causing people to defy or ignore the indigenous authority's regulation of forest use.

Regional Variations Among Kenyan Coastal Forests

There are over 60 forest remnants that have been identified as kaya forests (see figure 4.2), ranging in location and altitude from the Indian Ocean shoreline (Chale Island, Kaya Kinondo and Kaya Tiwi) to over 50 km inland and 200 m above sea level (Kaya Fungo). Some are on relatively flat land (Kaya Kinondo, Kaya Muhaka) while others, such as the five Rabai kaya forests (Mudzimuvya, Bomu, Fimboni, Mzizima and Mudzimwiru) cover hill slopes and ridges. They are underlain by varying geology; Kaya Kinondo lies on recent coral rag (limestone), the Rabai kaya forests, Kaya Chonyi and Kaya Fungo are on Triassic Duruma sandstones, while Jurassic sediments (shales and limestones) underlie Kaya Kambe (Caswell 1956). Each kaya forest has its particular surroundings, differing according to vegetation, land use and settlement history. The kaya forests are recognized by different Mijikenda sub-groups, details of whose belief systems and practices vary; the influence of Islam and Christianity also vary across the region. Few if any scholars of the Mijikenda would disagree that the kaya is important (if not central) to their sense of cultural identity; the most detailed and nuanced interpretation is probably that of Parkin, in which he describes the Giriama Kaya Fungo as 'a sacred

---

[7]   An old term for the ethnic groups today broadly identified as Mijikenda. The modern version 'Wanyika' is now generally considered as derogatory.

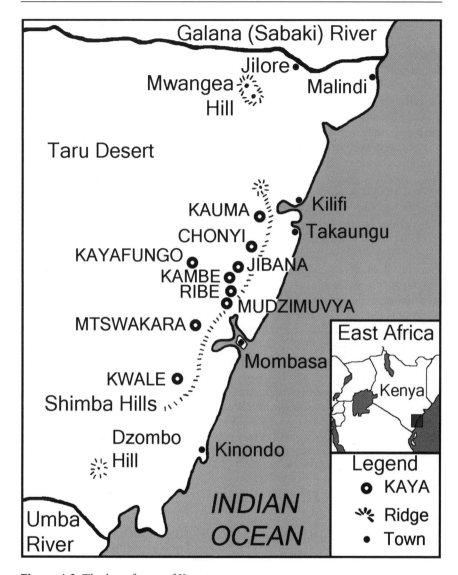

Figure 4.2 The kaya forests of Kenya

Source: East African Database and Atlas Project of UNEP, 27 March 2001

centre [that] is indeed regarded as the ultimate provider of ritual knowledge' (1991:52). It is also generally recognized that everywhere in coastal Kenya the kaya forests are under threat. However, the sense in which the kaya are important to cultural identity, and the precise nature of the threats, varies from one forest to the next. In the following sections we look at three particular kaya forests and the ways in which human activity is currently affecting their vegetation.

Background to the Fieldwork

Pakia's fieldwork, carried out in 1998 in the communities around Kaya Mtswakara[8] and Kaya Fungo,[9] focused on the extraction of building poles. Pakia interviewed men about the different tree species they preferred and used in house building, and the sources from which they obtained the poles. He investigated the extent to which distance from the kaya forest influenced people's choice of source of building poles. His study also sought to establish how effective the traditional management systems continue to be in controlling the extraction of plant resources from these two kaya forests. To do this he spoke with kaya elders, community kaya guards[10] (responsible for surveillance in the forests) and community members.

Kibet spent fourteen months (November 1999 to February 2001) in and around Kaya Mudzimuvya investigating how human disturbance (past and present) was affecting species composition, structure and their regeneration. Preliminary observation had shown that there was physiognomic variation in vegetation with six identified vegetation zones. He collected vegetation data and subjected them to statistical analysis to test the validity of these preliminary observations. Once the reality of these vegetation zones had been confirmed, it was necessary to establish whether they could be explained purely in terms of the physical environment, namely factors such as soil, slope/topography and altitude. Finally, Kibet looked at past and present uses of the forest to work out the influence of human activities on the vegetation, including investigating the historical uses of the kaya forest and how those uses were being regulated, who regulated the uses in the past, and whether any of the regulations controlling access to kaya resources are still being followed today. Kibet's data on forest use and regulations were collected through semi-structured questionnaires and participant observation.

[8] According to Willis 'Several sources agree that this, just south of the Mwache, was the first Duruma kaya ... damaged by troops of the Sultan of Zanzibar in the late nineteenth century, but continued to serve as a ritual centre' (1996:94–5).

[9] 'This is now the principal Giryama kaya ... Fungo ... was a mid-nineteenth century individual who seems to have acquired a great deal of power in Giryama society ... Some Giryama reject the use of his name for the kaya, insisting that it is kaya Giryama, not kaya Fungo' (Willis 1996:86).

[10] Kaya guards are relatively young men, recruited from the local community, and often members of the same families as the kaya elders. When the Coastal Forest Conservation Unit began to work with kaya elders' groups (from 1992 onwards) to prevent uncontrolled extraction of wood products from the kaya forests, CFCU provided funds to pay moderate monthly stipends to 2 or 3 kaya guards at several of the forests. Since CFCU's funding was drastically cut in the late 1990s, the kaya guards, if they are active at all, do so in a voluntary capacity or with occasional minor donations from the kaya elders' groups. At the time that Pakia and Kibet did their fieldwork, there were still kaya guards employed at their research sites.

The Study Area

Kaya Mtswakara, in Kwale District, is the primary kaya of the Duruma sub-group of the Mijikenda and covers about 248 hectares. Kaya Fungo, in Kilifi District, is the primary kaya of the Giriama and covers about 205 hectares. Kaya Mudzimuvya, also in Kilifi District, is one of five kaya forests of the Rabai people, yet another Mijikenda sub-group. Its area is about 171 hectares, including some quite steeply sloping land that ranges between 20 and 200 m above sea level. Kaya Mtswakara is a dry/wet coastal forest with dense forest vegetation (*Scorodophloeus fischeri* and *Hugonia castaneifolia* communities) found on hill tops, and gentle undulating and steep slopes that run into river valleys (Pakia 2000). Kaya Fungo, the furthest inland of the three forests, lies in an area that experiences significantly less rainfall than the other two, with occasional prolonged droughts, and is a coastal dry forest. The 'dense forest' vegetation in Kaya Fungo was the *Uvariodendron kirkii* community, recorded in the inner part of Kaya Fungo forest surrounding the central clearing and sacred sites (Pakia 2000). The greater area of Kaya Mudzimuvya forest (almost 68 percent of the sampled area) is covered by the *Bridelia* community group, consisting of scattered trees among open woody shrubland and bushland (less than 5 m high), interspersed by areas of grasses. The smaller area (about 32 percent) of Kaya Mudzimuvya is made up of the *Asteranthe* community group, which forms much of the closed forest, characterised by a continuous understorey cover, above which rise large emerging tree species, with occasional interlocking canopies in some sections of the forest (Kibet 2002).

The land use around all three kaya forests is partly pastoral (indigenous cattle and small stock) and partly agricultural (annual crops such as maize and millet; perennials such as bananas; tree crops such as coconuts, cashewnuts and mangoes). Pastoralism is probably relatively more important in the communities around Kaya Mtswakara and Kaya Fungo than around Kaya Mudzimuvya (a moister and more densely populated area). One thing characterizes all these communities and that is poverty. Except for those households lucky enough to have access to off-farm sources of income, people have little money to spare, even for such necessities as school fees and medical care. Thus there is heavy reliance on locally obtainable raw materials for house construction, and the majority of households cook on open hearths using locally obtained fuel wood. Houses are commonly built by men, the individual family heads. The traditional Mijikenda house was the grass house over a framework of poles, and older community members still expressed preference for this kind of house, though overall this housing type is on the decline. Pakia's study recorded grass houses in 71.7 percent of the homesteads of the Giriama around Kaya Fungo, but in only 34 percent of the homesteads of the Duruma around Kaya Mtswakara. In the settlements around Kaya Mudzimuvya very few grass houses remain. Where they are present, the grass houses are mainly used as granaries, livestock barns or kitchens and most of the primary dwelling houses are the rectangular type made of a framework of different sized poles filled in with lumps of mud, clay and/or cement. Standing poles/posts (*Nguzo* or *viguzo*) are the vertical poles fastened into the ground. They are usually between 4 and 10 cm base diameter. Rafters (*Pau*) are medium sized poles that hold the roof to the wall frame and are usually between 3 and 6 cm base diameter. Finally, withies (*Fito*) are the small size sticks, tied horizontally to hold *Nguzo* or *Pau* together, which range from 1.5 cm to 4 cm base diameter.

Use of Wood from Kaya Forests

The Mijikenda use timber and non-timber products from the kaya forests for a variety of purposes (Kibet 2002, Pakia and Cooke 2003a and b). The main uses of wood from the kaya forests are for building poles (harvested mainly though not exclusively by men) and fuel wood (harvested almost exclusively by women). Both these commodities may be used in the household of the harvester, or sold to others. In the following discussions we focus on the harvesting of building poles, while recognizing that the harvesting of firewood is an important activity that deserves separate discussion. Building poles are selected on the basis of species (durability and cultural acceptability), form (straightness) and size.

Preference and Use of Building Poles

The people Kibet interviewed in the homesteads around Kaya Mudzimuvya named their most preferred species for building poles as *Grewia plagiophylla, Combretum schumanni, Millettia usaramensis, Scorodophloeus fischeri* and *Cynometra suaheliensis.* Closed forest species (e.g. *Scorodophloeus fischeri* and *Cynometra suaheliensis*) made up over 35 percent of the 39 favoured species cited. Open woody shrubland species cited included *Grewia plagiophylla* and *Millettia usaramensis, Brachystegia spiciformis, Dalbergia melanoxylon,* and *Flueggea virosa.* Kibet's field observations, based on identifying the species of recently cut stumps, confiscated poles and those cut and hidden in the forest, confirmed the informants' expressed preferences. The implication is that despite some concern about the 'legality' of their pole collection (shown by their hiding of poles for later collection when the guards[11] or elders are less likely to be around), the people of this area are able to get hold of their preferred species to build their houses.

Pakia's informants from the households around Kaya Mtswakara named a total of 48 plant species used for building, of which 15 were the most commonly used species, used in more than 10 percent of homesteads.[12] Most

[11] Collection of building poles is time-consuming and tiring and harvesters can usually only carry home part of what they collect in a given day. Pakia reports that they hide poles, not only from elders and kaya guards, but also to prevent them being stolen by other people, including those who may be collecting legally.

[12] Pakia found a very wide variety of tree species used as building poles and rather few that were used in a significant proportion of the houses he analyzed; hence this rather low percentage of 10% to define the 'most favored' species.

of these commonly used species were described as 'best' for building, including species from different vegetation types occurring both within and outside the kaya forest. However, three of the most commonly used species were *not* the most preferred for building, while some of the less commonly used species (utilized in less than 10 percent of homesteads) were described as 'best' for building poles. This meant that although the informants were able to categorize species in terms of preference and suitability, the utilization levels were not based only on preference; local species population abundance was also important, with the most abundant species being used more frequently. Results from the households around Kaya Fungo showed that a total of 53 species were used for building, of which 15 were the most commonly used species for building in 10 percent or more of the sampled homesteads. The number of commonly used species is thus the same at Kaya Fungo as at Kaya Mtswakara, but only six of the 15 species were common to both communities. In the households around Kaya Fungo, although most of the commonly used species were considered 'best' species for building, five of the 15 commonly used species were not. *Croton talaeporos,* the species ranked fifth highest in utilization, was regarded as supplying poor quality poles for building. Several of the species described as being best for building, such as *Manilkara sulcata, Manilkara sansibarensis, Ochna thomasiana, Craibia brevicaudata* and *Agave sisalana,* were among the less commonly used.

Sources of Building Poles

In Pakia's interviews, the sources from which people might obtain building poles were divided into bought (locally or from further away) or collected (from the kaya forest, private farm land or bushland). 'Private farmland' referred to the land area that belonged to the family of the informant. 'Bushland' referred to communal land areas and other 'farmland' areas from which building poles could be collected. Around Kaya Mtswakara, the kaya forest was reported as the main source of building poles and 'private farmland' was the least important source. Most of the dense forest species such *Craibia brevicaudata, Scorodophloeus fischeri, Croton pseudopulchellus, Combretum schumannii, Manilkara sulcata* and *Cynometra suaheliensis,* as well as *Diospyros consolatae* (a woodland species) were collected from the kaya forest. The other major source of these dense forest and woodland species was 'bought near', indicating that collection from the kaya for local village sale occurred. These species are no longer available in areas outside the kaya forest due to habitat destruction from clearing and farming activities. They are collected from the kaya both for household use and by people who sell all or some of the wood they collect to other local users. Thus informal trade in building poles at the local level exists. The elders and guards described the trade in poles collected from the kaya forest as 'illegal', and they all acknowledged that such trade was taking place. Building poles 'bought far' were mainly mangrove species and the cultivated species *Casuarina equisitifolia* and *Agave sisalana.* The only species collected in significant amounts from 'private farmland' was *Thevetia peruviana,* an exotic and a 'poor' species for building poles, grown on homesteads mainly as an ornamental plant (it has beautiful flowers).

Contrasting sharply with Mtswakara, the principal source of building poles for communities around Kaya Fungo was 'Bushland', contributing more than three times the poles collected from any of the other sources. Only two species, *Croton pseudopulchellus* and *Cynometra schumannii*, were collected from the kaya in high proportions (>80 percent) relative to the bushland and other categories. This was most likely due to the unavailability of these species outside the forest. Even though both these species were in the 'best' category their utilisation was relatively low (in less than 18 percent of homesteads). Ten of the most commonly used species were collected from 'private farmland' although in small amounts. These data suggest that collections from the 'bushland' were made both for home use and for sale, although bought poles were a low frequency source of total poles used. Additional information and observations made in the urban markets indicated that poles collected in and around Kaya Fungo were traded in the neighbouring urban markets of Kaloleni and Mariakani, while mangrove species, *Agave sisalana* and *Coconus nucifera*, were purchased from 'far' localities.

Controls on the Extraction of Plant Resources from the Kaya Forests

Pakia's work at Kaya Mtswakara and Kaya Fungo showed that, historically, building poles were collected from both of these kaya forests with permission from the elders. The would-be collector provided the elders with a token or *kadzama*,[13] in the form of local palm wine, which the elders drank as they discussed the request. When accepted, the collector had to present his poles for inspection by the elders. Collection of building poles was prohibited for people not granted permission by the elders, and from the sacred sites within the kaya forests. Defaulters were subject to traditional fines on a scale reflecting the severity of the offence. A maximum fine included an animal (sheep or bull), a black chicken, some pieces of cloth, seeds of *Ricinus communis*, and *kadzama*, paid to the elders. The foodstuffs and drinks were taken into the kaya forest, and a traditional ceremony conducted to appease the spirits.

About two decades ago, the management protocols and the plant resource extraction procedures were reviewed by the elders in both kaya forests. The authority of elders to grant permission to pole collectors was maintained. However, the review instituted an additional monetary token in Kaya Mtswakara. The amount charged depends on the quantity of poles required, while the elders define the period and site for collection, and the guards supervise the collection. No collection of building poles for commercial purposes is allowed. The information Pakia obtained from his informants around Kaya Fungo on the current indigenous controls on pole collection was inconsistent. The majority of his informants told him that collection of all plant

---

[13] *Kadzama* is literally a certain kind of gourd (calabash), and by extension firstly the offering of palm wine contained in such gourds and secondly any kind of material or monetary offering to the elders.

resources from the kaya forest had been banned, due to severe degradation of vegetation as a result of excessive collection of firewood and poles for commercial purposes. The ban was intended to give the vegetation in the kaya forest time to recover, and the community was supposed to meet all its needs for plant resources outside the kaya, thus confirming the importance of the bushland. The situation was complicated further by yet other informants who explained that pole collection was allowed only after permission had been granted by the elders. At the time when these interviews were conducted, the elders were planning for a meeting to re-examine the protocols in plant resource collection. The elders were aware of the genuine domestic needs for plant resources, but were concerned about the commercial interests of some community members.

In both these communities, those who break the regulations on collection of plant resources are still subject to a traditional fine, which includes the customary components of foodstuffs, palm brew and materials used in a cleansing ceremony. Eating and drinking is done in the kaya, and when necessary a traditional ceremony is conducted. A monetary component has been added to the traditional fine. In Kaya Fungo the money collected is used to buy additional foodstuffs, while in Kaya Mtswakara the money collected, including the money paid by pole seekers, is shared between elders. A perceived unfair sharing of the money was reported to have led to internal conflicts and formation of rival factions among the elders and guards at Kaya Mtswakara. Some respondents complained that the money was originally intended to meet costs of cultural functions in the kaya forest, and the sharing among individual elders was a new development.

From his interviews in the community around Kaya Mudzimuvya, Kibet learned of a number of rules governing access to the kaya forest, several of which have direct implications for vegetation structure and composition. Fear of divine retribution played a significant role in the enforcement of these rules; in the past people believed that breaking them would result in undesirable events such as madness, death, or the birth of a handicapped child (Kweja Berau, pers. comm.). Some of these beliefs survive to the present day, though they are considerably weakened and the degree to which these rules are followed is much more limited than in the past. The rules were:

1 All non-Mijikenda were prohibited from entering the kaya forest.
2 *Moroni* and *Fingo* (central sacred sites) were out of bounds for all non-initiates, whether or not they were Mijikenda or even members of the Rabai community.
3 No modern clothing was allowed inside the kaya forest, such as shoes, wrist watches, caps, shirts, trousers.
4 No grazing of livestock was allowed inside the kaya forest, and all livestock that strayed into the kaya should be slaughtered and eaten there.
5 What belongs to the kaya must be retained there, for example if an animal was slaughtered in the kaya, all the meat must be eaten there and should not be taken outside.
6 People who died inside the kaya were buried inside and those who died

outside were buried outside (special rituals were required to change burial sites).

7 No tree felling was allowed inside the kaya forest; it was permitted to collect deadwood as fuel wood from certain specified zones.

8 Poles for building huts were collected from *Chanze*, which is a locality bordering the forest where cultivation was also permitted (but nowhere within the forest).

9 Forest burning was strictly prohibited.

10 The traditional huts that were built inside the kaya were made from two tree species (*Grewia plagiophylla* and *Dalbergia melanoxylon)* and were thatched with certain particular grass species.

In his fieldwork Kibet also learned of a number of taboos concerning the use of particular tree species. His 36 respondents named a total of 18 species as being protected, with *Bombax rhodognaphalon*, *Sterculia appendiculata*, *Milicia excelsa*, *Ficus spp.* (Mgandi) and *Adansonia digitata* most frequently named. One of the kaya elders gave a variety of reasons for their protected status. Some species (e.g. *Milicia excelsa*) were protected from casual use to ensure their availability for domestic or ritual items. Medicinal, popular fruit or shade trees on the farms were also commonly preserved. Species considered unacceptable for building poles among the Rabai people included *Canthium kilifiensis*, *Brackenridgea zanguebarica*, *Vangueria infausta*, *Allophylus rubifolius*, *Grewia forbesii*, *Deinbollia borbonica* and a species of *Euphorbia* that the Rabai indentify as *Mtudi*. *Canthium kilifiensis* was believed to cause misunderstanding and antagonism amongst family members if it was used for building or as firewood. *Bracken-ridgea zanguebarica* and *Euphorbia spp.* are identified as being poisonous and causing skin irritation. Traditional healers used to store their medicines and charms underneath some of the huge tree species, particularly *Adansonia digitata* or *Ficus spp.* and therefore the populace feared to cut them. All huge trees were believed to shelter guardian spirits (in the form of large snakes) as well as attracting rainfall, and therefore they were usually spared from logging. This regulation may explain the existence of remnants of huge *Bombax rhodognaphalon*, *Milicia excelsa* and *Adansonia digitata* near settlement areas.

The Impact of Human Activities on Forest Composition

As Pakia and Kibet's fieldwork has shown, controls on the extraction of wood products from these kaya forests exist, but conservation fieldworkers, elders and guards agree that they are not as effective as they would wish them to be. The guards in Kaya Fungo complained to Pakia that some elders failed to take legal action against defaulters, particularly their own relatives. This discouraged the guards from arresting culprits. In addition, in the past decade in-fighting between clans over the spiritual leadership has divided the community around Kaya Fungo. Some community members at Kaya Mtswakara have begun to complain that access to poles from the kaya forest is only for the 'rich' who can afford the monetary token to the elders. Despite these complaints, evidence from the pattern of use of different species (e.g. the relatively low use of *Craibia brevicaudata* in the homesteads around Kaya Mtswakara and *Combretum schumannii* in the homesteads around Kaya Fungo) suggests that the indigenous controls on the extraction of plant resources still have some force.

At both Kaya Mtswakara and Kaya Fungo there is evidence that harvesting of building poles is having a significant impact on forest composition. The potentially best plant resources for the pole types needed are found in the dense forest vegetation and from the species that form the emergent and short tree canopy layers, and this is where the impact is most obvious. It is recognizable from the removal of the canopy tree species, the transformation of dense forest to wooded grasslands and scrub-lands (especially *Acacia* communities), and the presence of invasive species such as *Lantana camara* and *Opuntia vulgaris*. Pakia's observations, using these indicators, suggest that the level and intensity of historical human impact is greater in Kaya Fungo than in Kaya Mtswakara (Pakia 2000). Informants in the households around Kaya Fungo presented a picture of continued spreading of the thorny scrub and wooded grassland vegetation types at the expense of the dense forest, and they identified anthropogenic fire as the main cause of this transformation.

Kibet's field observations and interviews provided a strong indication that at present less preferred and sometimes culturally prohibited species are being increasingly utilized, due to scarcity of preferred species. For example, *Canthium kilifiensis* is currently being used for building poles, while *Brackenridgea zanguebarica, Vangueria infausta* and *Grewia forbesii* are being utilized as firewood. Kibet's field work also showed a recent drastic reduction in the number of mature *Milicia excelsa* trees, while *Bombax rhodognaphalon* are increasingly being targeted for commercial timber production. Thus the evidence from the Rabai area points to weakening of the indigenous controls on extraction of wood from the kaya forests.

Kibet's fieldwork also showed there to be a fairly obvious correlation between former and current uses of particular areas within the kaya forest, and the status of the vegetation. Areas which have been cultivated have been subject to regular burning, as the traditional Rabai farming system involved the use of fire to clear the land. Open woody vegetation was more common in all areas traditionally used for cultivation and extraction of poles, testimony to the impact of clearing and burning. The cultivated sites (*Chanze, Bendeje* and *Mwakonde*; see Figure 4.3) are areas covered by open woody vegetation that is low in species richness and diversity. The relative lack of biodiversity in these areas as compared to other parts of the kaya forest reflects differences in their intensity of extraction.

Floristic composition varied both between and within the areas of open woody vegetation, despite their similarity in physiognomic appearance and historical use. *Chanze* and *Bendeje* seem to have suffered more degradation than *Mwakonde,* perhaps due to their proximity to settlements and thus their exposure to intensive use over a longer period. Easy access to *Chanze* and *Bendeje* compared to *Mwakonde* may contribute particularly to intense present use. Illegal resource extraction such as firewood or pole cutting tends to concentrate close to the forest edge (i.e. *Bendeje* and *Chanze*) because of

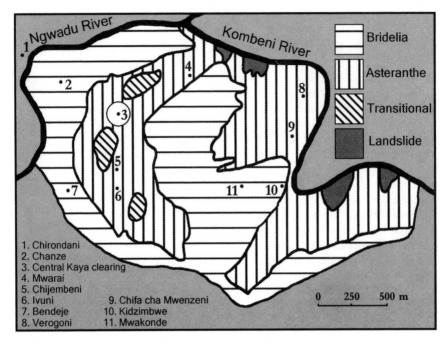

Figure 4.3 Sites and vegetation at Kaya Mudzimuvya

Source: Redrawn from Kibet 2002

people's fear of being apprehended if they venture further into the forest interior. Not much disturbance has occurred within *Mwakonde* area since the early 1980s, with lots of resprouts as tall as 5 m. Much of *Mwakonde* is under the *Catunaregam* plant community, while the *Keetia* community dominates *Chanze* and *Bendeje*. The presence of seedlings of species considered as forest species such as *Hymenaea verrucosa* and *Parkia filicoidea* (Beentje 1994) underneath cashew trees, which is common at *Bendeje* and *Chanze,* supports the hypothesis that the two major community groups had similar vegetation in the past and that conservation of the site has the potential to allow re-colonization by 'past' vegetation. The areas that were more recently encroached upon seem to have regenerated faster after the site was put under community protection, compared to the zones encroached upon earlier that have been under cultivation for a longer period. The reason for this development could be linked to existence of living stumps, and nearness to forest edges; such sites receive 'rain seeds' (seeds shed from nearby trees) from seed dispersers easily, compared to sites further away from the forest.

Closed forest vegetation dominates in all areas to which access is limited by taboos, secrecy and the existence of supernatural powers. All these areas are rich in species and more diverse. The closed forest representing the relatively intact forest patch dominated by tall trees over 15 m high with a continuous understorey cover occurs in all areas containing the most sacred sites of the

Table 4.1 Sacred and other sites in Kaya Mudzimuvya

Site	Location and significance	Traditional controls on use	Vegetation composition
Mwarai[14]	The most sacred place in Kaya Mudzimuvya; centre of spiritual and cultural practices. Near the central Kaya clearing where earlier settlement occurred at the hill summit.	All forms of resource extraction strictly prohibited.	Closed forest.
Chanze ('outside' in the KiRabai dialect)	A piece of land about a mile west of the central Kaya clearing. Borders Kaya Bendeje and extends down to Ngwadu stream.	Used for economic activities e.g. cultivation, grazing, firewood collection and pole harvesting.	Open woody vegetation.
Chijembeni	The former settlement area with an extension of a burial ground within the forest. Sometimes the area is identified as a kaya in its own right. Located SW of Mwarai.	No extraction of poles, firewood or farming activities allowed within the margins of the settlement area.	Currently covered by shrubby bushes.
Mwakonde	Located on the lower slopes, south of the hill summit.	Farming activities and extraction of plant resources were allowed.	Open woody vegetation, though less degraded than Chanze and Bendeje.
Ivuni ('ashes' in the KiRabai dialect)	A secluded area with several open hearths (Mafiga) with broken cooking pots. Located S of Chijembeni.	Women prepared food and other cultural materials for kaya ceremonies. Women could collect dry firewood nearby for use at Ivuni.	Closed forest.

[14] According to Robertson and Luke, Kaya Rabai consisted of nine separate Kayas, of which they visited Fimboni, Bomu and Mwidzimwiru [sic] in the early 1990s. They also mention Kaya Mudzimuvia (area and location not known) and go on to say 'Other Rabai kayas were named (by the Chief in 1987) as Chijembeni, Mwakonde (some forest), Mwarai, Mbwadu, Mwakatama, Mbura, Ivuni and Bendeji, but there appears to be a good deal of confusion over current accepted names and location, and whether these were true kayas in forest patches or clan areas' (1993:13-14). As Kibet's fieldwork shows, several of these names refer to sites within Kaya Mudzimuvya.

Table 4.1 cont.

Site	Location and significance	Traditional controls on use	Vegetation composition
Chirondani ('the place of a wound' in the KiRabai dialect)	Located outside the kaya forest, north of the kaya central clearing; said to be where the missionary Ludwig Krapf established a temporary home after he was denied permission to settle inside Kaya Mudzimuvya. So named because Krapf used to treat people suffering from wounds there.	Includes a spring where women fetched drinking water for home consumption.	The spring is surrounded by a small forest within a coconut farm.
Chifa cha Myenzeni	Located down slope and SE of the hill summit overlooking another Rabai kaya forest, Kaya Bomu.	Borders Verogoni, a site traditionally used to throw children born with deformities to die. Associated with spirits; people normally avoid this area.	Closed forest. The site is named after a huge *Parkia filicoidea* (Myenze) tree growing nearby.
Bendeje	Kaya Bendeje was considered an entrance to the main Rabai Kaya (Mudzimwiru). Provided a stop over and resting point for people moving between the different Rabai kaya forests.	No specific traditional or cultural functions, other than as a homestead; this may explain the encroachment for cultivation.	Covered entirely by coconut palms and cashew nut trees; occasional forest species e.g. *Hymenaea verrucosa* and *Parkia filicoidea*.
Ngwadu ('sour' in the KiRabai dialect)	The name of a stream separating two villages (Mbarakani and Mwele) from Kaya Mudzimuvya forest. A natural landmark defining the northern Kaya boundary.	The stream borders a site used traditionally for cleansing purposes when a dead body had to be relocated for burial from the Kaya to outside or vice versa.	Coconut palms, secondary bushland.

Kaya. They include the burial site (*Ivuni*), the prayer shrines (*Mwarai*), *Moroni* (meeting point for Kaya elders) and the spot where a traditional charm (*Fingo*) is buried. These sites are highly respected and extraction of forest resources is prohibited, so they have remained relatively undisturbed over the years as other surrounding areas have been targeted for cultivation, grazing and logging.

Historical uses of *Mwarai, Chijembeni, Ivuni* and *Chifa cha Myenzeni* may not give a complete explanation of their differences in floristic composition; present uses also have to be considered. *Mwarai* and *Chijembeni* have low stand density for tree and understorey species and high extraction levels for poles, firewood and withies as seen from cut stems and high livestock grazing frequency. Like *Bendeje* and *Chanze*, the areas *Mwarai* and *Chijembeni* lie close to modern settlements, and are thus likely to be subject to more intensive resource use, especially as respect for traditional controls on resource use weakens. In contrast, *Chifa cha Myenzeni* lies on the furthest corner from settlement and the vegetation is not easily penetrated due to the thick understorey and absence of established footpaths. This area has a high stand density for both tree layer and understorey species. Past logging as indicated by old stumps may have triggered the development of thick undergrowth, as light penetration into the lower vegetation strata increased, but at present logging does not seem to be active in this area.

Table 4.1 and Figure 4.3 show the different sites identified by Kibet with the guidance of his Rabai informants, as well as the vegetation composition at the time of his fieldwork.

Conclusion

The vegetation of coastal Kenya has been subject to changes in moisture availability over many millennia, reflecting changes in global and regional temperatures and rainfall. The record of environmental change here is sparse, compared to our knowledge of events in lake basins and on many of East Africa's highlands, but the reality of this change, and its probable impact on the forest/grassland boundaries, should not be denied. Herbivorous animals, both domesticated and wild, have doubtless also influenced coastal vegetation over the millennia and centuries. One cause for intensive human impact on forest vegetation is overtly stated in the Mijikenda myths of origin; land was cleared to create the original kaya settlements and large trees were cut to make the fortifications observed by early European travelers such as Charles New. Alternative models of Mijikenda history as outlined by Helm and others extend the period of agricultural, iron-working settlement back over many centuries, with concomitant impacts on woody vegetation. The impact of many smaller settlements on the surrounding vegetation would have been extensive, rather than the intensive impact that might be associated with the 'original nine kayas' of the Mijikenda foundation narrative. The transition from fortified settlements to the current sacred sites, however and whenever it occurred, must have been linked to a change in the use of forest products in the surrounding areas, possibly including an increased formalization of taboos and controls on the use of certain species and certain localities.

It is therefore important to recognize the remaining kaya forests not as dwindling remnants of an ancient vegetation community, but as dynamic spatial and temporal phenomena that have been changing under multiple external influences over several millennia. The dynamism does not only apply to the physical forces that have shaped these plant communities, but also to the human institutions embedded in these forests. The social significance and functions of the 'kaya elders' have changed greatly since the first contact with missionaries, explorers and colonial officials beginning in the mid-nineteenth century, and surely the terms of access to kaya forest resources have changed as well. While many aspects of this story remain to be uncovered, we must recognize that the kaya elders, as primary custodians of the kaya forests, have been able to maintain some degree of control over the land, timber and non-timber forest products of these forests. While the kaya forests were probably never totally free from human influence, it would be foolish to ignore drastic increases in demand for land and forest products in coastal Kenya that are driven largely by economic forces, among them poverty, population increase, and global forces such as those that drive tourism and the search for mineral deposits. We have to recognize that some kaya forests have been completely destroyed over recent decades, among them Kaya Ganzoni, Kaya Miungoni and Kaya Kiteje in Kwale District. Others, such as Kaya Chonyi (Kilifi District) and Kaya Bate (Malindi District) face severe threats (A. Githitho pers. comm.). Though the indigenous controls on the extraction of plant resources still have force in some situations, and they are increasingly supported by outside conservation organizations, there is reason for serious concern as to the ability of such coalitions to protect the kaya forests in the long term.

There is scope for much research in coastal Kenya, including palaeo-ecological work such as the analysis of pollen from soil and sediment samples, tree-ring studies (dendrochronology) and the study of coral growth patterns as an indicator of ocean water temperatures. More archaeological fieldwork around and (where possible) within the kaya forests will cast more light on settlement history and, combined with the palaeoecological research mentioned above, would allow us to put together the physical and human story and thus establish the environmental history of this region. Equally, if not more important than scholarly research are further conservation initiatives, aimed at involving the local Mijikenda communities as full partners with Kenyan and foreign government and non-government organizations. Understanding the history of the kaya forests will have little significance unless we can also ensure the future of at least some of them.

References

Barker, P., M. R. Talbot, F. Street-Perrott, F. Marret, J. Scourse, and E. Odada, 2004, 'Late Quaternary climatic variability in intertropical Africa'. In *Past Climatic Variability Through Europe and Africa*. R. W. Battarbee, F. Gasse and C. E. Stickley, eds, pp. 117–38. Dordrecht: Springer.

Battarbee, R. W., F. Gasse, and C. E. Stickley, eds, 2004, *Past Climatic Variability Through Europe and Africa*. Dordrecht: Springer.

Beentje, H. J., 1994, *Kenya Trees, Shrubs and Lianas*. Nairobi: National Museums of Kenya.

Brooks, K., C. A. Scholz, J. W. King, J. Peck, J. T. Overpeck, J. M. Russell, and P. Y. O. Amoako, 2005, 'Late Quaternary lowstands of lake Bosumtwi, Ghana: Evidence from high-resolution seismic-reflection and sediment-core data'. *Palaeogeography, Palaeoclimatology, Palaeoecology* 216:235–49.

Burgess, N. D., G. P. Clark, and W. A. Rodgers, 1998, 'Coastal Forests of Eastern Africa: Status, endemism patterns and their potential causes'. *Biological Journal of the Linnean Society* 64: 337–67.

Caswell, P. V., 1956, *Geology of the Kilifi-Mazeras Area*. Nairobi: Government Printer. Report No. 34, Geological Survey of Kenya.

Cole, J. and R. B. Dunbar, 2000, 'Tropical Pacific forcing of decadal SST variability in the western Indian Ocean over the past two centuries'. *Science* 287: 617–20.

Dublin, H. T., A. R. E. Sinclair, and J. McGlade, 1990, 'Elephants and fire as causes of multiple stable states in the Serengeti-Mara woodlands'. *Journal of Animal Ecology* 59:1147–64.

Goudie, A. S., 1996, 'Climate: Past and present'. In *The Physical Geography of Africa*. W. M. Adams, A. S. Goudie, and A. R. Orme, eds, pp. 34–59. Oxford: Oxford University Press,

Håkansson, N. T., 2004, 'The human ecology of world systems in East Africa: The impact of the ivory trade'. *Human Ecology* 32(5):561–91.

Hawthorne, W. D., 1993, 'East African coastal forest botany'. In *Biogeography and Ecology of the Rain Forest of Eastern Africa*. J. C. Lovett and S. K. Wasser, eds, pp. 57–99. Cambridge: Cambridge University Press.

Helm, R., 2004, 'Re-evaluating traditional histories on the coast of Kenya: An archaeological perspective'. In *African Historical Archaeologies*. A. M. Reid and P. J. Lane, eds, pp. 59–89. New York: Kluwer/Plenum.

Kibet, S., 2002, 'Human disturbance and its impact on vegetation structure, composition and regeneration of Kenyan coastal forests (a case study of Kaya Mudzimuvya forest)'. M.Sc. thesis, Jomo Kenyatta University of Agriculture and Technology.

Krapf, J. L., 1860, *Travels, Researches and Missionary Labours during an Eighteen Years' Residence in Eastern Africa*. London and Boston, MA: Ticknor and Fields.

Kusimba, C. M. and S. B. Kusimba, 2005, 'Mosaics and interactions: East Africa, 2000 b.p. to the Present'. In *African Archaeology*. A. B. Stahl, ed., pp. 392–419. Malden, MA and Oxford: Blackwell.

Makaya: the sacred forests (film), n.d., Dir. Richard Vaughan, created by Quentin Luke. World Wide Fund for Nature – National Museums of Kenya.

Morton, R. F., 1972, 'The Shungwaya myth of Mijikenda origins: A problem of later nineteenth century coast history'. *International Journal of African Historical Studies* 5(3):397–43.

—— 1977, 'New evidence regarding the Shungwaya myth of Mijikenda origins'. *International Journal of African Historical Studies* 10(4):628–43.

Mutoro, H. W., 1987, 'An archaeological survey of the Mijikenda kaya settlements on hinterland Kenya coast'. Ph.D. thesis, University of California at Los Angeles.

New, C., 1971 [1873], *Life, Labours and Wanderings in Eastern Africa*. London: Frank Cass.

Nyamweru, C. K., 1996, Sacred groves threatened by development'. *Cultural Survival Quarterly* 20(3):19–21.

—— 1997, 'Report on socio-cultural research carried out in Kwale and Kilifi Districts of Kenya, March to May 1997'. Consultancy report submitted to the Coastal Forest Conservation Unit.

—— 1998, 'Sacred groves and environmental conservation'. 1998 Frank P. Piskor Faculty Lecture, St. Lawrence University, Canton, NY.

—— 2003, 'Women and sacred groves in Coastal Kenya: A contribution to the ecofeminist debate'. In *Ecofeminism and Globalization*. H. Eaton and L. Lorentzen, eds, pp. 41–56. Lanham, MD: Rowman and Littlefield.

Pakia, M., 2000, 'Plant ecology and ethnobotany of two sacred forests (kayas) at the Kenya Coast'. M.Sc. thesis, School of Life and Environmental Sciences, University of Natal (Durban).

Pakia, M., and J. Cooke, 2003a, 'The ethnobotany of the Midzichenda tribes of the coastal forest areas in Kenya: 1. General perspective and medicinal plant uses'. *South African Journal of Botany* 69(3):370–81.

—— 2003b, 'The ethnobotany of the Midzichenda tribes of the coastal forest areas in Kenya: 2. Medicinal plant uses'. *South African Journal of Botany* 69(3):382–95.

Parkin, D. J., 1991 *Sacred Void: Spatial Images of Work and Ritual Among the Giriama of Kenya.* Cambridge: Cambridge University Press.

Robertson, S. A., and W. R. Q. Luke, 1993, 'Kenya Coastal Forests: The report of the NMK/ WWF Coast Forest Survey'. Nairobi: World Wide Fund for Nature.

Russell, J. M., T. C. Johnson, and M. R. Talbot, 2003, 'A 725 yr cycle in the climate of central Africa during the late Holocene'. *Geology* 31(8):677–80.

Schmidt, P. R., 1997, 'Archaeological views on a history of landscape change in East Africa'. *Journal of African History* 38:393–421.

Spear, T., 1978, *The Kaya Complex*. Nairobi: Kenya Literature Bureau.

Stager, J. C., P. A. Mayewski, and L. D. Meeker, 2001, 'Cooling cycles, Heinrich event 1, and the desiccation of Lake Victoria'. *Palaeogeography, Palaeoclimatology, Palaeoecology* 183:169–78.

Talbot, M. R., D. A. Livingstone, P. G. Paloner, J. Maley, J. M. Melach, G. Delibrias and S. Gulliksen, 1984, 'Preliminary results from sediment cores from Lake Bosumtwi, Ghana', *Palaeoecology of Africa and the Surrounding Islands* 16: 173–92.

Thompson, L. G., H. Mosley-Thompson, M. E. Davis, K. A. Henderson, H. H. Brecher, V. S. Zagorodnov, T. A. Mashiotta, P-N. Lin, V. N. Mikhalenko, D. R. Hardy, and J. Beer, 2002, 'Kilimanjaro ice core records: Evidence of Holocene climatic change in tropical Africa'. *Science* 298:589–93.

Verschuren, D., 2004, 'Decadal and century-scale climate variability in tropical Africa during the past 2000 years'. In *Past Climatic Variability through Europe and Africa*. R. W. Battarbee, F. Gasse, and C. E. Stickley, eds, pp. 139–58. Dordrecht: Springer.

Vincens, A., D. Williamson, F. Thevenon, M. Taieb, G. Buchet, M. Decobert and N. Thouveny, 2003, 'Pollen-based vegetation changes in southern Tanzania during the last 4200 years: Climate change and/or human impact', *Palaeogeography, Palaeoclimatology, Palaeoecology* 198:321–34.

Walsh, M., 1992, 'Mijikenda Origins', *Transafrican Journal of History* 21: 1–18.

Willis, J., 1996, 'The Northern *kayas* of the Mijikenda: A gazetteer, and an historical reassessment'. *Azania* 31:75–98.

Wilson, A., 1993, 'Sacred forests and the elders'. In *The Law of the Mother*, E. Kemf, ed., pp. 244–48. San Francisco, CA: Sierra Club Books.

World Meteorological Organization, 1999, 'The 1997–1998 El Niño event: A scientific and technical retrospective'. WMO-No. 905.

WWF (World Wide Fund for Nature), 1998, 'Fortified Villages Surrounded by Forests'. In *From Theory to Practice: Incentive Measures in Developing Countries*, pp. 20–22. Gland, Switzerland: WWF. Published in the series 'Benefiting from Biodiversity'.

5

Sacred Groves in Morocco
Vegetation Mosaics & Biological Values

ULRICH DEIL, HEIKE CULMSEE
& MOHAMED BERRIANE

The 'complex and diverse arena of spiritual, emotional, intellectual and practical activities at the interface of religion and ecology' (Sponsel 2001) can be observed at sacred natural sites in many parts of the world. Examples include the sacred groves of Christian Orthodox communities in Greece, Shinto shrine groves in Japan, Himalayan village groves in India (Ramakrishnan 1996), and tropical African groves with multiple levels of sacredness (Michaloud and Dury 1998). In the Maghreb countries of northwest Africa (Morocco, Algeria, and Tunisia), the surroundings of Muslim saints' tombs, and cemeteries of local Muslim communities, are often declared to be holy forests (commonly known as '*bois sacrés*' or '*forêts maraboutiques*'), and protected from clearing for religious reasons (see Photo 5.1). The cultural and spiritual importance of these Marabout forests is well known (Lang 1992, Verdugo and Kadiri Fakir 1995). The non-commercial values of these sites' biotic, aesthetic and spiritual resources pre-dated the development of scientific conservation. Within the sacred space, trees are protected, not as actual objects of veneration, but rather because such sites are important for the identity and social organization of the people that live with them (Bourquia 1990).

The interrelations among sacred sites, cultural integrity, and management of biological diversity have become matters of interest for conservation practitioners in recent years (Hay-Edie and Hadley 1998). Nevertheless, there are few studies that deal with the scientific aspects of these sites, with detailed investigation of the vegetation, habitat diversity, and conservation value of holy places (for Middle Europe: Graf 1986; for the Sahel: Guinko 1985, Neumann and Müller-Haude 1999; for Togo: Tchamié 2000; for India: Alemmeren Jamir and Pandey 2003, Mishra *et al.* 2004, Upadhaya *et al.* 2003, Ramanujam and Praveen Kumar Cyril 2003, Ramanujam and Kadamban 2001).

For the Maghreb countries, such studies are not available. Quézel and Barbero (1990) and Benabid (1991) make general statements about the conservation value of the Marabout holy forests in Morocco and they mention that these sacred groves might represent once widely-distributed ecological forms. However, a detailed floral inventory of such sites is still missing. Until now, sampling of vegetation data at Marabout sites was restricted to their forested areas, and all other ecological zones were ignored (see for example the vegetation studies by Barbero *et al.* 1981, Deil 1984, and Fennane 1986 for Northern Morocco). Thus, the full ecological characteristics of these holy forests remain unclear, and the extent to which traditional usage of sacred groves can complement scientifically driven conservation agendas in Morocco remains unexplored.

This paper analyzes the vegetation and characterizes the ecology of two sacred groves in northern Morocco. After a brief introduction into the traditional saints cult and pilgrimage practises in Morocco with an outline of the cultural background of the holy places, the results of this preliminary case study are presented to answer the following questions:

• Which plant species and plant communities occur on such burial grounds?
• Are the holy forests virgin forests or are they subject to grazing pressure by livestock and other anthropogenic impacts, other than burial activities? In the latter case, which vegetation patterns have been created by the traditional land use pattern?
• Do sacred sites shelter rare plant species or rare genotypes of common species?

Finally, the results from the vegetation inventory and the ecological analysis lead to a discussion of the potential role of sacred grove sites for nature conservation in the Maghreb, the anthropogenic character of their vegetation, and their longterm sustainability.

The Religious and Cultural Meanings of Sacred Sites in Morocco

Orthodox Islam does not allow any veneration of saints, yet the religious practices of many Moroccan Muslims revolve around the spiritual authority of patron saints. For hundreds of years, the faithful have gathered around Islamic scholars called Marabout and formed religious brotherhoods with important political, economic and social roles. These Marabout institutions were particularly influential in the fight against Spanish and Portuguese forces' occupation of the Atlantic coastal areas of Morocco in the fifteenth century.

The Marabout movement, and the authority of the saints upon which it depends, are still alive (Geertz 1968, Gellner 1969, Lang 1992). Marabout followers express their faith through collective pilgrimages (called *moussem* or *maoussim*) to the saints' tree-shaded tombs (*qubba*) (Verdugo and Kadiri Fakir 1995). The pilgrimages follow an annual cycle that ties into the agricultural calendar (Berriane 1990). Sixty percent of the celebrations occur in August and September after the labor bottleneck of harvest time. Other *moussem* events are linked to religious festivals, mainly to the *Maoulid* (the birthday of the Prophet, usually in April or May).

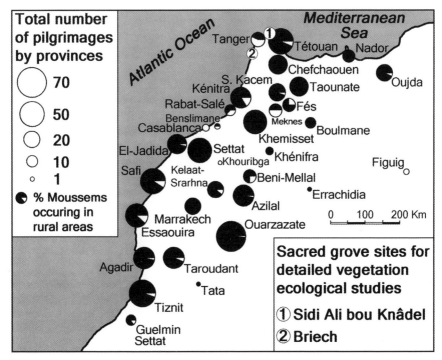

Figure 5.1 Distribution of pilgrimage sites in Morocco and locations of geobotanical case studies.

Figure 5.1 illustrates the number and distribution of *moussem* events in Morocco (based on Berriane 1992). Pilgrimages to sacred sites are not isolated events but a social phenomenon throughout Morocco. About 735 pilgrimages happen every year, most commonly in rural areas and in the western and southern parts of the country. The varying popularity of the pilgrimages can be explained by the high population densities near some sacred sites, these areas' agricultural productivity, the historical significance of certain places for the Marabout movement, and the distribution of tribal groups.

Originally, the ritual triad of pilgrimage, religious celebration, and popular festival developed out of pre–Islamic Arabian religious festivals with economic and social aspects. Furthermore, this ritual complex was influenced by the indigenous Marabout movement and the cycles of traditional markets (*souks*), as well as by the agricultural rites of Berber-Mediterranean societies. In the socio-cultural context of Morocco, it is a prime example of a popular event with religious, recreational, and entertainment values. When it occurs at the end of the agricultural season, the *moussem* is the most important, often the only, entertainment event in rural areas.

The importance of sacred groves as sites for domestic Moroccan tourism has been described by Berriane (1990). Some *moussem* events, like the pilgrimage to the Marabout grove of Moulay Abdessalam in the Western Rif Mountains, assemble thousands of pilgrims from vast areas and last several days. Others are

Table 5.1 Vegetation types occurring at the Sidi Ali bou Knâdel and Briech marabout sites

Relevé plot #		1	2	3	4	5	6	7	8	9	10	11	12	13	14	15	16	17
Location		Sidi	Sidi	Sidi	Briech	Briech	Sidi	Sidi	Briech	Briech	Briech	Briech	Sidi	Sidi	Sidi	Sidi	Briech	Briech
		Ali	Ali	Ali			Ali	Ali					Ali	Ali	Ali	Ali		
Character species of evergreen forests	*Olea europaea sylvestris* (tree)	A	A	F	A	A			A	A								
	Olea europaea sylvestris (shrub)	F	F				F	R								R	R	
	Clematis cirrhosa	F	R	F				R										
	Smilax aspera			F			R											
	Arisarum simorrhinum	R	F	F	R	R	R	R										
	Arum italicum	R	F	R			R											
Character species of maquis thicket	*Pistacia lentiscus* (tree)	F	F	A	F	A	F	F	R	F								
	Pistacia lentiscus (shrub)	F	F		F	F	F	F	R									
	Chamaerops humilis (shrub)	F	F	F			R	F	R	R		R					R	
	Quercus coccifera (tree)	F	F				F	F		R								
	Quercus coccifera (shrub)	F	F				A	A										
Character species of the spiny mantle community	*Calicotome infesta intermedia*		R		R	R	A	R									R	
	Asparagus aphyllus				F	R	R										R	
	Rubus ulmifolius					F												
Fire succeeder and sub-spontaneous ornamental	*Cistus monspeliensis*				R			A										
	Iris germanica											F						
Ombrophytic ruderals	*Geranium rotundifolium*	R	R															
	Torilis nodosa	F	F															
	Geranium purpureum			R				R										
Mesophytic ruderals	*Mercurialis annua ambigua*		R						F	F	R							
	Urtica urens								A	A								
	Malva parviflora								R	F								

Sisymbrium officinale				F	F							
Hordeum leporinum			F	F	F							
Chrysanthemum coronarium			R	A	R	A				R	R	
Verbascum sinuatum			R	R		R				R	R	
Dry resistant												
Trifolium scabrum	R	R						R	A			
ephemerals Trifolium stellatum	F							R	A			
Cleonia lusitanica							F	F			
Daucus muricatus					F			R	R			
Aegilops geniculata	F	F		F	F	R	F	R	R	F	A	A
Brachypodium distachyon	R	F	F	F	F	F	F	R	R	F	F	F
Trifolium angustifolium			R	R	R	R	R	R	R	F	F	F
Character species												
R *Hordeum bulbosum*					F	R		R		R		
F												
of productive *Hedysarum coronarium*			F				F	F	A		F	
grassland *Leontodon marocanus*		F						R	R			
Pasture weeds Galactites tomentosa	R	F			R	R	F	F	F	R	F	F
and ruderals Avena barbata s.str.				R	R				R	F	F	F
Scabiosa simplex dentata								R		A		
Bromus diandrus		R				R					F	F
Desmazeria rigida			R						R			
Atractylis cancellata	R				F			F	R	R		
Cynara humilis	R	R		R	R			R	R	R	R	R
Scolymus hispanicus	R	R		R		R				R	R	F

Key: blank = very rare or absent (< 1%)

R = rare (1 – 2.5%)

F = frequent (5 – 25 %)

A = abundant (25 – 100 %)

Notes: This table is reduced to constant respectively diagnostic species. The full species list is documented in Deil 2000. This table is based on the relevé method of sampling vegetation, which was developed in Europe and standardized by the Swiss ecologist Josias Braun-Blanquet. This method is particularly useful for classifying the diversity of plant cover over large units of land. Each column shows the relative frequency of plant species in relevé plots, each of which is representative of the vegetation of the entire stand.

of more local importance, and receive just a few dozen visitors over a period of one or two days. Amongst the principal pilgrimage events, the one at Moulay Abdellah is the most famous. This Marabout tomb-grove complex is situated at the Atlantic coast close to El Jadida and the metropolitan area of Casablanca. Recently, this pilgrimage has undergone an interesting transformation. It is now host to more than 74,000 visitors, mainly urban Moroccans. These tourists come in August to enjoy its seaside location, and although veneration of the saint remains the event's central objective, the religious aspects have been decreasing. This pilgrimage is becoming more and more a recreational event, and a variety of commercial entertainment services have emerged to serve the holiday-makers. This secularisation trend is also occurring at urban pilgrimage sites (Lindner 1999).

Location and Physical Environment of the Study Sites

To assess the biotic diversity, vegetation structure, and traditional land use of rural Marabout sacred groves, two localities near the city of Tangier (Figure 5.1) were selected for detailed geobotanical analysis. Each cemetery is situated in a different ecological zone.

The first cemetery, named Sidi Ali bou Knâdel, is located in the ecoregion 'Crêtes du Détroit' (André 1971, Deil 2003), a few kilometers south of the Straits of Gibraltar. The site is situated at the top of a marl hill near the sandstone ridges of Jebel Sanduc, at an altitude of 140 meters above sea level. Mean annual rainfall ranges from 750–850 millimeters, with its maximum precipitation in winter. The occurrence of the Kermes oak (*Quercus coccifera*) indicates that the dry summer season is moderated by an oceanic variant of the Mediterranean climate. The area is frost-free, and often buffeted by high winds.

The second place is Briech, named after the village nearby. It is located at an altitude of 40 meters above sea level in an ecoregion called 'Sahel du Nord,' a littoral sand plateau bordering the Atlantic Sea between Tangier and Azilah, and has an annual precipitation of 650–700 millimeters. The climate is sub-humid with mild, frost-free winters. These evergreen forests are dominated by the Wild Olive (*Olea europaea*), the Dwarf Palm (*Chamaerops humilis*) and the Mastic Tree (*Pistacia lentiscus*) (Emberger 1939).

Apart from their different edaphic and climatic conditions, both sites have characteristics in common: they are locally significant spiritual places and are therefore not pressured by regional and national pilgrimage. They have small Qubba (tombs) in their centres, and the graveyards are unfenced. Both sacred groves are used by the local populations as burial sites and grazing areas for livestock.

Methodology of the Geobotanical Analysis

Both cemeteries were studied in order to document their plant species and vegetation types and to assess their biological conservation value. The botanical analysis of the sites was performed in three stages:

1. Data sampling: The whole area of each cemetery was first classified accord-ing to the dominant vegetation, and its vertical structure identified (e.g., as closed forest, open woodland, maquis, lawn with annual plant species, etc.). Seventeen representative sampling areas were selected from these pre-stratified vegetation types, and all vascular plant species were recorded. The abundance of each species was also estimated.
2. Data treatment: These floristic samples from both Marabout forests were grouped according to floristic similarity to define plant communities, that is, vegetative stands with similar species combinations and common ecological conditions. The data set is presented in Table 5.1, shortened to the most common indicative species (the full data set is given in Deil 2000). The nomenclature of the plant species is according to Valdes *et al.* 1987.
3. Both study areas were mapped (Figures 5.2 and 5.3) to document the cover value of the different plant communities, to demonstrate how the vegeta-tion mosaic was created by the multipurpose usage of these sites, and to serve as a baseline for monitoring future change.

Results of the Geobotanical Case Studies

The studied Marabout groves present fine-scaled mosaics of different plant communities. These include evergreen sclerophyllous forests, thorny thickets, and many annual flowering plants, particularly in areas with disturbed soil profiles (i.e., near gravesites). They are very heterogeneous from a structural point of view (Table 5.1, Figures 5.2 and 5.3).

On both graveyards, the central area around the tomb is covered by a closed evergreen forest. At Sidi Ali (Table 5.1, col. 1–3), the mixed forest is domi-nated by Wild Olive (*Olea europaea* var. *sylvestris*), while Kermes Oak (*Quercus coccifera*) and Mastic Tree (*Pistacia lentiscus*) compose a second tree layer. In springtime, species that sprout from subterranean bulbs (*Arum italicum, Arisarum simorrhinum*), and those adapted to shade, like *Torilis nodosa,* cover the forest floor.

At Briech, *Olea europaea* is the only species of the actual tree layer. The undergrowth varies according to grazing intensity: in some parts (Table 5.1, columns 4–5), *Pistacia lentiscus* and *Chamaerops humilis*, both degraded to small shrubs, form a dense thicket under an over-aged tree-layer of Wild Olive. In other parts of the sacred site, permanent browsing by livestock has removed the shrub layer altogether, and the undergrowth is dominated by short-living herbs like *Mercurialis annua* ssp. *ambigua* and *Urtica urens*. These species are favoured by the microclimatic conditions under the tree canopy, such as shade and higher humidity, and by the high nitrogen content of the topsoil, a product of the manure deposited by livestock resting in the shade of the sacred grove.

At Sidi Ali, *Olea europaea* is regenerating in the shelter of dense *Pistacia* thickets, due to the limited grazing pressure on the sacred site. At Briech, on the other hand, the sacred grove is situated close to the village and grazing intensity is strong year-round. The wild olives have not been regenerating for

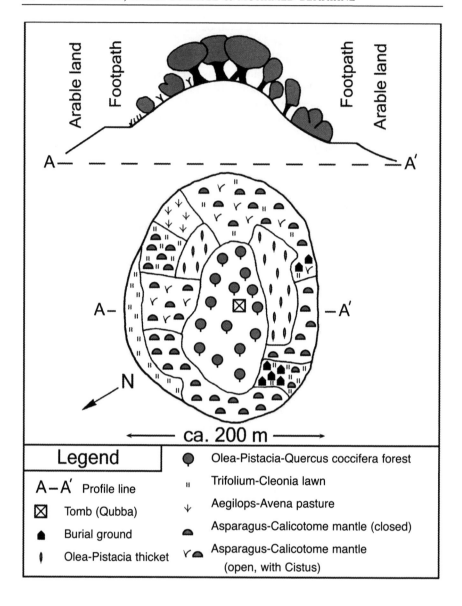

Figure 5.2 Vegetation map of the Sidi Ali bou Knâdel sacred grove

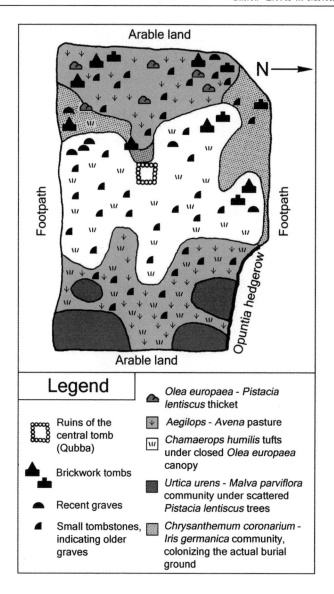

Figure 5.3 Vegetation map of the sacred grove near Briech

Photo 5.1 Marabout forest near Sidi Yamani (Province of Larache). The canopy is dominated by over-aged Wild Olive trees (*Olea europaea*). Permanent strong grazing prevents tree regeneration and favours the establishment of ground vegetation with nitrophilous herbs and grasses. (© Ulrich Deil)

Photo 5.2 The Qubba of Sidi Bourhaba is located in the dune belt near the city of Kenitra. The shrub and grassland vegetation can support traditional grazing, but would likely be destroyed if the pilgrimage develops into a domestic tourism event as in the cases of other Marabout sites situated close to the coast. (© Ulrich Deil)

decades. The canopy is still closed, but the tree population is becoming over-aged. In the long term, this forest patch will disappear. Quézel and Barbero (1990) call this type of degradation the 'therophytisation of forests.' Such 'subfossil' forest stands without any true forest species in the herb layer are nowadays quite common in Morocco (see Photo 5.1).

At Sidi Ali, the central woodland is surrounded by a dense mantle com-munity. There, shrubs like *Calicotome infesta* ssp. *intermedia* or *Asparagus aphyllus* occur (Table 5.1, column 6). This thorny thicket is opened from time to time by burning. This facilitates the establishment of a low maquis, dominated by the rockrose *Cistus monspeliensis* (Table 5.1, column 7). The mantle also shelters some rare tall growing herbs like *Cirsium scabrum* and *Origanum compactum*.

On sunny and sandy sites, the *Malva parviflora, Urtica urens, and Mercurialis annua* community is replaced by another ruderal community, dominated by the Wild Chrysanthemum (Table 5.1, column 10–11). In springtime, this plant community features the striking flowers of *Chrysanthemum coronarium, Hedy-sarum coronarium, Galactites tomentosa* and *Verbascum sinuatum*. This attractive indigenous flora is enriched by planted and subspontaneous species like *Pela-gonium capitatum* (*Chrysanthemum-Iris* community in Figure 5.3) and *Iris* species (*Iris germanica, I. albicans*). *Iris* species are often planted at Muslim cemeteries, and can persist for centuries. Former Islamic graveyards in Southern Spain, abandoned since the Reconquista, are still characterized by the occurrence of *Iris* populations (Valdes *et al.* 1987).

The outer fringes of both sacred groves are subject to strong and permanent grazing pressure and to periodical disturbances of both vegetation and soil for human burials. The plant communities in these areas are dominated by tiny ephemeral herbs (*Trifolium scabrum, T. stellatum,* and *Cleonia lusitanica*; Table 5.1, columns 12–13), weedy annual grasses (*Aegilops geniculata* and *Avena barbata),* and higher growing thistles (*Galactites tomentosa, Cynara humilis,* and *Scolymus hispanicus*; Table 5.1, columns 14–17).

At both sites, pasturing, small scale burning and burial activities have resulted in a fine-grained mosaic of different vegetation types. In total, they form a vegetation complex with a repetitive spatial pattern. A typical zonation ranges from the Qubba in the centre, surrounded by a forest with a shade-adapted herb layer, a spiny mantle community and scattered shrubs, and via a high growing pasture to a dwarf ephemeral lawn at the outer fringes with recent grave-mounds. The central forest is less degraded at Sidi Ali (which is far from the village) than in Briech (which is much closer to the settlement).

The Potential Role of Sacred Grove Sites for Nature Conservation

Usually, Marabout tomb-grove complexes are not nature reserves, in a legal sense of areas protected by Moroccan law, and it is certain that protecting certain organisms is not the direct intention of the people conserving these sites. Only a few sacred sites have been included in priority programmes for nature conservation in Morocco, such as the Marabout grove at Sidi Bourhaba (Photo 5.2). But even without any official status, sacred sites function to a degree as nature reserves (Quézel and Barbero 1990, Benabid 1991). Conservation is the by-product of other social purposes. Their conservation value can be summarized as follows:

- **Landscape aesthetic elements**: Marabout groves have high structural and floristic diversity. Especially in the nearly totally deforested lowlands of Morocco, sacred groves are important structural elements in the monotonous landscape. Striking tree forms and ornamental flowers have high aesthetic value.
- **Models for the potential forest vegetation**: Since nearly all Moroccan forests have disappeared due to millennia of agricultural pressure, sacred groves represent the only places where the natural or semi-natural structure and floristic composition of Maghreb forests might be reconstructed. They could serve as models for reforestation projects that aim to rebuild Mediterranean forests with a structure similar to the potential natural vegetation. Holy forest patches have not, however, yet been systematically investigated for their environmental and topographical values for Moroccan landscapes, so conservationists should be cautious with such analogies. It remains unknown to what extent sacred groves represent the natural vegetation of the area's pre-agrarian past.
- **Biodiversity conservation**: Marabout sites offer habitats for many plant species. On the few hectares of the sacred sites of Sidi Ali and Briech, about 170 vascular plants were found. This outstanding floristic diversity is correlated to a small-scale variability of moderate anthropogenic impact. This result is in accordance with the intermediate disturbance hypothesis of biodiversity.
- **Protection of rare plant species**: Two rare vascular plant species were found on the study sites. The orchid *Cephalanthera longifolia* is restricted to the central part of the Sidi Ali forest which offers suitable environmental conditions by permanent shading and an undisturbed humus layer. *Cirsium scabrum* is a thistle that gains biomass in a vegetative phase over several years and then flowers once. This life cycle makes this species particularly sensitive to grazing (Gálvez and Hernández Bermejo 1990). In the Tangier Peninsula it occurs nearly exclusively in sacred groves. Most of the rare endemic plant species in Morocco, are not found in closed forests and sacred sites, but are rather adapted to extreme edaphic conditions and open habitats (Deil 1993, Fennane and Ibn Tatou 1998).
- **Protection of genetic resources**: Marabout forests can be regarded as genetic reservoirs for tree species of interest for forestry. Many of the species tend to build ecotypes such as *Pinus halepensis*, *Pinus nigra* and *Pinus pinaster*. One of the rare populations of a *Quercus coccifera*-ecotype finds shelter in the sacred grove site of Sidi Ali. This ecotype differs from the widespread Western-Mediterranean Kermes-oak-taxon, but is close to *Quercus calliprinos*, the Eastern Mediterranean taxon (Benabid 1985, Quézel 1991).
- **Habitat function**: We can expect that sacred sites offer habitats for many animal species. They might function as stepping stones for mobile organisms and for diaspores. None of these assumptions have been investigated so far, however.

This chapter represents the first botanical investigation of sacred grove sites in Morocco. There has been, as yet, no nationwide survey of Moroccan sacred grove vegetation. We do not know whether sacred grove sites contain many of the species valued for biodiversity conservation in Morocco. Thus, at the present state of knowledge it remains unclear to what extent the traditional use of sacred grove sites can support the agendas of scientists and conservation managers.

Human Impact on Sacred Grove Sites

The Mediterranean region is extremely rich in biodiversity due to the long-term influence of moderate human impact (Médail and Quézel 1997, Naveh 1998, Pignatti and Pignatti 1984). In particular, short-living plant species have co-evolved with man, agriculture, and the domestication of animals. The recent decline in biodiversity in parts of the Mediterranean basin results from intensive resource exploitation and the abandonment of traditional land management practices (Plieninger and Wilbrand 2001, Seligman and Perevolotsky 1994). As shown in the case study above, sacred grove sites in the Maghred are usually not virgin forests. If they were, the sacred spaces would comprise pure forest stands and be poorer in species diversity. The structural variability and the floristic richness of the study sites are created by repeated small-scale impacts by humans (such as digging and pilgrimage) and livestock (such as grazing and defecation). Excluding people and livestock from these ecosystems would therefore diminish their floristic and structural diversity and eventually reduce anthropogenic vegetation patches.

To maintain the structural and floristic diversity of sacred sites, conservation policy and traditional utilization need to be balanced. Since the trees on sacred sites are traditionally taboo, they are protected against cutting. As observed for the Briech study site, however, regeneration of the Wild Olive has been impossible for decades because of overgrazing. This problem is common for the tree populations of many Moroccan sacred groves (Photo 5.1). Although the trees are protected, grazing in the forest patches is often too intensive and not sustainable. Some sacred groves will disappear if the pressure on their resources is not reduced.

In the present form, the vegetation mosaic of sacred grove sites is the result of pilgrimage, burial, and pastoralism. The trend toward ever-larger pilgrimages, and their transformation into domestic tourism events, suggests that the plant cover around many Marabout sites may soon become threatened (Photo 5.2).

Socio-cultural Contexts and Long-term Conservation Perspectives

An individual's perception and evaluation of the environment depends on the cognitive systems of their society, as experienced within a particular landscape. The structural composition of landscape, such as its field geometry, can be linked not only to land tenure and agricultural economics, but also to its cosmology and mythology (Krings 1991, Yoon 1991). The organisms in Maghreb sacred groves are protected for these social and symbolic contexts rather than their biological value, and so it is in these holy forests that cosmology and imagination become tangible in the biosphere.

The combination of traditional religious activities and moderate land use favors biodiversity and the conservation of sacred grove sites in Morocco. The conservation of these holy forests is highly dependent on trends in modern Moroccan society. Lang (1992) states that the religious importance of the saints, and the Marabout sites these practices support, are not likely to disappear as long as they play important roles in Moroccan society. At the same time, however, the ecology of Maghreb sacred groves may soon be endangered by modern socio-cultural trends such as the conversion of traditional pilgrimages into commercialized events for domestic tourism (Berriane 1990, 1992).

References

Alemmeren Jamir, S., and H. N. Pandey, 2003, 'Vascular plant diversity in the sacred groves of Jaintia Hills in northeast India'. *Biodiversity and Conservation* 12:1497–510.

André, A., 1971, 'Introduction à la géographie physique de la péninsule tingitane'. *Revue de géographie du Maroc* 19:57–76.

Barbero, M., with P. Quézel and S. Rivas-Martinez, 1981, 'Contribution à l'étude des groupements forestiers et pré-forestiers du Maroc'. *Phytocoenologia* 9:311–412.

Benabid, A., 1985, *Étude phytoécologique des peuplements forestiers et pré-forestiers du Rif centro-occidental (Maroc).* Rabat: Travaux de l'Institut Scientifique, Série Botanique 34.

—— 1991, 'La préservation de la forêt au Maroc'. In *Conservation des Ressources Végétales*. M. Rejdali and V. H. Heywood, eds, pp. 97–104. Rabat: Proc. I. A. V.

Berriane, M., 1990, 'Tourisme national et migrations de loisir au Maroc: acculturation ou évolution interne?' In *Le Maroc – Espace et Société*. A. Bencherifa and H. Popp, eds, pp. 195–214. Passau: Passauer Mittelmeerstudien.

—— 1992, 'Tourisme national et migrations de loisir au Maroc (Étude géographique)'. Rabat: Publ. Fac. Lettres Université Mohammed V, Sér. Thèses et Mém., 16.

Bourquia, R., 1990, 'Espace physique, espace mythique. Réflexion sur la représentation de l'espace tribal chez les Zemmour'. In *Le Maroc – Espace et Société*. A. Bencherifa and H. Popp, eds, pp. 247–54. Passau: Passauer Mittelmeerstudien.

Deil, U., 1984, *Zur Vegetation im Zentralen Rif (Nordmarokko).* Berlin: Dissertationes Botanicae, 74.

—— 1993, 'Le Tangérois – Aspects biogéographiques et problèmes des conservation des resources végétales'. In *Tanger – Espaces, économie et société.* M. Refass, ed., pp. 17–30. Tangiers: Faculté des Lettres et Sciences Humaines de Rabat, Ecole Supérieure de Traduction de Tanger.

—— 2000, 'Heilige Haine als Naturschutzgebiete? Zur Vegetation von Marabut-Wäldchen in Nordmarokko'. In *Aktuelle Beiträge zur angewandten physischen Geographie der Tropen, Subtropen und der Regio Trirhena.* G. Zollinger, ed., pp. 147–66. Freiburg: Freiburger Geographische Hefte, 60.

—— 2003, 'Characters of "traditional" and "modern" vegetation landscapes – A comparison of northern Morocco and southern Spain'. *Phytocoenologia* 33:819–60.

Emberger, L., 1939, 'Carte phytogéographique du Maroc 1:1,500,000'. In *Aperçu general sur la vegetation du Maroc. Veröffentlichungen des Geobotanischen Institutes Rübel* 14:40–157.

Fennane, M., 1986, 'Contributions à l'étude phytosociologique des tetraclinaies marocaines'. *Bulletin de l'Institut Scientifique* (Rabat) 10:57–78.

Fennane, M., and M. Ibn Tattou, 1998, 'Catalogue des plantes vasculaires rares, menacées ou endémiques du Maroc'. *Bocconea* 8.

Gálvez, C., and J. E. Hernández Bermejo, 1990, 'Life cycle and adaptive strategies of three non-annual, ruderal Cardueae: *Onopordum nervosum*, *Carthamus arborescens*, and *Cirsium scabrum*'. *Plant Systematics and Evolution* 171:117–28.

Geertz, C., 1968, *Islam Observed: Religious Development in Morocco and Indonesia*. Chicago: University of Chicago Press.

Gellner, E., 1969, *The Saints of the Atlas*. Chicago: University of Chicago Press.

Graf, A., 1986, 'Flora und Vegetation der Friedhöfe in Berlin (West)'. *Verhandlungen des Berliner Botanischen Vereins*, volume 5.

Guinko, S., 1985, 'Contribution à l'étude de la végétation et de la flore du Burkina Faso. 1. Les reliques boisées ou bois sacrés'. *Revue Bois et Forêts de Tropiques* 208:29–36.

Hay-Edie, T., and M. Hadley, 1998, 'Natural sacred sites – A comparative approach to their cultural and biological significance'. In *Conserving the Sacred for Biodiversity Management*. P. S. Ramakrishnan, K. G. Saxena and U. M. Chandrashekara, eds, pp. 47–67. New Delhi: Oxford and IBH Publishing.

Krings, T., 1991, 'Agrarwissen bäuerlicher Gruppen in Mali/Westafrika'. *Abh. Anthropogeographie*, Sonderheft, 3. Berlin: FU Berlin.

Lang, H., 1992, 'Der Heiligenkult in Marokko'. *Formen und Funktionen der Wallfahrten*. Passauer Mittelmeerstudien, 3. Passau: Passavia Universitätsverlag.

Lindner, P., 1999, 'Lieux saints ou lieux de cures? Le processus de transformation des centres traditionels de pélerinage: cas de Sidi Hrazem et de Moulay Yacoub (Maroc)'. In *Le Tourisme au Maghreb*. M. Berriane and H. Popp, eds, pp. 305–23. Rabat: Publ. Fac. Lettres, Sér. Colloques et Seminaires, 77.

Médail, F., and P. Quézel, 1997, 'Hot-spots analysis for conservation of plant biodiversity in the Mediterranean basin'. *Annals of the Missouri Botanical Garden* 84:112–27.

Michaloud, G., and S. Dury, 1998, 'Sacred trees, groves, landscapes and related cultural situations may contribute to conservation and management in Africa'. In *Conserving the Sacred for Biodiversity Management*. P. S. Ramakrishnan, K. G. Saxena and U. M. Chandrashekara, eds, pp. 129–43. New Delhi: Oxford and IBH Publishing.

Mishra, B. P., with O. P. Tripathi, R. S. Tripathi and H. N. Pandes, 2004, 'Effects of anthropogenic disturbance on plant diversity and community structure of a Sacred grove in Meghalaya, northeast India'. *Biodiversity and Conservation* 13:421–36.

Naveh, Z., 1998, 'Culture and landscape conservation: A landscape ecological perspective'. In *Ecology Today: An Anthology of Contemporary Ecological Research*. B. Gopal, P. S Pahak and G. K. Saxena, eds, pp. 19–48. New Delhi: International Scientific Publications.

Neumann, K., and P. Müller-Haude, 1999, 'Forêts sèches au sud-ouest du Burkina Faso: végétation - sols - action de l'homme'. *Phytocoenologia* 29:53–85.

Pignatti, G., and S. Pignatti, 1984, 'Sekundäre Vegetation und floristische Vielfalt im Mittelmeerraum'. *Phytocoenologia* 12:351–8.

Plieninger, T., and C. Wilbrand, 2001, 'Land use, biodiversity conservation, and rural development in the dehesa of Cuatro Lugares, Spain'. *Agroforestry Systems* 51:23–34.

Quézel, P., 1991, 'Structures de végétation et flore en Afrique du Nord: leurs incidences sur les problèmes de conservation'. In *Conservation des Ressources Végétales*. M. Rejdali and V. H. Heywood, eds, pp. 19–33. Rabat: Proc. I. A. V.

Quézel, P. S., and M. Barbero, 1990, 'Les forêts Méditerranéennes – problèmes posés par leur signification historique, écologique, et leur conservation'. *Acta Botanica Malacitana* 15:145–78.

Ramakrishnan, P. S., 1996, 'Conserving the sacred: from species to landscapes'. *Nature and Resources* 32:11–19.

Ramanujam, M. P, and D. Kadamban, 2001, 'Plant biodiversity of two tropical dry evergreen forests in the Pondicherry region of South India and the role of belief systems in their conservation'. *Biodiversity and Conservation* 10:1203–17.

Ramanujam, M. P., and K. Praveen Kumar Cyril, 2003, 'Woody species diversity of four sacred groves in the Pondicherry region of South India'. *Biodiversity and Conservation* 12:289–299.

Seligman, N. G., and A. Perevolotsky, 1994, 'Has intensive grazing by domestic livestock degraded Mediterranean Basin rangelands?' In *Plant-Animal Interactions in Mediterranean-Type Ecosystems*. M. Arianoutsou and R. H. Groves, eds, pp. 93–103. Dordrecht: Kluwer.

Smith, E. A., and M. Wishnie, 2000, 'Conservation and subsistence in small-scale societies'. *Annual Review of Anthropology* 29:493–524.

Sponsel, L. E., 2001, 'Do anthropologists need religion, and vice versa? Adventures and dangers in spiritual ecology'. In *New Directions in Anthropology and Environment*. C. Crumley, ed., pp. 177– 200. Walnut Creek, CA: Altamira Press.

Tchamié, T. K., 2000, 'Évolution de la flore et de la végétation des bois sacrés des Massifs Kabyè et des régions environnantes (Togo)'. *Lejeunia* 164:1–36.

Upadhaya, K., with H. N. Pandey, P. S. Law, and R. S. Tripathi, 2003, 'Tree diversity in sacred groves of the Jaintia hills in Meghalaya, northeast India'. *Biodiversity and Conservation* 12:583–97.

Valdes, B., with S. Talavera and E. Fernández-Galiano, 1987, *Flora Vascular de Andalucía Occidental*. Barcelona: Ketres.

Verdugo, D., and J. Kadiri Fakir, 1995, 'Cultural Landscapes: Maraboutic sites in Morocco'. In *Cultural Landscapes of Universal Value*. B. von Droste zu Hülshoff, M. Rössler, and H. Plachter, eds, pp. 96-105. Jena: G. Fischer.

Yoon, H.-K., 1991, 'On Geomentality'. *GeoJournal* 25:387–92.

PART TWO
The Social Organization of Sacred Groves

6

The Socio-Politics of Ethiopian Sacred Groves

TSEHAI BERHANE-SELASSIE

In his classic work, *The Golden Bough* (1890), James Frazer identified sacred groves as relics of past stages in the social evolution of religion. Studies of sacred groves have since transcended such assumptions and begun to focus on the social forms of the human agency that plants trees, tends forests, and declares some of this vegetation sacred or divine. This approach has been called 'the spiritual dimension of forest conservation' (Omohundro 1999). Recent scholars of political ecology have advocated a dialectical approach to human ecology that focuses on how various levels of asymmetrical power relations shape ecological systems (Paulson, Gezon, and Watts 2004). This paper explores human agency in conservation, with particular reference to the power of religious beliefs and the contrasting power of politics. It starts with the premise that societies with traditions of forest veneration imprint their spiritual and social relationships on the ecology around them. In much of sub-Saharan Africa, a critical relationship is the power differential between autochthonous 'firstcomers' in a particular landscape and subsequent settlers. Autochthones may ritually legitimize their claims to landscape features, such as forests, and invoke ancestral property rights, yet 'latecomers' often dominate the local political economy. The later settlers, in turn, rely on the 'firstcomers' to perform the rituals that maintain social and ecological order (Mitchell 1961). Religious beliefs therefore inform the social construction of power, which then shapes ecological relationships.

This ritual and ecological process reflects the division of labour in Ethiopia's agricultural societies. Rather than relating to autochthonous and immigrant status, the dynamics of both social ranking and sacred groves in rural Ethiopia correspond to occupational specialization. The rituals that occur in sacred groves are typically performed by ritual experts who are usually individuals of low social status, or who are members of socially marginal and despised occupational groups. These experts ostensibly control non-human space and therefore preserve the environment, but this authority stands in contra-

Figure 6.1 Ethiopian sites mentioned in this chapter.

distinction to social elites' control of local political economy, particularly through land ownership. In other words, the symbolic and social construction of Ethiopian human ecology is persistently in conflict with the material differences of political inequality. This tension has become increasingly pronounced in rural Ethiopia in recent decades due to the political dynamics of centrally planned land reform efforts, war, and reconstruction.

To show this dialectical process of human ecology, this chapter draws on three examples from my anthropological fieldwork among artisan communities. The first is based on research near Lake Abaya in the Wolayta region of south-central Ethiopia, where I carried out field work in 1972–75 and 1989–93.[1] Another is from my 1992–93 work on the polytheistic religious traditions, agricultural economics, and the potential for conservation in Dizi, western Ethiopia.[2] My third example draws on the doctrines of the Ethiopian Orthodox Church (EOC) and their manifestations in popular practice. This paper

[1] As described in Tsehai Berhane-Selassie 1997a and 1997b.
[2] The research was carried out on behalf of the Soil Conservation Research Project (SCRP), and was reported in Tsehai Berhane-Selassie 1994a.

contributes to the literature on Ethiopian land tenure by demonstrating how religion, social organization, and ecology intersect to form particular human ecological relationships. I argue that religious precepts highlight the dialectical relations of tension in controlling and organizing human space, especially the politics of land ownership. That is, sacred groves become socially important in ritual; this reinforces belief systems and also exacerbates the political tensions of land ownership.[3]

Sacred Groves, Trees, Forests and Land

In a dialectical approach that deals with both sacred groves and the politics of land tenure in Ethiopia, a focus on the social meanings of place is of central importance. Ethiopian forests are often perceived as 'non-human' spaces, and people avoid these dangerous areas where wild animals, spirits, and deities reside. These beliefs gloss the dynamic process of ecological management with a seemingly static cosmological state. Some Ethiopian sacred groves mark the grave sites of political or spiritual leaders; others comprise the archetypal forests from which social groups' first ancestors are said to have emerged; a few protect sources of holy water, and many surround the churches and monasteries of the EOC.[4]

The level of protection that these social meanings confer upon both ordinary forests and sacred groves range from strict taboos on resource extraction (as is the case at many Oromo ritual sites) to the limited exploitation of resources for religious purposes such as tree felling to fill monasteries' timber needs (Melakeselam Dagnachew Kassahun 2002). Although sacred groves are fixed ecological features and relatively fixed cultural features (as representatives of supposedly primordial forests once encountered by the ancestors) their meanings and social values tend to shift according to the forests' changing symbolic and material uses. Ritual experts mediate social groups' relationships with cosmological forces in these groves, and therefore they are the crux of these shifting values and meanings.

[3] EOC doctrines and practises regarding Ethiopian forests were surveyed at a conference on Ethiopian land use and religion held at the University of Wales, Bangor, UK, in 2002. The papers, along with a comprehensive bibliography, are available at: http://members.lycos. co.uk/ethiopianplants/sacredgrove/. On the politics of land tenure in Ethiopia, see Hoben 1996. This chapter also expands the themes developed in Tsehai Berhane-Selassie 1994b.

[4] Generally, there has been a rapid depletion of Ethiopian forests, and despite some afforestation programs, the lack of comprehensive land-use policies is increasingly affecting the forest and woodland cover. Absolute figures of vegetation cover are unavailable, as there has been no systematic compilation of the necessary data. Estimated figures accepted by international agencies such as the FAO and the UNDP hold that the forest cover was roughly 16% of Ethiopia's land area in the 1950s and 3.1% in the early 1980s. Only 2.8% of the land surface was forested as of 2000, most of which is in the south-western and central parts of the country (FAO 1984). Information on the size of primary forests, the subject of this article, is difficult to come by, but a FAO document claims that it is 4,377,000 hectares (which is roughly 3.96% of Ethiopia's land area, FAO 2000). A slightly higher percentage was given during an inter-governmental workshop in FAO 2003.

Trees, people, and social status combine in this process. Indeed, because of the symbolic alternation of trees and human beings, a cultural continuum exists from church forests to sacred groves and significant individual trees. Many Ethiopians plant indigenous trees, especially African Wild Olive (*weira*) and African Pencil Cedar (*tid*), around churches to enhance their social standing. Local notables plant these trees, and decades later particularly large specimens serve as markers of their high social status. These trees often become sites for the annual veneration of female fertility deities in most of central and southern Ethiopia, irrespective of prevailing monotheism. These trees develop into protected and cherished representations of the spirit of neighbourhood (*adbar*), and those who planted them gain some of the trees' prestige as focal points for the neighbourhood. At the other end of the continuum lie more mundane and pragmatic uses of forest products. Ethiopians rely on forests for firewood, game, honey, fruit, and a variety of wild plants with medicinal, craft, and seasoning values. In some areas of the north, farmers plant indigenous trees with medicinal values in their fields and preserve others for hanging bee hives.[5]

Despite these ecological and social practices that contribute to conservation, politics often contributes to the destruction of forests in Ethiopia. In general, Ethiopian forests represent the territorial markers of social groups, and every Ethiopian has a sense of 'belonging' to some locality by virtue of having been born there. Forests are therefore deeply embedded in the politics of local identity and land tenure. Rights to land in Ethiopia have long been shaped by ruling elites, and in the twentieth century Ethiopia's rulers often abrogated local claims to land by giving their political clients plots of land. The 1976 abolition of private property by the socialist government, however, increased tenurial insecurity by further centralizing land matters. This uncertainty intensified in rural Ethiopia after 1991, when the post-revolutionary government introduced its policy of exclusive ethnic territoriality (*killil*). These policies overrode the complexities of local land claims, ignored the ways that trees, forests, and sacred groves had mediated identity and land tenure in pre-revolutionary Ethiopia, and further centralized the state's control of land (under the guise of decentralization). In addition, the *killil* policy made ethnic identities more rigid and defined as static primordial categories rather than negotiated social processes. These new forms of identity politics undermined the authority of ritual experts and reduced (but did not destroy) the significance of sacred groves.

The Specialists of Sacred Groves

Although most Ethiopians consider sacred groves to be mysterious and incomprehensible places, there are groups of specialists that link the social and the cosmological worlds through ritual action. Although these ritual experts

---

5   On the widespread use of herbal medicine in Ethiopia, see Fullas 2001, Dawit Abebe and Ahadu Ayehu 1993, and Tsehai Berhane-Selassie 1971. Examples of trees planted in fields include *Cordia africana, Acacia negrii* (endemic), *Albizia schimperiana, Erythrina abysisnica, Syzygium guineense* subspecies *afromontanum*, and *Prunus africanus*. See also Fichtl and Admasu Adi 1994.

have crucial roles in the complex of material and symbolic relationships that constitute Ethiopian human ecology, most belong to endogamous low status groups with occupational specializations other than agriculture. Scholars have variously labelled these liminal groups in Ethiopian society as artisans, occupational groups, and low castes.[6] The dominant ethnic groups label these groups as Shinahsa, Weyto or Qemant in the north; Tebib in the western and central highlands; Chinasha among the Wolayta; Fuga among the Gurage; Hadicho among the Sadama; and Wata among the Boran of the far south. Some of these groups, such as the Shinahsa, Weyto, and Wata were specialized foragers living on riverbanks. The Qemant were a Jewish artisan group, and most of them have migrated to Israel. Although it is difficult to ascertain the population of artisans, given Ethiopia's lack of reliable census data, the artisans numbered between 250,000 and 330,000 people in 1993, when the total population of Ethiopia was approximately 52 million (UNDP 1993).

Farmers usually allocate dry, remote, and generally marginal areas to the artisans, who then provide services and products such as pottery, ironwork, and honey to their benefactors. Farmers also expect their dependants to ensure the health and well-being of their own farms by performing rituals in sacred groves. Differences in the material access to resources and the performance of symbolic work thus form the Ethiopian division of labour, a particular social hierarchy, and a version of balanced reciprocity. The ritual experts are therefore both powerful and powerless, and viewed with a mixture of contempt and fear. Occupational groups such as potters and iron-mongers are believed to command powers ranging from an 'evil eye' that can cause living things to wither to the ability to transform themselves into were-hyenas. The occupations that these groups rely upon for their livelihoods – such as hunting, pottery, ironwork, tanning, beekeeping, woodcarving, specialized trade, and medical services such as scarification and cliterodectomy – are denigrated by the landholding agriculturalists (Tsehai Berhane-Selassie 1994c, 1997c). These attitudes are bolstered by mythological charters describing the artisans as descendants of elder brothers who had lost their land rights to younger brothers through error, foolishness, and trickery. Material poverty and low status keep these ritual experts socially marginal and therefore prone to manipulation by local elites.

Although some of these artisan-experts are members of the EOC, their ritual practice is wholly independent from church supervision. Christian and non-Christian experts command different and separate sacred groves. Ethiopians are often, however, syncretic in their veneration of forests and sacred groves. Examples include the worship of the fertility goddess Atete next to the eight-hundred-year-old Christian monastery on Mount Zeqwala, Muslims' use of sacred groves around the St. Gabriel Church of Qulubi, and the veneration of the *adbar* trees planted by prominent individuals in various areas. Christian ritual experts may invoke various deities in non-EOC sacred sites, and non-Christian experts often include Christian and Muslim prayers in

---

[6] For a discussion of these classifications, see Tsehai Berhane-Selassie 1994c. See also Silverman 1999:13, Shack 1964, Todd 1978, and Pankhurst and Worku Nida 1999.

their incantations. In the studies presented below, the local farmers and artisans who want to placate forest spirits are members of the EOC.

The Sacred Forest of Illubabor

The sacred grove of Illubabor in Dizi, western Ethiopia, is embedded in a long-fallow system of horticulture in which forests and fields alternate in thirty-year cycles. The farmers of Dizi practice slash-and-burn agriculture in montane forests and valley bottom swamps. The forest stands both on the plateau and the sides of the mountain, and some of its areas are considered sacred and accessible only to ritual experts. Living in scattered hamlets on the mountainside, the farmers clear forest plots according to the amount of labour they can muster. They also build raised fields in the swamps and irrigate the swamps' drier margins. Each farmer leaves lone trees standing amidst some undergrowth in the middle of each plot. After cultivating the land for a few years, the farmers allow their plots to lie fallow for thirty years, during which time the protected trees and their undergrowth spread to revegetate the fields. The new growth becomes part of the forest and the sacred woodland. Although this horticultural cycle means that forest boundaries shift back and forth over time, the sacred forest is still perceived as a fixed entity. The sacred sites for ritual practice therefore move around the forested landscape, so the sacred forest of Illubabor is a mobile one.

After the 1974 Marxist revolution, the new government decided to resettle farmers from the drought-prone areas of northern Ethiopia in Dizi, which added new complexities to the socio-political relationships intersecting in the sacred forest of Illubabor. The government's resettlement plan encouraged newcomers to clear the forest, drain the swamps, and begin intensive farming and cash crop production. The planners insisted that increasing livestock herds was the key to increasingly large harvests, because the additional manure would make up for the loss of soil nutrients in a short-fallow system. The newcomers cleared land as quickly as possible in order to establish tenurial rights. As one newcomer said, 'All we have to do is clear more forests if we need more land to cultivate' (Alemneh Dejene 1990). The Marxist government condemned both spirituality and inequality, and suppressed discourse about despised groups and ritual experts in order to destroy exploitation and status inequality. The land redistribution programs of 1976 were supposed to benefit the marginalized. However, when farmers from the drier north settled in Dizi, they displaced the 'crafts producers' (the polite new terminology for low-status artisans) from their traditional holdings next to the sacred forest. Bureaucrats explained that the artisans' removal was voluntary and necessary to 'avoid burning down farmers' villages' when firing pottery, or that the artisans had left the forest because they 'liked marginal lands' elsewhere.

It was indeed difficult for me to identify and speak with former artisans in Dizi. A few had found employment in the area's coffee and tea plantations; others had found shelter with newly arrived religious sects. Historically, the artisans in Dizi had specialized in tanning, ironwork, and pottery, and had lived among the farmers as a despised group with mystical powers. Some artisans had been re-located in a villagized neighbourhood[7] close to Nopa, the capital of Dizi district. In my interviews with them, they downplayed their loss of traditional occupational roles, ritual skills, and access to land, but instead asserted that their skills were actually recent acquisitions. Some potters, for example, claimed that they learned pottery from government agents in 1976. They therefore denied the stigma attached to their work as artisans, and were clearly mute about the hardships they had endured during villagization.

Significantly, the farmers of Dizi approved of these changes in the 1970s. Public discourse held that the artisans were overburdening the land, and that new farming techniques were necessary. After the overthrow of the Marxist junta that ruled Ethiopia from 1974 until 1991, however, the farmers of Dizi spoke of their desire to return to the pre-revolutionary hierarchy of farmers and artisans. Farmers spoke of the absent and once-subordinate artisans as being responsible for the shortage of labour for cutting fodder, controlling forest-based wildlife pests, draining swamps and maintaining irrigation channels. The farmers avoided talking about the officially promoted change of attitude towards the artisans they had once used as labourers for these mundane tasks and ritual experts for spiritual services. Instead, they linked current land use and social concerns, such as food insecurity, to problems placating forest deities such as the sky god Waqa and the fertility goddess Atete. They discussed the ecological and social disasters that they believed had been caused by producers selling the items customarily used for sacrifice, such as dairy products, in local markets. Sacred substances had been exposed to market forces instead of ritual channels, and settlers and artisans were buying sacrificial foods for their own consumption.

The farmers blamed several catastrophic crop failures on the 'evil eyed' artisans and immigrant strangers living in Dizi. The inactive ritual experts were needed, they said, to use their esoteric powers to control the unknown by sacrificing dairy products and new crops to the deities in the sacred forest. They criticized the revolutionary government for having prohibited the rituals that maintained the fertility of land, cattle and people, and they complained that the youth were turning away from these traditional religious practises. Ecological problems therefore emerged into common discourse in the familiar idioms of ritual and social inequality.

The Illubabor forest was a symbol of the legitimate land tenure claims of Dizi farmers, and they relied on ritual experts to perform the sacrifices necessary to maintain regional fertility and well-being. The land reforms and resettlement projects of the revolutionary government created new uncertainties about both access to resources and the causation of natural disasters. Government intervention had tried to change the older socio-politics which had made artisans subordinate to farmers, but instead of creating equity, these

---

[7]   Villagized neighbourhoods were sites where people who had formerly lived in scattered rural dwellings were obliged to live in close proximity with each other in order to access government services. In practice, this policy was designed to increase the government's control of its rural areas.

efforts caused the artisans to lose land rights. The new immigrants from the north were clearing the forest without due regard for the local fallowing system, and the artisans lost their role as stewards of the forest landscape and its sacred areas. The current situation is contradictory and ambiguous. The farmers would like the artisans to perform fertility rituals in the sacred grove, but also want to restore the old hierarchy. The artisans evade a long-standing social stigma by downplaying low-status occupational and ritual roles. The result of these political tensions is that sacrifices do not occur in the sacred grove of Illubabor although this is desired by most Dizi residents.

The Sacred Forest of Lake Abaya

Neither villagization nor the denial of land rights and deskilling of the artisans were isolated occurrences in Ethiopia. In a move rather similar to the villagization programs of the early 1980s (but without the *Dergue's* overt intention to control and conscript), a 1960s development project removed a group of potters from their position as a subset of Wolayta society and resettled them within the sacred forest around Lake Abaya. The resettlement project was supported by the government, the World Bank, and an NGO (World Vision), but led to both environmental degradation and rapid social change (Tsehai Berhane-Selassie 1997b).

Lake Abaya and its sacred forest are located in a depression between two mountain blocks, and are home to several groups with disparate political systems and forms of social organization. The lake acted as a boundary to separate the various ethnolinguistic groups into political entities. All of these groups venerated the forest around the lake, but few attached any importance to the lake itself. Some groups recognized ancestral gravesites on their lands adjacent to the forest, and others avoided the forest as a metaphysically dangerous place. Only the ritual experts had access to the forest.

The Wolayta divided their society into farmers (*Qoga*), artisans (*Chinasha*), and 'others' (*Ayle*, a term for slaves and immigrants who had become the farmers' dependants). Wolayta artisans, as elsewhere, were denied direct entitlements to land, although local belief systems held them to be the original 'owners of the land' and masters of arcane power. *Chinasha* men and women were subject to deeply institutionalized prejudice and discrimination. Except in the rare cases when an ancestor had become a successful warrior and been rewarded with good land by his lord, members of this community had long been destitute. Women made pottery and offered ritualized medical services (such as cliterodectomy), and men worked as (in status ranking from high to low) farmers on marginal lands, beekeepers, ironworkers, musicians, and tanners. Some men specialized in medicine, the performance of funerary songs, and as hunters.

In the 1960s, a commercial coffee scheme supported by the World Bank initiated a regional project called Wolayta Agricultural Development Unit (WADU). It encouraged the dominant *Qoga* farmers to grow coffee and other commercial crops. In order to maintain food production, these farmers turned to the marginal lands occupied by the artisans to grow the staple crop of ensete (false banana). Decreasing access to land contributed to *Chinasha* immiseration, and when a sugar factory and cotton plantations were established south and east of Wolayta, *Chinasha* men were the first to emigrate. In that economic context, the local governor, a strong supporter of WADU, decided to settle some *Chinasha* as farmers in order to retain them in the Wolayta area. Ignoring local perceptions about the sacred groves surrounding Lake Abaya, this official made them clear the sacred forest (where they had once conducted rituals for all of Wolayta society) and create new farms and homes there.

Converting the artisans into successful farmers turned out to be a hard task. The area was unsuitable for growing ensete, so the *Chinasha* were persuaded to grow and consume maize. As the once-forested soil lost nutrients and became exposed to leaching and erosion, the former artisans needed commercial fertilizers. These were initially provided by foreign aid, and later solely by World Vision. The *Chinasha* farmers found themselves locked into an endless cycle of indebtedness and dependency on an NGO with an overtly Christian message. Evangelization and generational discontinuity contributed to the loss of their detailed ethnobotanical knowledge and their pottery skills. Within a decade, the clearance of the forest had increased surface temperatures enough to allow malarial mosquitoes to spread into the Lake Abaya area, and the lakeside *Chinasha* were among the first to suffer this new public health problem.

The *Chinasha* who remained embedded within Wolayta society continue to practice pottery, but very few have access to the marginal lands (those seized by *Qoga* farmers for ensete) needed to maintain forest-based specializations. The only beekeeper I found at Gununo village in 1993 blamed the decline of his craft on the general 'lack of law and order' in Ethiopia to which the 'kings of bees' are sensitive, and to his children's loss of interest in the occupation. *Qoga* farmers dismissively said that apiculture, a specialization with obvious economic and ecological benefits, was 'dangerous except for those from families traditionally engaged in the occupation.' Clearly, artisan trades in Wolayta are still perceived as both socially and metaphysically hazardous. The results of this development project contradicted its goals, as has often been the case in Africa (Hobart 1993). Instead of agricultural intensification and economic diversification, the relocation of *Chinasha* to the Lake Abaya sacred grove led to environmental degradation and the destruction of a particular division of labour in society that had bound the various subgroups of Wolayta society together in a particular human ecology relationship.

Although the socialist reforms of the 1970s attempted to change the land tenure status and socio-political position of the *Chinasha,* most people in Wolayta responded to the reforms with caution. The *Chinasha* potters, who were normally the women, were organized into workers' and farmers' cooperatives, but their claims to the lands allocated to them by the socialist government became invalid after the end of the revolutionary period in 1991. Since then, the *Chinasha* have taken the initiative to reverse changes in land use and social organization (unlike in Dizi, where it had been the farmers who took the initiative). They are resuming their subordinate position to *Qoga* farmers, partly in order to access marginal farm lands. Many have reclaimed their customary plots, where they now farm with permission from the landowning farmers. Rather than simple economic interests, the *Chinasha* have argued that they also seek to restore what they see as their rightful role as managers of the cosmological and social well-being of the entire Wolayta area. The forest around Lake Abaya had virtually disappeared by 1993. By 2000, farmers in nearby Abela and the adjacent district of Boroda were receiving food aid from development agencies, as they tried to develop irrigation schemes in the deforested landscape (Save the Children 2002, World Vision 2000).

The Groves of the Ethiopian Orthodox Church

Unlike the ritual experts of the sacred groves in Dizi and Wolayta, the lives and activities of the clergy, monks, hermits and nuns who inhabit and manage the EOC groves are, to a large extent, centrally regulated. The sacred groves of the EOC are the woodlands immediately around churches (which number about 35,000 throughout Ethiopia), monasteries, nunneries, and healing centres such as holy springs, wells and rivers. The size of the groves depends on the importance and age of these religious sites. In many parts of Ethiopia, EOC institutions are defined in part by the presence of trees, so these areas comprise a network of *in situ* conservation areas (Bingelli 2002).

The doctrines and practices of the EOC concerning its groves cite Biblical injunctions to preserve trees, and emphasize that EOC sacred groves express human commitment to the glorification of God (Taye Bekele *et al* 2002, Melakeselam Dagnachew Kassahun 2002).[8] They also provide important material benefits for the EOC. It is commonly believed in Ethiopia that forests are associated with the presence of God, and that aromatic herbs, shrubs and trees enhance acts of worship. Many EOC officials strongly believe that local climatic conditions are God's response to the quality of their belief in him. Priests, some of whom express the idea that forests symbolize life after death, lead public prayers to ask for improved health conditions.

The clergy responsible for the conservation of church woodlands are usually knowledgeable about ethnobotany and the local flora and fauna. They conduct public religious festivities in the forests, use them for prayer and meditation, and teach others in the shade of church trees. Monks, hermits, priests and nuns find solitude as well as incense and beeswax in the monastery forests. They also obtain fruit, fuelwood, timber, and wood for various ritual purposes. These forests are, to some degree, centrally managed. The EOC development department provides seedlings to the monasteries, sometimes free of charge, and monasteries cannot cut trees without the consent of their diocesan office. Extensive tree clearance and over-extraction of resources, therefore, are prevented by the ecclesiastic bureaucracy.

---

8 A typical Biblical passage cited by the EOC to support their conservation policy is Deut. 20:19, 'When thou hast besieged a city a long time, and hath compassed it with bulwarks to take it, thou shalt not cut down the trees that may be eaten of, neither shalt thou spoil the country round about with axes: for it is a tree, and not a man, neither can it increase the number of them that fight against thee' (King James Bible 2006).

According to the EOC, the existence of the forests around its holy sites demonstrates the church's tenure over forest resources. Until the socialist revolution of 1974, the state recognized EOC ownership of land, buildings, and sacred groves. This changed during the revolutionary years, when the state confiscated many of the EOC's economically useful lands. About 30 percent of all lands nationalized after the 1974 revolution were EOC lands, and the EOC has, in general, been unable to recover these lands since the end of socialism in 1991 (Bingelli 2002). Sacred sites are not recognized as a category of forest ownership by the Ethiopian government, so the tenurial status of EOC forests is at best ambiguous (Taye Bekele *et al.* 2002). In theory, the state still retains ultimate authority over all woodlands in the immediate surroundings of monasteries and churches, and it assumes that these forests' sacred status is enough to prevent them from over-exploitation. The church has, however, lost the authority to enforce respect for its lands and its forests. It was closely associated with the monarchy prior to the 1974 Marxist coup, and prejudice against the EOC has become deeply entrenched in the secularist adminis-tration. The resurgence of ethnic politics, most forcefully after the post-socialist government's 1991 policy of dividing Ethiopia into exclusive ethnic territories (*killil*), also sapped the EOC's legitimacy as a forest management institution. By asserting ethnic identities as exclusive and static models of people and territory, many groups were able to challenge the church's land claims in their areas. One of the major ways that such groups assert these claims is by cutting trees.

Even where the church's teachings prevail, the general loss of land owner-ship and the associated revenue has obliged local devotees to support, and in effect manage, some churches through their financial contributions alone. Many Ethiopian monks and nuns themselves face acute food shortages, leaving them unable to help the poor and vulnerable as they once did. Many monas-teries and nunneries, therefore, have been forced to turn some of their protected woodlands into fields to grow food and generate income.

Dramatic examples of the church's loss of authority over its wooded areas comes from the destruction of sacred groves at the 800-year-old monastery of Gebre Menfes Qidus at Zeqwala, and the 500-year-old monastery of Assebot. The Zeqwala monastery is about 45 kilometers south of Addis Ababa in the Great Rift Valley, and stands by a sacred crater lake associated with its founder (Taye Bekele *et al.* 2002). The monastery of Assebot (with the two churches of Debre Wegeg Kidist Selassie and Abune Samuel), is located about 300 kilometers east of Addis Ababa, on the Rift Valley route to Harar. A strong indicator of the change of attitude towards the EOC has been the unauthorized destruction of sacred groves in these areas, which has aggravated soil erosion and downstream sedimentation (EOC 1999). Research by the Forest Genetic Resources Conservation Project of the Institute of Biodiversity Conservation and Research in Addis Ababa investigated farmers' use of resources from monastery groves. Other sources having been depleted, the farmers rely on trees in the monasteries' groves for timber and fuelwood. According to the farmers themselves, the most threatened tree and shrub species are *Juniperus procera*, *Olea europaea*, *Calpurnia aurea*, *Dodonaea angustifolia*, *Schefflera abyssinica*, and *Ehertia abyssinica*. The researchers fear that monastery forests may soon be destroyed completely unless drastic measures are taken, and noted that both government authorities and the EOC administration 'have not taken appropriate measures' to stop the high rate of deforestation (Haase and Janssen 1995). Resource conflict has even led to violence. At Assebot monastery, members of a particular ethnic group have been responsible for cutting trees and claiming property rights within forest boundaries. The Assebot monks have been physically threatened, intimidated, and occasionally killed by members of this group, all in the name of asserting a primordial connection between a social group and territory. Ecological destruction and violence are therefore the direct results of the government's *killil* policy of ethnic territoriality and its lack of forest policy defining the status of sacred sites.

Despite these political changes, some EOC sacred groves continue to survive. This is not because of the efficacy of the church's formal teachings, but rather because of informal and popular views of forests as places of power (Berhane-Selassie 1994b). Many Ethiopian Orthodox Christians look to churches, monasteries, and nunneries to protect their localities through the piety and prayers of EOC priests, monks, and nuns. Popular beliefs also posit that EOC groves are inhabited by spirits able to possess any human who strays into these 'wild spaces' unprepared. The church occasionally confronts these spirits through exorcism rituals, but usually allows informal ritual experts from among the laity to mediate relationships with these nature spirits.[9]

The Ethiopian classification of the physical environment into 'human' and 'non-human' spaces means that the formal blessings of the church authorities are not required for the public recognition of certain sites as sacred. Wild and non-human spaces are characterized as inhospitable, fearsome, unhealthy, and unsafe, and are therefore associated with spirits, both evil and benign. Led by their experts, followers of polytheistic religions seek to influence general ecological conditions by participating in rituals in the woodlands around churches and monasteries. Spatial and symbolic overlaps thus occur among the worshippers of various religious orientations in the same sacred groves, although the ritual experts overlap very rarely. The monastery at Zeqwala is a prime example of this multiplicity. The crater lake and its surrounding sacred forest serve as a pilgrimage site for Christians, but the same trees (and a particular slab of natural rock near the lake) comprise the major site for the worship of Atete, a female fertility deity. The local people hold annual celebrations for Atete on the EOC's annual feast day of Abbo, which commemorates the Ethiopian Orthodox saint who founded the monastery. The same people who pass the night in the forest celebrating the goddess join the priests at the lake to enact the Christian celebration of Abbo the next morning (Mirgissa Kaba 1991).

---

[9] These beliefs posit that humans and animals share the physical world with spirits descended from half of the thirty children of Adam and Eve. Eve, finding it embarrassing that God was counting her children whenever he visited, hid fifteen of them from him. He therefore cursed her unseen children to turn invisible. They nonetheless continue to have all the attributes of humans, and conduct lives similar to our own.

Conclusion

This chapter argues that various hierarchical political processes have tended to dissolve the linkages between Ethiopian sacred groves and community belief systems. The sacred groves do not, however, simply become irrelevant. The parallel worlds of human and non-human space continue to meet in the dynamic micropolitical contestations of status, ownership, legitimacy, authority, and rights throughout Ethiopia. The ability of several categories of ritual experts to mediate social relationships and ecology in both wild forests and sacred groves shows that neither the EOC nor the Ethiopian state has a firm grip on the meanings and organization of personhood, property, and environmental resources. Nor do local elites simply dominate ecological relationships in both material and symbolic processes. The local socio-politics of sacred ecosystems is dynamic, yet most social actors treat the meanings, categories, and values of sacred groves as fixed and static. The ongoing dialectic of political economy and cosmology ultimately drives Ethiopian land use and challenges development planners and conservationists to examine culture-specific forms of inequality and ways of valuing landscapes.

References

Alemneh Dejene, 1990, 'Peasants, environment, resettlement'. In *Ethiopia: Rural Development Options*. Siegfried Pausewang, Fantu Cheru, and Stefan Brune, eds, pp. 174–86. London and Atlantic Highlands, NJ: Zed Books Ltd.

Bingelli, Pierre, 2002, 'Workshop discussions. Conference on biodiversity and sacred sites in Ethiopia'. http://members.lycos.co.uk/ethiopianplants/sacredgrove/. Online document, accessed May 14, 2006.

Dawit Abebe, and Ayehu Ahadu, 1993, *Medicinal Plants and Enigmatic Health Practices of Northern Ethiopia*. Addis Ababa: B. S. P. E.

Ethiopian Orthodox Church Development and Inter-Church Aid Commission, 1999, *Management Plan for Zequala Monastery*. Addis Ababa.

Fichtl, Reinhard and Admasu Adi, 1994, *Honeybee Flora of Ethiopia*. Weikersheim, Germany: Margraf Verlag.

Food and Agriculture Organization (FAO), 1984, 'Land use, production regions and farming systems: Assistance to land use planning'. Technical Report no. 3. Rome: FAO. Available online at http://www.fao.org/documents/show_cdr.asp?url_file=/DOCREP/003/ X6684E/ X6684E10.htm

——— 2000, 'Global Forest Resources Assessment, 2000'. Rome: FAO. Available online at ftp://ftp.fao.org/docrep/fao/003/Y1997E/FRA%202000%20Main%20report.pdf

——— 2003, 'Proceedings of Sub-Regional Workshop on Forestry Statistics IGAD'. FAO: Rome. Available online at ftp://ftp.fao.org/docrep/fao/003/X6684E/X6684E00.pdf

Fullas, Fekadu, 2001, *Ethiopian Traditional Medicine: Common Medicinal Plants in Perspective*. Sioux City, IA: F. Fullas.

Haase, G., and A. Janssen, 1995, *Project Appraisal Report*. Forest Genetic Resources Conservation Project. Addis Ababa: GTZ.

Hobart, Mark, ed., 1993, *An Anthropological Critique of Development: The Growth of Ignorance*. London: Routledge.

Hoben, Allan, 1996, 'The cultural construction of environmental policy: Paradigms and politics in Ethiopia'. In *Lie of the Land: Challenging Received Wisdom on the African Environment*. M. Leach and R. Mearns, eds, pp. 186–208. London: International African Institute.

King James Bible, 2006, 'King James Bible'. Great Books Online, Bartleby.com. Accessed May 14, 2006.

Melakeselam Dagnachew Kassahun, 2002, 'The role of the Ethiopian Orthodox Tewahdo Church in preserving trees and woodlands', http://members.lycos.co.uk/ethiopianplants/sacredgrove/. Online document, accessed May 14, 2006.

Mirgissa Kaba, 1991, 'Pilgrimage to Zeqwala Abo', *Sociology Ethnology Bulletin* 1(1):3–4. Dept. of Sociology and Social Administration, Addis Ababa University

Mitchell, J. Clyde, 1961, 'Chizere's tree: A note on a Shona land-shrine and its significance'. In NADA: *The Southern Rhodesia Native Affairs Department Annual* 38:28–35.

Omohundro, John T., 1999, 'Forest issues in anthropology in the 1990s'. Online document, http://www.potsdam.edu/ANTH/forest.html. Accessed Feb. 13, 2004.

Pankhurst, Alula and Worku Nida, 1999, 'Menjiye Tabeta – Artist and Actor: The Life and Work of a Fuga Woodworker'. In *Ethiopia: Traditions of Creativity*. Raymond A. Silverman, ed., pp. 113–32. East Lansing, MI: Michigan State University Museum.

Paulson, Susan, Lisa Gezon, and Michael Watts, 2004, 'Politics, ecologies, genealogies'. In *Political Ecology across Spaces, Scales, and Social Groups*. S. Paulson, and Lisa Gezon, eds, pp. 17–37. New Brunswick, NJ: Rutgers University Press.

Save the Children UK, 2002, 'Nutrition Assessment Wolayita Zone, Ethiopia'. Electronic document, http://www.savethechildren.org.uk/foodsecurity/documentation/pdfs/ NS%20 Wolayita.pdf. Accessed May 31, 2006.

Shack, William, 1964, 'Notes on occupational castes among the Gurage of south-west Ethiopia.' *Man* 64(54):50–2.

Silverman, Raymond, ed., 1999, *Ethiopia: Traditions of Creativity*. East Lansing, MI: Michigan State University Museum.

Taye Bekele, Getachew Berhan, Sisay Zerfu and Kumlachew Yeshitela, 2002, 'Perspectives of the Ethiopian Orthodox Tewahido Church in forest biodiversity conservation', http://members.lycos.co.uk/ethiopianplants/sacredgrove/.

Tsehai Berhane-Selassie, 1971, 'An Ethiopian medical textbook written by Gerazmach Gabrawald Aragahan Daga Damot'. *Journal of Ethiopian Studies* 9(1):95–179.

—— 1994a, 'Social Survey of the Soil Conservation Areas Dizi, Anjeni and Gununo, Ethiopia', Soil Conservation Research Project, Research Report 24. University of Berne in association with the Ministry of Natural Resources Development and Environmental Protection, Ethiopia, and the United Nations University.

—— 1994b, 'Ecology and Ethiopian Orthodox theology'. In *Ecotheology – Voices from South and North*. David Hallman, ed., pp. 155–72. Geneva and New York: WCC Publishers and Orbis.

—— 1994c, 'The Wolayta conception of inequality; or is it inclusivity and exclusivity?' In *Proceedings of the Eleventh International Conference of Ethiopian Studies*. B. Zewde, R. Pankhurst, and T. Beyene, eds, pp. 341–58. Addis Ababa: Institute of Ethiopian Studies, Addis Ababa University.

—— 1997a, 'The politics of womanhood in occupational inequality'. In *Transitions, Environments, Translations: The Meaning of Feminism in Contemporary Politics*. Joan Scott, Cora Kaplan and Debra Keates, eds, pp. 226–52. London: Routledge.

—— 1997b, 'Ethiopian rural women and the state'. In *African Feminism: The Politics of Survival in Sub-Saharan Africa*. Gwendolyn Mikell, ed., pp. 182–205. Philadelphia, PA: University of Pennsylvania Press.

Todd, D., 1978, 'The origins of outcasts in Ethiopia: Reflections on an evolutionary theory'. *Abbay: Documents pour servir à l'histoire de la civilisation éthiopienne* 9:145–58.

United Nations Development Program (UNDP), 1993, 'Human Development Report 1993'. Electronic document, http://hdr.undp.org/reports/global/1993/en/. Accessed May 31, 2006.

World Vision – Ethiopia, 2000, 'Food Security Report of May 2000'. Addis Ababa: Grants Division, Early Warning Unit.

7

Behind Sacredness in Madagascar
Rules, Local Interests & Forest Conservation in Bara Country

NADIA RABESAHALA HORNING

Known for its biological diversity, Madagascar has caught the world's attention for its enduring deforestation problem. According to some estimates, annual deforestation rates range from 1.4 percent to 4.7 percent humid tropical forests (Achard *et al.* 2002) and from 1 percent (Andriamalala 2003) to 8.3 percent for all forests (Myers 1989), with a prospect of total deforestation within as little as twenty years.[1] Because of its negative impact on biodiversity and rural livelihoods, researchers and policy makers have focused their efforts on understanding the causes for deforestation in the hope of putting a halt to this phenomenon. Not surprisingly, and as is the case in other parts of the world, relatively less attention has been given to situations where forest users have successfully conserved forest resources over time (Banana and Gombya-Ssembajjwe 2000; Fairhead and Leach 1998). This chapter's purpose is to analyze the conditions under which positive conservation outcomes are possible by looking at the case of Analavelona sacred forest, in southwestern Madagascar.

A discussion of my methods of inquiry follows, after which I present some background information on this case before discussing rules regulating forest uses and access and the differential effectiveness of state and community-devised rules in inducing compliance and, therefore, forest conservation. I conclude that the forest's 'sacredness' serves a specific function, that is, the protection of local leaders' socio-economic interests.

Methods

The case presented in this chapter is one among five that were part of a study of conditions under which rules promote or do not promote forest conservation in Madagascar. The methods of inquiry for this research were both

[1] Except for Myers' rate, the rates are average figures for 1990–2000.

quantitative and qualitative, as is the analysis. Several instruments of investigation were combined to collect data on forest products, the rules governing product access and uses, forest users' perceptions of the rules and rule enforcers, communities' compliance behavior, and conservation outcomes.

At the community level, household surveys of randomly selected individuals (15 men, 15 women in each community) were conducted. The questionnaire contained 33 main questions (some with follow-up questions) organized in four parts: (1) Markets and Administrative Centers; (2) Livelihood Choices and Forest Products; (3) Local Governance; and (4) Rules on Forest Products and Rule Compliance. All surveys were conducted in Malagasy.

At higher administrative levels, semi-structured interviews were conducted with politicians, *Eaux et Forêts* (the Malagasy forestry department, hereafter referred to as E & F) personnel, officers in the state agency for land administration, professors and students from the universities of Antananarivo and Toliara, provincial legal professionals, international and national NGO representatives, and government officials. The individuals interviewed were selected based on their likely knowledge of the particular village communities and for their understanding of the general context of environmental conservation in Madagascar.

Key informant, focus-group interviews, and rapid appraisal techniques were used at different analytical levels to complement the survey and semi-structured interview data. These additional interviews were also conducted in Malagasy, except for those with high-ranking officials (who mixed French and Malagasy).

In order to gather data on conservation outcomes, I relied on two measurements, one objective and the other subjective. To get as objective a measure of resource conservation and degradation as possible, I utilized quantitative data on forest cover change for all sites. To determine changes in forest cover over a 51 -year period (1949 to 2000) topographic maps from 1957, based on 1949 aerial photographs, and Landsat Thematic Mapper satellite imagery (path 160, row 76) acquired on 11 April 1989, 3 November 1994, and 23 August 2000 were compared for each site. The 1989 image was orthorectified as part of NASA's Geocover project and the two other TM images were co-registered to the 1989 image. Each of the images had a spatial resolution of 28.5 meters.[2]

Finally, I gathered information on the ground to get some idea of the extent of compliance and non-compliance with rules at the level of communities. This was no easy task for two reasons. Given that non-compliance with rules is construed as illegal, I could not hope that all informants would trust me and open up to discuss freely the motivations behind their choices to degrade forests. However, once informants confessed to breaking a rule (or several rules), it became easy for them to discuss not only the form and frequency of non-compliance, but their motivations for not complying. In eastern Analavelona, where the rates of confession to non-compliance with state rules were highest, informants openly said that they had no need for state regulations given that the community had effectively and successfully preserved its sacred forest.

---

[2] Ned Horning provided his expertise on the subject in order to quantify the extent of deforestation within the areas under investigation.

Analavelona Sacred Forest: A Case of Successful Forest Conservation

A quick look at the evolution of forest cover for the two areas for the period of 1949–1989, using visual comparisons of 1949 aerial photographs and 1989 satellite images, reveals how exceptionally conserved Analavelona sacred forest is.[3] For the eastern side (Andranoheza area), spatial data show evidence of some pasture activities inside the forest. For instance, there is a patch northwest of Andranoheza (patch 'A' on Figure 7.1) that was cleared and subsequently burned on a regular basis; however, in forty years this deforested patch of about 12.5 acres has not expanded.

On the western side (Mikoboka area), changes in forest cover are practically undetectable. The most obvious evidence of clearing appears in the southern tip of Analavelona (patch 'B' on Figure 7.1) where burning for pasture also occurs and where a passage linking Andranoheza and Mikoboka areas was established over time. The visual aids show that an area of approximately 5 to 7 acres has been cleared between 1949 and 1989 (Figure 7.1, left and center picture, respectively).

Although some degradation, most likely due to fires set to create pasture, is observable on the southeastern and southern edges of the forest, these changes are negligible when compared to the ecological stability of the surrounding forests. The negative effects of fire and swidden cultivation have been quite limited in this area, as recent scholarship has also demonstrated for other parts of Madagascar (Kull 2004). A comparison of 1989 and 2000 satellite images confirms the trends observed for the preceding forty years (Figure 7.1). The 2000 image clearly shows burning scars around the sacred forest, at a distance safe enough to protect the sacred forest from burning (N. Horning 2004, personal communication).

Analavelona: The Forest, The People and Their Livelihood Strategies

Mount Analavelona, the site of Analavelona sacred forest, lies between latitude 22°36.5'south and 22°43.5'south and longitude 44°7.9'east and 44°12.7'east. It is located north of the portion of Route Nationale (RN) 7 that links Toliara to Sakaraha, some 25 kilometers northwest of the town of Mahaboboka. The area falls under the jurisdiction of Sakaraha district, in the province of Toliara. The two sites presented in this chapter are located southeast (Andranoheza area) and southwest (Fanjakana community, Mikoboka area) of Analavelona sacred forest.

Andranoheza Bara (eastern Analavelona)

Andranoheza Bara is made up of the main settlement of Anjiomena (30 households) and five hamlets (46 households) located east of this main village and commonly referred to as Andranoheza Bara. The average household size is 5.1

---

[3] Unfortunately, this method does not allow the detection of changes in forest structure and species composition.

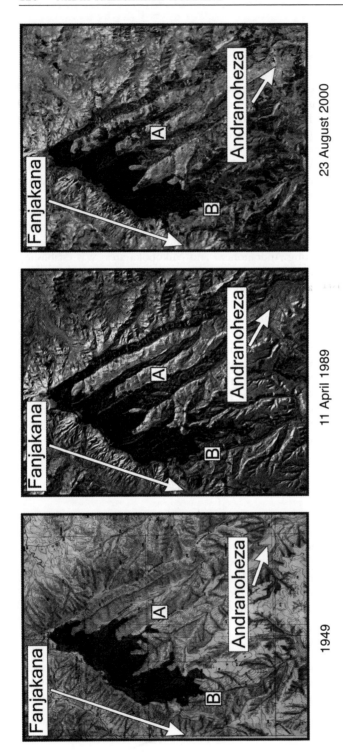

Figure 7.1 Changes in Analavelona sacred forest 1949–2000

people. Most Andranoheza inhabitants self-identify as members of the Bara ethnic group, and practise exogamous marriage and patrilineal descent. From the sample surveyed, 93 percent of men and 73 percent of women were Bara. The other ethnicities represented in the various settlements were Tanosy, Betsileo, Masikoro (women) and Tandroy-Sihanamena (one man). Once married to a Bara man, a woman is expected to adopt Bara customs.

The main subsistence activities are gathering various forest products (as reported by 97 percent of informants), paddy rice cultivation (80 percent of informants), and cultivating various vegetables to complement the staple crop (97 percent of informants). In addition, 97 percent of male informants own zebu cattle. Fifty-three percent of survey respondents said that they were self-sufficient for food throughout the agricultural calendar.

Mikoboka (western Analavelona)

The region west of Analavelona is called Mikoboka, whose name means 'sunken,' and it is notorious for its isolation and inaccessibility. In this area, Fanjakana residents are the principal users of Analavelona forest. Fanjakana is a cluster of village settlements including Mahavatsy (19 households), which is divided into two hamlets, as is Betsingily (also 19 households). Compared to Andranoheza, the sacred forest is easier to access, not only because of the shorter distance separating the settlements from the forest, but also because the terrain is less steep. Another big difference between the two sides is the existence and availability of alternative forests (other than gallery forests), on the western side, that are used to meet some of the villagers' needs. The average household size in Fanjakana is 4.8 people. Fanjakana residents are ethnically homogenous in that all people surveyed claimed Bara identities. Only membership in particular clans distinguishes inhabitants of the different hamlets. Two clans dominate, however, the Bara Zafindravola and the Bara Ndrevola (also known as the Andriavola). Ninety-four to 100 percent of informants cultivate paddy rice and complementary vegetable crops.

Nearly everyone harvests products from the forest (94 percent), while 80 percent and 97 percent of informants own cattle and poultry, respectively. Overall, 94 percent of those surveyed considered themselves self-sufficient year round, which shows that livelihoods are much more secure in Fanjakana than they are in Andranoheza.

Both village territories are far from the closest weekly market in Mahaboboka and the administrative centers (Mahaboboka and Sakaraha) that the villagers use. From Andranoheza, it takes a little over two-and-a-half hours to walk to the market. Most Andranoheza respondents (59 percent) consider the market to be 'far away,' and yet their access is better than that of Fanjakana residents, who need to travel for 12.3 hours on average, with an overnight stopover. In general, therefore, Fanjakana villagers go to the market much less frequently than their Andranoheza counterparts.[4]

---

4   Six months a year, many farmers produce a surplus to sell at the market, in which case some go to Mahaboboka once a week. For the rest of the year, the frequency of trips to the market drops to once a month for most villagers.

Table 7.1 Forest products for Analavelona (Andranoheza and Fanjakana)

Forest Products	Percentage of informants who mentioned product	
	Andranoheza (N=30)	Fanjakana (N=30)
Fuel Wood	90	50
Construction Timber	67	47
Food (game meat and honey)	47	43
Pasture	13	0
Coffin timber (*tamango*)	3	3
Place of worship	3	0

How Analavelona Forest is Used

Fuel wood, construction timber and supplementary food are the main forest products extracted by Fanjakana and Andranoheza residents (Table 7.1). For all products, the sacred forest itself and the gallery forests surrounding it are the main source. For coffin timber and some pasture, only the sacred forest can accommodate users' needs. On the eastern side, Analavelona is also a place of worship.

Rules Pertaining to the Sacred Forest

Two types of rules apply for forest products in Andranoheza and Fanjakana. State rules dominate when it comes to harvesting construction lumber and burning land to create pasture. These rules apply to all forests in Madagascar, regardless of their legal status. That is, gallery forests are not distinguished from the forest of the Analavelona Massif as far as forest legislation is concerned. In the specific case of construction lumber and lumber for coffins (*tamango*), state rules and community rules overlap because the appropriate species of sufficient size that are required for these particular purposes can only be found in Analavelona sacred forest.

General community rules about Analavelona

When people from one side of Mount Analavelona talk about the other side, they tell you that they share ownership of Analavelona because they are related (they are *mpilongo*). The term *mpilongo* loosely refers to relationships that tie individuals, families or clans, to one another. Researchers who studied this area invariably note that Bara clans share attributes that distinguish them from one another but also allow them to share characteristics. Among these attributes are ethnonyms, oral histories of forest use, and taboos on particular uses of the forest and its products (*fady*, see Moizo 1997 and Saint Sauveur 1998:77). A close examination of proscriptions in this community rule system allows one to see how traditional rules about the sacred forest define communities of users along the cultural lines of kinship and ethnicity. It is important, when

Table 7.2 Summary of Community Rules for Analavelona Forest (Eastern Side)

Proscriptions and Prescriptions	Sanction
Light Offenses	
1. One must not call someone by their name in the forest	… or else one will get lost from a few hours to a few days.
2. One must not wear gold or silver jewelry in the forest	… or else one will lose one's jewelry (to the spirits).
3. One must bring rum (*toaka mena*), incense (*ramy*) and ask for the blessing of the ancestors upon entering the forest with new visitors	… or else one will get lost and may run into a series of annoying events.
Serious Offenses	
1. One must respect cleanliness, especially in sacred spots	… or else serious illness, possibly leading to death, awaits one.
2. One may not bring pork meat into the forest	… or serious illness or death may result
3. One must not have sexual relations in the forest[5]	… or serious illness or death may result
4. One must not cut down trees, especially large ones, in the forest	… or else serious illness, death, and curse on descendants await one.

Source: Rakotonirina 1999:42–3

discussing rules pertaining to the forest, to distinguish between the sacred forest located on Mount Analavelona and the surrounding gallery forests whose structure and legal status differ. In the local jargon, *ala* refers to Mount Analavelona; *monto* refers to surrounding savanna; and *sakasaka* refers to gallery forests found alongside of rivers just outside of the forest.

Rakotonirina (1999) shows that community rules are mainly prohibitive in nature ('one must not…or else') and prescriptive ('one must… or else'). In addition, he distinguishes between light and serious offenses, noting that the worst possible offense has to do with deforesting Analavelona. Table 7.2 summarizes his findings.

A closer examination of the rules governing the access and utilization of Analavelona gives a more balanced picture in terms of proscriptions, prescriptions and permissions (Table 7.3). The rules seek to maintain orderly ecological, social, and moral relationships. Community and state rules apply to both gallery forests surrounding the sacred forest and the sacred forest itself (i.e., the Massif). Though the Analavelona Massif itself has no legal 'protected area' status, this forest, as any forest in Madagascar, falls under E & F administrative jurisdiction. Specific requirements on species and size of construction wood and wood for coffins cause users to look to Analavelona forest, where the largest trees (up to 80 cm DBH) and valued species (such as

---

[5] It used to be forbidden to bring women into the forest at all because of the temptation of sexual relations and also because of menstruation.

Table 7.3 Rules pertaining to Analavelona Forest, Andranoheza Community (East)

Proscriptions	Percentage of respondents surveyed who mentioned particular rules (N=10)
Killing birds inside the forest	90
Doing 'dirty' or 'bad' things	60
Taking pork, sheep and goat meat into the forest	30
Taking women into the forest	30
Selling products from the forest	20
Killing animals (especially lemurs)	10
Permissions	
Hunting tenrecs and harvesting honey (for self-consumption only)	70
Hunting lemurs and other animals	10
Selling products from the forest	10
Harvesting large trees to make coffins	10
Prescriptions	
Observing Bara customs and rituals (rum, honey, incense, money, tobacco, zebu)	70
Getting a cutting permit from E & F prior to cutting trees inside the forest	30
If an outsider, getting permission from the community prior to entering the forest	20

Source: Horning 2004: 131

hazo malañy and *karabo*, species unknown; and *Dalbergia trichocarpa*, locally known as *mañary*) are found. Because these species belong to categories (*première* and *deuxième*) protected by Madagascar's forest legislation, state rules apply to the Analavelona Massif.

According to the data in Table 7.3, the rules most frequently invoked are community rules in all three categories (the state rule about cutting permits is the exception). Also, some contradictions are apparent regarding selling products from the forest and hunting lemurs, and these contradictions pertain to certain kin groups' taboos (*fady*) on particular forest products, such as lemur meat. Finally, no informants mentioned the state restrictions on the timing and location of pasture fires, although 13 percent of Andranoheza respondents had specifically said that pasture is a forest product. This could indicate either that villagers are not aware of this particular rule, or that they are aware of it but do not acknowledge it because they deem it illegitimate. Table 7.3 also shows that community rules control access to fuel wood and food, whereas state rules apply to construction lumber. Especially in Fanjakana, where residents acquire timber in the sacred forest, community rules for cutting trees combine with state rules.

Rules governing access to fuel wood

There are two key rules for firewood collection: (1) one must not collect wood in sacred places, and (2) one must not cut *Mampisaraka* trees, or else the ancestors will punish transgressors with marital problems, illness and even death. *Mampisaraka* spp. is relatively abundant, so these community rules are not efforts to conserve as much as they are the means of defining both acceptable behavior and terms of access. By forbidding cutting of *Mampisaraka* spp. and establishing certain sacred spots as off-limits, Bara communities remind guests and newcomers that Bara customs must be observed on Bara land. These rules are therefore a form of 'entitlements mapping' (Leach, Mearns, and Scoones 1999) that assert the tenurial rights of a particular autochthonous group. I refer to these rules as definitional rules because they define people's membership in Bara society.

Rules for harvesting lumber for construction

State rules dominate patterns of access to wood for construction, though they overlap with community rules in Fanjakana because the Analavelona sacred forest is the main source for this product there. Knowledge of state rules varies from one side to the other. For example, twice as many Fanjakana informants mentioned that it is forbidden to sell construction wood or to use particular species for building. Because Analavelona forest is not the main source of construction wood on the eastern side (where gallery forests are readily available), more informants in Andranoheza think that it is acceptable to sell timber (41 percent) than do those on the western side (7 percent) of Mount Analavelona.

Informants expressed the two most frequently cited rules in the form of a proscription (93 percent of Fanjakana respondents said that selling harvested lumber is forbidden) and a legal prescription (91 percent of Andranoheza respondents said that one must obtain a cutting permit from E & F prior to harvesting lumber for construction). Interestingly, respect for a specified tree size does not appear among respondents' prescriptions, even though season for cutting, tree species, and tree size are all specified in E & F permits.

Rules pertaining to hunting and gathering in the sacred forest

Rules pertaining to supplementary food harvested in the sacred forest are the most telling of the differences between the two community case studies. Since Analavelona sacred forest is the sole source of honey and tenrecs for both sides, informants mentioned only community rules although E & F regulations clearly restrict tenrec hunting.[6] Community rules differ in number and, more importantly, in content. Andranoheza informants mentioned seven proscriptions while Fanjakana respondents cited four. Despite their shared ethnic identity as Bara, each community has its own set of rules about the sacred forest. The community rules mentioned by one set of respondents were not

---

6   Tenrecs are small insectivorous mammals, and most species are endemic to Madagascar.

mentioned at all in the other community. This is evident for both proscriptions and prescriptions. It is likely that livestock mediate this crucial difference between these two Analavelona communities. In Fanjakana, a local leader asserted that, 'we used to have many zebus around here. But it has become too expensive to own cattle. People steal them, or they get sick and we cannot afford to take care of them.' Since no such changes in the desirability of owning cattle were expressed in Andranoheza, this could explain why the rules of forest management are stricter on the eastern side than they are on the other side.

However, respondents agree when it comes to selling tenrecs and honey. In fact, this is true of all Bara communities that I studied. Just as people do not harvest *Mampisaraka* spp. for fuel wood, no one may sell honey or tenrec meat within a Bara community. Selling the resources given by *Zañahary*, the supreme being, is considered shameful in Bara culture mainly because it is a public admission of one's poverty and is thus shunned, concealed, and avoided. This is a norm, therefore, rather than a proscriptive rule. This was expressed in Andranoheza discourse as 'it is permissible to harvest honey and tenrecs for one's own consumption only' (70 percent of respondents) rather than the rule that 'one may not sell honey and tenrecs … or else' (20 percent).

Equal portions of Fanjakana respondents consider it acceptable to sell forest products such as honey, whereas no one from Andranoheza mentioned that it is. This is not so much a discrepancy as it is a reflection of the fact that Fanjakana respondents do not consider 'being shunned' a form of sanction in the way that being cursed by the ancestors or being fined by state authorities is. This could actually indicate that social pressure is weaker in Fanjakana than it is in Andranoheza. Honey in general, but especially Analavelona honey, which is considered 'cold', is a praised commodity in surrounding communities and markets. In the area, honey is valued for its sweetness (it is considered a delicacy) but most importantly for its medicinal properties. It could be that Fanjakana residents are more interested in the material benefits than the social costs of selling Analavelona products.

Overall, the most striking observation is that Andranoheza residents are stricter about access to the Analavelona forest. The first indicator of this is that 39 percent of respondents who answered the question in Fanjakana said that there are no restrictions on the harvest of honey and the hunting of tenrecs in Analavelona forest. No one said so in Andranoheza. More respondents cited community rules governing forest foods on the eastern side than on the western side (percentages vary from 10 percent to 90 percent in Andranoheza whereas they are at 8 percent in Fanjakana).

The Fanjakana people have more lenient terms of access to Analavelona forest than Andranoheza residents, and opinion is divided equally in Fanjakana about the acceptability of selling honey. Among the terms of access mentioned in Andranoheza, the most frequently cited rule (mentioned by 70 percent of informants) specifies that food harvested in Analavelona is for self-consumption only. No one mentioned this in Fanjakana. Again, rules are signals to other forest users that restrictions apply on the eastern side of Andranoheza. This is most likely because there are more than spirits to protect in the forest.

Andranoheza residents also keep zebu cattle hidden in the forest, and the area's regional reputation suggests that many of these are stolen.

Prescriptions expressed about food are no different from those expressed for other products specifically harvested in Analavelona forest. This explains why almost 70 percent of respondents who answered the question in Fanjakana said that no particular prescriptions apply for harvesting food in the forest. The rule that one must observe various rituals before and after visiting the forest is a general community rule on both sides of Mount Analavelona. Prescriptions are another form of definitional rule to the extent that they distinguish local users from outsiders when it comes to entering the sacred forest. When those considered part of the large community of Analavelona owners want to enter, they must ask for the spirits' blessing. The process of asking permission comes with various rituals, which for the most part require minimal material expenditure. Once in the forest, they must respect customs at the risk of getting lost or even dying. The same set of rules applies to outsiders, but a local person must accompany visitors while in the forest. These rituals demonstrate the differences between locals and visitors, and engage the outsiders in a moral economy of symbolic exchange.

Enforcement and Leaders' Legitimation Capabilities

There is a clear distrust of strangers and outsiders, who villagers group into a *vazaha* category, be they foreign or Malagasy. How do villagers make this us-them distinction? In general, anyone who does not act like a Bara is a *vazaha*, and that includes anyone who is educated, who has seen the city and has embraced (even if just partially), the ways of the outside world in their manner of dress, speech, and mode of argument.[7] Administrative officials are the quintessential *vazaha*, and local Bara think of them as 'messengers' and spies of the state. Why is this?

Local histories of interactions with the outside world help us to understand why villagers discriminate against outsiders. One needs to keep in mind the history of settlement in Andranoheza and Fanjakana. Migrants from other parts of southern Madagascar in search of pasture for their livestock approached Bara farmers (in the west) and Bara *mpanjaka* (political leaders in the east) during the mid- to late 1800s to secure rights to settle in the area. These migrants were already well-established when colonial administrators began collecting taxes in the first half of the twentieth century (tax collectors routinely encountered abandoned villages because locals had elaborate plans for alerting one another of these officials' movements and fleeing into the forest to avoid taxation). When the country became independent in 1960, Malagasy civil servants replaced colonial administrators, and villagers witnessed a progressive reduction in the provision of public services such as agricultural extension and health care. By the mid- to late 1970s, civil servants' visits had become rare, and when

---

[7] Locals who have left an area to pursue opportunities (educational, professional, social, etc.), even if bound by the same rules or taboos (*fady*), are labeled *vazaha* upon re-entering village territory.

they took place, it was often to extract bribes from local villagers arbitrarily accused of stealing cattle or breaking forest service rules. Though some villagers bemoan the fact that they are isolated and ignored by their state, it is not unreasonable to suspect that this isolation is partly self-imposed for the simple purpose of containing outsiders who have long been, and are likely to remain, regarded with a great deal of suspicion.

It is interesting to note in Andranoheza, however, that residents have edged toward 'domesticating' state power by selectively educating two young men who, at the time of this research, occupied key political positions (as Mayor of Mahaboboka and agent for the conservation NGO, World Wide Fund for Nature). Clearly, for people who pride themselves in resisting outsiders' ways (including literacy), this reflects a successful strategy for containing the intrusive behavior of outside authorities. The young men's families are the wealthiest, in terms of herd size, in the entire Analavelona area. It is significant that the mayor's father is Andranoheza's *mpisoro*, the community's spiritual leader, despite being an ethnic Antandroy, not a Bara. By marrying into a Bara family, he has been able to prosper locally. Taking advantage of the fact that the legitimate *mpisoro* has shown little interest in leadership (and is known for being mentally challenged), this Antandroy man seized the opportunity to assume the role of guardian of the forest. He therefore uses Bara community rules in order to protect his wealth.

Given that the current *Chef de Cantonnement Forestier* has not visited these two remote areas at all since 1991, and that monitoring and enforcement activities have been sporadic and scarce, it is puzzling that villagers should claim that they fear repression by the state.[8] In reality, other state authorities occasionally travel to the area. On both sides of Mount Analavelona, villagers reported abuses of power by military officers who had come to arrest cattle rustlers, monitor compliance with E & F regulations on construction and the use of fire. More often than not, the *gendarmes'* visits result in arbitrary arrests, extraction of bribes, verbal abuse, and even physical torture. E & F regulations allow the *Chef de Cantonnement* to delegate his power to sanction rule-breakers to the *gendarmes*. These officials only have to glance at houses and fields to detect violations. New construction is easy to detect, as are recently burned areas amid acres of open savanna. In Fanjakana, several respondents commented that people comply with the rule for obtaining cutting permits at the Mayor's office simply in order to protect themselves from abuse by these unaccountable and unmonitored military officers. The implication is that compliance is motivated more by self-protection rather than concern for environmental degradation and conservationist values.

If villagers' bad experiences with the state's armed forces largely contribute to a collective fear of repression, there are nonetheless respondents who stated that state rules were 'good' and 'necessary' because they reinforce community rules. Villagers in the Analavelona area appreciate state rules when they do not clash with their need for forest access, which supports both their production system and, by extension, their Bara cultural identity. Monitoring activities are

---

8   According to some informants, a forestry agent came to Andranoheza in 1990, which is the year before the current *Chef de Cantonnement* arrived in Sakaraha.

erratic, however, and villagers perceive that the likelihood of detection is remote. Costs of breaking state rules are therefore low. Although this perception is not as strong in Andranoheza, where surveillance is more frequent than in Fanjakana, villagers are aware that there are ways to avoid the state's harsh punishment. When found in the wrong, villagers feel relieved rather than burdened by the bribes or fines that they are required to pay to the authorities to avoid punishment or prolonged contact with the state.

State rules differ from community rules. Under state rule systems, it is easier to avoid sanctions for rule-breaking than it is with community rules. With formal rules, fines may be paid to avoid incarceration, or bribes can be offered to prompt authorities to overlook the infraction. Rule-breakers therefore have options. When a community rule is broken, on the other hand, the spirits do not negotiate, and harsh sanctions are perceived as imminent and inescapable.[9]

Why Forest Users Comply with the Rules

Superior local enforcement capabilities

Although community rules about the sacred forest are no less strict and sanctions no less harsh than the state rules, community rules are better able to steer local behavior in the direction of conservation. Even though there is some flexibility in terms of what are acceptable forms of resource extraction, the most frequently cited rules were prohibitions or prescriptions for the three principal forest products of wood, honey, and tenrecs.[10] What is more, sanctions for rule-breakers range from having to sacrifice a *aomby mazava loha* (the most expensive kind of zebu) to a supernaturally caused death without any descendants, all of which represent significant material and social costs.

The Bara people of Analavelona comply with community rules because the resource system is relatively small and makes access to the sacred forest easy to monitor. In addition, entering and exiting the forest is readily visible given the proximity of settlements to the isolated forests surrounded by savanna. Should anyone be tempted to break a community rule about the forest, they know that the chances of getting caught are high because public monitoring of rule compliance is strict in Analavelona. All visitors must ask for community permission to enter the sacred forest, which allows the community to ascertain the visitors' purposes. To access the forest from the eastern side, one has to travel through Anjiomena territory. Beyond this settlement, and as one gets closer to the edge of the forest, visitors inevitably have to pass through the growing cattle camp of Analabenday, where pastoralist families take turns to maintain occupancy throughout the year. Once inside the forest, the *mpiarakandro* herders (usually young men or boys), informally but effectively serve as resource monitors.

---

[9] Sacrificing a zebu may appease some angry spirits, but this option is expensive and the spirits' decisions are often arbitrary.

[10] There is one outstanding exception: for firewood collection, 88% and 100% of respondents who answered the question in Andranoheza and Fanjakana, respectively, said that nothing in particular was obligatory.

Overall, villagers' comments indicate that there is not an open-access situation in Analavelona because of these three layers of regulation. Not only are there community regulations, but state rules also apply (though their effectiveness is, at best, questionable); and ultimately, spiritual powers protect the forest against transgressors. There is also a multi-layered local monitoring system that renders the probability of detection high, which in turn has a deterrent effect on potential resource abusers.

Legitimacy of local rule enforcers

The local belief that the ancestral spirits (called the *lolo* or *angatsy*) watch over those who enter the forest has a clear effect on forest users' decisions to comply with community rules. There are widely held spiritual beliefs about the powers and efficacy of forest spirits in Madagascar, and forest users usually choose to be safe rather than sorry. Rumor and anecdotal accounts of spiritual rule enforcement, rather than personal experience, seem to provide sufficient motivation for Analavelona residents to comply with Bara community rules. By and large, the legitimacy of these community rules, and the existence of the Bara ancestral spirits, are never questioned. The terms of resource access are therefore deeply rooted in the Bara cosmological system.

The legitimacy of local leaders (*olobe*) also supports rule compliance. *Olobe* play influential roles in local affairs, and only they are entrusted with the enforcement of community norms. Survey results clearly indicate that villagers are comfortable with their local leaders because they know them well, and this social embeddedness makes them accountable. The opposite is true of state authorities.

There are sometimes subversive reasons for breaking state rules, and one such reason has to do with these Bara communities' aversion to *vazaha* (strangers) and suspicion of outsiders' authority. The Bara Mitiria area of Andranoheza, for example, has long been characterized by villagers' efforts to maintain Bara traditionalism. This is a closed society that is proud of its closure. The oral histories collected there consistently omitted a key incident in local history, when French forces chased them out of their territory and burned down their settlements (as part of a larger effort to eradicate small kingdoms around Madagascar during the colonial period).[11] It is no surprise therefore, that this community feels that it has protected Analavelona on its own and that its members are capable of containing intrusions into the forest by outsiders without state assistance and intervention. In the process of regulating forest access, they re-assert themselves as an autochthonous group and rehearse the political legitimacy of their settlement.

Livelihood strategies

On both sides of Mount Analavelona, at least two-thirds of respondents claim

---

[11] Villagers' historical accounts omit this dark part of their past. Our guide, who is from the village, was the one who informed us of this passage because his own interest in the community's history led him to this discovery, which he kindly shared with us.

to own cattle, and cattle are kept in the forest for pasture, shade, tax evasion, and secrecy. Customary rules have therefore been devised to control entry into the forest because the Bara keep their most precious (and sometimes illegal) assets there. Access rules are stricter in Andranoheza because, unlike Fanjakana residents, influential Andranoheza residents are still keenly interested in owning (and hiding) zebus. Arguably, the reason why only about half of Andranoheza informants claim to be self-sufficient year round (compared to Fanjakana residents) is because the purchase of cattle absorbs all extra income that households make. Villagers on both sides of Analavelona depend on the forest as an aquifer vital for their irrigated rice agriculture, and the vast majority of people depend on forest products for their livelihoods. Finally, cultural practices require large trees of particular species for funerary rituals and coffins. Customary rules are therefore backed by collective concern for economic, social, and cultural survival. To this extent, they make sense, they are legitimate, and so they are followed.

Local cost/benefit calculations

Ultimately, the balance of incentives and disincentives for complying with community rules is stronger than that for complying with state rules. As discussed above, it is less costly to observe community rules than it is to observe state rules. For instance, the transaction costs of getting a cutting or burning permit from E&F (not only is there a fee, but it costs travel time and accommodation) far exceed the costs of observing community rules which usually require consideration of what one is wearing, awareness of who is entering the forest, and offerings of short prayers, honey, rum, and small change to mollify the spirits. The cost of breaking community rules often exceeds the cost of breaking formal rules. For instance, illegal bush fires are sanctioned by the state at rates that barely reached a third of the cost of sacrificing a zebu for breaking a community rule, like a *fady* taboo. Likewise, though incarceration by the state is viewed as highly undesirable, chronic illnesses and the loss of loved ones are permanent conditions and, therefore, worse punishments that the spirits can impose.

Concluding Remarks

What can we learn about conservation from the case of Analavelona sacred forest? In Analavelona, communities protect the forest, and the forest protects the spirits of the ancestors and the cattle of the living. Cattle, in turn, protect and enhance local economic, social, political and even spiritual power. The analysis of these material relationships shows that the sacredness of the forest is ecologically and economically functional, and so the persistence of the sacred forest ceases to be a mystery. What conditions, therefore, are necessary to promote the conservation of sacred groves in Africa? The first condition is maximum community autonomy and institutional self-sufficiency. This case clearly shows that, unlike in many other cases, these communities in Madagascar have, by and large, contained intrusion by outsiders into the management of community affairs. The second condition is that state and community interests in forest conservation should converge. When local rules serve both community and state conservation interests, it becomes possible for local communities to manage resources autonomously. This, in turn, reduces the chances of political ambiguity contributing to resource degradation. The third condition is that rules should be compatible with local livelihood strategies and production systems. If these three conditions are factored into conservation policy, then both state and community rules can induce compliance and promote resource conservation. This, however, requires that the social groups whose interests the rules protect recognize and legitimize both the rules and their own authority as rule enforcers. Communities must also devise and adapt monitoring and enforcement mechanisms strong enough to induce users to comply with the rules. Conserving Africa's sacred groves therefore requires that community rules and state rules be woven together.

References

Achard, Frédéric, *et al.*, 2002, 'Determination of deforestation rates of the world's humid tropical forests'. *Science* 297:999–1002.

Andriamalala, Clarah, 2003, 'Etude de la dynamique de la déforestation entre 1967 et 2000'. Traitée par un SIG: Case de Tsinjoarivo, Madagascar. Université de Bâle, NLU-Biogéographie.

Banana, Abwoli and William Gombya-Ssembajjwe, 2000, 'Successful forest management: The importance of security of tenure and rule enforcement in Ugandan forests'. In *People and Forests: Communities, Institutions, and Governance*, Clark Gibson, Margaret McKean, and Elinor Ostrom, eds. Cambridge, MA and London: MIT Press.

Fairhead, James and Melissa Leach, 1998, *Reframing Deforestation: Global Analyses and Local Realities – Studies in West Africa*. London: Routledge.

Horning, Nadia Rabesahala, 2004, 'The Limits of Rules: When Rules Promote Forest Conservation and When They Do Not – Insights from Bara Country, Madagascar'. Ph.D. Thesis. Cornell University.

Kull, Christian , 2004, *Isle of Fire: The Political Ecology of Landscape Burning in Madagascar*. Chicago: University of Chicago Press.

Leach, Melissa, Robin Mearns, and Ian Scoones, 1999, 'Environmental entitlements: Dynamics and institutions in CBRNM'. *World Development* 27(2):225–47.

Moizo, Bernard, 1997, 'Des esprits, des tombeaux, du miel et des bœufs: perceptions et utilisations de la forêt en pays Bara Imamono'. *Recherches pour le Développement. Série Sciences Biologiques* 12:29–51.

Myers, Norman, 1989, *Deforestation Rates in Tropical Forests and Their Climatic Implications*. London: Friends of the Earth.

Rakotonirina, Bruno, 1999, 'La Forêt Sacrée d'Analavelona et les Villageois d'Andranoheza'. Master's Thesis. Université de Toliara.

Saint Sauveur, Armelle de, 1998, 'Gestion des Espaces et des Ressources Naturelles pour une Société Pastorale, les Bara du Sud-Ouest Malgache'. Ph.D. Thesis. Université Michel de Montaigne-Bordeaux 3.

8

Palaver Trees Reconsidered in the Senegalese Landscape
Arboreal Monuments & Memorials

ERIC S. ROSS

Palaver trees, the large shade trees which serve as loci for political gatherings from Senegambia to Madagascar, have long been recognized as embodiments of traditional political practice in sub-Saharan Africa.[1] The term 'palaver' derives from the Portuguese *palavra*, meaning speech, parley or discussion. Portuguese mariners and traders were the first Europeans to observe the practise of palaver beneath trees in the coastal communities where they transacted business. At the time, the practice was seen by these observers to be essential to public life, including the management of the polity's economic affairs. For example, in Mbanza Kongo, capital of the kingdom of Kongo, sixteenth century Portuguese diplomatic and commercial missions were received publicly by the king and his entourage of courtiers beneath a great fig tree which grew in the city's central square (Ki-Zerbo 1978:184). Similarly, Alexander Cleeve, the Royal Africa Company's chief agent along the Gambia River (c. 1685), records having parleyed with the *mansa* of Niumi 'at the foot of a great tree' in the capital of Juffure (Wright 1997:109). Palaver trees of this sort were symbols of authority, legitimacy and sovereignty.

More recently, Africanists have understood the stereotypical palaver tree in the middle of the village square as a manifestation of the continent's intrinsic tradition of decentralized governance. Ideally, all members of society, regardless of age or gender, wealth or status, attend a palaver, and everyone has the right to speak ... and to be heard. This understanding of palaver retains much of its political and social potency to this day and is manifest in many contemporary political and social processes in Africa. Simon Obanda (2004) has argued that palaver constitutes Africa's contribution to the global culture of political dialogue. UNESCO has used the term palaver to promote the building of grass-roots democracy, particularly in Mali where a successful process of

---

[1] A more detailed discussion of palaver trees may be found in Ross 2006.

national consensus-building was undertaken in the mid-1990s.[2] Several web-based programs have also adopted the palaver tree as central theme: a Senegalese discussion forum uses the *arbre à palabre* as an organizing theme, while the Georgia Institute of Technology has created *Palaver Tree Online*, a forum that links community elders with children for the purpose of fostering a shared sense of community history through the narration of life stories and oral histories.[3]

Given the continued relevance of the palaver tree as an African political concept, this essay will analyze these trees as physical realities and as part of the cultural landscape of Senegal especially. In many cases the historic palaver trees of past centuries still exist, while in others it is the political and social space formerly marked by such trees which endures. This chapter will first demonstrate that palaver trees were effectively the principal *monuments* of an otherwise non-monumental type of settlement; secondly that these trees have had a lasting impact on the spatial configuration and designation of the modern Muslim towns of Senegal; and finally that in certain cases trees continue to serve symbolic political functions today. Thus, more than a useful metaphor for good governance, the palaver tree should be considered as part of the country's living cultural heritage.

The existing historical literature related to Senegambian polities provided much of the following data on monumental trees, while a supplementary inventory of trees was compiled during a rapid tour of Senegal's historic capitals in December 2001 and January 2002. Accompanied by my research assistant and Touba resident Cheikh Oumy Mbacké Diallo, I visited Mboul, Lambaye, Diakhao and Kahone, as well as a number of other historic sites in the Wolof-Serer heartland. Wherever possible, the most senior informants were interviewed in the field, as close as possible to the actual historic trees. These informants included senior members of old political lineages and local officials.[4] Moreover, this survey of historic and monumental trees follows many years of field investigation and cartographic analysis of Senegal's contemporary Sufi shrines, and some of this data has also been used herein.

A Complex Phenomenon

The term *palaver tree* as used in European languages is misleading. It designates what is in reality a number of different phenomena which make political, social

---

2 http://www.undp.org/poverty/docs-civilsociety/community-experiences.pdf. See also *Consensus and Peace*, UNESCO, 1980, and a study on 'The palaver in Ethiopia' published in the UNESCO quarterly *Cultures*, Vol. IV, No. 3, 1977. http://www.unesco.org/courier/1999_05/uk/signes/intro2.htm *The UNESCO Courier*, accessed 8 October 2003.

3 http://www.cc.gatech.edu/elc/palaver/.

4 The data collected during this field session remain fragmentary. What is really needed, given the lack of published research on the topic of Senegal's old royal capitals, is a proper study conducted by a team which would include an historian specializing in oral traditions, an archaeologist and a cartographer. On-site there is a great deal of local knowledge about the history and configuration of these places.

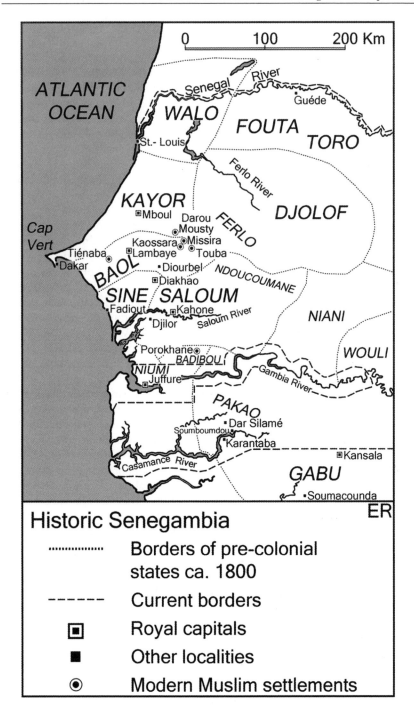

Figure 8.1 Historic Senegambia

or religious use of individualized trees. Historically, in Senegambia and the Western Sudan, specially designated trees served as sites for the public administration of justice, and for public displays of royal or elite prerogatives. Other trees marked sites for coronations or the administration of oaths. Yet others had religious functions, and were used for rituals conducted by traditional griots or by Muslim clerics. Rather than a single 'palaver tree' serving as locus of public debate, polities were marked by a number of different trees, of various species, which served a variety of public and collective functions, only one of which was the 'palaver' process. These trees often had individualized proper names, which could be descriptive (such as the 'Baobab of Circumcision' in Kahone for instance), or they could be known generically, as in the 'baobabs of writing' and the 'baobabs of griots' which occur in many towns. The palaver tree as a place of public assembly for political debate needs to be understood within this wider context whereby a plurality of trees served as a community's public monuments and memorials, and so marked its principal social institutions. For want of a better generic term, 'palaver tree' will be used here to designate the complex phenomenon of individualized trees which served public, social and political functions, as opposed to the more strictly 'sacred' type of trees or groves that were used for initiation or secretive religious rituals (such as masquerades, circumcisions, royal burials, altars, etc.), though this distinction between 'public' and 'secret' is not always so clear in West Africa.

Senegalese oral traditions and historical sources point to palaver trees as important political sites in the origin of the first Wolof and Serer states, in the fifteenth century. The traditions of the Empire of Mali and of satellite Mandinka polities indicate that this was the case even earlier, as far back as the thirteenth century. In the Mandinka and Serer areas palaver trees are usually kapok trees (*Ceiba pentandra*). The kapok is one of the tallest trees in the West African flora, with heights of 40 m. quite common in the mixed forest-savanna belt (Dalziel 1937: 119). The towering monumentality of kapok trees is further emphasized by the prominent 'buttresses' which support what are otherwise very slender trunks. Further north in Wolof areas palaver trees are more likely to be baobabs (*Adansonia digitata*, or *guy* in Wolof). Baobabs are extraordinary trees in many regards, their most distinctive attribute being their enormous girth. Though the trees are not very tall (between 20 and 25 m. for mature specimens), their massive trunks can reach up to 9 m. in diameter, and circumferences of over 25 m. have been measured (Adam 1962:35). The second distinctive feature of these trees is their great longevity, which can stretch well over one thousand years (as attested by radio-carbon dating, Hora 1981:267). There is even reason to believe that certain baobabs are far older still, but these ancient trees are invariably hollow — the wood at the center having disintegrated to create a cavity — so their age is impossible to determine by carbon dating or dendrochronology. The cavities within the trunks of old baobabs are sometimes quite large, and depending on configuration, can be put to a variety of uses, ranging from shrines, altars, and tombs to roadside kiosks and workshops. These cavities are useful in other ways too, as they can contain beehives or pools of rain water. Due to their size and longevity, baobabs are important landmarks in Senegal's dry savanna plain, which generally lacks other types of spatial markers such as hills or streams. Some of the most venerable baobabs are true historical landmarks in that they predate human settlement as recorded in oral histories. Their physical presence reaches beyond human time horizons and thus they are often known by proper names. In Senegalese oral histories such baobabs are often mentioned as loci of battles, and as markers of political boundaries.

In addition to baobabs and kapok trees, cola trees (*Cola cordifolia, taba* in Wolof and Mandinka), acacias (*Acacia albida, kàdd* in Wolof) and *mbul* trees (*Celtis intergrifolia*), have played important historical roles in the construction and maintenance of collective identities. Moreover, these identities were often articulated both in spiritual and political terms. Trees were considered the 'souls' of West African polities; they were their *genii loci* (Parrinder 1951:149). They represented the unity and destiny of a community as a whole. They actualized and synthesized notions of foundation/creation, duration/continuity and harmony/order, in both cosmic and temporal senses. The tree as *genius loci* represents first of all the notion of foundation. Historians regularly encounter accounts of West African kingdoms and cities being founded beneath particular trees, such as the *linke* tree (*Afzelia africana*) which grew in the sacred grove of *Kouroukan Fougan* in the holy city of Kangaba in Mali. This tree marked the 'great gathering' which had witnessed the foundation of the world (Prussin 1986:117). A more recent example of political foundation is that of Segou, capital of the Bambara kingdom of the same name. Early in the 18th century this city was established when the king came to live beneath a *karité* tree (*Butyrosperum parkii*) on the banks of the Niger (Ki–Zerbo 1978: 241). 'Foundation' trees are common to many smaller polities as well. Dar-Silamé in Pakao (Casamance) began after a hunter slept under a *linke* tree and dreamt of building a village, while the neighboring village of Karantaba takes its name from the cola tree where the founder, Fodé Heraba Dramé, recited the Koran with his students (Schaffer and Cooper 1980:69).

Foundation trees such as these were regarded as the spiritual guarantors of their communities. As embodiments of political legitimacy, they also played key roles for the institution at the very summit of West African social organization, the monarchy. Kings were crowned beneath certain trees, they held court and administered justice beneath others, and were buried beneath yet others. Trees were destinations along the routes of coronation processions. Oaths were taken beneath them. Newly crowned monarchs circumambulated and sometimes physically ascended them. In Djilor (in the delta of the Saloum River), since the thirteenth century, every newly crowned chief has circumambulated the tree on the town's central square seven times (Sarr 1986:231). Likewise, kings of the Asante, upon enthronement, took oaths beneath certain trees, where they would swear before the assembled people to rule wisely (Thompson 1993:116). In Ouidah's Tové ward there is a tree-shrine (possibly an *iroko* tree, *Chlorophora excelsa*) called *Kpasséloko*, in a sacred grove called *Kpassézoumé*, which was created to commemorate King Kpassé's parley with Portuguese traders in the sixteenth century (Sinou 1995:68). Every new head of the local Adjovi lineage spends several weeks in seclusion at the foot of this tree prior to his enthronement ceremony. Another interesting case is that of

Guédé, in Fouta Toro (Senegal). Guédé is one of the oldest continuously inhabited towns in the Fouta. It was an important political capital and center of Islamic instruction. Oral tradition records how starting in the fifteenth century the Fouta's Muslim Denianké kings were crowned beneath a great tamarind (*Tamarindus indica*) before proceeding to the river bank for a sacrifice. Before it died in 1996, Guédé's tamarind, which stood next to the town's mosque, was estimated by forestry officials to be over one thousand years old (Chavane 1985:65).[5]

Trees could also mark politically important tombs. It is believed that Samba Sarr, the founder of the kingdom of Sine (died *c.* 1286 CE), was buried next to the mosque which he had erected in Djilor's Ngaraf ward. He is said to have predicted that a tree would grow over his tomb, and declared its fruit forbidden to his descendants. The mosque of Ngaraf has long since disappeared but a great baobab still marks Samba Sarr's tomb, and his injunction is still respected today by members of the former royal lineage (Sarr 1986:231). In another case, a single great baobab in the village of Soumboundou (in Pakao, Casamance) marks the grave of Mankoto Ba Camara, the village's saintly Muslim founder (Schaffer and Cooper 1980:69). Many historic Senegambian graves are similarly shaded by great baobabs. To a certain extent this might be an accidental or involuntary association, because baobabs may sprout from seeds present within the stomachs of those buried.[6]

Whatever the origin of the association, baobabs and cemeteries have been inextricably linked in West Africa since ancient times. Serer cemeteries especially appear as extensive baobab forests. Moreover, cemeteries which have been abandoned for centuries can still be discerned in the landscape by observing the configuration of baobabs. The famous cemetery of Fadiout is dominated by baobabs. Fadiout lies in the maritime delta of the Saloum River, an area characterized by numerous seashell middens, the archaeological remains of fishing villages dating back to the seventh century CE. As baobabs thrive in calcareous soil (Adam 1962:39), these middens are invariably crowned by one or several baobab trees. The island town of Fadiout, which served as main port for the kingdom of Sine, is built on one such midden, and the public square in its center is dominated by an enormous palaver tree called the *Baak no Maad*, or 'King's Baobab' (Martin and Becker 1979:161). Its cemetery, on a separate island midden one hundred meters away, is crowned by as many as a dozen baobabs in the midst of which a tall iron crucifix has been erected. This cemetery is remarkable in that it contains both Christian and Muslim graves.[7] Another example is from Dakar. In the 1930s Dakar's Catholic cathedral was built in what had formerly been the Muslim cemetery of the pre-colonial town of Ndakarou. The two mature baobabs which had loomed over that burial-ground still rise above the cathedral garden today.

---

[5] Personal communication, Ibrahima Thiaw, archaeologist at IFAN–UCAD, Dakar, January 2005.

[6] This botanical explanation was provided by Hamady Bocoum, *Département de la pré-histoire*, IFAN–CAD, Dakar, December 1994. The contents of the baobab gourd-fruit are popular in Senegalese cuisine.

[7] Personal observation, August 1988.

Historic trees have also symbolized justice in West Africa, as in Niani, capital of the Empire of Mali. Affairs of state were conducted in the shade of a great kapok tree which stood in the city's central square (Niane 1989:21). According to the fourteenth century Moroccan traveler Ibn Battûta (1995: 1033), the *mansa* sat enthroned upon a dais beneath this tree. This was also the case in Ouagadougou, where the *mogho-naba* rendered justice beneath a tree (Ki-Zerbo 1978:251), and in Ouidah, where the *yovogan*, or governor, settled disputes beneath a tamarind that still stood in the 1950s (Guide Bleu 1958:512). In other cases, monumental trees could represent state sovereignty. For example, Juffure, the capital of the kingdom of Niumi at the mouth of the Gambia River, lay slightly inland from the shore, but was identifiable from the sea because of two tall trees (most likely kapoks) which rose higher than the surrounding vegetation. The largest tree was known as the ensign ('pavilion') of the *mansa*, who insisted that all passing vessels fire a salute; if they neglected to do so, he would stop trade (according to the mid-eighteenth century French cleric Abbé Demanet, cited in Brooks 2003:264).

Those trees which represented a society's political charter (hereafter referred to as 'constitution trees') were also sometimes the objects of popular political celebrations. The *Guy Njulli* (Baobab of Circumcision) in Kahone, for example, was visited each year by representatives from each province of the kingdom of Saloum. They arrived in the capital ostensibly to pledge their fealty to the king beneath the great tree, but the ceremony also involved public festivities which lasted for days (B. Diouf 1989:12–13). In Diourbel it was a large kapok named *Doumbe Diop* that was the focal point of a great festival (Marone 1970:155). It is important to stress here that these constitution trees were not 'worshipped.' They were the locus of public political acts similar to those that modern states orchestrate around monuments such as cenotaphs, commemorative columns, triumphal arches, and tombs of unknown soldiers.

Palaver trees were important for West African political administration and rule, but not necessarily in today's terms of democratic governance. This is illustrated for example by Kansala, the capital of Gabu established in the thirteenth century. To the east of the royal palace were a public square and a tree called the *tabadjou* (most likely a cola). It was in this central square, beneath the *tabadjou*, that young princes would congregate with their retinues for drinking parties and amusement (Niane 1989:64). In the city of Soumacounda, a provincial capital of the Gabu Empire, a great kapok tree occupied the public square. Here the provincial court assembled to settle disputes, accompanied by much palm wine and millet beer (Niane 1989:44). Far from reflecting an idyllic state of democracy, such palaver trees were sites for ostentatious public displays of power and class privilege. They were places of power, marking social inequality and conferring political legitimacy by invoking the process of settlement foundation.

Palaver Trees as Urban Monuments

Throughout much of pre-colonial Senegambia, public architecture tended to be neither monumental nor permanent. Perhaps as a result, great trees such as those described above assumed the symbolic functions of monumentality and permanence which in other parts of the world took architectural form. Polities and communities were marked topographically by these individualized trees which served collective political, social and religious functions. Many of these trees still stand today – thirteen of them have been classified as historic monuments by the Senegalese Government.[8] In effect, West Africa's palaver trees often survived the fleeting rise and fall of its cities and states, and throughout the area great kapok trees and solitary giant baobabs are often the last remaining traces of almost forgotten settlements (Niane 1960:149). A good example of this is Niani, the historic capital of the Empire of Mali, which has shifted its location four times since the fall of that empire at the close of the fifteenth century. Each successive site is still marked by a great baobab (Hervé 1959:53).

In Wolof, it is the term *pénc* (pronounced 'pench' as in the English 'bench') which designates the palaver tree. *Pénc* also designates, by extension, the central public square of a village, town or neighborhood (Fal, Santos and Doneux 1990:168). Both meanings can be said to refer to a political and social *place*, but it is likely that the designation of the palaver tree predates that of the town square. It is easy to assume, for instance, that the tree beneath which people gathered for public debate in time came to symbolize the public political process and its spatial institutionalization as central square. In today's usage the term *pénc* can designate any public assembly, including the National Assembly in Dakar and, in the religious term *péncum Yalla*, even designates the gathering of the resurrected for God's final judgment. It is important to stress here that this term does not designate a species of tree; *pénc* designates an institution that takes the form of a tree – of whatever species.

A variety of monumental trees marked the configurations of Senegal's most important pre-colonial settlements, its royal capitals. These included coronation trees, constitution trees, tree altars and tree cemeteries, and, most importantly, *pénc* trees – trees which mark the central public squares of these capitals. For example, Mboul, Kayor's first capital, was founded c. 1550 CE when a Muslim cleric named Amadi Dia, at the behest of the first *damel* (king), attached a talisman to a pigeon and set it loose. The first tree on which the pigeon alit was designated as the palaver tree for the center of the public square of the new capital. The bird happened to land on an *mbul* tree, and the capital was named Mboul after the tree (Fall 1974:105). Mboul is now a very small village and the original *mbul* tree no longer exists, but the spot where it stood in the center of the former capital's *pénc* is still known to residents. During my brief visit in January 2003, the wife of the village head provided a guided tour of Mboul's major tree monuments. The *Kàddou Pallou Kaye* is an acacia beneath which *damels* were crowned (M. Diouf 1990:224). The *Guy Werugën* is a baobab which was used during coronation ceremonies to measure the height of the new *damel*. Its trunk still carries numerous incised marks consisting of vertical and oblique strokes and aligned dots. Another great baobab whose trunk is incised with horizontal strokes is the *Guy Sanar Akanan*, or 'idol tree,' which was used by traditional priests. Mboul also had a Muslim neighborhood (now

---

[8] The list of Senegal's registered historic sites and monuments is available online at the official site of the Ministry of Culture, http://www.culture.gouv.sn/.

abandoned) where the *Ndiangou Kàdd Laye-Laye* stands. This acacia gets its name from the Muslim recitation 'Allâh Allâh' and is commonly referred to by local residents as *l'arbre du marabout*, or 'tree of the marabout.' The social and political history of Mboul is therefore literally embedded in the landscape through these trees.

Lambaye was the royal capital of the kingdom of Baol. It is now a large village consisting of a number of distinct hamlets, each of which marks a neighborhood of what was once a much larger urban complex. During my visit in January 2003, Dame Diaw, the village head, identified many of its historic trees. The *Guy Ndange* is one of two great baobabs – the second has collapsed from the weight of age – still marking the capital's oldest public square. Its trunk is incised with many short vertical and horizontal strokes. Lambaye's second public square is marked by a third baobab called the *Guy Pénc*, and another large baobab marks the location of the former royal compound nearby. Another tree, the *Ngicie Bàkku* (species unidentified), was where nobles and soldiers took oaths before departing for battle. Several other baobabs in Lambaye are associated with the activities of the priests and griots attached to the court. The *Guy Tan*, for instance, was where priests left sacrifices for vultures. It has a large inner cavity which is accessible at ground level through a high open 'doorway.' Further a field, the *Guy Bateñ* marks the neighborhood where the griots lived, while another baobab, the *Guy Géwél*, was their primary religious shrine. The latter tree has an inner cavity with a wide opening creating a semicircular architectural space which may have been conducive to public observation of rituals. Its trunk is incised with numerous vertical strokes. The use of baobab trunks to support arcane inscriptions is common throughout the region. Such trees are known generically in Wolof as *guy mbind* (baobabs of writing).[9]

Pénc trees characterized the processes of urbanization and political organization throughout pre-colonial Senegambia. Diakhao, for example, was the capital of the kingdom of Sine from the sixteenth century to the onset of colonial rule. Diakhao is still the administrative center for an *arrondissement* (or county) and its original *pénc* is still the town's principal public square. In January 2003, Dieng Sarr (a village elder) and Hadi Diouf (daughter of the last king) showed me the central *pénc* and the royal compound. Originally, four *mbul* trees stood on the *pénc* and marked political continuity during coronation ceremonies. Only one of these trees still stands. The royal compound, on the north side of the *pénc*, is still occupied by the descendants of the former royal family[10] and is dominated by a towering baobab. Senegal's Ministry of Culture has recently classified Diakhao's *Guy Kanger* tree, a secluded baobab outside of

---

[9] In the city of Diourbel one *guy mbind* in particular, the *Guy Kodiouf* of Ndounka ward, was the object of a lengthy scholarly controversy between Cheikh Anta Diop and Raymond Mauny (Diop 1954:vol. 2, 352, Gard and Mauny 1961:11, Diop 1967:246). Diop was convinced that this tree constituted an important archaeological artifact and that the glyphs inscribed on its trunk could be deciphered. Mauny, on the other hand, was of the opinion that the markings constituted 'graffiti' and was dismissive of the entire phenomenon.

[10] The last Buur Sine, Mahecor Diouf, died in 1969. By that date his title was honorific and his duties entirely ceremonial. His mausoleum lies in the first court inside the royal compound.

town where kings would formerly have offered libations, as a historic site.

Kahone was established as the capital of the kingdom of Saloum in the sixteenth century. It was a great tree, venerated by the local Serer, that gave its name to the city (Ba 1976:830). Today Kahone is an industrial suburb of Kaolack, the city that has replaced it as administrative capital of the Saloum region. During my visit in January 2003, El Hadj Malik Sarr, *farba* of Kahone[11] and member of its municipal council, explained the old capital's configuration. The original central square still exists; it harbors the remnant stump of an old shade tree and the mausoleum of the last Buur Saloum, but the former royal compound, on its south side, is entirely abandoned. All that really remains of Kahone's past glory as royal capital are two baobab trees which stand on its eastern outskirts. The *Guy Géwél*, or 'Baobab of Griots,' is truly huge and towers over the landscape. Its large inner cavity can only be reached through narrow apertures eight meters above ground and, because of this, it may have once served as burial chamber for griots.[12] The enormous *Guy Njulli* (the 'Baobab of Circumcision'), classified as a national monument, is carefully tended behind a protective fence. This tree was the locus of an annual festival, called the *gàmmu*, which lasted for days and during which representatives of all the kingdom's provinces would pledge their loyalty to the king (B. Diouf 1989: 12-13). One part of this unusual and ancient baobab towers skywards while the other grows horizontally along the ground for some distance before rising.

It is clear from these cases that monumental trees of various types played significant roles in the spatial, political and spiritual configurations of settlements in West Africa. Palaver trees were topographical markers, and they constituted the principal 'places of power' of polities (Colson 1997). They were political institutions and they were monuments. Their presence in the landscape helped give material expression to such abstract political concepts as foundation, constitution, sovereignty, authority and identity. Moreover, these arboreal embodiments of political concepts are still relevant to Africa's cultural landscapes today. The city of Dodoma, for example, which was planned as Tanzania's new national capital in the mid-1970s, was supposed to be centered on a monumental metal acacia tree in the center of Ujamaa Square (Vale 1992:152). This abstraction of the palaver tree, never actually built, was to serve as the capital's chief monument. In Senegal, on the other hand, monumental trees are still active phenomena, and have contributed to the configuration of modern Muslim settlements in particular.

---

[11] Historically, the *farba* of Kahone was the Commander in Chief of the army, chosen by the Buur Saloum from among the oldest free families of the capital (Ba 1976:818). Today, the title is honorific and is bestowed on (or inherited by) a senior elder among these lineages.

[12] Some of Senegal's historic baobabs were once used as sepulchers for griots. Griots are a caste-like social group of experts in oral tradition, and have long been both feared and revered for the power they command. As a consequence, griots were not buried in the ground lest their power make the soil sterile (Diop 1967:93). Sometimes they were entombed in suitably configured baobabs, which thus became natural funerary monuments. On the outskirts of Dakar, one such sepulcher-baobab was found to contain the remains of no fewer than thirty individuals (Mauny 1955:73).

Contemporary Islamic Practice

Of particular interest here is the Mouride *ṭarîqah*, or Sufi 'order,' established by *shaykh* Ahmadou Bamba Mbacké (1853–1927) in the late nineteenth century. One of the defining characteristics of the Mouride movement has been its policy of 'internal colonization,' which was part of the expansion of cash-cropping in colonial Senegal (Searing 2002, Sy 1969). Between the 1880s and the 1950s a large number of villages were established by the brotherhood in what had previously been the sparsely inhabited pastoral areas of Ferlo and Ndoukoumane. Amongst these basically agricultural villages, the order created a number of religious and spiritual centers as well, such as Touba and Darou Mousty. In the decades since independence, these ritual centers have become important towns and cities. It is in these modern Muslim settlements that one can discern the continuity of palaver trees as political phenomena.

The most important Mouride settlement is Touba, the spiritual metropolis and 'capital' of the order (Ross 1995, Guèye 2002). Touba is currently a booming city of about half a million inhabitants – making it Senegal's second largest city after Dakar. A large *mbéb* tree (*Sterculia setigera* or gum plane) figures prominently in Touba's founding legend. This tree marked the spot in the uninhabited wilderness that was revealed to Ahmadou Bamba Mbacké in 1887 as the site where the holy city was to be built (Samb 1969:743, Sy 1969:314). The Sufi city of Touba is named for *Ṭûbâ*, the tree of paradise of Islamic tradition. The moment and place of its foundation were manifest in an *mbéb* tree. This spot is now occupied by Touba's great mosque, but the foundation tree lives on in the form of an 87-foot-high central minaret, the *Lamp Fall*, which dominates the entire holy city and surrounding countryside.

There are several other foundation trees in Mouride tradition. For example, one of Ahmadou Bamba's brothers, Mame More Diarra Mbacké, founded the village of Missirah in 1913 on a site marked by a baobab called *Ndeglu*. The founder is said to have spent a month in prayer and Koranic recitation beneath the tree before the first house was built (Copans 1980:91). Likewise, in 1926 the Mouride village of Kaossara, named for the Koranic *Kawthar* (the 'Pool of the Prophet' described in *ḥadîth*), was founded beneath a baobab that had a reservoir of fresh water within its trunk (Copans, Couty, Roche and Rocheteau 1972:140). The Mourides were not the only Sufi order involved in the creation of new shrines and settlements at this time. In 1882 the Tijânî *shaykh* Amary Ndack Seck founded Tiénaba on the spot revealed to him through a 'luminous sign' at a *sambam* tree (species unidentified, D. Diop 2003:47). It is only after having spent three days in spiritual retreat at this tree that the *shaykh* left to obtain a land grant for the place from the king of Baol. The recurrence of foundation trees in modern Muslim towns seems to confirm Igor Kopytoff's 'internal African frontier' hypothesis; new societies in frontier zones tend to construct their identities, and their topographical configurations, based on the conceptual toolkits and ideological resources of the older cultures from which they had grown (Kopytoff 1988:10).

Apart from foundation trees, other types of trees mark *lieux de mémoire* (Nora 1984). These are not so much 'places of power' as they are places of collective memory. A variety of trees figure in both the official historiography and the popular legends associated with the life of Ahmadou Bamba Mbacké. For example, in the Mouride town of Porokhane, where Ahmadou Bamba spent several years as a child, there is still the stump of the tree in the shade of which he is believed to have memorized the Koran (Mbacké 1981:56). Several arboreal memorials can also be found in Touba's central shrine-complex, next to the great mosque. These include a palm tree said to mark the locus of the first birth in the holy city,[13] and a lote tree (*Ziziphus mauritiana*) said to mark the spot where Ahmadou Bamba buried some of his most potent mystic writings (Guèye 2002:371). Both trees still thrive and are well known to residents of the city. There is also the case of the *Guy Siyare* (from the Arabic *ziyârah*; 'pious visitation'), also called the *Guy Jàkka* (or 'Baobab Mosque') in Touba's Mbal neighborhood. The large inner cavity of this baobab, entered through a 'doorway,' is configured like a mosque, complete with a properly aligned *miḥrâb* prayer niche. It is popularly believed that Ahmadou Bamba used to pray in this tree during his ascetic retreats in the wilderness (Dieye n.d.:75). This is also the case of a *sexaw* tree (*Combretum micranthum*) which stood in Touba's southern outskirts, and which gave its name to the neighborhood of Sékhawgui. Local residents insist that Ahmadou Bamba Mbacké used this tree for spiritual retreat and they have constructed a local community identity around the legend (Guèye 2002:78, 466).

Of equal interest to our discussion of the legacy of Senegal's historic palaver trees is the continued association of baobabs with burial and inscription. Touba's central cemetery, for instance, was established by Ahmadou Bamba Mbacké at the foot of a baobab following the death of one of his wives by snake-bite.[14] Until it died in 2003, this baobab was known as the *Guy Texe* (pronounced 'Gouye Tékhé'), or 'Baobab of Felicity,' and its trunk was inscribed all over with names in both Arabic and Latin script. According to Samb (1969: 743), pilgrims and pious visitors would write their names and those of loved ones on the trunk of the *Guy Texe* in order to 'register' themselves for entrance to Paradise. The *Guy Texe* thus actualized to a certain extent Touba's connection to *Tûbâ*, the Islamic tree of paradise. There was also a second 'baobab of writing' in Touba, in the ward called Gouye Mbind, a little to the south-east of the cemetery. People used to visit this baobab in order to inscribe their names, occasionally driving into its trunk nails or wooden pegs with names attached. In 1983 the *guy mbind* of Gouye Mbind ward succumbed under the weight of this popular devotion and collapsed.[15] At the time of writing, a third

---

13 This is 'Bara's palm tree.' Bara (d. 1936) was Ahmadou Bamba Mbacké's third son, born in 1888 to Sokhna Aminata Lo soon after Ahmadou Bamba had established himself and his family on the holy site. The story of this tree was related to me by one of Bara Mbacké's grandsons, Cheikh Oumy Mbacké Diallo of Touba's Gouye-Mbind ward, in October 1994.

14 This was the same Sokhna Aminata Lo, mentioned above as being the first to give birth in Touba. Interview with the guardian of Touba cemetery, October 1994.

15 The story of this *guy mbind* was related to me by Cheikh Oumy Mbacké Diallo of Gouye Mbind ward in October 1994.

Photo 8.1 The palaver tree in the central square of Touba's Darou Marnane ward

guy mbind still stands on the central square of Touba's Darou Marnane ward. It is covered with inscribed names and is approached barefoot by pious visitors.

Baobabs also mark the central shrine of Darou Mousty, the Mouride's 'second city.' Darou Mousty was founded in 1912 by Mame Tierno Birahim Mbacké (d. 1943), one of Ahmadou Bamba's younger brothers and a Sufi in his own right. The cemetery, called *Baïti*, where the principal members of the lineage are buried, is laid out as a series of courts on the west side of the city's central public square, facing its great mosque, right in the center of the town. The mausolea of members of this Mbacké lineage lie in the third and last court. The second court, which precedes it, is dominated by eight ancient baobabs, one of which is used for the inscription of names.[16] Many other large baobabs stand in the compounds of the important *shaykhs* which surround this central necropolis. It is apparent to this observer that this modern Sufi town was established in the middle of a very old baobab grove. The modern Sufi movement in Senegal, in sum, has organized space on older principles of settlement design, in which political and spiritual legitimacy are embedded in palaver trees.

Conclusion

Many of Senegal's historic arboreal institutions and monuments are still standing. These monumental trees constitute important elements of Senegal's cultural heritage. Without them our understanding of the historic landscape would be impoverished. Moreover, for local residents, palaver trees are still part of living collective memory; some still stand, others lie where they have

[16] Interview with guardian of Darou Mousty's *Baïti*, 30 December 2001.

collapsed, while yet others may have disappeared altogether, though not without leaving an indelible mark on toponymy.

The significance of contemporary Muslim practices lies in that, as in the past, people continue to use such trees to configure the social landscape. Trees have played important roles in configuring Sufi shrines and urban fabrics. They serve as markers, as memorials and as monuments. These functions are spatial in that they contribute meaning to the landscape, but they are also social and political, in that they 'fix' identities while also articulating a spiritual worldview. By helping to build up collective and community identities, these monumental trees have helped to anchor newly configured places in Senegal's emergent landscapes; just as in other cases they might constitute the last physical reminders of abandoned historic settlements.

Data from Senegal and elsewhere in Africa indicate that the palaver tree remains a potent embodiment of political and social concepts. Like much of the world, Africa is currently in the midst of rapid urbanization. New landscapes are being created and new identities are being forged in the process. The palaver tree, as political symbol, social institution and urban monument, is being put to good use. This may largely have to do with the *signal* and symbolic quality of the tree. For Umberto Eco, trees are 'natural signs' (1986: 117). As perceptible elements of the phenomenal world, they are common occurrences but, not withstanding their great physical diversity, their form tends to be prototypical: roots in the ground, vertical trunk, branches in the sky. Trees have also been categorized as 'natural symbols' (Douglas 1970), conveying a host of related political, social and religious ideas which are widely shared across cultures. In Jungian terms, the tree is an *archetype*, a manifestation of an instinctive trend residing in the subconscious of all humans (Jung 1968).[17]

Whatever the reason, the palaver tree continues to embody a variety of social, political and spiritual concepts, and these concepts are still being re-formulated and re-embodied as trees as new social, political and religious needs arise. Palaver trees are thus part of the living cultural heritage of the continent. The value of a *living* heritage lies not only in its connection to history, but in its ability to contribute to resolving contemporary issues. Development is, Ismaïl Serageldin says, 'like a tree. It is nurtured in its growth by feeding its roots, not by pulling on its branches' (1995).

[17] In this Jungian sense, the tree would be a *universal* archetype, while the palaver tree might be a specifically African contribution to the genre.

References

Adam, J. G., 1962, 'Le Baobab'. *Notes Africaines* 94:33–44.

Ba, A. B., 1976, 'Essai sur l'histoire du Saloum et du Rip'. *Bulletin de l'IFAN* (série B) 38(4): 813–60.

Brooks, G. E., 2003, *Eurafricans in Western Africa: Commerce, Social Status, Gender, and Religious Observance from the Sixteenth to the Eighteenth Century*. Oxford: James Currey.

Chavane, B., 1985, *Villages de l'ancien Tekrour: Recherches Archéologiques dans la Moyenne Vallée du Fleuve Sénégal*. Paris: Karthala.

Colson, E., 1997, 'Places of power and shrines of the land'. *Paideuma: Mitteilungen zur Kulturkunde* 43:47–57.

Copans, J., Ph. Couty, J. Roche, and G. Rocheteau, 1972, *Maintenance sociale et changements économiques au Sénégal*. Paris: ORSTOM.

Copans, J., 1980, *Les Marabouts de l'arachide*. Paris: Le Sycomore.

Cruise O'Brien, D. B., 1971, *The Mourides of Senegal: The Political and Economic Organization of an Islamic Brotherhood*. Oxford: Clarendon Press.

Dalziel, J. M., 1937, *The Useful Plants of West Tropical Africa*. London: Crown Agents for the Colonies.

Dieye, Ch. A. (no date, ca. 1998), *Touba: Signs and Symbols*. Self-published document in possession of the author.

Diop, Ch. A., 1954, *Nations nègres et culture: de l'antiquité nègre égyptienne aux problèmes culturelles de l'Afrique noire d'aujourd'hui*. Paris: Présence africaine.

—— 1967, *Antériorité des civilisations nègres: mythe ou vérité historique?* Paris: Présence Africaine.

Diop, D., 2003, 'La Tidjannyat Mahdiste de Thiénaba Seck: son implantation et son évolution (1875–1973)'. Master's thesis in history, Université Cheikh Anta Diop de Dakar.

Diouf, B., 1989, 'Le Gamou de Kahone: mythe ou réalité'. *Le Soleil*, Dakar, August 11, pp. 12–13.

Diouf, M., 1990, *Le Kajoor au XIXe siècle: Pouvoir ceddo et conquête coloniale*. Paris: Karthala.

Douglas, M., 1970, *Natural Symbols: Explorations in Cosmology*. New York: Vintage Books.

Eco, U., 1986, *Semiotics and the Philosophy of Language*. Bloomington, IN: Indiana University Press.

Fal, A., R. Santos, and L. Doneux, 1990, *Dictionnaire Wolof-Français*. Paris: Karthala.

Fall, T. L., 1974, 'Recueil sur la vie des damel'. *Bulletin de l'IFAN* (série B) 36(1):93–146.

Gard, J., and R. Mauny, 1961, 'Découverte de tumulus dans la région de Diourbel'. *Notes Africaines* 89:10–11.

Guèye, Ch., 2002, *Touba: La capitale des Mourides*. Paris: ENDA/Karthala/IRD.

Guide Bleu, 1958, *Guide Bleu Afrique de l'ouest, 1958*. Paris: Hachette.

Hervé, H., 1959, 'Niani: ex-capitale de l'empire Manding'. *Notes Africaines* 82:51–5.

Hora, B., 1981, *The Oxford Encyclopedia of Trees of the World*. Oxford: Equinox.

Ibn Battûta, 1995, 'Voyages et périples (Riḥlah)'. In *Voyageurs arabes: Ibn Fadlân, Ilon Jubayr, Ibn Battûta et un auteur anonyme*. Translated from Arabic and edited by P. Charles-Dominique, Paris: Gallimard.

Jung, C., 1968, *Man and his Symbols*. New York: Bantam Doubleday Dell Publishing.

Ki-Zerbo, J., 1978, *Histoire de l'Afrique Noire*. Paris: Hatier.

Kopytoff, I., 1988, 'The internal African frontier: The making of African political culture'. In *The African Frontier*. I. Kopytoff, ed., pp. 3–85. Bloomington, IN: Indiana University Press.

Marone, I., 1970, 'Le Tidjanisme au Sénégal'. *Bulletin de l'IFAN* (série B) 32(1):136–215.

Martin, V., and Ch. Becker, 1979, 'Lieux de culte et emplacements célèbres dans les pays Sereer'. *Bulletin de l'IFAN* (série B) 41(1):133–89.

Mauny, R., 1955, 'Baobabs – cimetières à griots'. *Notes Africaines* 67:72–76.

Mbacké, B., 1981, 'Les Bienfaits de l'Eternel ou la biography de Cheikh Ahmadou Bamba Mbacké'. *Bulletin de l'IFAN* (série B) 43(1-2):47–108. Translated from Arabic by Kh. Mbacké.

Niane, Dj. T., 1960, *Soundjata ou l'épopée Mandingue*. Paris: Présence Africaine.

—— 1989, *Histoire des Mandingues de l'Ouest*. Paris: Karthala.

Nora, P. 1984, *Les Lieux de mémoire, Vol. 1, La République*. Paris: Gallimard.

Obanda, S., 2004, 'La Palabre, un apport à la mondialité'. *Géopolitique Africaine* 14:219–26.

Parrinder, G., 1951, *West African Psychology*. London: Lutterworth Press.

Prussin L., 1986, *Hatumere: Islamic Design in West Africa*. Berkeley, CA: University of California Press.

Ross, E. S., 1995, 'Touba: A spiritual metropolis in the modern world'. *Canadian Journal of African Studies* 29(2):222–59.

—— 2002, 'Marabout republics then and now: configuring Muslim towns in Senegal'. *Islam et Sociétés au sud du Sahara* 16:35–65.

—— 2006, *Sufi City: Urban Design and Archetypes in Touba*. Rochester: University of Rochester Press.

Samb, A., 1969, 'Touba et son "magal"', *Bulletin de l'IFAN* (série B) 31(3):733–53.

Sarr, A., 1986, 'Histoire du Sine-Saloum'. *Bulletin de l'IFAN* (série B) 41(3–4):211–83.

Schaffer, M., and C. Cooper, 1980, *Mandinko: The Ethnography of a West African Holy Land*. New York: Holt, Rinehart and Winston.

Searing, J., 2002, *'God Alone is King': Islam and Emancipation in Senegal, the Wolof Kingdoms of Kajoor and Bawol, 1859–1914*. Oxford: James Currey.

Serageldin, I., 1995, *Nurturing Development: Aid and Cooperation in Today's Changing World*. Washington, DC: World Bank.

Sinou, A., 1995, *Le Comptoire de Ouidah: Une ville Africaine singulière*. Paris: Karthala.

Sy, Ch. T., 1969, *La Confrérie Sénégalaise des Mourides: Un essai sur l'islam au Sénégal*. Paris: Présence Africaine.

Thompson, R. F., 1993, *Face of the Gods: Art and Altars of Africa and the African Americas*. Munich: Prestel-Verlag.

Vale, L. J., 1992, *Architecture, Power, and National Identity*. New Haven, CT: Yale University Press.

Wright, D. R., 1997, *The World and a Very Small Place in Africa*. London: M. E. Sharpe.

PART THREE
The Symbol of Forests

9

Loggers v. Spirits
in the Beng Forest, Côte d'Ivoire
Competing Models

ALMA GOTTLIEB

The first time I set foot inside the rain forest in West Africa, I felt over-whelmed. Birds and mammals whose names I didn't know were chirping (the Beng would say 'crying') above me and making a variety of quiet moans and noisy howls around me, hidden by canopied foliage so tightly interwoven I could scarcely detect where the leaves of one tree separated from those of another. The rain forest of Côte d'Ivoire was an organic, singular place whose massiveness seemed forever unknowable.

A village elder, Kona, was leading my husband and me to his fields inside the forest that day. He'd recently adopted us for the time we'd be living in his small village in the Beng region some 200 miles north of the Atlantic coastline, and this was Kona's first time serving as forest guide to Westerners. Kona was amused by our wide-eyed wonder at the vast, overarching forest, our incessant barrage of questions. To him, the space through which we were walking was powerful – but hardly undifferentiated: indeed, every spot oozed economic, cultural or religious significance to him.

Kona knew the names of every insect that crawled or flew by, and whether or not it stung people; he recognized which part of each plant at our feet (bark, leaves, roots) might be used to cure which disease; he could predict when and where he'd be likely to find the game he was so skilled at hunting, from forest snail to majestic elephant; he could easily identify the *zɔ* tree whose bark men strip off and process to make bark cloth bags and mats;[1] and he could point out the *kpraw kpraw* fruit that produces oil-bearing seeds that children of years past strung on thin sticks and lit as small, portable lamps.[2]

Yes, Kona's ecological knowledge of the rain forest was impressive; but equally fascinating, Kona commanded a second layer of knowledge of the rain

---

[1] For a description of the difficult work involved in this craft, see Gottlieb and Graham (1994:305).

[2] For a description of how these lamps are made, see Gottlieb and Graham (1994:305–6).

149

forest that was initially less visible to me. This is the sort of knowledge we might call social, for Kona easily saw the human contours of the forest, not just its natural foundations. He recalled which farmer owned rights to tap which palm trees and pick fruits from which banana plants; he remembered how many years each patch of earth had lain fallow since it was last planted; he easily identified the owner of each field (whose contours sometimes faded seamlessly into the surrounding forest to me) as it was staked out as a wedge in a pie-like circle; and he readily noticed the picket (initially camouflaged to me by the surrounding trees) that had been planted in the forest to mark the halfway spot on the path that connected two neighboring villages, indicating where the residents of one village could stop working while doing their annual path-clearing work that their village chief mandated, in order to maintain their half of the road. This invisible but nonetheless tangible social landscape started slowly to open itself to me as I began to study local socio-ecological knowledge and came to appreciate the enormous understanding of the local geocultural landscape that lay inside each Beng farmer's mind.

Humbling as this knowledge of Kona's was, what came to amaze me even more was a third layer of his knowledge that proved the most invisible of all. As I studied the Beng universe, I understood that the forest was alive with an entire unseen cosmos, a cultural imaginary whose contours are charted by the Beng as precisely as were the more tangible components of the forest. It is this cultural imaginary that is the focus of the pages that follow. For the Beng world is populated not only by flora and fauna visible to the human eye, but also by forces imperceptible to humans yet decisive in their effects on humans. This invisibility is the subject of much Beng thought.[3]

A Beng folktale explains that a gulf now separates the world of humans from that of spirits . . . although this gulf did not always exist. This version of the folktale was told to me by master storyteller, Akwe Kouadio Baa, who himself heard it recounted by an elder and liked it so much that he became moved to put it to song when entertaining a small audience. This is the story Baa told:

> A certain man and a certain spirit went to construct a village. Every day, they ate *foutou*, but there were always leftovers.[4] They ate meat, but there were leftovers. They drank palm wine, but there were always leftovers. When they were done eating, the man would roll a cigarette, every day he would roll a cigarette! One day, the spirit said, 'When we eat *foutou*, we always leave leftovers. When we eat meat, we always have left-overs. When we drink our palm wine, we always have leftovers. In addition, when you "eat your fire," I can't stay by your side.'
>
> The man asked, 'Why is that?'
>
> The spirit replied, 'If the day comes that we don't find anything to eat or drink, you'll come and eat me!'[5] Then the spirit ran off into the forest. The next morning, the man

---

3 For more on Beng religion, see Gottlieb (1996:19–45; 2004), Gottlieb and Graham (1994).

4 *Foutou* is a starch dish common throughout much of the rain forest area of West Africa; women make it from cooked yams pounded into an elastic ball and eaten with an accompany-ing sauce.

5 The spirit thought that the man smoking the cigarette was literally 'eating fire.' The spirit imagined that a man who could 'eat fire' could eat anything, including the spirit. In earlier times, the Beng used to smoke tobacco in wooden pipes; cigarettes, either commercially rolled in paper or home-rolled in corn stalks, are a more recent introduction.

said he was going hunting. The spirit went ahead to where the man would be coming. The spirit asked him, 'In your village, when women pound something, between the mortar and the pestle, which of the two of them makes the noise that resounds the farthest?' The man replied, 'It's the mortar whose noise resounds the farthest.' The spirit then asked him, 'But if the pestle hadn't hit against the mortar...?' The man said, 'Ah! It's the pestle whose noise resounds the farthest! It's true: if the pestle hadn't hit against the mortar...!' The spirit then beat up the man. The man ran off, ran off to his village. Every day in the forest, the spirit hit the man when he was out hunting. Finally, the man's child said to him, 'Papa, why haven't you killed anything the past five days when you've been out hunting?'

He said, 'Little boy, it's not my fault. The spirit that left went and waited for me in the forest. Every day he beats me up! In beating me up, he asks me, "Between the noise of the mortar and the noise of the pestle, which resounds the farthest?" If I don't know, he beats me up!'

His son said, 'Papa, tomorrow I'm going along too.'

The next morning, the boy and his father went off to go hunting. As soon as they got there, they saw the spirit right away. He came and asked the man, 'In your village, between the noise of the mortar and the noise of the pestle, which travels the farthest?'

The child ran up to his father's side and went and smacked the spirit on his cheek, *kpao*. Then he asked the spirit, 'Between my hand and your cheek, which one sounds the loudest?'

The spirit answered, 'I beat up your father, beat him up, beat him up, and he wasn't able to ask me about it at all. You, just a child, you've come and hit me and you've asked me about my affairs. But I'm not able to do the same to you. This is a great source of shame to me. Therefore, from now on, I'll be able to see people, but people themselves will no longer be able to see me.' Then he put darkness between us. And that's why we don't see spirits any more – that's the reason.

We see that this fable chronicles an irrevocable rupture that distances humans from spirits because of the superior wisdom of a human child that a spirit finds humiliating. Nevertheless, the Beng continue to maintain active relations with the spirits, of whom they recognize several types. One major group contains two distinct subgroups living in the bush: *gaŋwroŋ* and *alufy#*.[6] The second major group of spirits (*bɔŋzɔ*) is directly associated with the Earth, which is accordingly conceived as spiritually powerful. These *bɔŋzɔ* spirits prefer to congregate around spots in the forest where a small pool of water is adjacent to a hill – a combination that the spirits reputedly find especially hospitable. Thus people put shrines at such places, and indigenous priests come once every six days to make offerings at these shrines.[7]

The Beng have imagined much about the existence of the forest-dwelling spirits. Despite the gulf separating them from humans, there are myriad connections between the two worlds – connections that constitute a virtual hallmark of Beng eco-thought.

[6] The latter are pygmy-sized spirits – some say, powerful beings rather than spirits *per se* – living on the village/forest border.

[7] Another group of spiritual beings, called *wru* (souls), exists as ancestors in the afterlife (*wrugbe*, lit. 'soul village'); these figure prominently in the lives of the living and especially in infants and young children (see Gottlieb 2004) but are not affiliated with the forest and hence are not discussed here further. The Beng also recognize a deity called *eci* that I translate loosely as 'sky/god.'

Thus, every village is affiliated with a specific patch of Earth (in some cases, two or even three Earths) that is given a proper name; while known to most adults, the names of these Earths are considered too powerful to utter in normal discourse.[8] Some Earths are also considered to be affiliated with a specific matriclan. Each such Earth is considered to have precise contours localized in a particular spot, and particular *bɔŋzɔ* spirits are said to reside at these spots. In fact, the terrestrial orientation of the Beng places its emphasis on these spirits of the Earth.[9] Many villagers frequently make offerings to the spirits connected with the named patch of forest-based Earth that is associated with their village. The *bɔŋzɔ* spirits affiliated with certain named Earths are said to be especially powerful. On occasion, people may travel to other villages to make offerings to particular spirits that a religious specialist has told them are responsible for their wellbeing.

Two kinds of indigenous religious practitioners maintain ties with these various spirits. Diviners (who may be male or female) use a variety of techniques – including interpreting the patterns made by cowry shells thrown on a mat, or the patterns made by water mixed with kaolin when swirled around in a brass bowl. Spirits are temporarily drawn from the forest to these items. Once the bush spirits have entered the village to congregate around the objects, diviners communicate with the invisible spirits and then interpret the spirits' communications to concerned clients.

Clients often consult a diviner because of sickness or misfortune in the family. Depending on what the spirit recommends, the diviner may offer a simple herbal remedy to the client and/or prescribe a sacrifice to (a) particular spirit(s) affiliated with the bush at large, or with a particular named Earth, or with the land of the ancestors.

Masters of the Earth (who are virtually always male) officiate over the offerings that diviners prescribe. These religious figures worship the Earth spirits once every six days (according to the six-day Beng calendar) by offering prayers and animal sacrifices on behalf of individuals (or, occasionally, groups) who seek protection against evils such as witchcraft; relief from afflictions that are deemed to have a spiritual cause; atonement for past sins committed; or thanks for past wishes granted or good luck experienced. Individuals who sacrifice a sheep at such a shrine may hope that the spirits that reside in the shrine may make the person very successful at work and thus wealthy. Occasionally, a village chief may offer a sheep to sacrifice to the resident shrine spirits to ask for a plentiful coffee crop for the whole village. In making such a request, the chief would promise that should the wish be granted, he would later return to thank the shrine's bush spirits by offering a cow, which all residents of his village would take up a collection to buy. All these sacrifices create a strong continuity between the village-based world of humans and the forest-based world of spirits.[10]

---

[8] To honor this strong preference, I do not divulge their names in any of my writings.

[9] As with many African religious systems, the sky deity is rather remote and, while evoked frequently in casual speech, is never the direct object of sacrifice. For some discussion of this trend comparatively in sub-Saharan Africa, see Ray 1999.

[10] Until very recently, most Beng villagers have maintained an active commitment to the religious

The forest spirits themselves are considered powerful in a particular way that is referred to as *kalɛ*. Although one might be tempted to translate this term as 'sacred,' the English concept does not map the same conceptual sphere as that limned by the Beng term. For one thing, the semantic field covered by the Beng term includes spirits, some humans, and some animals; for another thing, beings who are *kalɛ* are morally neutral. It is true that forest spirits are said to be invisible, hence invincible. And the Earth is also classified as *kalɛ* in those forest spots where *bɔŋzɔ* are said to reside. Yet some very visible forest-dwelling animals are also classified as *kalɛ* if they, too, are said to possess spiritual powers. For example, porcupines are *kalɛ* as they are considered to be the diviners of the forest, with their tails serving as their instrument of divination. It is said that great hunters may know of additional animals that possess spiritually based powers and hence are *kalɛ*.

Despite the gulf chronicled in the folktale cited above that now separates village-dwelling humans from forest-dwelling spirits, some people routinely transcend this geo-mythical divide and maintain intimate relations with the spirits. As with the bush spirits themselves, such people are also classified as *kalɛ*. Indeed, such people are said to be protected by forest spirits; as the Beng put it, 'If there are spirits behind someone, then s/he is *kalɛ*' (*a bɔŋzɔ sõ fe a klɛ na, o kalɛ na*). Their association with forest-based spirits affords such people protection from the ordinary stresses of daily village life. Thus someone who is *kalɛ* seems both fearless and invulnerable. People may say that their skin is so tough that they do not get cuts, even if they are slashed with a machete. Likewise, they cannot normally be bitten by mosquitoes because their blood is not sweet; if they are bit, their skin will not swell up. People who are *kalɛ* reportedly cannot be killed by ordinary people or even by witches; due to protection by bush spirits, it is said that only god (*eci*) can kill such people, usually at a very advanced age.

Bush spirits are said to know beforehand when the death of a person who is considered *kalɛ* will occur, if that person lives in a village near the spirits' forest abode. When they foresee the death of such a person, the *bɔŋzɔ* reportedly drum and sing in the forest to celebrate the person's funeral in advance of the actual death. People who live nearby may say that they hear mysterious drumming and singing in the forest that they can't identify; this is interpreted as the spirits' anticipatory funeral. If this occurs during the dry season (usually October through February/March), villagers may say that they see a light that burns very brightly from the same spot from which they hear singing and drumming, but they aver that the bright spot is not a fire. It is said that this light is the light of gold that the spirits own. Soon after seeing and

---

[10] (cont.) practices I have summarized here. However, in the past few decades – far more recently than in many other regions of sub-Saharan Africa – a small but increasing number of Beng have become attracted to Christianity, and even more to Islam. Yet, as with many Africans, most Beng who have adopted one of the 'world' religions see the different faiths as complementary rather than competing, and most continue to practice at least an attenuated version of their local religious tradition while simultaneously endorsing the major precepts of a new religion. Put simply, for most, the Christian or Muslim god is added on to the Beng pantheon, rather than replacing that pantheon.

hearing these mysterious sounds, villagers say that they always hear announced the death of one of their villagemates who was indeed a person classified as *kalɛ*.

Certain kinds of humans are routinely assumed to be *kalɛ*. At the malevolent end of the spectrum of people, witches are considered *kalɛ*, as evidenced by their superhuman powers. But many benevolent people are also able to maintain relations with spirits and are thus considered *kalɛ*. These include diviners and some exceptionally talented artists – sculptors, musicians and dancers.[11] Since all diviners are regularly in touch with spirits, they are categorically considered *kalɛ*.[12] One diviner I came to know, Kouakou Ba, is said to have been born *kalɛ* having begun to divine when he was just a child. Because his gifts are said to derive directly from god (*eci*) and he maintains close relations with the bush spirits, Kouakou Ba is said to be incapable of lying when he divines; for this he is greatly respected, and his wide reputation draws him clients from as far as the coastal city of Abidjan. Diviners use a variety of methods to attract spirits to communicate with them; some diviners (called *siawoli*, or 'spirit dancers') own statues that are said to please and draw the spirits to them. When these diviners wish to become possessed by spirits so as to perform a divination, they bring out their statues to attract the forest spirits to the figures, so that the spirits will possess and communicate to the diviner while dancing; the diviner can then diagnose the cause of the client's problem. In this case, the statues are considered to constitute a kind of sacrifice to the spirits. Thus as part of the divination session, the diviner should crack an egg onto the statue as a sacrifice to the spirits when making a request on behalf of a client – whether good health, financial success, a productive harvest, a healthy child, or good luck. Great artists also maintain intimate relations with the spirits. As an example, let us consider the case of 'Kouakou,' a talented sculptor, musician and herbalist I knew who was said to 'have spirits behind him'. Although middle-aged, Kouakou had never married – a striking anomaly in Beng villages. His neighbors explained that Kouakou didn't need a human wife because he had a spirit wife who left him content. Some neighbors speculated that spirits might even live in Kouakou's drums and statues. Although, as the folktale quoted above indicated, spirits are generally said to reside in the forest and eschew human habitations, there are exceptions: spirits are attracted to ritual paraphernalia kept by certain spiritually powerful people such as Kouakou. Another talented musician I knew was rumored to be *kalɛ* because his mother always applied white clay or kaolin (*sɛpe*) on his forehead while he danced and sang. The white clay known as *sɛpe* is considered to be the 'powder of the spirits' (*ŋo fwɛ*); the spirits are said to like it (*ŋo vi a ni*) and to dust their own (invisible) bodies with it. Thus when a human uses kaolin, spirits are reportedly attracted to the person and may then protect him or her. Likewise, diviners who perform divinations by drawing spirits to statues sprinkle *sɛpe* on the plate on which they place the statues, to attract the spirits to it. In similar

---

[11] In fact, the distinction between witches on the one hand and diviners/artists/healers on the other hand is not as sharply drawn as Westerners might think. For a discussion of the continuum between good and evil use of occult powers in Beng practice, see Gottlieb 1989.

[12] For more on Beng diviners, see Gottlieb 1996: Ch. 2, Gottlieb and Graham 1994.

fashion, when offering a sacrifice to forest spirits, people put some *sɛpɛ* on the ground next to the item being left for the spirits.

Beyond diviners and artists, ordinary people may be said occasionally to have 'spirits behind them.' For example, if someone falls sick and consults a diviner, the diviner may diagnose that the patient 'has spirits behind' him or her. The diviner may specify that these spirits 'want' statues carved for them; the sculptures would generally be carved to represent the same gender as is attributed to the spirit. Once having commissioned a sculptor to carve such a statue to draw or even house the forest spirit, the sculpture's owner should clothe the statue and keep it inside the house.

More dramatically, some people are said to 'come from' the world of the bush spirits. In this case, some identifying feature usually distinguishes them visually from most of their peers. For example, people with red hair are said to be gifts from particular forest spirits, who bestowed the person as a newborn on a human family. Generally, a spirit gives a red-haired infant to a parent (of either gender) who is a member of the clan that is associated with that spirit's shrine. While such red-haired people are still children, their parents must regularly offer sacrifices to the donor spirits to thank them for their gift; when they are grown, these redheads offer the necessary sacrifices themselves.

Such a child, as a 'child of the spirits,' can often 'see clearly,' being attributed powers of a clairvoyant. As with other people who are judged *kalɛ*, a red-haired child can often predict when there will be a death in the village. Foreseeing the death, the clairvoyant will start privately celebrating the funeral by tapping drums, crying, and singing funeral songs, without revealing the name of the person whose death he or she has forecast.

A red-haired child may be given certain ritually powerful objects with which to dance, to attract spirits that would allow the child to become a diviner and a healer. When a red-haired girl is initiated to be married, she may announce that because of her connection with bush spirits, she needs certain items as gifts to maintain her ties to the *bɔŋzɔ*, such as a white chicken, a white *pagne* cloth, and a white dress. The red hair itself is considered to be both powerful and a source of vulnerability. When red-haired children get a haircut, they put the cut hair in a separate covered pot that is kept by their father (as adults, red-haired individuals may maintain the pots themselves). This is to protect them: if someone were to get hold of some of their locks of hair, it is thought, the thief might sell the hair to witches in exchange for some 'meat' to 'eat.'

A woman may experience a premonition that she may bear a red-headed child in the future as a gift from the spirits. Here is a case I recorded from my field notes of one such instance:

> One day 'Akissi' was in bed and thought she saw a bush spirit on her, wearing a white *pagne*. She told this to the Master of the Earth in her village, who explained that the being she had seen was a particular male *bɔŋzɔ* from the forest. The spirit had appeared as a way to announce that he intended to bestow a daughter on Akissi some time in the future. The Master of the Earth instructed Akissi to perform a sacrifice to the spirit the following Friday. The sacrifice was to be of a particular sort that the Beng call called *folie*, which consists of yam *foutou* [see Note 4] with red palm oil plus an egg, all wrapped

together in a broad leaf. From then on, the Master of the Earth continued, every so often on a Friday, Akissi should offer this same sacrifice to the bɔŋzɔ, along with a liter of palm wine.

Akissi followed the instructions of the Master of the Earth, and some time later, she became pregnant and gave birth to a girl. The baby had somewhat reddish hair and was said to be a gift from the male forest spirit that had visited Akissi much earlier. After the birth, the Master of the Earth instructed Akissi that every Friday, she should continue to offer a *folie* sacrifice to the spirit, to thank him for having given her the baby girl.

The range of people discussed above who have unusual relations with the forest spirits clearly indicates how the spirits, while long ago rendered invisible and relegated to the forest, nonetheless continue to noticeably influence the lives of humans. But it is not only through their relations with exceptional people that the spirits remain connected to the human world. The spirits themselves reportedly maintain strong continuity with people's daily practices in their own quotidian lives: as with the ancient Greek gods, the lives of forest spirits recognized by the Beng are said to parallel in uncanny ways the lives of humans.

Thus the spirits are said to live in villages much like human villages. The cultural geography of the rain forest includes specific places that the Beng say are 'spirit villages,' and these are located in specific sites that Beng adults can readily identify. People attempt to steer clear of these sites so as not to disturb the spirits. Children are taught never to approach such places, which are considered exclusive property of the spirits. Should any human approach such an area, it is said that the spirits will take that person and never allow him or her to leave that part of the forest. The spirits are especially likely to congregate in the afternoons at the spots that the Beng have marked as shrines. It is said that any ordinary person who approaches a spirit at such a shrine will perceive the spirit in human form, into which it has changed, and will immediately die. It is taboo for people other than a Master of the Earth to approach these shrines in the daytime.

With the slash-and-burn method of agriculture that Beng farmers employ, Beng women are charged with burning off fields that were planted the previous year. Women are extremely careful to control their fires so as to prevent the fire from spreading to any part of the forest that is said to house an invisible spirit village. Most women are highly skilled at setting and containing their field burning, but occasionally a fire burns out of bounds. If a woman's fire accidentally goes out of control and an area identified as a spirit village is burnt down, the farmer leaves herself vulnerable to terrible punishment by the angry spirits, and disaster is said to ensue. One madwoman I knew was said to have been cursed by the spirits and gone mad after inadvertently burning down a part of the forest that is said to be the abode of spirits.[13]

In some spots where many spirits reportedly live, people say that the spirits want the nearby forest paths to remain well cleared, because many spirits share the paths with people. If the paths are left overgrown, the spirits are said to become angry and send illnesses to the village(s) that they consider responsible for maintaining the path.

---

[13] For another perspective on this madwoman, cf. Gottlieb 2004:105.

Not only do the spirits live in human-like villages; according to the Beng, the spirits also have the same bodily desires that rule humans. For example, they get hungry as humans do and they like to eat human food; however, being invisible, the forest spirits do not grow such food themselves. Instead, they rely on food provided to them by people. Some farmers plant fields near the places that humans have identified as spirit villages, and these farmers expect that the local bush spirits will help themselves to their crops. For this reason, people do not ask questions if they discover some crops missing from their fields, as they assume the absent items must have been taken by spirits who were feeding themselves.

Indeed, people say that the bush spirits come out of their villages once every six days (the length of the traditional Beng week) to eat yams and other crops growing in people's fields. Since this occurs every six days, the sixth day in the Beng week is designated as a 'rest day' from work for people: on this day (called *ba fɛ* for villages in the savanna region of the Beng area, and *po fɛ* for villages in the forest region), it is taboo (*sɔ̃ pɔ*) for people to enter into the forest to work in their fields or even to chop down trees or fetch water from forest ponds. On these days, the hill spirits are said to be out and about eating in the humans' fields, and if a farmer were to see the spirits, his or her life would be in danger. The spirit would flee, and the farmer would be required to apologize to the spirit by sacrificing a chicken; even so, death might be the spirits' punishment for having been seen by a human.

Within their 'villages,' spirits are said to be especially partial to living in certain species of trees in the forest. The tall *iroko* tree (*Chlorophora excelsa*, in the mulberry family) – sometimes called a West African teak because of its high-quality wood – is said by the Beng to be a spirit-sheltering tree *par excellence*.[14] If a Beng sculptor wishes to carve a statue from *iroko* wood, before cutting down the tree, he must first make an offering to the spirits that he assumes live in the tree.[15] With such an offering, the sculptor both apologizes for disturbing the spirits, and warns the spirits to vacate the tree and find another tree to serve as their abode elsewhere in the forest. Only by engaging in such a propitiatory sacrifice can a sculptor avoid disaster when he chops down the forest giant that is the *iroko* tree.

Not only do bush spirits reportedly live in human-like 'villages,' they are also said to be gendered. Male and female spirits are said to marry, have children, and generally structure their lives in ways that resemble the lives of human families. The *bɔŋzɔ* are reportedly partial to the colors red and white and wear a human style of clothing (*pagnes*) made from red or white cloth. People say that if a spirit sees a human child wearing red or white clothing while in the forest/fields, the spirit might be drawn to the child and might even think that the child is a spirit; in either case, the spirit is likely to take the child

[14] Technically an *iroko* tree is considered spiritually powerful – we might say, 'sacred' – only if it hosts a spirit. However, technically, any *iroko* tree might host spirits so in effect all *irokos* are regarded as 'sacred' because of their potential. The Beng also prize *iroko* trees because their hard wood makes excellent furniture; however, I never heard anyone claim that this was the reason for the tree's sacred connections.

[15] I use the masculine pronoun here intentionally because all Beng sculptors are male.

to raise as its own. To present such a tragic scenario, some human mothers avoid dressing their children in red or white clothes if they will be entering the forest, so as to reduce the likelihood that their children will be kidnapped by forest spirits.

Nevertheless, kidnapping does reportedly occur. In one case, a woman took her young grandson to the fields and lost track of him there. The village chief sent a messenger around the village to ask everyone present to look for the child, but no one was able to find him, and the boy stayed all night in the forest. The family sacrificed several white chickens to the spirits to ask that they release their child. The next day, the family found the child: reportedly, the spirits had returned him to the same spot from which they had taken him the previous day.[16]

Another case also involving a grandmother includes a more dramatic return. One day, a young boy went to the fields with his grandmother and wore red underpants. Having arrived at the fields, he lay down for a nap. His grandmother walked a short distance to throw away some garbage, and when she returned, the boy was gone. The grandmother screamed for him and walked all around the nearby fields but did not find her grandson. She returned to the village and also failed to find the boy. The village chief announced that every villager must immediately begin to look for the child both in the village and the forest, and that no one would be allowed to sleep until the child was found. Meanwhile, a diviner, Ajua, was consulted; after communicating with bush spirits, Ajua announced that a female spirit had taken the boy. Apparently this particular forest spirit had only one child and wanted a second child. She had seen the little boy, had been drawn to him – presumably because of his red underpants – and had taken him. However, her spirit husband had told her to return the child to his human family because the child was not eating and might die of hunger. If he died, his human family would be upset and realize that it was the spirits who had killed the boy, and then people would no longer plant fields in that area of the forest. In this case, how would the spirits eat? The next day, the spirit husband threatened to kill his wife unless she returned the child to his human grandmother.

Hearing all this from the bush spirits, the diviner instructed the villagers to offer a guinea hen to the female spirit, who might be willing to accept this domesticated fowl as a replacement for the child and would then return the boy to his family. The fowl was soon offered, and a woman who went to the fields saw the young child standing all alone in the forest, a bit dazed, and hungry. Reportedly, the female spirit had taken the boy's red underpants, which she had liked. To replace them, she had wound together a black and white string and had tied this cord around the child's waist; on these, she had threaded several items that are considered to have spiritual significance in the Beng world: two small horns of a certain species of duiker (*gbɛ*), two small brown beads (called *cecɛŋwlɛ*), two large black beads (called *bomblo trì*), and two cowry shells – one on each duiker horn. The diviner instructed the boy's

---

[16] For another perspective on the close relations between young children and spirits, see Gottlieb 2004.

family always to guard this special cord carefully. When he outgrew it, his family kept the spirit's waistband hanging on the wall inside the house.

As these cases suggest, the bush spirits maintain an active presence in the lives and minds of village-dwelling Beng. Despite the fact that the two sets of beings inhabit different worlds and that the spirits are said to be invisible to humans, their disparate worlds are nevertheless clearly interconnected. Indeed, this interconnection is actively maintained in both directions to the point that each discursively depends on the other for existence, despite the fact that these interconnections are hedged by rules, and each tries to maintain respect for the other by way of these rules. A delicate balance should be achieved as long as the rules for engagement are followed.

Nevertheless, the respect that Beng people routinely try to accord the spirits is not shared by all visitors to the region. When 'strangers' (*tiniŋ*) enter the area, they may be unaware of the invisible spirits that the Beng see in the forest; alternatively, if the visitors are monotheists – whether Christian or Muslim – they may ridicule the claim of the spirits' existence altogether.[17] Such visitors to the region may either inadvertently or even deliberately flout the rules that the Beng say the spirits demand of humans when entering their territory. A clash of cultural systems inevitably ensues. As an example, let us consider this story.

The rainy season had begun, and two large trucks bearing molasses from the sugar plantations in the north were heading down the road south to Abidjan to unload their sweet cargo. But the rains had degraded the dirt roads so much that one of the trucks became mired in a mud ditch on the side of a road leading through a hilly portion of the Beng region. The driver of the second truck endeavored to hitch his rig up to his colleague's vehicle and pull the first truck free, but this only resulted in the second truck getting stuck as well. A third rescue truck met the same unhappy fate. Beng villagers watching the spectacle unfold informed the drivers that as far as they were concerned, the trucks had by no means been subject to an 'accident.' Rather, bush spirits that live in the forest surrounding the hillside road had been offended by the weight, noise and polluting fumes of the trucks traveling through their territory; in protest, the forest-dwelling spirits had derailed the vehicles. Beng elders suggested that the drivers offer the bush spirits a chicken sacrifice by way of apology.

Now, not only were the drivers not Beng, they were also Muslims. Still, on hearing the Beng interpretation of the religious foundation of their unfortunate situation, the drivers agreed to sacrifice a chicken to the local forest spirits that their Beng hosts averred were the cause of the trucks' problems. Soon after the chicken was offered, a rescue truck arrived from the closest town and effectively pulled the trucks back onto the road. The Beng took the finale to this saga as legitimation of their dealings with the forest spirits.[18]

In this case, despite their own monotheistic orientation, strangers to the region demonstrated respect for the local polytheistic landscape in agreeing to

---

[17] For another perspective on 'strangers' in the Beng region – especially their effect on and relation to young children – see Gottlieb 2004:146–64.

[18] For a longer narration of this story, see Gottlieb and Graham 1994:204–8.

acknowledge the forest spirits' existence by offering them a sacrifice. A few years later, a somewhat similar event – this time involving loggers – had a much darker outcome.

To many actors in the contemporary world, the rain forest of the Beng region offers an entirely different source of power from that which the Beng attribute it. Rather than spiritual wealth, logging companies now view the forest as a source of financial wealth. According to the current Director of Waters and Forests in Côte d'Ivoire (who is a Beng man), the *iroko* is currently 'the most expensive tree on the market' (Boussou Koffi, August 3, 2004). In the Beng region, commercial logging began in the 1980s, especially focusing on irokos.[19] Currently, a large *iroko* tree might sell for up to 250,000 CFA in Côte d'Ivoire (Boussou Koffi, Aug. 3, 2004), with the Beng enjoying none of the profits when such a tree has come from their region.[20] The financial incentive is strong for logging companies, and the resultant level of deforestation already accomplished in Côte d'Ivoire by logging companies has now been well established for much of sub-Saharan Africa:

> [A]ccording to the FAO, Africa lost the highest percentage of rainforests during the 1980s of any biogeographical realm, a trend that continued from 1990-1995.
>
> Around the turn of the century, West Africa had some 193,000 sq. miles (500,000 sq. km) of coastal rainforest. However, the tropical forests of West Africa, mostly lowland formations easily accessible from the coast, have been largely depleted by commercial exploitation, namely logging, and conversion for agriculture. Now, according to the FAO 1997, only 22.8% of West Africa's moist forests remain, much of this degraded... countries like Cote d'Ivoire have suffered extensive forest loss as a result of commercial logging and agriculture...
>
> (Butler 2002)

Indeed, as of 1999-2000, Côte d'Ivoire was experiencing an annual loss of 4.3 percent of its forests (*ibid.*). Where the Beng see the large trees of the surrounding forest as the abode of invisible but powerful spirits whose complex demands must be vigilantly accommodated, capital flows redefine those same trees as the abode of cash that must be sought by any means and at all costs. Marx long ago argued that cash itself has become the ultimate fetish; in the Ivoirian rain forest, one sees two kinds of symbolic treasure locked into an irreconcilable, even fatal competition.

This competition is now being written on the bodies of loggers. Some years ago, several lumberjacks were sent by logging companies to chop down *iroko* trees in the Beng part of the rain forest. Well trained in the technicalities of their trade but ignorant of the hidden Beng landscape, the loggers chopped

---

[19] The two companies that have most recently logged in the Beng region are F.I.P. and INPROBOIS. (F.I.P. and INPROBOIS are members of the European Foundation for the Preservation of the African Forest Resource; see http://www.ifiasite.com/index.php?rub= Foundation&langue=en.) A third company, a subsidiary of MOBIO, was active in the Beng region early on but has not sent in loggers to the region in recent years (Boussou Koffi, August 2004). Loggers typically made deals with Beng villagers that resulted in the Beng receiving a relatively modest gift from the company, which they might or might not be able to use, in exchange for logging rights.

[20] As of June 2005, the exchange rate was 536 CFA = US$1.

down several *iroko* trees – those same trees that the Beng claim are the abode of local forest spirits – without offering the resident spirits any propitiatory sacrifices in advance. According to Beng reports, the spirits that made their home in the *iroko* trees were angered by the loggers destroying their residence without either asking forgiveness ahead of time or offering compensation after the fact. In cutting down the giant trees, some of the outsider lumberjacks were severely injured; others were killed by the very trees they were endeavoring to fell. Their surviving colleagues interpreted the tragedy as the result of the forest spirits' revenge. According to Beng reports, many loggers hearing of the events became fearful of the local forest spirits, and some refused to work in the region.

In short, those who have visited, or have even just passed through, the Beng area from afar have often experienced firsthand what they consider as the force of the Beng spirits, and they have then brought stories of their frightening adventures back to the cities. In these ways, to the extent that they are known outside their immediate region, the Beng have occupied a somewhat respected, somewhat feared place in the nation's cultural imaginary. While modernity makes its seemingly one-way march, the fiercely held religious traditions of the Beng have served as a potent counterweight to the seeming inevitability of social and religious change. Yet Beng spirits are not universally accepted. Spiritual and mechanistic causal schemes compete for discursive dominance in the local setting.[21]

Ecologists witness with increasing urgency the relentless destruction of the earth's forests, especially rain forests. According to some specialists, 'Today only one fifth of the world's original forest cover remains, and Global Forests Watch is predicting another 40 percent of the remaining forest will be lost in the next 10 to 20 years' (Semillero Africa 2000). In Ivory Coast, this trend is particularly insidious:

> Ivory Coast, the biggest timber exporter in Africa, lost about two-thirds (over 56%) of its closed forest in 20 years from 12 million ha in 1956 to 4 million in 1977 (Timberlake 1991). The annual rate of deforestation is 6.5%
> (Organization for Social Science Research in Eastern and Southern Africa n.d.).

More recently, the ongoing civil war in Côte d'Ivoire (for which a peace accord was signed in January 2003 but which is still causing continued local upheaval as of this writing) has fully disrupted logging activity in the Beng region.

In any case, although three companies retain interests in the Beng rain forest, it is unclear whether logging will recommence when the political disturbances are finally settled. Regardless of the national outcome of the civil war, according to the director of the nation's Waters and Forests Ministry, nearly all of the *irokos* in the Beng region have already been cut down, with no efforts at replanting (Boussou Koffi, August 4, 2004). The timber companies seem to have focused entirely on short-term gain with no thought of sustainability even of their profits, let alone of the forest itself.

---

[21] For another set of perspctives on how different forces are vying for dominance in a complex geopolitical Ivoirian landscape, cf. Hellweg 2004.

As I have suggested, with each felling of a tree in the Beng section of the rain forest, another trunk of cultural significance was felled too. As the Beng see it, not only the trees but the spirits who they say inhabit those trees are under siege. When a spirit's abode is destroyed, the spirit will endeavor to find another nearby *iroko* to inhabit; failing that, the Beng say, the spirit will have to go farther afield to locate a new home. Unlike in northern Benin, where forest-based deities may remain despite dwindling resources (Siebert, personal communication, Jan. 31, 2005), in the worst-case scenario the Beng can imagine that all the spirits would abandon the Beng region altogether.

While this is barely thinkable to most Beng, it remains to be seen which regime of the forest – economic and discursive alike – prevails.

* For support of my research among the Beng, and for granting me the luxury of time to write up the material over the years, I am grateful to the John Simon Guggenheim Memorial Foundation, National Endowment for the Humanities, Wenner-Gren Foundation for Anthropological Research, Social Science Research Council, United States Information Agency, and several units at the University of Illinois (Center for Advanced Study, Research Board, and Center for African Studies). For intellectual support during my field research, I owe a continuing debt to more members of the Beng community than I have space here to enumerate. Here, let me acknowledge in particular Bertin Kouakou Kouadio (currently a Beng doctoral student in international relations at Florida International University) and Boussou Koffi (a Beng currently serving as Directeur Général des Eaux et Forêts de Côte d'Ivoire) who helped update information concerning contemporary forestry practices in the Beng region.

For perspicacious comments on this chapter, I am grateful to Ute Siebert. Small portions of this chapter appeared in different form in Gottlieb 2004.

References

Butler, Rhett, 1996–2002, 'Tropical rainforests: African deforestation and forest data'. Mongobay.com. Available online at: http://www.mongabay.com/rates_africa.htm.

Gottlieb, Alma, 1989, 'Witches, kings, and the sacrifice of identity; or, the power of paradox and the paradox of power among the Beng of Ivory Coast'. In *Creativity of Power: Cosmology and Action in African Societies*, W. Arens and Ivan Karp, eds, pp. 245–72. Washington, DC: Smithsonian Institution Press.

—— 1996 [1992], *Under the Kapok Tree: Identity and Difference in Beng Thought*. Chicago, IL: University of Chicago Press.

—— 2004, *The Afterlife is Where we Come From: The Culture of Infancy in West Africa*. Chicago: University of Chicago Press.

—— and Philip Graham, 1994 [1993], *Parallel Worlds: An Anthropologist and a Writer Encounter Africa*. Chicago: University of Chicago Press.

Hellweg, Joseph, ed., 2004, Special issue: 'Mande hunters, civil society and the state'. *Africa Today* 50 (4).

Organization for Social Science Research in Eastern and Southern Africa, n.d., Social Science Research Report No. 13. Organization for Social Science Research in Eastern and Southern Africa. Available online at: http://www.ossrea.net/ssrr/no13/no13-01.htm

Ray, Benjamin, 1999, *African Religions: Symbol, Ritual, and Community* (2nd edn). Upper Saddle River, NJ: Prentice-Hall.

Semillero Africa, 2000, 'Developments in development – Global forests watch monitors threatened forests worldwide'. *Semillero Africa* 1 (3). Washington, DC: International Center New Forests Project. Available online at: http://www.newforestsproject.com.

Timberlake, L., 1991, *Africa in Crisis: The Causes, the Cures of Environmental Bankruptcy*. 2nd edn. London: Earthscan.

Tockman, Jason, 2001, 'The IMF: Funding deforestation. American Lands Alliance'. November 2001. Available online at: http://www.wrm.org.uy/bulletin/54/Co.

10

Are Sacred Forests in Northern Bénin 'Traditional Conservation Areas'?
Examples from the Bassila Region

UTE SIEBERT

This chapter addresses the question of whether sacred forests in the Bassila Region of northern Bénin can be regarded as 'traditional conservation areas' and whether such areas can form a basis for forest conservation today. There is a new trend in international conservation programs, stressing the importance of cultural and religious values of local populations in their interaction with the environment. The following will discuss these new conservation ideas from a social science perspective and assessments will be made based on empirical examples. The chapter is based on findings from anthropological fieldwork carried out in 1999 and 2000. It will present some of the arguments made in my Ph.D. thesis on sacred forests of five villages of the Bassila region (Siebert 2004). While the thesis looks at people's actions towards sacred forests from both a diachronic and a contemporary perspective, I focus in this chapter on diachronic processes in relation to sacred forests in northern Bénin.

During fieldwork, an actor-oriented approach was chosen in order to take into account the roles, interactions and interests of relevant actors in relation to sacred forests. These actors included male and female farmers belonging to different age groups and religions; the traditional authorities such as village chiefs, priests, and healers; officials of the state forest service and members of conservation NGOs; agents of a forestry project financed by German development aid, and loggers. Research methods included participatory observation, semi-structured and structured interviews, group discussions, non-structured conversations and oral history methods.

Culture and Religion in Conservation Programs

Within the context of a shift in the development paradigm from top-down to participatory approaches and community-based natural resource management

164

schemes, a new trend developed within conservation organizations in the 1990s. In contrast to conventional conservation approaches, which often aim at excluding people from their environment, many conservation organizations have become more interested in 'integrative approaches' and 'cultural factors.' While the former approaches stressed the separation of nature and people, the new position underscores the fact that people often shape their environments and biodiversity in a positive way. The chief scientist of the International Union for the Conservation of Nature (IUCN) stresses that the protection of biodiversity requires conservation of the culture and traditional lifestyle of people who interact with specific forms of biological diversity (McNeely 2002:1-2). Other conservation organizations such as UNEP (Posey 1999), Greenpeace (2001) and the German Association for Nature Conservation (NABU) (1998) in their publications and programs also emphasize the important role of 'traditional cultural values' for sustainable behavior towards the environment.

In the new 'cultural policies' of many conservation organizations, spiritual and religious values are frequently mentioned for their significant function in conservation. A good example of the new cultural approach is the 'Natural Sacred Sites' project, which was formed between 1996 and 1998 within the ecology division of UNESCO. This project asserted that hotspots of biodiversity in Africa, Asia and Latin America may be conserved through religious values and taboos. Sacred forests, mountains, rivers and lakes were mentioned as 'examples of traditional conservation' (UNESCO 1997) and a sacred forest in Northern Ghana appeared on a list of potential project sites. The project founder suggested that 'religious beliefs as a determining factor in human behavior have often been ignored by Western conservationists or development experts' (Schaaf 1999:342).

The new conservation trend assumes that biodiversity can be conserved by preserving culture and religious norms. Conservationists also often understand so-called 'natural' sacred sites as traditional conservation areas. Translating sacred sites in such a way often assumes that religious norms are readily compatible with conservation goals. For example, Amoaka-Atta has emphasized that the 'study of the taboos and practices surrounding sacred groves ... lends great credit to the conservationist instincts of the rural forefathers' (Amoako-Atta 1995:87). Embedded in these assertions is the assumption that religious norms determine human action and that people act sustainably based on such norms.

It is important to note that, in the sources cited above, there is a significant lack of empirical evidence for justifying the assumptions made by the cultural conservationist position on religious norms. From the perspective of social anthropology, this new policy trend appears to rely on a rather static, isolated and romanticized concept of culture. Furthermore, determining relationships between norms and action has been sharply questioned within social anthropology. Current research in Africanist social anthropology and sociology underscores the malleable character of social structures and the flexibility of individuals in dealing with social norms. Instead of asking how well individual interests adapt to social norms, more recently the focus is on ways in which social actors adjust norms to fit their interests. In this respect, the work of Anthony Giddens (1988) is especially relevant since he stresses the flexible scope of action of social actors in the face of social norms and emphasizes the constant potential for social change.

Social scientists such as Helbling (1999) and Pedersen (1995) have recently discussed some of the assumptions made by the new cultural conservationist approach. They doubt that norms *determine* action and simultaneously call into question the assumption that one can infer ecological action from the existence of norms. However, the authors present their arguments rather briefly based on scant empirical data. Since there is a near-complete lack of empirical evidence to support the conservationist position on religious norms in Africa, and relatively little empirical data on this issue in the social science literature, my research examines norms and actions regarding sacred forests from a historical and contemporary perspective. In this chapter, I evaluate the conservation potential of African sacred groves. I discuss the question of whether sacred forests of the Bassila region of Bénin can function as 'traditional conservation areas,' and how the relationship between norms and action regarding sacred forests can best be understood.

Empirical Examples

The setting

I chose the Bassila region of northern Bénin for this study because it has the richest forest resources in the country. It is situated 350 kilometers from the Atlantic coast in the northern Guinea savanna zone, close to the Togolese border. A mosaic of savanna and dense semi-deciduous forest prevails. In this region, the Anii and the Nago are the two major language communities. Their ancestors settled in the region several centuries ago, coming from other regions in Bénin, Togo, Ghana, Burkina Faso, and Mali. Due to their mixed ethnic origins, it is more correct to speak of Nago- or Anii-speaking people rather than labeling them as two separate ethnic groups (Elwert 2001:136, Siebert 2004:104). These societies were independent closed corporate communities that strongly identified with their shared settlements, and due to frequent external attacks they built up a 'highly organized community of defense' (Elwert 1997:174). Each village developed a unique form of ceremonial and religious life. Even though many aspects of social organization are similar in Nago and Anii villages today, elements of local religion (such as gods and ceremonies) still tend have a rather localized character.

The following discussion presents the cases of two Anii-speaking villages (Kodowari and Mboroko) and two Nago-speaking villages (Kikélé and Igbéré). Two of the villages are located next to big roads while the other two are situated in rather isolated areas. Shifting cultivation of food crops is the predominant form of land use in the area among both men and women. Agroforestry and non-timber forests products supplement the local diet. In Kikélé and Kodowari, men also engage in the cultivation of cash crops such as cotton. Resources such as forests, sacred groves, creeks and rivers are owned by lineage groups. The lineage head distributes land, hunting and fishing rights to the male lineage members who grant temporary use rights to their wives and new settlers.

Local concepts of sacred forests

It is important to note that terms such as 'sacred forests' and the French expression 'forêt sacrée,' commonly used in the local French jargon of the Bassila Region, are external categories that do not fully grasp the local notions of such forests. Generally speaking, there is neither a concept of 'sacredness' in the local languages, nor is there an opposite notion of 'profanity.' Instead, supernatural and spiritual elements and beliefs are often intertwined with the normality of daily life. 'Forest' in the Nago language can be translated as *igbo*, and in Anii as *gudo*. Both concepts apply to dense forest vegetation that is hard to penetrate. In contrast, the concepts of *odan* (Nago) and *ukuraka* (Anii) indicate savanna and grassland with occasional trees (tree savanna) and herbs.

When people speak of sacred forests they add modifiers to their general concept of forest, describing the forest's function or content: 'Taboo forest' (Nago: *igbo iwo*, Anii: *amara gudo*), 'god forest' (Nago: *igbo ɔnsa*, Anii: *ukono gudo*) or 'ceremony forest' (Nago: *igbo oro,* Anii: *asile gudo*). Taboos or norms for sacred forests consist of prohibitions against cutting trees or lighting fires. The whole village population works to prevent bushfires from entering a sacred forest. Today there are two main physical forms of sacred forests in the Bassila region: some forests surrounding a village are called 'forest of the village' (Nago: *igbo ilelu*, Anii: *gufaldo*), and in the past most villages of the region were situated in the middle of a small forest in order to defend the settlement against intruders. These forest circles contained gods (Nago: *ɔnsa*, Anii: *ukono*)[1] who protected the village inhabitants against wars, raids, droughts, infertility of both land and women, poverty, accidents and sickness. By establishing reciprocal relationships and humanizing these forest gods, the villagers sought to control external forces. The forest gods were formerly ambivalent and free-floating spirit-beings (in Nago: *anjɔni*, in Anii: *ijini*) who materialized into gods in the forest.[2] The forest gods demand respect, but since they are soothed by regular feeding, they are generally well-disposed towards humans. The second type of sacred forests is more common today. These forests are remnants of the forest circles and consist of small forest patches close to the village that still accommodate the protective forest gods. Thus, they are either called 'god forest' (Nago: *igbo ɔnsa*, Anii: *ukono gudo*) or carry the name of a specific forest god.

Even though their physical traits are different, both types of sacred forests still bear the same social and religious meanings. It is important to note that for both forms of forests the expression 'sacred forest' is misleading because from

---

[1]   In local French jargon they are called 'fétiche' (without the negative European connotation attached to this term).

[2]   The gods either materialized themselves, indicating their location to a clairvoyant, or the spirits were called by powerful priests into a forest or tree and thus turned into localized gods.

a local perspective, a forest is not worshipped in itself but is rather the location of a god or a shrine. Since forest gods favor cool, moist air and shady areas, they prefer to dwell among large trees such as *Khaya senegalensis*, *Ceiba pentandra*, *Adansonia digitata* or *Chlorophora excelsa*. Such trees cannot, however, be considered as 'sacred species' in the Bassila Region since they lose their special status if a god decides to move elsewhere.

According to local perceptions of the land, there is a marked dichotomy between domesticated human space and wilderness.[3] Sacred forests belong to the human sphere of villages and farms, because humans maintain close and reciprocal relationships with the forest gods. Unlike sacred forests, other forests belong to an ambivalent sphere of semi-human space (when close to a settlement) and to the more remote wild sphere of 'bush' inhabited by spirits.

From 'Village Forests' to 'God Forests'

Evidence from oral history data suggests that sacred forests in the Bassila region of Bénin underwent considerable physical transformations starting in the 1960s, namely the conversion from 'village forests' (large forest circles enclosing villages) to 'god forests' (small patches of forest). A diachronic perspective is important to show what this change means for people's uses of both sacred forest resources and the norms that protect them. It is crucial to note that oral history data consist of subjective memories, perceptions and judgments which are embedded in the interests and perspectives of the present. Even though oral history data can serve as a source for tentative reconstructions, the historical processes presented below are based on congruent data from many informants in different villages. Also, the meanings of village names support the data given by my informants.

In the following, the first example of Kikélé will be presented. Today, Kikélé is a village of approximately 800 Nago-speaking inhabitants. It is located seven kilometers from Bassila (a town of approximately 3000 inhabitants) on the road to the city of Parakou, which is located about 100 kilometers to the east. According to village elders, the ancestors of the current population arrived as several small lineage groups from Southern and Central Bénin and from Togo in the early sixteenth century. Seeking security in unity, the ancestors settled in the center of a forest island in the savanna in order to defend themselves against raids of slave hunters from the kingdom of Allada and Dahomey in the south and the Baatombu kingdom of Nikki in the north. The name Kikélé is derived from *man kekere oke* (in Nago, 'children of the small hard village'), referring to its successful defense against external attacks. The people of Kikélé called the forest encircling their village *igbo laku* ('big forest'). They built large ramparts within the forest and reinforced them with thorny plants from the savanna to keep aggressors at bay. Only a small path led through *igbo laku* into the village, which could be closed up by a thorny thicket. This

---

[3]   For similar understandings of the environment in West Africa, see Croll and Parkin 1992, Van Beek and Banga 1992, Leach 1992 and Van den Breemer 1992.

defensive forest was further enhanced by the spiritual powers of the forest god *osumare*. This god was responsible for the protection against raids, illness, droughts and infertility. *Osumare* lived in a shrine under a big tree in the forest because he preferred cool and shady areas. Protective norms (*iwo*) for the forest were established, which included the prohibitions on cutting trees and lighting fires. Since the danger of attacks from other villages was constant, women and children stayed in the village as much as possible. Only during planting and harvest seasons did they leave the village and help the men at work in the fields located outside of the defensive forest. As they toiled, an elder would sit in a tree and scan the area for enemies.

According to my oral history interviews, changes in the physical form of this defense forest occurred due to several factors, starting with the growing presence of French colonial power from 1910 onwards. Around 1920, the French enforced their *pax colonialis* in the region by prohibiting slave raiding, feuding, and attacking neighboring villages. The new peace enabled village populations to move more freely around the region and to increase interactions with the northern town of Djougou, a regional religious and economic center. In the 1930s, the colonial peace fostered population growth in Kikélé. Informants gave the following reasons for this expansion: due to peace, there were no casualties in attacks anymore and people felt that there was no need to limit family size in order to maximize flexibility in case of attack. This population growth led to a rather cramped situation inside the boundary of the *igbo laku*.[4] According to oral history data, however, the people of Kikélé endured overcrowded conditions until 1960 because the presence of the French colonial power was threatening to them: the French had not only introduced peace but also forced labor (construction of roads), recruited soldiers by force, and collected a poll tax. The people of Bassila were more exposed to such dangers because the small town hosted the regional colonial administrative headquarters. In contrast, the inhabitants of Kikélé preferred to hide inside the forest circle when colonial officers came close to the village. Consequently, they were able to selectively establish contacts with the world outside the village. For example, Chabi Ota Imorou (75 years old) remembered how the French frequently passed the forest of Kikélé without realizing that there was a village inside. Thus, *igbo laku* maintained its function as a physical and spiritual defense against external threats until the end of the colonial regime. It was only after the political independence of Dahomey (today's Bénin) in 1960, when the last French colonial officer had left the region, that people in Kikélé gave up their defensive strategy. By this time, the village was bursting demographically. The negative effects of the overcrowded village were most intensely felt by the younger men and women who, due to lack of space, had to stay with their parents. Chabi Ota Imorou remembered:

> At the time when the colonials took slaves for their own wars, the people of Kikélé conserved their dense forest. But when they realized that the French had left, after

---

4 Due to a lack of official statistics on the region's demographic development for the mentioned period, it is not possible to supplement oral history accounts with exact numbers. However, since oral history interviews in five villages and the town of Bassila provide congruent information, it is likely that population growth was considerable in the region.

independence, many young men said: Ah! Now, we can destroy the forest, there is no problem anymore. We can now build our own houses and work on our own fields
(Siebert 2004:124)[5]

Thus, after the end of external threats in the 1960s, young men debated issues concerning the forest circle with traditional authorities of Kikélé. The young men wanted to build houses and establish farms on the land of the *igbo laku* forest. Based on the social structure of the village community, most of them were economically and socially dependent on their fathers. Before they were married, they had to work in their father's fields and train as warriors in order to defend the village. However, they were only allowed to marry once their elder brothers had married. Only after the wedding did they receive their own fields and become eligible to build their own houses. Very often, young men had to live with their parents and work for their father for many years; in some cases they were never able to marry and establish their own households. In the 1960s, therefore, after the youth's work as soldiers had become obsolete, they realized that they had new economic opportunities in trade if they oriented themselves beyond the boundaries of the village. In this process, they began to perceive *igbo laku* as an obstacle in the quest for new economic and social independence.[6] Many of the young men embraced new identities as Muslims, although only a few of them were in fact sons of the first Muslims of the village. The new faith had emerged in Kikélé in the 1920s through trade relations with Djougou, and the village's first mosque was established in 1940.[7] The young men started to interpret the old ceremonies and taboos around the forest god as pagan practices. Maman Ousmane (59 years old) was one of the young Muslims. He recalls: 'For us, preserving the old defense forest did not make sense anymore. We reasoned that as Muslims, the norms and taboos for the forest god did not apply to us and we did not accept the old order of things any longer' (Siebert 2004:126). Therefore, the young Muslims were not impressed when the elders threatened them with the old sanctions of supernatural illness or death. But since the young men could not completely ignore traditional land regimes, they started to discuss options with the traditional authority figures of the village chief, the forest priest, and the earth priest.[8] In these negotiations, the young men asked for permission to cut some sections of the forest. When the three elders refused them, the young men threatened

---

[5]   The original interviews were in French; the English translation is that of the author.

[6]   Sheridan (2004) shows how similar socio-economic developments and changes in actions towards the environment occurred in post-independence Tanzania. In the region of North Pare in the 1960s, young men were more interested in the fertile soil of sacred forests than in preserving them as ceremonial areas (2004:89).

[7]   In the Bassila region, Sunnite Islam is predominant. Contrary to studies on Islamic practice in West Africa which analyze forms of Islam influenced by Sufism and local religions (for example Hunwick 1997, Rosander 1997, and Westerlund 1997), Islam in Bassila follows the teachings of Mohammed very closely and is characterized by rather modest and sober prayers, weddings, and funerals. There is no integration of elements of local religions.

[8]   The earth priest is the head of the lineage whose ancestors founded the village. This lineage owns the land on which the village is located. Sometimes, the earth priest is also responsible for the god in the village forests. But in some cases like in Bassila, the forest priest is another member of the same lineage that established the village.

to leave the village. This threat proved effective, since many young people were leaving the region for better economic options in bigger towns or neighboring countries. The elders were afraid of losing the labor contributions of the younger generation for agriculture, construction, and other community tasks. The forest priest, village chief and earth priest and other elders were now faced with the dilemma of keeping the forest god satisfied while simultaneously accommodating the needs of the young people. In 1967, at last, the elders consulted *osumare*, the forest god, to explain the generational and economic problem to him. The god proved to be understanding of the situation and offered a compromise: in exchange for a compensatory sacrifice,[9] the young men were allowed to cut part of the forest circle if they left enough trees around his shrine to keep him hidden and shaded from the sun. The village chief and forest priest showed the young men the areas open for clearing. Consequently, the forest circle was opened up for village and farmland expansion, and so was finally reduced to a relatively small grove surrounding the shrine of *osumare*. What was formerly called *igbo laku* or village forest was re-labeled *igbo çnsa*, the 'forest of the god'. With this compromise, the elders felt that the forest had not completely lost its importance because the god's will had been respected and thus his spiritual protective functions remained intact. In negotiating with the forest god they had to make concessions to the young men, but they were nonetheless able to assert their social and cultural capital and interpretative power concerning the norms and taboos. Furthermore, this compromise secured the existence and relevance of *osumare*.

Similar developments occurred in the Anii-speaking village of Kodowari (which now has approximately 850 inhabitants), which is located on the road to Djougou. Originally, Kodowari was located in a dense forest, roughly two kilometers away from the road to Djougou. Its name is derived from the term *nkondowar*, which means 'people of the house in the forest' in Anii. Until the end of the colonial period, the people of Kodowari remained inside their defensive forest in order to avoid contact with the colonial state, as 80-year old Akoui Moumouni and other elders recalled. As in Kikélé, however, oral history data indicate that the village population had increased dramatically since the 1920s and that when the colonials left the region, young men of the village wanted to settle on the road to Djougou. Most of these young men were Muslims and traders, so the road promised enhanced commercial activity. At first, their elders prohibited the young men from leaving the village, arguing that they could not live without the protection of the forest god *gudoni*. The young men were not intimidated by such statements, citing the power of their new faith. Finally in 1963, the elders gave in and agreed to move the whole village to the new site along the road.[10] Some villagers who had been labor

---

[9] Since *osumare* prefers white and sweet food, he asked for bananas, milk and white roosters.

[10] Some informants of Kodowari remember their childhood in the village in the forest circle. They talk about the comforting cool climate provided by trees and mention that they felt secure in the forest. Today, they deplore being exposed to the sun and destructive winds. Some of them have started to plant teak trees around the village in order to protect themselves against storms. Also, old people in Bassila say that they now live in the open savanna (some even say 'desert') and that they feel insecure and uncomfortable. Most male and female

migrants in Ghana suggested transforming the old forest into a plantation of banana and teak. They reasoned that in the absence of war, the functions of the forest circle were well outdated. The forest priest of *gudoni* realized that it was time to negotiate with his god. In exchange for a compensatory sacrifice, *gudoni* approved of the transformation of large parts of the forest circle. Later, when bush fires for clearing land in the new farming zone threatened the *gudoni*, the forest priest asked the forest god to move closer to the village. Lacking an alternative forest adjacent to the new village site at the side of the road, *gudoni* accepted a single large tree as substitute for his dense forest.

In contrast to Kikélé and Kodowari, there are very few villages in the region whose forest circle is still intact. Igbéré with its *igbo ilelu* (forest of the village) and Mboroko with its *gufaldo* (village forest) are two cases in point. In comparison with the first two settlements, it is interesting to ask why these villages preserved their forest circles. Are the inhabitants of Igbéré and Mboroko more in line with religious norms?

Both villages are relatively isolated, located next to small bumpy roads off the main roads of the region. Igbéré is a Nago-speaking village of approximately 600 inhabitants, situated 45 kilometers east of Bassila. Mboroko, a small Anii-speaking village of roughly 160 people, is located 30 kilometers north of Bassila. According to oral history accounts, despite a population increase between 1940 and 1960, there was less pressure on village lands within the forest circles because so many young people had left the villages in the 1960s. Many of them migrated to bigger towns or cities in Bénin, others found work in Nigeria and Ghana. Whereas young farmers in Kikélé and Kodowari were able to engage in trade from the 1960s onwards, this option was not available for the young men of Igbéré and Mboroko. Even today, young men in both villages have scarce economic possibilities and look for sources of income elsewhere. For example, whereas young farmers in Kikélé and Kodowari can engage in lucrative cotton farming today, this is not possible in Igbére and Mboroko because access to both villages is still so difficult that the trucks from the state agency for cotton marketing do not pick up the harvest.

In the 1970s and 1980s, however, the people of Igbéré were confronted by a saw mill located 20 kilometers to the west.[11] The loggers were especially keen to cut large trees located inside of the forest circle, so the forest priest asked the forest gods *ilelu* and *okuta laku* for permission to cut trees in their abode. Both gods agreed in exchange for compensatory sacrifices. In Mboroko, on the other hand, there was no need to negotiate with the forest gods because the people had decided to move outside of the forest circle when the village finally proved to be too small in 1990. This happened because the ground of the

[10] (cont.) informants (over 40 years) say that felling of forests causes climate change and droughts today. They often link forests with moisture and abundant fertility whereas savanna is associated with limited fertility and drought.

[11] The first logging activities in the Bassila region started at the end of the 1950s with the arrival of a French entrepreneur who installed the first saw mills. By the 1980s, five saw mills with over 200 loggers operated in the area. At the end of the 1980s, when timber resources grew scarce, the saw mills closed down and logging shifted to small-scale local entrepreneurs organized in informal networks (Siebert 2004: 157–8, cf. also Siebert and Elwert 2004).

gufaldo forest circle is very rocky and bumpy, and it was not considered suitable for expanding the settlement and fields. Therefore, the people of Mboroko decided that it was better to leave the forest circle intact, move the village outside, and use the former village site for horticulture and agroforestry. The new village is situated about 200 meters away from the *gufaldo*, and is now surrounded by open savanna, which poses no problem for further expansion of field and village.

In the cases of Kikélé and Kodowari, the older defensive and metaphysical institutions of the village forest were questioned by young men in the context of drastic political and economic changes. These oral history data show that actors are constructively engaged with their own social norms, and that they have the power to change or reproduce the social structure. These examples of changing social norms and resource use patterns support Giddens' notion that norms help social actors to make sense of social structure and order (1988:70). 'Making sense' in this context also means that the effect and goals of certain norms are comprehensible and legitimate for members of that society. Of course, sense alone is insufficient: norms and sanctions in case of non-compliance are only socially accepted if people consent to the power that enforces the norms and sanctions (*ibid.*:229).

In the cases of Kikélé and Kodowari, the process of questioning the usefulness of the institution of the village forest and the legitimacy of the power enforcing the protective norms led to an altered reproduction of the norms. During precolonial periods of political and ecological uncertainty, it is likely that there was a tremendous desire for security in the region. The norms that secured the effectiveness of the physical and spiritual protection of the forest comprised symbols and practices that enhanced and institutionalized order. Of course, there may have been breaches of these norms, and the existence of sanctions points to this possibility. However, it is likely that such acts of noncompliance happened only at an *individual* level. In contrast, the *collective* act of calling into question the institution of the defense forest only occurred in the context of drastic political and economic changes, leading to new social and economic interests within larger groups of village societies.

The following factors shaped the reevaluation of the village forests and their norms: after the end of external threats (wars and colonial regime), the physical protection of the forest circles was no longer necessary. Simultaneously, the end of wars resulted in demographic growth. Due to this population increase, the forest circles turned into obstacles for the expansion of villages and fields. A new era of peace and mobility created more economic options. Young men established trading networks with the town of Djougou, and thus came into intense contact with the teachings of Islam. They began to strive for a degree of social and economic independence their fathers themselves had never had.[12] Islam became a means of self-emancipation in northern Bénin because it promised an alternative, more egalitarian social order to young men. One of the first young Muslims of the town of Bassila, 80-year-old Soulé Gomina,

---

[12] Similarly, Van den Breemer (1992:102f.,106) shows in the case of Aouan society (in Ivory Coast) how the struggle for social emancipation resulted in ecologically damaging practices towards forests.

stated: 'According to Islam, each man can build his own house, he can have several wives and work on his own fields.' (Siebert 2004:132). Sunnitic Islam, which is now common in the region, was a powerful tool for deconstructing obstructive cultural norms since it is characterized by a clear dichotomy of orthodox Islam and the practice of ('pagan') local religion. This form of Islam 'defines clear alternatives where change is sought, and raises the threshold for change by forcing any other system into a direct and open competition' (Elwert 1995:225). However, this does not mean that strategic values were the only reasons that young men turned to Islam. Most young men in northern Bénin at the time were convinced of Islam's superiority over local religions.

Young men did not only reject the old forest institutions with their norms and sanctions, they also threatened to leave the villages in case the traditional authorities did not pay attention to their new claims to land in the forests. In Kikélé and Kodowari, young men caused the old authorities to differentiate between the physical and the spiritual protective function of the forest. The village chiefs, earth and forest priests finally agreed that the physical protective function had become obsolete and that it was now possible to diminish the physical form of the forest circle. In this way, the old authorities both attended to the demands of the young men and avoided a loss of their own economic, social and cultural capital, which derived from their roles relating to the forest gods.[13] The result of these negotiations with the forest gods was a physical transformation of circular village forests into building sites, fields of crops, and small forest patches called 'god forests.' With regard to the cases of Igbéré and Mboroko, oral history data shows that the preservation of forest circles in both villages was not linked to a higher commitment to protective norms. Instead, there were no vested interests against diminishing the village forests and thus there was no need to negotiate for access to the forest circles.

Conclusion

Oral history data show that sacred forests in the Bassila region of Bénin functioned as a physical and spiritual defense against external threats until the 1960s. Local concepts of sacred forests reveal that the forests were not conceived as 'sacred' *per se*; they did not embody gods but merely served as *abodes* for them. Thus, gods and trees are not identical. Also, the protective norms did not actually protect the trees in the forest, but instead referred to the forest gods. There is no evidence that trees and forests in themselves were conceived as sacred or that they were protected for their own sake. Likewise, there is no evidence that trees were preserved for ecological reasons. Instead, trees and forests were only protected against felling and fire when they hosted forest gods. The example of Kodowari shows that once the forest god *gudoni* moved to a new site, it was unproblematic to transform its former abode into

[13] Economic capital in the form of payments for their ritual services, social capital in the form of social prestige and social relations, and cultural capital in the form of their knowledge of ritual procedures and language (see Bourdieu 1983 for a theoretical discussion of the three kinds of capital).

a plantation. Thus, it is not possible to infer an ecological consciousness or motivation from the existence of protective norms around sacred forests. In the same vein, it is impossible to deduce that rural Béninois lose some of their ecological sensitivity by cutting down sacred groves. Although conservationists often deplore the loss of a people's formerly harmonious relationship with the environment, empirical data show that there is a clear difference between the goals and motivations of local sociocultural norms and scientific conservation. The former protection of the forest circles had an *ecological side-effect* but did not aim at nature conservation itself. Thus, it is incorrect to interpret sacred forests in the Bassila region as 'traditional conservation areas' and take protective norms as examples of traditional conservation mechanisms. Such translations are ahistoric interpretations imposing contemporary Western conservation ideas on social institutions embedded in a completely different historical, social and political context.

Even if protective norms attached to sacred forests did not aim at conserving the forests themselves, is it still possible to use their ecological side-effect for conservation goals today? First, it is important to note that because the goals behind protective norms are radically different from the motivations of contemporary conservation, compatibility between the two is problematic. Second, in order to serve as a stable basis for conservation, such norms would have to considerably shape, if not determine, peoples' actions towards sacred forests. But the oral history accounts of Kikélé and Kodowari reveal flexible treatment of protective norms, resulting in the diminution of the forests or even in the substitution of a forest by a single tree. Even though there is not always general ambiguity between norms and action in society, there is always much room for maneuver between norms and action, especially in the context of rapid political and economic change. This is even more apparent as new social and economic interests develop and relationships of power within society change. The examples of Kikélé and Kodowari show that sacred forests are not static institutions. The existence of forest gods and protective norms did not prevent a reduction or destruction of sacred forests. As 75-year-old Soulé Maman of Kikélé explained, 'the gods go with our needs if we respect their desires, if we nourish them during our ceremonies' (Siebert 2004:134). Despite physical changes, sacred forests still play a central and lively role in village life today. Notwithstanding the strong influence of Islam, approximately 80 percent of the villagers still turn to the forest gods and their priests in case of need. The powers and attractiveness of the forest gods do not seem to have decreased with the transformation of their abodes.

Rather than basing forest conservation on religious norms around sacred forests, my empirical data have revealed that it is crucial to create economic incentives for conservation and sustainable management of forests. In interviews and conversations, many farmers showed interest in forest conservation if they were also able to use part of both sacred and non-sacred forests commercially for agroforestry, especially using cashew, teak, citrus, mango, and timber trees. Under such conditions, the historical and spiritual aspects of sacred forests may enhance the motivations for investment and conservation. However, they do not present sufficient motivation in themselves. But in case there are no alternative sources of income in the future, many informants pointed to the need to exploit the remaining forests. Consequently, in most villages in northern Bénin, forest priests are prepared to ask the forest gods for permission to further reduce the sacred forests.

References

Amoako-Atta, Boakye, 1995, 'Sacred groves in Ghana'. In *Cultural Landscapes of Universal Value.* Bernd von Droste, Harald Plachter, and Mechtild Rössler, eds, pp. 80–95. Jena: Gustav Fischer Verlag and UNESCO.

Bourdieu, Pierre, 1983, 'Ökonomisches Kapital, kulturelles Kapital, soziales Kapital'. In *Soziale Ungleichheiten: Sonderband Soziale Welt.* Reinhard Kreckel, ed., pp. 183–98. Göttingen: Schwartz.

Croll, Elisabeth and David Parkin, 1992, 'Cultural understandings of the environment'. In *Bush Base: Forest Farm: Culture, Environment, and Development.* E. Croll and D. Parkin, eds, pp. 11–36. London: Routledge.

Elwert, Georg, 1995, 'Changing certainties and the move to a "global" religion: Medical knowledge and Islamization among the Anii (Baseda) in the Republic of Bénin'. In *The Pursuit of Certainty: Religions and Cultural Formulations.* Wendy James, ed., pp. 215–33. London: Routledge.

——— 1997, 'Bénin'. In *Encyclopedia of Africa South of the Sahara.* John Middleton, ed., Vol. 4, pp. 168–79. New York: Charles Scribner's Sons.

——— 2001, 'Herausforderung durch das Fremde – Abgrenzung und Inkorporation in zwei westafrikanischen Gesellschaften unter wechselnden evolutiven Bedingungen'. In *Begegnung und Konflikt – eine kulturanthropologische Bestandsaufnahme.* Wolfgang Fikentscher, ed., pp. 132–44. Munich: Bayerische Akademie der Wissenschaften.

German Association for Nature Conservation (NABU), 1998, *Cultural Landscapes and Nature Conservation in Northern Eurasia.* Berlin: NABU.

Giddens, Anthony, 1988, *Die Konstitution der Gesellschaft.* Frankfurt/Main: Campus.

Greenpeace, 2001, *Greenpeace 2001.* Amsterdam: Greenpeace International.

Helbling, Jürg, 1999, 'Der Einfluss religiöser Vorstellungen, Normen und Rituale auf die Ressourcennutzung in einfachen Gesellschaften am Beispiel der Cree und der Maring'. In *Die Wahrnehmung von Natur und Umwelt in der Geschichte.* Peter Sieferle, ed., pp. 19–41. Frankfurt/Main: Campus.

Hunwick, John, 1997, 'Sub-Saharan Africa and the wider world of Islam: Historical and contemporary perspectives'. In *African Islam and Islam in Africa. Encounters between Sufis and Islamists.* Eva E. Rosander and David Westerlund, eds, pp. 28–54. London: Hurst.

Leach, Melissa, 1992, 'Women's crops in women's spaces: Gender relations in Mende rice farming'. In *Bush Base: Forest Farm: Culture, Environment, and Development.* E. Croll and D. Parkin, eds, pp. 76–96. London: Routledge.

McNeely, Jeffrey, 2002, 'The Nature of Biodiversity Protection'. Unpublished manuscript in possession of the author.

McNeely, Jeffrey, and William Keeton, 1995, 'The interaction between biological and cultural diversity'. In *Cultural Landscapes of Universal Value.* Bernd von Droste, Harald Plachter, and Mechtild Rössler, eds, pp. 25–37. Jena: Gustav Fischer Verlag and UNESCO.

Pedersen, Poul, 1995, 'Nature, religion and cultural identity. The religious environmentalist paradigm'. In *Asian Perceptions of Nature. A Critical Approach.* Ole Bruun and Arne Kalland, eds, pp. 258–76. Richmond: Curzon Press.

Posey, D. ed., 1999, *Cultural and Spiritual Values of Biodiversity.* Nairobi: UNEP.

Rosander, Eva E., 1997, 'Introduction: The Islamization of "tradition" and "modernity"'. In *African Islam and Islam in Africa. Encounters between Sufis and Islamists.* Eva E. Rosander and

David Westerlund, eds, pp. 1–27. London: Hurst.

Schaaf, Thomas, 1999, 'Environmental conservation based on sacred sites'. In *Cultural and Spiritual Values of Biodiversity*. D. Posey, ed., pp. 341–42. Nairobi: UNEP.

Sheridan, Michael, 2004, 'The environmental consequences of independence and socialism in North Pare, Tanzania, 1961–1988'. *Journal of African History* 45:81–102.

Siebert, Ute, 2004, 'Heilige Wälder und Naturschutz. Empirische Fallbeispiele aus der Region Bassila, Nordbénin'. Spektrum – Berliner Reihe zu Gesellschaft, Wirtschaft und Politik in Entwicklungsländern, No.88. Münster: Lit.

Siebert, Ute and Elwert, Georg, 2004, 'Combating corruption and illegal logging in Bénin, West Africa: Recommendations for forest sector reform'. *Journal of Sustainable Forestry* 19(1/2/3): 239–61.

UNESCO, 1997, 'Sacred Sites, Project Preparatory Phase'. Paris: UNESCO. UNESCO Project Document. Unpublished manuscript.

UNESCO, 1998, 'Sacred Sites – Cultural Integrity and Biological Diversity, Criteria'. Paris: UNESCO. Unpublished manuscript.

Van Beek, Walter and Pieteke Banga, 1992, 'The Dogon and their trees'. In *Bush Base: Forest Farm. Culture, Environment and Development*. E. Croll and David Parkin, eds, pp. 57–75. London: Routledge.

Van den Breemer, Jan, 1992, 'Ideas and usage: Environment in Aouan society, Ivory Coast'. In *Bush Base: Forest Farm. Culture, Environment and Development*. E. Croll and David Parkin, eds, pp. 97–109. London: Routledge.

Westerlund, David, 1997, 'Reaction and action: Accounting for the rise of Islamism'. In *African Islam and Islam in Africa. Encounters between Sufis and Islamists*. Eva E. Rosander and David Westerlund, eds, pp. 308–33. London: Hurst.

11

Archaeological Perspectives on Sacred Groves in Ghana

GÉRARD CHOUIN

Small clusters of trees, groves, and thick woods punctuate the landscape of southern Ghana. In the coastal area, these groves are often bounded by an almost impenetrable forested edge and stand in clear contrast with the surrounding farms and the savanna fallows made of shrubs at different stages of ecological succession (see Guelly, Roussel and Guyot 1993). Farmers know them by name, for they are visual references and geographic markers that structure the local perception of space. Drawing on recent discussions about forested landscapes in West Africa (e.g., Fairhead and Leach 1996, 1998), and locating the Ghanaian evidence within West Africa more broadly, I argue that sacred groves are human artifacts that may be studied for their historical, symbolic, and socio-political significance.

It was in the mid-1990s that I first came across these forests when I was recording oral traditions in Komenda-Edina-Eguafo-Abrem District, in the Central Region of Ghana. This area of approximately 400 square kilometers includes Elmina, one of the most important European fortified trading posts on the Gold Coast from the fifteenth to the nineteenth centuries. In Nsadwer, a small village northwest of Dutch Komenda, people told me about a forest called Aprem Enntum, which literally means 'cannon was not able.' I was struck by the word cannon, its associations with European military activities, and the use of the past tense. All suggested that this particular forest was related to a historical event. This drew my attention to sacred forests as places of memory (Juhé-Beaulaton 1999, Moniot 1999, Nora 1984), which might offer clues to reconstitute aspects of the pre-colonial social and political history of the area and facilitate our understanding of past landscapes and systems of symbolic representations.

Sacred Groves and Past Settlements in West Africa

Several social scientists working in West Africa have noted the connection between old settlement sites and sacred groves. As early as 1923, the British anthropologist Rattray identified a major archaeological site next to the sacred grove of Asantemanso. Located about 20 miles south of Kumasi, Ghana, the place was presented by the Ashanti as the spot where 'the first human beings came forth from the ground' (Rattray 1923:121). Excavations by Peter Shinnie and Brian Vivian confirmed the importance of the Asantemanso site for our understanding of long-term human occupation of the forest zone of Ghana. Several overlapping settlements have been discovered and dates provided by carbon-dating of charcoal suggest that the site was founded circa 800 AD (Shinnie 1988, Shinnie and Vivian 1991).

Overall, a growing body of documented evidence, gathered throughout the forest zone of West Africa, shows a strong correlation between past settlement sites and the occurrence of sacred groves (Davies 1964, Perrot 1982). Dominique Juhé-Beaulaton described a similar process in Bénin by explaining that 'an old settlement, abandoned for historical reasons, is respected because ancestors were buried there' (1999:111, my translation) – and therefore becomes a sacred grove. Togudo (the first capital of the Allada kings), Savi (capital of the kingdom of Whydah, conquered by Abomey in 1727), and many other abandoned historic settlements of the pre-colonial Slave Coast are still embedded in the Ghanaian landscape by such groves (Fairhead and Leach 1998:105).

Much evidence attests that the spatial correlation between old settlement sites and cemeteries and the existence of sacred groves is no coincidence. Old settlements were frequently turned into burial grounds and gradually recolonized by forest. The sacredness of these sites comes first from their association with the mortal remains of important ancestors, and consequently from their roles as territorial markers for local elites. Such a correlation is not ubiquitous, however; not all sacred groves are associated with archaeological sites, and conversely, not all archaeological sites are signaled by a sacred grove. This suggests that different historical processes might have led to the formation of similar anthropogenic environments.

Sacred Groves as Processes and Lieux de Mémoire

While a complex chain of ecological processes can account for the formation of a forested landscape, its consecration as a spiritual place is a historical event that converts the forest from a natural to a social entity – a sacred grove. In this process, members of a community identify a specific area in the landscape as a point of contact between the invisible and the human worlds, and establish a ritualized alliance with spiritual entities that dwell there. This process cannot be described in ecological terms alone.

In her discussion of sacred groves in Bénin, Juhé-Beaulaton (1999) distinguished 'created groves' (*bois créés*) from 'pre-existing groves' (*bois préexistants*). Such a typological distinction suggests the existence of different processes leading to the creation of sacred groves. In a preliminary account of Ghanaian sacred groves (Chouin 2002a), I suggested four categories:

- Groves 'discovered' during the clearing of new agricultural lands, often in

the case of a newly created or expanding settlement
- Groves used for ritual purposes by a particular group within a community
- Groves associated with a specific event (e.g., a battle) which revealed the sacred character of the forest to the community
- Groves used as burial grounds

The four processes were not neatly bounded, however, and some of the forests discussed below could clearly have resulted from a combination of several processes. While this four-fold categorization was useful, it ignored the local categories of sacred sites. In southern Ghana, people differentiate between *asamanpow* (groves associated with burial places and seen as the home of ancestral spirits) and *abosompow* (groves seen as the habitat of nature spirits).[1] This distinction fits the earlier observation that only a limited number of sacred groves are associated with archaeological remains and that these are generally related to burial grounds. A revised typology, then, distinguishes between

- Sacred Groves associated with burial grounds and old settlements
- Sacred groves associated with 'nature spirits,' and showing the archaeological remains of ritual practices rather than settlement[2]

Further, it is useful to distinguish between processes of creation (why and how a particular sacred grove was established) and processes of usage (how the forest was re-interpreted and used through time), which leave different material remains in the archaeological record.

A central question in archaeology concerns the validity of causal relationships between material remains, landscape features, and past events. If very different historical processes produce the same archaeological record, how can we accurately infer the past from artifacts and features? We need theories to link the typology of sacred groves in Ghana to the fact that the existing landscape has been crafted by a complex, multi-vocal, and intertwined array of historical, ecological, and socio-political factors. Beyond the different processes that produced (processes of creation) and conserved sacred groves (processes of usage), there is a common mechanism at work: the making of memory. I suggest that looking at sacred groves as '*lieux de mémoire*' (places of memory), allows a series of correspondences between history, memory, and material remains to be established.

The concept of *lieux de mémoire* has been the nexus of one of the most creative historical pursuits of the last two decades of the twentieth century in France. First explored by Pierre Nora in the early 1980s, the *lieux* included not

---

[1] See, for example, McCaskie 1990:135.

[2] Some of the 'nature spirit' sites as well as some of the 'burial/settlement' sites are also associated with iron slag. They may form a third category of groves, which could be termed 'iron-smelting related' sites. This, however, is alien to the local typology which I adopted here. Also, the association between sacred grove and slag mounds or slag-saturated fields may be due to the fact that the latter were avoided by farmers because of their physical characteristics. Such unfarmed parcels – like the sites of ancient settlements – were rapidly colonized by woody plants.

only geographical spaces but also a variety of mnemonic devices such as symbolic artifacts and concepts. Thinking in terms of *lieux de mémoire* means treating memory as representing a complex amalgam of strategies rather than simply reflecting the past (Nora 1984:viii). A distinction was made between the 'recomposed memory,' which remains dynamic and negotiable, and the 'persistent memory,' which is more positivist and absolute. For Nora, recomposed memory is a living force that constantly re-interprets the past in the light of the present, and is opposed to history, the intellectual reconstruction of the past. As Moniot noted, Nora's work was inspired by French historical specificities, which creates difficulties in transposing the *lieux de mémoire* concept to another setting (Moniot 1999:13). Nevertheless, the variety of innovative concepts and ideas it contains can fruitfully inspire work in the tropics. By using this method for grounding historical accounts on particular small-scale objects, such 'trifles of history' can demonstrate how different perceived realities exist at different scales through memory-making (*ibid.*:17). Sacred groves can usefully be seen as such objects that provide transformed but crucial evidence of the past. Conceptualizing sacred groves as *lieux de mémoire* allows the archaeologist to explore – beyond the diversity of site formation processes – an overall process of memorization that gives cultural meaning to natural phenomena.

In insisting on the dynamics of memory, the concept of *lieux de mémoire* emphasizes that a landscape should be interpreted both as a diachronic accumulation of sedimented memories extending deep into the past, and also as a synchronic construction that reshapes the past to serve the purposes of the present. This awareness is central to better contextualization of oral historical and archaeological material, as the following example illustrates.

Nsadwer Case Study

Nsadwer is a settlement located in a narrow belt of marshy land that runs, discontinuously, parallel to the Ghanaian seashore from Côte d'Ivoire to Nigeria. These lowlands are watered by a network of coastal lagoons alternating with narrow ridges. Many of these coastal lagoons and their associated wetlands were drained by urban and agricultural development during the twentieth century, and the overall environment is clearly much drier today than it was in the pre-colonial period. Although remnants of mangrove ecology can still be found along riverbanks and in estuaries, one must walk in the flooded countryside during the rainy season to get a sense of how watery the environment once was, before industrial plantations and unplanned urban development transformed it. At Nsadwer, for example, powerful machines reshaped large tracts of land to establish a sugar cane plantation and factory in the 1950s and '60s (an industry which collapsed in the early 1980s).

People, however, had not waited for the colonial and postcolonial era to occupy and change the landscape of these lowland areas. From the first millennium up to modern times, people had settled in this area and modified its landscape. Sacred groves are markers of these long-term uses of coastal West Africa. Here, through observations made during archaeological surveys, oral traditions and documentary sources, I aim to produce a series of dialogic microhistorical narratives about people and their environment: on one hand, I attempt to decipher the social history of a landscape created and reinterpreted by local communities over time; on the other hand, I look at landscape features as clues for the reconstruction of the little-documented social history of the coastal communities that created the groves.

The Founding of Nsadwer

The history of Nsadwer is largely undocumented. In a previous article, on the basis of an analysis of oral traditions and scarce documentary sources, I suggested that the village had been founded in the early 1870s (Chouin 2002a). A new set of documentary and oral traditions collected in 2001 and 2002 reinforces this hypothesis. Small kin groups came from various areas to settle in Nsadwer in the second half of the nineteenth century:

> Before Nsadwer was founded, there was enough land around Kankan [Dutch Komenda] and people did not need to travel far. Where you can farm, it becomes your property. People came from Elmina and Ankwandah. When they started clearing various parts of the lands, stools were carved. Stools need land and land needs stools. But people still go to the original place to maintain the relationship with the original family.[3]

Land was readily available in the hinterland of Dutch Komenda at that time, due to insecurity generated by the Mfantse-Asante wars, as well as generally low population density in the rural areas of the Ghanaian coast in the nineteenth century compared to crowded urban centers such as Edina. Also, like most lowland areas located along the coast, Nsadwer was, at best, a marginal ecological zone for agriculture. The productivity of its soil is rather poor, and the land is either too dry or subject to destructive floods during the rainy season. Large areas of land are unsuitable for farming. During the dry season, when the concentration of soluble salts peaks, the ground water is salty and unfit for human consumption and watering fields. The only sources of drinking water are the river Hua (which flows from Eguafo into the lagoon at Dutch Komenda) and an artificial pond for collecting rainwater.[4] The river dries up, however, during the dry season, and leaves only small ponds of greenish turbid water. When I first visited the village in 1994, the community had recently eliminated guinea worms from the Hua River. This combination of biophysical factors, along with a rainfall pattern that allows only one yield a year, seriously impairs the development of Nsadwer. It is one of the poorest communities in the Komenda-Edina-Eguafo-Abrem district of the Central Region of Ghana.

---

[3] Chouin field notes, hereafter cited as 'FN/Note #.' Kofi Atta, elder of the Ntwea Nsona family, Nsadwer, FN/2001, interview 02/14/2001.

[4] An analysis of the mineral content of the Hua river conducted in 1994 by the Water Research Institute, the Center for Scientific and Industrial Research, Accra showed that it was suitable for human consumption. I thank Mr. Jean-Daniel Neveu for supporting the cost of the analysis. The shallow pond is known as 'Afamuna Pond,' and quickly dries up during the dry season.

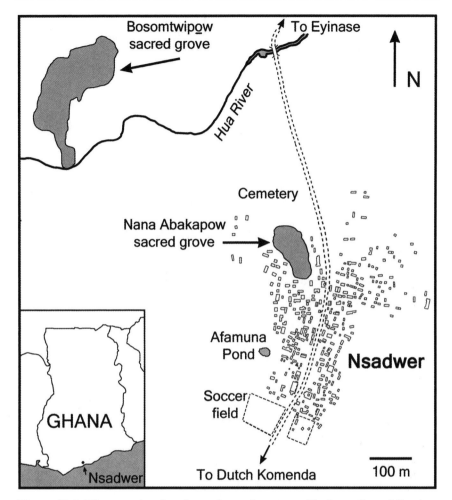

Figure 11.1 History and archaeology of sacred groves at Nsadwer, Central Region, Ghana

In 2003, I collected a short, hand-written history of the Ntwea family of Nsadwer. It was written in 1953 (in the Mfantse language) by Joseph Eshun.[5] Although there is much chronological mixing, the document is interesting because it clearly echoes old fragments of oral traditions connected to Dutch Komenda, and embeds them in the Nsadwer landscape. It relates the founding event that led to the establishment of Nsadwer, when the Ntwea kin group fled conflict-ridden Dutch Komenda *ca.* 1860–1870. Rival paramilitary associations known as 'Asafo companies' struggled throughout the Komenda area, while the Dutch colonists launched a punitive expedition against Komenda in 1869:

Wombir Asafo members were bellicose ... One fight made the Wobir (sic) people to lose

5 Joseph Eshun, 'Short history of the Ntwa family of Nsadwer', dated 13 July 1953. Copy in possession of the author.

all their elders. The death toll was so great that the resulting stench made it impossible to remain there. Nana Kojo Itue therefore advised that since they were all brothers he would not like such incidents to occur again in future. Moreover, the stench produced by the decomposing bodies made it impossible to live where they were and so he advised his people to relocate. They therefore moved to a new site, which they named Nsadwer, 'the war is over'.

(Baesjou 1979: 35)

Other echoes of the flight from Dutch Komenda of this group of people appear in oral histories that I collected in 1994:

> We were being chased and we came to hide around here. When the battle was over we assembled here and made a settlement called Nsadwer, 'the battle is over' ... We were fleeing together with the people of Dutch Komenda. The group consisted of fishermen and farmers. Those of us who were farmers separated ourselves from the fishermen and came to settle here. We all used to be in Kankan [Dutch Komenda].[6]

In their flight, they took refuge in the thick woods that then stretched behind the seashore. The high trees protected them from the gunshots of the pursuing Dutch, and 'no one was hurt while we hid in the forest' (FN/24/94).

Nsadwer was probably founded after these violent events, on the location of a previously existing farming hamlet: 'Nsadwer had already just been founded (but had no name) when they came to hide in the forest. The various families came together to hide. They were there during the day and would come back to the village in the night. After they came out of the forest, they named the village Nsadwer' (Kofi Atta, FN/2001).[7] This portion of forest, renamed *Perem Enntum*, literally meaning, 'cannon was not able' then became a sacred grove. Indeed, for the community, only the presence of a beneficial spirit dwelling in the forest could explain why none of the refugees were harmed: 'our safety was attributed to the powers of the inhabiting god of this forest which cannons could not harm' (FN/24/94). This is the only forest that can clearly be associated with the founding of the village. A random surface survey of the grove I conducted in December 2001 did not reveal any artifacts, but the survey was very limited in scope due to the dense vegetation cover. Also, it is probable that a small group of people hiding during the day in the forest would not have left much material trace, since cooking activities probably took place in the hamlet during the night.

Lineage, Land Use and Landscape History at Nsadwer

Part of Eshun's document tells us of tensions over leadership of Nsadwer, between different branches of the Ntwea Nsona kindred. Although members often present themselves as a unified lineage, it is actually a complex of relationships resulting from the incorporation of different groups of kin (with

---

[6] Ebusuapanyin Kofi Atta, Nsadwer, FN/24/94, interview 06/18/1994. Transcription and translation by Ernest Quayson, Elmina.

[7] A local document dated 1942 mentions three of such old hamlets; 'Of the three Amanpe, Anumii and Nsadwirdir, I do not know or cannot tell which is the oldest.' Kodwo Awotwi vs. Kofi Bonku, suit. N°66/42, April 1942, p. 6. Copy in possession of the author.

various origins) over time. Within the lineage, competition exists between the descendants of these different groups for the control of the symbolic regalia of leadership, political power and access to land. These tensions over material and symbolic power lead to disputes, and the archives of the colonial and post-independence courts are full of such cases. In court, defendants and plaintiffs usually rely on family oral history to support claims. The English transcriptions of these oral testimonies thus form a unique source of history, as close as possible to lineage history. Elders of these Nsadwer groups usually keep copies of these documents.

Kojo Atta, an elder from the Ntwea Nsona family, allowed me to read the papers in his possession. They included records of legal disputes adjudicated in the 'Native Tribunal of Edina' in April 1942 and March 1943. These documents are useful for reconstructing the local history of land use and understanding how Nsadwer farmers perceive their landscape. Streams, silk cotton trees (*onyina*), lime trees, anthills, old paths, bamboo groves and sacred groves are used to demarcate farmland and are often precisely mentioned in proceedings. For example, in one of Atta's documents from a 1945 case, the oral testimony included a description of the Nsadwer landscape; 'Kweku Esson was my late uncle. He has a boundary with Kow Akyer. The boundaries are Hyiro Bonkam, then Tennie's stream, then to a tree called Nkrunpa, the Kyiakwapow (Kyiakwa forest), then to Ntsitse Kwanm (old road) then one goes to Kow Akyer's land facing mine or where I had ploughed then to Bonka silk cotton tree.'[8] Court proceedings are useful sources from which to compile lists of the sacred groves extant in the colonial period for comparison with those collected during interviews with elders.

Particularly interesting for my survey of Nsadwer sacred groves was a map produced as an exhibit to a case probably heard in 1945.[9] The document presents a map of all Ntwea Nsona lands around Nsadwer. It shows detailed boundaries and major topographical features such as major roads, rivers, and main pathways. It also shows long-abandoned hamlets and sacred groves.[10] It was only in 2001 that I learned of the existence of the 1945 map, six years after I had first obtained a list of Nsadwer groves from elders. The two lists matched almost perfectly.[11]

[8] We recognize here the *Kyeakopow* sacred grove, see Table 11.1. Kodwo Awotwi vs. Kofi Bonku, suit. N°66/42, April 1942, p. 6. Copy in possession of the author.

[9] Kofi Mamfur and Kobina Awotwi, etc. (plaintiffs) vs. Kobina Bogya and 20 others (defendants) and Kobina Bonku and 4 others (co-defendants). I do not know the exact reference to the proceedings of this court case, which I could not find in the archives. The map is dated 8 January 1945. The map is in possession of the Ntwea Nsona family of Nsadwer.

[10] The words *abosompow* or *asamanpow* are not used on the map. Rather, names of groves are followed by the word *Asori* [modern Asoye] which means 'the spot where libation is poured.' Kofi Atta, Nsadwer, FN/2002, interview 01/18/2002.

[11] There were two exceptions. First, one grove, Aba Nsu, was on the map but had never been mentioned to me. Elders readily admitted they had forgotten to mention it. In 2002, little was left of Nana Aba Nsu, a grove that had served as a shrine for a river spirit dwelling in the Hua river. Located on the eastern bank of the river, the trees, mainly *Takuso* trees typical of mangrove environments, were meant to give shade to the river god. According to Kojo Atta, who accompanied me to the place, a farmer looking for more sunshine on his farm had

The Destruction of Sacred Groves

Some groves, represented both in the modern local discourse and on the 1945 map, have actually physically disappeared from the landscape. Two of them, Nana Abaka and Nana Agyinagyina Nkwantapọw, were indeed cleared in just the last decade of the twentieth century. Nana Abaka was still in existence when I first came to Nsadwer in 1994, and appears on a map of the Nsadwer settlement prepared that year by the Electricity Company of Ghana.[12] Both groves had been located within the perimeter of the village, and were cleared to make room for urban development. Besides some stumps of the groves' trees, small cement enclosures now mark the sacred nature of these areas.

Although the destruction of sacred groves seems to have accelerated in recent decades, I believe this is not strictly associated with the colonial and postcolonial periods. Each of the cults associated with the Nsadwer groves formed in a particular process of creation, and in response to a specific problem or historical event. The groves were then revisited and reinvested with new meanings by subsequent generations, leading to new processes of usage. A great number of cults circulated in West Africa, and newly adopted cults might have rendered older ones less and less attractive, gradually resulting in the abandonment of their sacred places (Baum 1999). Sacred groves are embedded in social history and, as such, are neither pristine nor eternal features. Each of them was born under circumstances which gave them particular social meanings and physical features. The physical manifestations of sacred sites change according to their social and historical contexts, and these transformations can include the complete annihilation and destruction of a sacred grove's trees with no loss of its sacred character.

In West African urban and village contexts, rapid changes in settlement pattern can affect sacred groves. Once on the periphery of a community, sacred groves can quickly become islands of vegetation in expanding settlements. As they become part of the urban environment, their status and functions may change. Isolated sacred groves become more visible markers of power but can also embody older concepts of wilderness incompatible with the increasingly domesticated and transformed settlement. Urbanization may thus generate conflict between a local elite's need to maintain the spiritual relationships that legitimize their authority and the new symbols of status and power in the urban landscape. It therefore becomes necessary to build houses for the groves' spirits. This is generally done by clearing the grove and building walls around the focal place of the sacred. Today at Nsadwer, and throughout southern Ghana, such

[11] (cont.) cleared the surrounding mangroves, including Nana Aba Nsu, in the late 1990s (Nsadwer, FN/2002, interview 01/18/2002). Although he was fined by the community, his act illustrates the gradual disappearance of river/water god cults in the area. This decline probably explains why the elders forgot to mention it in the list I collected in 1994. Secondly, the Bosomtwi grove, prominent in the oral discourse, was not to be found on the 1945 map. This is simply because of its location, west of the Hua River, outside of lands represented on the map.

[12] Copy in possession of the author.

Photo 11.1 Cement block shrine at Nsadwer, showing a tree stump from the former grove (© Gérard Chouin)

built structures are square or circular enclosures made of cement blocks. These small enclosures often include a single tree decorated with a white cloth, and fragments of the glass bottles used during libations. The urbanization of sacred groves is completed by roofing the enclosure and installing a door to the new shrine. The sacred is now fully integrated into its built environment. During my observations of libations in forests, I noted that such transformation of sacred groves is often considered highly desirable by the people of Nsadwer, as this proclamation from a libation ritual attests:

> Nana Atwer! Here is your drink! We have not come to see your nakedness. We have come with Kwesi Bronyi to see where you live. Perhaps he has come to help us to provide you with suitable accommodation.[13]

It is therefore important to insist that sacred groves are, as all historical entities, subject to creation and destruction by people. The destruction of a grove, especially within a settlement, can actually mean an 'upgrading' of the sacred site rather than its loss. Indeed, we should not forget that, in sacred groves, most trees are not sacred but merely form an enclosure to protect the spiritual focal point. The most important trees are merely resting places for a spiritual entity. The protective function of the trees may well be transferred to a wall whenever it is thought appropriate. Processes of usage can thus lead to the ecological transformation of *lieux de mémoire* while maintaining social continuity.

The Birth of a Sacred Grove

The recent history of Nsadwer makes it a useful case study for understanding

---

[13] Kofi Attah, Nsadwer, FN/24/94, interview 06/18/1994. Transcription and translation by Ernest Quayson, Elmina.

the formation processes of West African sacred groves. After the community was formed, people gradually identified the guardian spirits of the land while simultaneously transforming the landscape. Traditions of origin sometimes still recall how such spiritual entities revealed their dwelling places, identities, taboos, and ritual expectations to the community by possessing people. This kind of direct revelation seems to occur most frequently when farmers are engaged in large-scale bush clearing activities, particularly after the founding of a new settlement when the farmers are taking full control of the landscape. In Nsadwer, at least three forests were identified and preserved in this way: Atwerpow, Bosumefipow and Ekyinakwapow. According to accounts, the first two were discovered and revealed by Esuon Komfo.[14] This event probably took place at the end of the nineteenth century:

> My grandmother was spiritually possessed and for a year she had vanished and all search for her whereabouts proved unsuccessful. It was after one year that they got to know that she was living in this forest [Atwerpow sacred grove]. She was a young woman during the incident. The day she came out of the forest it was raining heavily. ... The gods themselves directed that the forest should not be cleared and also revealed to them [the elders] the rituals they should perform. Nobody comes here on Tuesday. It is a taboo to do so.[15]

Part of a different oral account (by the same informant) explains:

> It was a forest which was being cleared for a settlement. When they were about to clear this portion [nowadays Atwerpow], the god inhabiting the place warned [through Esuon Komfo] that they should leave this site intact because it is his residence. The elders understood the warning and stopped clearing the place.[16]

Such forests result from compromises between humans and spiritual forces for the control of the land. By definition, they are sacred groves associated with nature spirits and are usually not old settlement sites. Indeed, all the surface material I observed in these groves consisted of artifacts used in ritual cooking activities.

Other groves, which are often presented as dwelling places of the guardian spirits of the community, are linked with traumatic events in local history. In the eyes of the people I interviewed in Nsadwer, four forests have a vital role to play for their survival as a community. These are Atwerpow, Agyinagyina Nkwanta, Nana Ebodem, and Akromapow. *Atwer* is a corruption of *yetwer* ('we lean'), and Atwerpow literally means 'we lean on the forest.' Atwerpow is thought to protect the village from disease: 'It is a god which has the power [to] prevent any disease or epidemic coming to our town. We all depend upon him. Our souls are dependent on him.'[17] The same power is attributed to

---

14 The term *komfo* indicates that she is remembered as a priestess who had been chosen to be the medium for this spirit.

15 Ebusuapanyin Kofi Atta, Nsadwer, FN/23/94bis, interview 07/16/1994. Translation by Thomas Montford, Elmina.

16 Ebusuapanyin Kofi Atta, Nsadwer, FN/24/94, interview 06/18/1994. Transcription and translation by Ernest Quayson, Elmina.

17 Ebusuapanyin Kofi Atta, Nsadwer, FN/24/94, interview 06/18/1994. Transcription and translation by Ernest Quayson, Elmina.

Table 11.1 Sacred groves at Nsadwer, Ghana

Sacred Groves	Type	Associated archaeological material
1. Nana Abakapow	Settlement site	Surface scatters of various types of pottery shards and oven-like features associated with a late first millennium/ early second millennium AD settlement; small mounds of slag and fragments of furnace walls associated with seventeenth-century iron smelting.
2. Agyinagyina Nkwantapow	Nature spirit site?	Scatters of local ceramics.
3. Nana Bosomtwipow	Settlement site	Lots of archaeological material visible on surface in and around the grove, including local and imported ceramics, local and imported tobacco pipes, lots of slag and human remains. Excavation documented a late first millennium/early second millennium AD settlement followed by a sixteenth/ seventeenth century settlement specialized in iron smelting. The burial ground postdates the abandonment of the latter site c. 1660.
4. Awaewae Abodwepow	Nature spirit site	No archaeological material found.
5. Atwerpow	Nature spirit site	No archaeological material found. Only a small part of the forest was surveyed.
6. Akromapow	Nature spirit site	No archaeological material found.
7. Aprem Enntumpow	Nature spirit site	No archaeological material found. However, oral traditions present the site as a hiding place in the 1870s. Traces of short stays in the forest are probably concealed in the forest.
8. Bosomefipow	Nature spirit site	No archaeological material found in 2001. However, during a visit in 1994, I saw recent ritual features in the form of a wooden figure dressed with some material and tiny beads, as well as the remains of a temporary hearth used for ritual cooking.
9. Nana Ebodempow	Nature spirit site?	Surface scatters of local ceramics including some pedestal pots. This could be a seventeeth-century settlement site but was not investigated.
10. Ntonton-bekumpow	Nature spirit site	No archaeological material found.
11. Ekyinakwapow	Nature spirit site	No archaeological material found.
12. Aba Nsu	Nature spirit site	No archaeological material found

Agyinagyina Nkwanta, which literally means 'someone who stands at the crossroad.' According to one informant, 'when an epidemic is being brought in from outside, when a sickness is about to break out, he [Agyinagyina Nkwanta] stands at the junction or entrance and can therefore prevent any bad sickness from entering.'[18] This informant was not able to be more specific about the nature of the diseases that could be prevented by the spirits, nor could he tell under which circumstances these beneficial gods were discovered.[19] The process of creation of these groves, however, seems linked to the widespread violence and disease on the Gold Coast in the late nineteenth century.

Nana Abodei shelters a spirit 'capable of giving us children'[20] while Akroma-pow is known for having 'helped our ancient people in wars. Akroma can perform wonders to prevent any attackers from invading us here. Enemies will be unable to enter Nsadwer.'[21] In both cases, the informant was not able to give more details about the events that led to the discovery of these beneficial spirits. Though there is no direct evidence of well-established links between historical events and the groves, such oral traditions provide us with a vivid description of the spiritual and psychological reactions of rural communities like Nsadwer in the last third of the nineteenth century, when confronted with warfare and deadly epidemics that regularly threatened life and the social order.

Recomposed History

Several sacred grove sites in Nsadwer are, in fact, archaeological sites (see Table 11.1), including Nana Bosomtwi and Nana Abaka.[22] Informants from the village were unanimous that the Bosomtwi forest was the ancient royal cemetery of the Eguafo chiefs, but only 'the very prominent ones among them, the important ones. They were buried here.'[23] When asked why the chiefs of Eguafo were buried so far from Eguafo (about 15 kilometers), the informants gave different answers. In Dutch Komenda, I was told that the four brothers

---

18   Kyeame Kojo Nketsia, Nsadwer, FN/22/94, interview 06/04/1994. Translation by Thomas Montford, Elmina.

19   This might have happened in reaction to threatening epidemics. In the late last quarter of the nineteenth century, smallpox was the most recurrent and deadly pandemic on the Gold Coast. To my knowledge, there is no study of that disease on the nineteenth-century Gold Coast. However, we know that a smallpox epidemic broke out in the end of the year 1871 in Elmina area and lasted several years (Baesjou 1979: 42, 210, 212). The influenza pandemic of 1891–1893 and that of 1918–1919 (Patterson 1995) could have also been involved in the creation of this sacred forest.

20   Kyeame Kojo Nketsia, Nsadwer, FN/22/94, interview 06/04/1994. Translation by Thomas Montford, Elmina.

21   Ebusuapanyin Kofi Atta, Nsadwer, FN/24/94, interview 06/18/1994. Transcription and translation by Thomas Montford, Elmina.

22   I will discuss these sites, and the test excavations conducted there, in greater detail in my forthcoming dissertation.

23   Kyeame Kojo Nketsia, Nsadwer, FN/22/94, interview 06/04/1994. Elders at Dutch Komenda Traditional Council, Dutch Komenda, FN/20/94b. Translation by Thomas Montford, Elmina.

who had founded the area's villages 'first settled at Bosomtwi but they did not remain there for long,' and that 'they did not like farming, so they went to Eguafo... All the four brothers settled at Bosomtwi from Tekyiman before dispersing.'[24] In Nsadwer, however, informants told me

> The reason why burials take place in Bosomtwi forest is that the god at Eguafo and the Bosomtwi god at Nsadwer were brothers. When a chief or any prominent person dies, he is buried here. At that time there were wild animals, which dug graves [in the interior, near Eguafo]... This is the reason why Eguafo buried their royals and prominent men in Nsadwer Bosomtwi forest.[25]

In 1994, walking through the Nana Bosomtwi forest for the first time, I noted the presence of scattered potsherds and some small-size whole pots. At the edge of the grove, I was told farmers often dug up pottery and human bones. Paradoxically, inquiries in Eguafo did not reveal the existence of a burial site in Nsadwer.[26] A traveler's account from the early seventeenth century seems to confirm the existence of an Eguafo royal cemetery near Nsadwer. Pieter De Marees, a Dutch merchant who traveled along the coast in the late sixteenth century, described the grave of a previous king of Eguafo (1987:91). The Bosomtwi grove is located within walking distance from Dutch Komenda and could be the royal cemetery that De Marees visited. Although archaeological investigations have confirmed the presence of a seventeenth-century burial ground and settlement at Bosomtwi, no evidence has yet been found to confirm it as the place visited by the early Dutch traveler.[27]

The Bosomtwi site illustrates a process of creation whereby a grove emerges

---

[24] Nana Kobena Esuon, Regent, and Ernest Acker, Oman secretary, Dutch Komenda, FN/20/94a. Translation by Thomas Montford, Elmina.

[25] Ebusuapanyin Kofi Atta, Nsadwer, FN/19/94, interview 05/15/1994. Transcription and translation by Ernest Quayson, Elmina.

[26] Nana Boampong Wreko, Eguafo Adontenhene, Eguafo, FN/23/94, interview 06/12/1994. Transcription and translation by Ernest Quayson, Elmina.

[27] De Marees wrote, 'in the year 1570, when Don Sebastian was king of Portugal and ruled over the Castle of Mina, and the Portuguese were waging war on the people of Comando [Eguafo] and Foetu, they came with a great number of soldiers and drove away the inhabitants and burnt their towns, namely Comando [Eguafo] and Foetu. The Negroes gathered in the forest watched the Portuguese returning to their Castle and murdered and killed over three hundred of them, whose heads I have seen, having counted up to fifty of them, lying ... above the ground around the grave of the late king who at that time ruled the Blacks or Negroes. ... This I learnt from the mouth of the Viador, who is the brother-in-law of the king. He told me that he took part in the battle and showed me that those were the heads of the very Portuguese who had died on that occasion' (De Marees 1987:91–92). There is further corroboration that De Marees actually saw this grave when he went ashore at Komenda. First of all, this port, also known as Akitekyi, was at that time the most important trading place for Dutch merchant vessels west of Mina. De Marees most probably traded there himself. The only other Eguafo port he mentioned was Ampenyi, which he certainly did not visit because this area was under the influence of the Portuguese. Finally, the term 'brother-in-law' or 'brother' of the king is a title or appellation which seems to have only been used for one of the most important officers of the state: the commander-in-chief of the military forces who was at the same time governor of the main coastal town of the kingdom. Accordingly, the 'viador' 'brother-in-law of the [Eguafo] king' who met De Marees was the headman of Akitekyi/Dutch Komenda.

from an abandoned settlement and its burial ground. The process of usage, in which a forest is reinterpreted and used over time, can also be tentatively reconstructed.[28] The partial excavation of the Bosomtwi cemetery in June 2003 showed that plundering had heavily impacted the site at some point in the past. Such a plundering might have occurred before (or after) the founding of Nsadwer, and as early as the eighteenth or nineteenth centuries. It involved extensive digging of pits that resulted in the mixing of disconnected human remains throughout the top ninety centimeters of soil. As a result, human bones and teeth remains (particularly teeth) are conspicuous in the topsoil, and any past farmer would have noticed these and identified them as human (as they still do today). The site was therefore rightly identified as an ancestral cemetery (*asamanpow*) by the people who founded Nsadwer, and toponyms were given that reflected this identification. Indeed, the riverside grove of Bosomtwi, for instance, gets its name from the god Twi, who is a river god associated with the passage of souls from life to death (Wilks 1993: 107).

It is worth noting that in the oral traditions, the presence of a cemetery somehow obliterated the existence of an old settlement. This, I believe, is due to the fact that the community discovered the burial site but did not inherit much historical knowledge about it. Memory was almost entirely recomposed. This recomposition became grounded in regional folk history. It is therefore not too surprising that local traditions link the site with Eguafo, the historic overlord of the coastal area. Several explanations could be given to explain the mythic association between the Bosomtwi grove and the ancient Eguafo royal cemetery. First, the association with the old Eguafo dynasty was likely considered prestigious. At Nsadwer, all sacred groves are under the authority of the matrilineage from which the chief (*odikro*) is selected. A recomposed historic association with the ancient elite might have been a strategy to strengthen the authority of the ruling matrilineage. Second, the myth might have spread after the plundering of the cemetery, as rich gold ornaments (mainly beads and pendants, typical of seventeenth to nineteenth-century burials) were probably recovered. Finally, the association between Nsadwer Bosomtwi and the Eguafo royal cemetery could also be a distorted and recomposed echo of an historic fact: the presence in the area of the royal burial ground described by De Marees in 1601. Such transfers of meaning are common artifacts of shifting *lieux de mémoire*.

Conclusion

Changes in the landscape reflect broad cognitive as well as sociopolitical changes in society. The virtue of landscapes, however, is that they remain generally more stable than society at the temporal scale of human lives. Landscape therefore comprises a source for the reconstruction of African history, and it is a source that is deeply rooted in African social realities which are otherwise very difficult for outsiders to apprehend through more traditional

---

[28] On the processes of creation and usage, see also Chouin 2002b.

documentary historical sources. Sacred groves are a form of landscape that exists only as a by-product of human societies. At Nsadwer Bosomtwi, for instance, the modern forest cover is a consequence of the abandonment of the site in the seventeenth century: the grove developed quickly on midden deposits rich in organic matter, and was protected by its function as an ancestral burial site. Sacred groves are created for social purposes and are typically used by local elites within the context of specific historical trajectories.

The social and historical dimensions of West African sacred groves are rarely analyzed for their conservation values. As we recognize that the 'meaning' of a sacred grove is temporally sensitive and dynamic, it is not enough to seek the meanings of African sacred groves in the terms of the present. Conservation policy is, in itself, a process of usage that changes the meanings and values of sacred groves as *lieux de mémoire*. Regional patterns of sacred groves in Africa should be read as palimpsests. They delineate old settlement patterns and provide a window onto pre-colonial socio-political practices and dynamics, but they also reflect current social, political, and ecological relationships.

In this chapter I have argued that sacred groves, as anthropogenic creations, are historical in nature. The main challenge for the archaeologist is to go beyond the groves' synchronic representations and to conceptualize them as dynamic objects that were created in quite different historical contexts. We must consider how their meanings have been constantly re-interpreted and re-crafted in the light of changing events, ideas and values. Here, I have adopted an approach to *lieux de mémoire* based on two intertwined concepts: processes of creation and processes of usage. The process of creation refers to the chain of events that explain the creation of a grove. Oral traditions are the main analytic tools used to explore such a process, but archaeological investigations should also be pursued if the sacred grove stands on a burial ground and/or settlement. The process of usage refers to both the cognitive and practical dynamics that have changed the meaning and role of sacred groves through time. While the creation of a sacred grove follows specific historical events, the rituals that embody its sacredness are usefully understood as *lieux de mémoire* in social action. As time goes on, the grove erases history but recycles memory through processes of usage. Long after the precise chain of events that gave birth to a sacred grove is forgotten, ritual activities recompose memory.

Further study of West African sacred groves is needed to organize long-term sequences showing their emergence and dynamics. The spatial analysis of sacred groves on a regional basis, together with the analysis of oral and written sources, the documentation of ecological patterns, and the careful archaeological excavation of a limited number of sites may improve our understanding of the history and culture of southern Ghana over the past millennium.

References

Baesjou, R., 1979, *An Asante Embassy on the Gold Coast: The Mission of Akyempon Yaw to Elmina, 1869–1872.* Leiden: Afrika Studiecentrum.

Baum, Robert, 1999, *Shrines of the Slave Trade*. New York: Oxford University Press.

Chouin, Gérard, 2002a, 'Sacred groves as historical and archaeological markers in southern Ghana'. *Ghana Studies* 5:177–96.

—— 2002b, 'Sacred groves in history'. *IDS Bulletin* 33(2):39–46.

Davies, O., 1964, 'Archaeological exploration in the Volta Basin, Accra'. *Bulletin of the Ghana Geographical Association* 9(2):28–33.

De Marees, P., 1987, *Description and Historical Account of the Gold Kingdom of Guinea (1602)*. A. Van Dantzig and A. Jones, trans. and eds. Oxford: Oxford University Press.

Fairhead, James, and Melissa Leach, 1996, *Misreading the African Landscape: Society and Ecology in a Forest-Savanna Mosaic*. Cambridge: Cambridge University Press.

—— 1998, *Reframing Deforestation: Global Analysis and Local Realities – Studies in West Africa*. London: Routledge.

Guelly, K. A., B. Roussel, and M. Guyot, 1993, 'Installation d'un couvert forestier dans les jachères de savane au sud-ouest Togo'. *Bois et Forêts des Tropiques* 235:37–48.

Juhé-Beaulaton, Dominique, 1999, 'Arbres et bois sacrées: Lieux de mémoire de l'ancienne Côte des Esclaves'. In *Histoire d'Afrique: Enjeux de Mémoire*. J. P. Chrétien and J. L. Triaud, eds, pp. 101–18. Paris: Karthala.

McCaskie, T. C., 1990, 'Nananom Mpow of Mankessim: An Essay in Fante History'. In *West African Economic and Social History: Studies in Memory of Marion Johnson*. David Henige and T. C. McCaskie, eds, pp. 133–50. Madison, WI: University of Wisconsin African Studies Program.

Moniot, H., 1999, 'Faire du Nora sous les Tropiques?' In *Histoire d'Afrique: Enjeux de mémoire*. J. P. Chrétien and J. L. Triaud, eds, pp. 13–26. Paris: Karthala.

Nora, Pierre, 1984, *Les Lieux de mémoire: La République*. Paris: Gallimard, coll. Bibliothèque illustrée des histoires.

Patterson, K. D., 1995, 'Influenza epidemic of 1918–1919 in the Gold Coast'. *Transactions of the Historical Society of Ghana* (New series) 16(1):205–25.

Perrot, C. H., 1982, *Les Anyi-Ndenye et le pouvoir au 18ème et 19ème siecles*. Paris: CEDA et Publications de la Sorbonne.

Rattray, R. S., 1923, *Ashanti*. New York: Negro University Press.

Shinnie, P., 1988, 'Excavations at Asantemanso, Ghana (1987)'. *Nyame Akuma* 30:11–12.

Shinnie, P., and B. Vivian, 1991, 'Asante research project'. *Nyame Akuma* 36:5–6.

Wilks, Ivor, 1993, *Forests of Gold: Essays on the Akan and the Kingdom of Asante*. Athens, OH: Ohio University Press.

PART FOUR
The Future of African Sacred Groves

12

Legal Recognition of Customary Forests in Uganda
An Approach to Revitalizing Sacred Groves[1]

ABWOLI Y. BANANA, JOSEPH BAHATI
WILLIAM GOMBYA-SSEMBAJJWE & NATHAN VOGT

There are 4.9 million hectares of natural forests and woodlands in Uganda, covering 24% of the land area. Private and customary forests make up 70% of all forests and woodlands while government forest reserves make up only 30% of the forest land (MWLE 2002). This includes 15% of forest land managed by the National Forest Authority (NFA) as Central Government Forest reserves and 15% managed as National Parks by the Uganda Wildlife Authority (UWA).

Presently, there is a concern in Uganda that customary forests are being degraded more rapidly than those forests managed under formal property rights. For example, a large number of cultural forests in Buganda, Bunyoro and Tooro Kingdoms of Uganda that lie outside state forest reserves have been degraded to the extent that only small fragments of formerly extensive cultural forests remain in a largely agricultural landscape (Gombya-Sembajjwe 2000). On the other hand, in Acholiland and Lira Districts of northern Uganda where customary land ownership is still widespread, customary forests are still in relatively good condition (MWLE 2002). Research on sacred groves in Buganda has revealed that informal rules and regulations alone are no longer sufficient to mediate the effect of the increasing demographic and market pressures on customary forestry resources (Gombya-Sembajjwe 2000). McKean (2000) has debated whether traditional institutions are relics of the past and too weak to mediate the underlying drivers of forest degradation today. In the concluding chapter of this book, Alden Wily poses the all-

[1] We are very grateful for the continuing support of the Ford Foundation which has enabled us to systematically collect data from more than 40 forests in Uganda over seven years. We also thank the residents within the villages around the study forests for sharing their knowledge with us. We thank Krister Andersson at the Workshop in Political Theory and Policy Analysis, Indiana University for devoting time to discuss and provide comments on this paper.

important question: 'Are sacred forests safe?'

The observed steady degradation of forests on land held under customary (communal) tenure in Uganda in general and in Buganda in particular has led scholars and policy makers to rethink how best these forest resources may be made secure again, in order to maximize their social and environmental benefits. In this chapter, we describe the informal rules used to manage sacred groves and other forests on communal land according to Baganda custom and show how the efficacy of these institutions has declined over time. We present a case study on the origin, management and condition of two sacred groves (Magezigoomu and Mukasa) that are managed through two different sets of informal rules. Traditional practices allow hunting and collection of non-timber forest products (NTFPs) in Magezigoomu, while these activities are not allowed in Mukasa. Given these different traditional management regimes, how do these forests differ today in ecology and level of human disturbance? Are these two sacred forests safe? Finally we discuss the emerging opportunities in Uganda to promote the linking of informal and formal institutions in order to strengthen and revitalize the management of customary forests.

The Origin of Forests and Sacred Groves According to Baganda Folklore

In the Luganda language the word forest (*kibira*) refers either to a group of trees or to a room in the tomb of the *kabaka*[2] where the jaws of the dead king are kept. According to Baganda folklore, fear and respect for forests started at the death of Kabaka Kintu around the fourteenth century AD, as it is believed that Kintu disappeared into a dense forest. People started referring to that community of trees as *kibira*, a Luganda verb meaning 'to cheat'. This is because the trees had cheated them of their beloved king (Gombya-Ssembajjwe 1997, Kagwa 1971). Since the first *kabaka* got lost in the forest, when a *kabaka* dies, the lower jaw is removed and kept in a room known as *kibira* located in Kasubi tombs near Kampala.[3] For fear of 'disappearing' forever in the forest, the Baganda developed rules and norms for managing this grove.

The norms of particular sacred groves in Buganda originate from clan and community experiences and are often linked to spirituality. Different historical events or beliefs determine the specific rules, responsibilities and obligations that form the basis of the traditional forest management patterns for each grove. According to Baganda custom, one clan member is selected by the ancestral spirits to be the guardian of the grove. The guardian, together with the elders and clan leaders, is responsible for monitoring the behaviour of sacred grove

---

[2] Kabaka: the Luganda word for the king, absolute monarch of the Buganda kingdom, which traces its origin back to the original Kabaka Kintu who is believed to have been in power during the late fourteenth century. The monarchy survived the colonial era and the early years of Uganda's independence, only to be abolished by President Obote in 1966. It was reconstituted in 1993 when President Museveni invited the son of the late Kabaka to return to Uganda and he was crowned as Kabaka Mutebi II in July 1993.

[3] The Kasubi tombs, in a suburb of the Ugandan capital Kampala, are maintained as a historic and cultural site and are the location for the tombs of three recent kabakas.

users and enforcing cultural norms. These sacred grove guardians are highly respected in the clan and are often consulted on other clan and family issues. There are no written rules or guidelines to regulate sacred grove use and management. Clan or community members are taught the 'dos and don'ts' relating to the sacred forests at an early age. The elders and the guardians often visit the sacred grove in the company of children in order to teach the younger generation these rules and taboos. The rules regarding access to and use of each sacred grove are different. However, there are some general rules that apply to all sacred groves in Buganda. No one is allowed to enter the sacred grove alone and a man must accompany a group of women when they visit the sacred grove. Women who are menstruating are not allowed to enter sacred groves. Urinating, defecating and making love in sacred groves are all prohibited (Gombya-Ssembajjwe 1997). This is because sacred groves are used for worship and social gatherings and therefore had to be pure and clean from human and cultural contamination.

Worship, spiritual consultation and sacrifice are the most common non-consumptive uses of sacred groves and customary forests. The level of extractive use varies; in some groves no extraction of forest products is permitted, while others provide people with a great variety of products. In some groves permitted activities include hunting for wild animals, collection of wild plant foods, fruits, medicinal plants and water. Thus customary forests also provide food security in times of droughts and famine. Occasionally, harvesting of mature trees for timber, firewood and charcoal may be allowed under the guidance of the guardian, elders and clan heads (Gombya-Ssembajjwe 2000).

In any African community, the level of adherence to traditional religion varies (just as it does with other religions such as Christianity and Islam). The degree of conformance to the cultural taboos therefore also varies; today in Buganda the majority of people with strong beliefs and high levels of conformance are traditional healers, their families and the elderly of the community. In recent years, however, there has been some resurgence of belief in elements of Baganda culture, which may be related to the revitalization of the Buganda kingdom and the re-installation of cultural leaders such as the kabaka, chiefs and clan leaders. Spiritual sanctions, in combination with material fines and penalties, enforce the norms and rules related to the use of customary forests. Elders constantly remind the community of the dangers that await those who abuse the customary forests. Such dangers include the invasion of the offender's household by strange insects and the destruction of their crops by the spirits. Offenders may also become impotent, infertile or insane.

Material sanctions for sacred grove abuses include the return of the illegally harvested produce to the forest, slaughter of an animal to appease the spirits, or payment of cash fines. Relatives of an offender, together with the sacred grove guardian and the elders, organize a ritual to cleanse the offender. These cultural norms and rules helped to build the social capital that was necessary to prevent overexploitation of forest resources and ensure the conservation of biodiversity (Gombya-Ssembajjwe 1997). There is, however, some debate as to whether indigenous peoples such as the Baganda consciously sought to conserve biodiversity. For example, Smith and Wishnie (2000) argue that there is a distinction between 'conservation' and 'sustainable coexistence.' They define conservation as practices that are designed to prevent or mitigate species depletion or habitat degradation. They also argue that conservation practices are costly because of the low discount rates the society must incur and the associated increase in short-term production costs in order to reap benefits in the future. This definition implies a design process (either intentional or evolutionary) and involves decision-making or adaptation by natural selection. On the other hand, sustainability may be a result of low human population density, low demand for a resource, or limited technology. In these instances, sustainability is not intentional or planned.

The 'design component' is often missing in the management of customary forests by small-scale subsistence societies. And thus, according to Smith and Wishnie (2000), cultural maintenance of customary forests may promote sustainable use of resources without any intention to conserve them, with conservation being just an incidental by-product. Nevertheless, harvesting restraint motivated by belief in supernatural sanctions as used in the management of customary forests plays a key role in limiting harvesting levels, leading to resource sustainability and eventually to resource conservation. This may be attributed to the fact that the forest management practices of different communities incorporate systems of incentive structures including markets, rules, norms, information, and knowledge that effectively expand social capacity to steer interactions between nature and society.

In addition, practitioners of what we may call 'ethnoforestry' have a variety of simple monitoring and feedback mechanisms that help them make harvest and management decisions through knowledge networks (Feeney *et al.* 1990; Ostrom 1990). For example, individual users of a sacred grove observe and communicate to each other about the changing condition of the resource. When these users observe degradation, this provides incentives to modify the application of their knowledge and craft durable institutions for managing the resource. This is especially true for small, less complex ecosystems being used by small homogenous communities, as is often the case with sacred groves. These practices, like many other common property regimes, are adaptive and have ingredients of adaptive management (McCay and Acheson 1987). Such adaptive knowledge systems can be integrated into the formal sector to design operational systems that are responsive to local needs and the changing resource conditions.

Case Studies of the Magezigoomu and Mukasa Customary Forests

The Uganda Forest Resources and Institutions Research Center (UFRIC), based at Makerere University, has collected data on forest resources and institutions since 1993 using research protocols developed by the International Forest Resources and Institutions (IFRI) research program. Several sites studied by the program contain culturally important forests. One such site, Katebo, is located on the shores of Lake Victoria in Mpigi District of the Buganda Kingdom. It contains two cultural forests, Magezigoomu and Mukasa. These forests are adjacent to each other (Figure 12.1), and are located

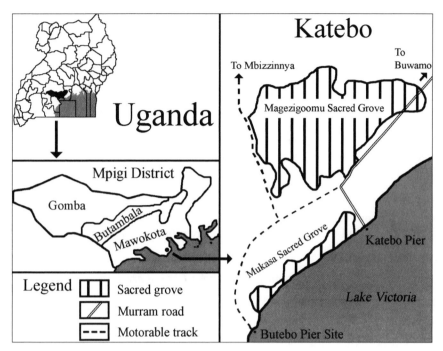

Figure 12.1 Map of Mpigi District showing the location of Magezigoomu and Mukasa cultural forests

in a rural setting where the main economic activities are fishing, subsistence agriculture and petty trading. The majority of the local population belongs to the Baganda ethnic group. The area is relatively densely populated with a density slightly above the national average of 100 persons per km².

The forests in this agro-ecological zone are classified as tropical moist, evergreen forests with closed canopies (Barbour, Burk, and Pitts 1987, Howard 1991). They are also medium altitude, semi-deciduous forests dominated by *Piptadeniastrum, Albizia* and *Celtis* forests tree species (Howard 1991). These forests are under the control of the Kayozi clan of the Baganda. The founder of the Kayozi clan is said to have come to this area from the Ssese islands in Lake Victoria with Kabaka Kintu around the fourteenth century. They occupied land on the shores of Lake Victoria at a place called Katebo. Some years later Kabaka Kimera[4] ordered the execution of some Kayozi clan members after they had betrayed him. When the executioners arrived at Katebo, Lukuyege, the founder of the Kayozi clan, then blind, ordered his clan members and his chief slave to run for safety.

Lukuyege was the last to flee from the advancing executioners but was easily located and killed. A *muwafu* (*Canrium schweinfurthii*) tree grew on his grave. With time more trees grew around his grave and formed a forest. The forest

---

4   Kimera was the third Kabaka of Buganda (following Kintu and Chwa I) and is believed to
     have reigned in the early to mid-fifteenth century.

was named 'Magezi goomu – gassa – Lukuyege' meaning 'a loner's wisdom' (or lack of consultation) led to Lukuyege's death. This name was shortened to Magezigoomu and the forest that grew around the grave was also called Magezigoomu. The slave, Mwogezi-Akkutanya, was buried near his master. A *mpewere* (*Piptadeniastrum africanum*) tree grew on his grave. Another *muwafu* tree grew on the site where Lukuyege's daughter Nambakire knelt to mourn for her father, and this tree was named Nambakire. The original trees that anchored the formation of the grove are still standing. The Magezigoomu tree is about 40 m high and 166 cm in diameter at breast height (dbh); the Mwogezi Akkutanya tree is about 35 m high and 153 cm dbh, while the Nambakire tree is about 20 m high and 110 cm dbh. The total area of this forest is about 16 hectares.

The Mukasa forest, located on the shores of Lake Victoria, is much smaller (about 4 ha). This forest was a shrine for Mukasa, who is one of the 'male gods' of Lake Victoria responsible for rain making, healing the sick and providing good luck. Members of the Kayozi clan used to pay tribute to Mukasa in this forest.

Access Rules to Magezigoomu and Mukasa Customary Forests

The landscape in which the forest patches are located is considered to be Kayozi clan land, and officially belongs to the head of the clan who controls land distribution among male clan members. Over the generations most of the land has been sub-divided for farming and settlement, but the two forest patches have not been not sub-divided.

According to the customary rules of access to Magezigoomu sacred grove, local community members may hunt for wild game and gather yams, fruit, and firewood for subsistence use. However, it is required that all the harvested food be consumed within the forest. This requirement limits the amounts that individuals can harvest. It also ensures that seeds are left within the forest to ensure regeneration. Individuals are allowed to harvest only one product per visit to the forest. If one goes to the forest to harvest yams, they should not gather firewood. This restriction raises harvesting costs, because repeated visits are required for an individual to harvest multiple products. Harvesting of forest produce is only allowed between noon and 3:00 pm. Regulating periods of access reduces the time available to harvest forest resources, promotes community self-policing, and consequently reduces monitoring costs.

The rules of access to Mukasa sacred grove do not permit any extraction of forest products. This forest is used as a shrine for worshiping the god Mukasa for his provision of rains, good health and good luck. The local people believe that there are many snakes in this sacred grove, and this may be one reason why community members seldom visit this patch of forest to collect forest products.

Assessment of Ecological Conditions

Twenty-two sample plots with a radius of 10 m. each were randomly laid in Magezigoomu Forest and eight in Mukasa Forest in 1995 and 2000. Data about trees in the sampled plots were compiled to determine the condition of the groves. Using stem density and mean diameter at breast height (dbh) of all trees with dbh above 10 cm, we calculated the basal areas of trees in each forest in 1995 and again in 2000.

In order to determine the level of compliance to rules of access, we looked for evidence of human disturbance due to timber harvesting, firewood cutting, charcoal burning, cultivation, and any other form of forest use. Our data allowed us to compare changes in basal area of trees between 1995 and 2000. Our assumption was that if traditional institutions in the area are strong and still mediating the forces leading to forest degradation, we would expect to find limited evidence of illegal harvesting and an increase in basal area in these two forest patches between 1995 and 2000.

Results

At Magezigoomu community norms do not permit clearing land for cultivation or harvesting wood for timber or charcoal production, but we found evidence of these activities in 50 percent of the plots in 1995 and 70 percent in 2000. In both surveys, we found widespread shifting cultivation of annual vegetable crops. Plots were abandoned after one season and trees were regenerating in the abandoned gardens. To investigate how unregulated use of this sacred grove affects its biophysical condition, we compared the number of stems per hectare, mean dbh and the total basal area observed in 1995 and 2000. Trees of 10–25 cm diameter dominated Magezigoomu forest in both years, giving a mean dbh of 20.7 cm in 1995 and 20.5 cm in 2000 respectively. It appears that the mature trees in this forest had been harvested for timber and firewood prior to the first visit. The high levels of harvesting coupled with the absence of mature trees from this forest indicate that the future of Magezigoomu sacred forest is not secure.

In Mukasa sacred forest where tradition does not allow extractive use of the forest by the community, no evidence of harvesting for firewood, timber, charcoal making and cultivation was observed in the first visit in 1995. In the

Table 12.1 Forest structure parameters in Magezigoomu and Mukasa cultural forests in 1995 and 2000

Forest Name	Forest structure parameter	Study period 1995	Study period 2000	T-test
Magezigoomu (n =22)	Mean tree density (trees/ha)	289 ± 22	245 ± 15	1.83★
	Mean DBH (cm)	20.7 ± 1.25	20.5 ± 0.6	0.19
	Basal area (M^2)/ha	11 ± 0.004	8 ± 0.003	1.15★
Mukasa (n =8)	Mean tree density (trees/ha)	400 ± 25	371 ± 8	2.04
	Mean DBH (cm)	28.4 ± 1.32	23.4 ± 1.29	1.72★
	Basal area (M^2)/ha	26 ± 0.009	24 ± 0.008	1.10

★ Significant at 5% level

second visit five years later, evidence of harvesting of these products was observed in less than 20 percent of the plots surveyed. The number of stems per hectare, mean dbh and the total basal area were significantly higher in Mukasa than in Magezigoomu (Table 12.1). In both visits, very large trees with diameters greater than 60 cm were common in this forest. Therefore, from the data collected there is evidence to show that the integrity of Mukasa forest is, at present, secure.

Discussion

Magezigoomu sacred forest, where tradition allows harvesting of non-timber forest products, shows signs of 'open-access' utilization. The cultural limits on extraction are only selectively practised in this forest. In addition, there is no evidence of self-policing or any other form of collective action by the community to protect this forest patch from encroachment. This bears out the observations by Gombya-Ssembajjwe (2000) that customary forests located outside state forest reserves have been degraded and only small fragments of formerly extensive cultural forests remain in a largely agricultural landscape. According to McCay and Acheson (1987), as well as Fortmann and Nihra (1992), long-term survival of common property systems (such as sacred groves) as institutions requires compliance with cultural norms and values. Interviews with clan leaders and community members revealed that Christians and Muslims who do not practice traditional religions presently dominate the study area. It is the traditional healers and their immediate family members who still use the sacred groves for worshipping or sacrifice. This partly explains why the majority of the people in the study area do not adhere to cultural norms and values. As Gibson et al. (2005) have shown, rules must be enforced for community forest management institutions to work. In addition, we found many ethnic groups and a large transhumant fishing population in the study area. Increased ethnic diversity and heterogeneity of the community can contribute to poor governance systems and increased degradation of the resource due to lack of shared vision, beliefs and norms (Ostrom 1990, 2000).

If traditional management systems of social control and regulation have broken down in the area, it is important to ask why Mukasa forest is less degraded than Magezigoomu. Explanations include not just the presence of an effective monitoring and rule enforcement institution at Mukasa, but also the fear of the snakes that populate in this forest. Fear of mythological large serpents is one of the harvest restraint mechanisms that is widespread in East African ethnoforestry practices. Whether the presence of snakes in Mukasa forest is real or myth needs to be investigated. However, it can be noted that these two forests are located on the equator where the hottest part of the day is between noon and mid-afternoon, which is the time when most community members would harvest forest products, since they are out on the lake fishing early in the morning and late in the evening. Snakes normally like to take shelter in the forest around midday for protection from the intense tropical heat. It is therefore possible that the presence of snakes in the forest is quite real. Since the canopy of Magezigoomu forest is more open and there is less litter on the ground, there are not enough shade and hiding places in this forest and hence there may be few snakes to scare away harvesters of forest products.

In light of the continued high degradation of sacred customary forests in Uganda as elsewhere in Africa, searching for other strategies that can help conserve these forests is crucial. In the next section, we discuss the emerging opportunities in Uganda for revitalizing ethnoforestry.

Linking the Informal and Formal Sectors: An Approach to Revitalizing Ethnoforestry

Ethnoforestry is a form of common property regime. The possibility of using common property regimes as alternative institutions for managing natural resources has attracted much interest among academics, policy makers, and development practitioners in the past two decades. Both community-based natural resource management (CBNRM) and International Conservation and Development Programs (ICDPs) are development efforts attempting to con-serve nature and maintain the economic flow of goods and services from the resources to increase benefits and incomes for present and future generation of local users. Such direct involvement of the local communities in resource management is a distinct shift from the 'fines and fences' approach that govern-ments have employed for decades with varying levels of success.

Why has interest in common property regimes increased in recent times? In the last two decades many governments in Africa, Latin America and Asia have implemented decentralized policymaking in the natural resources sector, in-cluding forestry. This has proceeded on the assumption that decentralization creates an enabling environment for the development of effective local institu-tions that can limit harvesting levels and set management strategies more reflective of local needs and at lower costs of monitoring and rule enforcement. Decentralization is varied and has different meanings for different local and non-local actors (Lind and Cappon 2001, Ribot 1999). Enabling practitioners of ethnoforestry to sustainably manage local forestry resources can be con-sidered as one form of decentralization. Strengthening and legally recognizing ethnoforestry, as part of Uganda's decentralization process, is a viable strategy for protecting biodiversity in both officially designated and informally protected areas. Legal recognition of ethnoforestry aims to limit access to cultural forests to clan members and registered user-groups only. This is critical because both theory and practice indicate that resources involving open access are much more vulnerable to overharvesting than those with restricted access (McKean 1992, Ostrom 1990).

We know that most common property regimes' management depends on relatively informal means to monitor access and to sanction free-riding and other violations of management rules. Using Magezigoomu and Mukasa sacred forests as a case study, we concluded that these mechanisms have become less effective and need to be revitalized. The following policies have been adopted in Uganda to enhance the management of customary forests:

i *Legal recognition of customary land tenure as one of the formal land tenure regimes in the country*
A clan or a formally registered group or association may register customary land and obtain a Certificate of Customary Ownership. The assumption is that a certificate of ownership would provide the incentives for long-term management of customary forests and sacred groves by the clan or by the registered association.

ii *Registered customary forest land has to remain under forest cover*
Under this strategy registered customary forest land would form part of the country's permanent forest estate, and the owners are bound to keep the registered customary land under forest cover in perpetuity, thereby preventing conversion of forest land to other uses.

iii *Legal recognition of indigenous forest management practices*
By recognizing indigenous forest management practices, the cultural norms and rules accepted by the clan and by-laws passed by the local communities become legally binding. This strategy of linking the informal and formal forest sectors builds upon traditional community management systems. It promotes the development of binding rules, rights, responsibilities and obligations within a community. Formalization of the traditional management systems with an emphasis on transparent and accountable governance and equitable distribution of economic and social benefits is likely to contribute to the sustainable management of forestry resources in Uganda by reinforcing weakened informal means of monitoring and sanctioning free-riding and other violations of cultural rules.

Supportive Legislation for Linking Practice to the Formal Forest Sector

In the past, there has been no formal policy specifying forestry as a preferred land-use on customary land. Recent legislation such as the Forest Policy of 2001, the Land Act of 1998, the National Forest Plan of 2002, and the National Forestry and Tree Planting Act of 2003 all respect the attributes of informal institutions in forestry resources management (MWLE 2002). In addition, the new Uganda Forestry Policy of 2001 emphasizes and promotes sustainable management of natural forests on private and customary land.

All the above legislation legally empowers cultural and traditional organizations to manage forests on customary land. For example, security of tenure for customary forests is clearly stipulated in the Land Act of 1998 and the Forest and Tree Planting Act of 2003. The Land Act states 'Where customary forests are considered to have significant subsistence, economic, environmental or cultural value, or where there is a history of communal management through traditional systems of regulation and control, a local community may decide to formally register ownership.' The National Forest and Tree Planting Act (2003) also provides the legal framework for the registration of Customary Land as

Community Forests. Community Forest Regulations and Guidelines (2004) have been put in place. The guidelines define the obligations and responsibilities of the various stakeholders. All that is required now is to widely publicize and increase public awareness of these guidelines.

Although these new legal regulations have created an enabling environment to link *de jure* and *de facto* property rights, legal regulations alone are not enough to stop degradation of forests on customary land. Other approaches such as providing economic and cultural incentives, improved forestry extension, training and information services are necessary, and have been put in place. For example, by registering a sacred grove or customary forest, a clan can demand that the District Forest Services provide forestry extension services. Under the National Forest and Tree Planting Act (2003) the District Forest Services must provide technical guidance for forestry on local forest reserves, and on private and customary land within the district. The District Forest Services are expected to facilitate and ensure public awareness of the cultural, economic and social benefits of conserving forests on customary land.

In addition to the District Forest Services, the National Agricultural Advisory Services (NAADS) under the Plan for Modernization of Agriculture, is expected to build the capacity of farmers, NGOs, and clan-based organizations to demand and use appropriate forestry advisory services. According to the National Forest Plan of 2002, owners and users of customary forests will be supported in the reinstatement of traditional systems of management and control. In addition, the Plan calls for the development of collaborative partnerships with rural communities and the District Forest Services for the sustainable management of forests. Collaborative Forest Management (CFM) provides a platform for linking and using both informal indigenous knowledge and the formal and scientific management of forest resources.

Conclusion

Using Magezigoomu and Mukasa sacred forests as a case study, we observed extensive harvesting of timber, charcoal production and crop cultivation in Magezigoomu cultural forest, and a low level of extractive use of Mukasa cultural forest. In agreement with the findings by Gombya-Ssembajjwe (2000) we can conclude that sacred control mechanisms have become less effective in regulating resource use in customary forests.

The future of sacred forests may become more secure if they are registered as Community Forests, because upon registration there is increased security of tenure. With increased tenure security and increased benefits, a clan or community may put more effort into monitoring and rule enforcement of customary forests and can receive forestry advisory services from the district forest service. This is likely to lead to enhanced protection of these forests.

References

Agrawal, Arun, 1994, 'Rules, rule making, and rule breaking: Examining the fit between rule systems and resource use'. In *Rules, Games, and Common-pool Resources*. E. Ostrom, R. Gardner, and J. Walker, eds, pp. 267–82. Ann Arbor, MI: University of Michigan Press.

—— 1995, 'Population pressure = forest degradation: An oversimplistic equation?' *Unasylva* 181(46):50–8.

—— 1996, 'The community vs. the markets and the state: Forest use in Uttarakhand in the Indian Himalayas'. *Journal of Agricultural and Environmental Ethics* 9(1):1–15.

Barbour, Michael G., Jack H. Burk, and Wanna D. Pitts, 1987, *Terrestrial Plant Ecology*, 2nd edn. Menlo Park, CA: Benjamin and Cummings.

Fairhead, James, and Melissa Leach, 1996, *Misreading the African Landscape: Society and Ecology in a Forest-Savanna Mosaic*. Cambridge: Cambridge University Press.

Feeney D. F., *et al.*, 1990, 'The tragedy of the commons: twenty two years later'. *Human Ecology* 18:1–19.

Fortmann, Louise, and Calvin Nhira, 1992, *Local Management of Trees and Woodland Resources in Zimbabwe: A tenurial niche approach*. Centre for Applied Social Sciences occasional paper. Harare: CASS, University of Zimbabwe.

Gibson, C. C., J. Williams, and E. Ostrom, 2005, 'Local enforcement and better forests'. *World Development* 33(2):273–84.

Gombya-Ssembajjwe, William, 1997, 'Indigenous technical knowledge and sacred groves (traditional forest reserves), Mpigi District, Uganda'. Uganda Forestry Resources and Institutions Center (UFRIC) Research Note No. 1.

—— 2000, 'Sacred forests: An alternative way of conserving forest resources'. In *Community-based Forest Resources Management in East Africa*. W. Gombya-Ssembajjwe and A. Y. Banana, eds. Kampala: Makerere University Press.

Howard, P. C. , 1991, *Nature Conservation in Uganda's Tropical Forest Reserves*. Gland, Switzerland: International Union for the Conservation of Nature (IUCN).

International Forestry Resources and Institutions (IFRI), 1998, 'International Forestry Resources and Institutions'. *Field Manual, version 8.0*, Bloomington, IN: Indiana University, Workshop in Political Theory and Policy Analysis.

Kagwa, Apolo, 1971, *Ekitabo kya basekabaka be Buganda*. Nairobi: East African Publishing House.

Lind, J., and J. Cappon, 2001, *Realities or Rhetoric? Revisiting the Decentralization of Natural Resources Management in Uganda and Zambia*. Nairobi: African Center for Technological Studies.

McCay, B. J., and J. M Acheson, eds, 1987, *The Question of the Commons: The Culture and Ecology of Communal Resources*. Tuscon, AZ: University of Arizona Press.

McKean, M. A., 1992, 'Success on the commons: A comparative examination of institutions for common property resources management'. *Journal of Theoretical Politics* 4:247–81.

—— 2000, 'Common property: What is it, what is it good for, and what makes it work?' In *People and Forests: Communities, Institutions, and Governance*. C. C. Gibson, M. A. McKean, and E. Ostrom, eds, pp. 1–26. Cambridge, MA: MIT Press.

Ministry of Water, Lands and the Environment (Uganda), 2002, *The National Forestry Plan*. Kampala: Government of Uganda.

National Environmental Management Authority (NEMA), 1998, *The State of the Environment 1998*. Kampala: NEMA.

Ostrom, Elinor, 1990, *Governing the Commons: The Evolution of Institutions for Collective Action*. Cambridge: Cambridge University Press.

Ostrom, Elinor, 2000, 'Reformulating the commons'. *Swiss Political Science Review* 6(1):29–52.

Ribot, J. C., 1999, 'Accountable representation and power in participatory and decentralized environmental management'. *Unasylva* 50:18–22.

Smith, E. A., and M. Wishnie, 2000, 'Conservation and subsistance in small-scale societies'. *Annual Review of Anthropology* 29:493–525.

13

Are Sacred Groves in Sub-Saharan Africa Safe?
The Legal Status of Forests

LIZ ALDEN WILY

There is little doubt that socio-cultural values of forests have played an enormous role in the existence of forests today – a fact all too frequently witnessed in the lonely survival of a small but intact sacred forest within the midst of cleared fields. In light of continuing high rates of deforestation in Africa, deepening understanding of what helps conserve forests is crucial.[1]

It is also important to be aware of the paradigms under which forests today are governed, for irrespective of whether primarily for socio-cultural, economic or environmental purposes, all forests in Africa are subject to policies that are broadly outside the control of those who have the most immediate vested interest in them – the local community. Whilst agricultural and other policies have played their role, this has been most obviously the case for forests which colonial and post-colonial governments have brought under their own jurisdiction as forest parks, reserves or otherwise classified state-owned resources. These embrace upwards of 250 million hectares today.[2] Consideration of whether or not these forests had local functions or were locally owned has rarely been a deterrent to the appropriation process (Alden Wily and Mbaya 2001: 162–77). Historically the central state has regarded itself both as the rightful beneficiary of their commercial values and as the only safe guardian of those forests perceived as requiring protection for biodiversity and other non-consumptive purposes. A multitude of sacred forests have been captured within this domain. It may reasonably be expected that local interaction with forests for social and other purposes is a good deal more active today in those forests which have not been brought under state jurisdiction. These remain substantial at around 400 million hectares (ibid.:41–2). By default, rather than design, customary or other informal regimes dominate in these forest areas – a

[1] Africa lost an average of 0.5 million ha of forest annually between 1990 and 2000 (FAO 2001; Table 3).
[2] FAO 2001: Table 4.

207

condition that does not necessarily bespeak formal recognition of local interests or rights, as will shortly become apparent.

Policies towards both reserved and off-reserve forests are dramatically changing. The task of this chapter is to examine how far these changes recognize the social values of forests and/or provide for local groups or communities to not only control the way these forests are accessed but to have their customary tenure over the forest acknowledged and formally protected. Accordingly the focus will be upon the extent of legal jurisdiction that is being afforded the community level. New national forestry policies will be noted but legislation is by its nature a good deal more precise and binding than declamatory policy and therefore the better witness of formal change.

Table 13.1 Examples of new legislation affecting African forests. Parentheses indicate a significant amendment to an older law.

Country	New Constitution	New Local Govt. Laws	New Land Laws	New Forest Laws
Benin	1990	1997	(1999) and Draft	1993
Burkina Faso	1997	1998	(1991,1996) and Draft	1997
Burundi	1992 and Draft	Draft	Draft	Draft
Eritrea	1997	1996	1994	1998
Ethiopia	1995	1992	2005	1994
Ghana	1992	1993	(1993) Proposed	1998
Côte d'Ivoire	2000		1998	
Kenya	Draft	Proposed	Proposed	2005
Lesotho	1993	1997	Draft	1998
Madagascar	1992	1994	Proposed	1997, 2001
Malawi	1994	1998	Proposed	1997
Mali	1992	1993, 1995, 1999	2000	1995
Mozambique	1990	1997	1997	1999
Namibia	1990	1992	2002	2001
Niger	1996		1993, 1997	1999
Rwanda	2003	1999	2004	Draft
Senegal	2001	1996	1994	1998
South Africa	1996	1997, 2000, 2002	9 laws: 1994-2004	1998
Sudan	2004	1991 Proposed	Proposed	2002
Swaziland	Draft Bill	Draft	Draft	Draft
Tanzania	Proposed	(1992, 1999)[3]	1999, 1999, 2002 (2004)	2002
The Gambia	1997	Proposed	Proposed	1998
Uganda	1995	1997	1998 (2004)	2003
Zambia	1991	(1992)	1995 and Proposed	1999

---

[3] Zanzibar Island makes its own laws with four new land laws 1989–1994 and a new forest law in 1996.

A Changing Governance Environment

New paradigms regarding the way in which forests on the continent are secured and managed do not exist in isolation. They gain a great deal from a more widely changing socio-political environment and one that is notable for a general shift towards more democratic and localised procedures for governing society and its resources. Developments in constitutional, land and local government law are most immediately relevant. Table 13.1 illustrates the extraordinary level of formal change under way in these sectors on the African continent.

Caution must be exercised in assuming that the new paradigms such laws embody are actively being exercised or enforced; the process of arriving at agreed ways forward is proving contentious, and usually for political reasons. For example, the South African Communal Land Rights Act passed in 2004 (but still not assented) began life in 1997 as a proposal to hand over private and community lands in the ex-Homelands to their occupants but eventually provided for these to be owned by tribal authorities, in a bid to secure the support of chiefs in the 2004 election. Even when safely entered into law, commencement dates are often delayed (e.g. Tanzania) or the will and resources needed to apply the law are not forthcoming (e.g. Uganda, Namibia).

Nonetheless the breadth and innovation in current law-making is substantial. Interestingly, the sphere where most widespread change is occurring is the forestry sector itself. At least 40 of Africa's 56 mainland and island states have new national forest policies and/or laws to hand (Alden Wily 2003a). Moreover, implementation is widespread. Common directions include reorientation of traditional forest management plans away from timber harvesting towards protection and use management, increased opportunities for private sector involvement, including non-government and community based organizations; imposition of more accountability in the way governments administer forests under their control; decentralization of operational authority to sub-national governments – and perhaps most pronounced of all – a dramatic rise in the legal opportunities for forest-local communities or groups to become forest managers or co-managers in their own right (Alden Wily and Mbaya 2001, FAO 2002, Kohler 2001).

Around half of these countries are also reforming land relations. The main thrust to this is reform in land administration regimes (Alden Wily and Mbaya 2001, Toulmin and Quan 2000). However, even the most modest of administrative reforms tend to result in (or be driven by) an overhaul of the legal treatment of rights in land themselves. Rural majorities are in particular being dramatically affected. As shown later, the status of local interests over sacred forests is accordingly affected – at least in law.

Local government reform often occurs hand-in-hand with land and natural resource reform, putting in place, often for the first time, elected bodies at the community level and endowing these (unevenly) with executive and legislative powers (Ribot 1999). The now well-established village governments of

Tanzania (1975) are proving potent examples, varying conceptions of which have been entered into the governance norms of neighbouring states and beyond.[4] The relative power of traditional authorities is predictably a matter of debate, including where chiefs have remained the dominant guardians of environmental and social values (FAO 2003).

As supreme law, new constitutions are laying the foundations for change including many of the specific developments discussed below. Almost all of the 30 or so new African constitutions since 1990 greatly enhance traditional bills of rights, including social, cultural and property rights. They lay the foundation for more participatory governance and widely introduce a new respect for community and custom. For example, Mozambique's new Constitution drew a clear distinction between community and individual rights (Article 47) and firmly protected free expression of traditions and values (Article 53) – both of immense importance to how subsequent new land and forest laws would in turn deal with communal forest interests. Uganda's 1995 Constitution liberated all customary lands from state ownership (Article 237). Kenya's draft Constitution recognizes community land as one of three main classes of tenure. Most new constitutions now introduce chapters on environmental protection and natural resource management on the one hand, and commitments to localize governance to the grassroots on the other.[5]

Discussion

Do new forest laws recognise sacred forests?

The first task is to determine whether or not the socio-cultural values and uses of forests are sufficiently appreciated in the terms of new laws. Thirteen cases were reviewed. The results were mixed. Neither new national forest policies nor new laws in Malawi, Namibia, The Gambia, Nigeria or Ethiopia make explicit reference to social or cultural values or acknowledge that a range of sacred forests or groves exists. There is one uniform exception: in all cases new forest laws in these states secure customary rights to collect plants for medicinal purposes.

Protection of socio-cultural values is only slightly better covered in the new laws of Zambia, Ghana, Uganda and South Africa. Zambia's forest law, for example, provides for chiefs to be *ex officio* members of local forest management committees (Forests Act 1999; s.26) and the South African National Forests Act 1998 permits the Minister to issue licences for cultural or spiritual purposes (s. 23).

The policies and laws of Lesotho, Tanzania (Mainland), Mozambique and Kenya make more concrete provision for sacred forests and socio-cultural values in general. In Lesotho, the Forest Act 1999 states that the customary forests of *liremo* and *matsema* (sacred groves or sites of ritual practices) are there-

---

4   For example, Uganda, Rwanda, Malawi, Lesotho and in constitutional proposals in Kenya.
5   An early example is Ghana's Constitution of 1992. A late example is the draft Constitution of Kenya.

after automatically classified as Community Forests under community control (s. 17). Tanzania's Forest Policy 1998 permits village religious institutions, associations or groups to manage forests (4.1.3) and provides detailed procedures for this in the new Forest Act 2002. The Forest and Wildlife Act 1999 of Mozambique echoes the earlier provisional Land Law 1997 that allows communities to declare areas of historical and cultural value for strictly non-commercial purposes (Article 13). These are to be managed in accordance with local norms and practices (Articles 1, 13, 21).

Finally, the Kenya Forests Act 2005 is the most explicit in its support for socio-cultural attributes. Sacred groves are defined (s.3) and protection of cultural forest sites listed as a factor to be considered in reserve creation (s.23). Mining or stone quarrying may not, for example, be undertaken where the forest has cultural importance or contains sacred trees or groves (s.41). Nature Reserves may be declared where there is 'environmental, cultural, scientific or other special significance' (s.32). Sacred groves within any other forest may not be interfered with and those wishing to use or conserve such areas may apply to do so (s.32). Management of forests may include 'cultural use and heritage' as its purpose (s.40). At the same time, all forests save Private Forests are vested in the State (s.20). Moreover full control is vested in local authorities where the forest is of 'cultural or scientific significance to the local community' (s. 23). Section 20 contradicts constitutional provisions for community land rights while the latter hands over such customary property to local authorities that are both socially remote from the community and not fully elected.

On the whole, attention to sacred forests is deficient in the thirteen laws reviewed. In addition, even in the cases last described, the *primary* concern of new policy and law is indisputably towards promoting the economic and productive use values of forests, including by communities. However, the gain to community interests in general is considerable under new forest laws and this presents a myriad of opportunities through which sacred forests may indirectly be sustained with legal support. Before examining this, it is necessary to turn first to developments in new land legislation that impact upon local land interests. For new forest enactments are being very strongly affected by new land laws.

Do new land laws support community interests?

Improved legal status for customary land rights. Virtually all rural occupants in Africa (and a significant proportion of urban dwellers) still occupy land today under arrangements that are neither recorded nor formally registered as their private property (Augustinus 2003). Change in the status of these customary or other informal land interests is one of the flagship characteristics of current land reform on the continent. In the past, the only means for an individual, family, group or community to gain statutory recognition of ownership was through a process which converted the land right into European-derived forms such as freehold or leasehold rights and these were generally issued to individuals. In some states (e.g. Zambia, Côte d'Ivoire) a main thrust of new legislation is to accelerate this conversionary process, much as was the intention of earlier reforms such as those launched by Kenya and Senegal in the 1960s (Bruce and Migot-Adholla 1994, Golan 1994).

A more innovative strategy is gathering pace. This halts century-long efforts to replace customary regimes and instead improves their legal standing and gives support for their operation. Thus, Uganda's Constitution (1995) and Land Act (1998) make customary tenure one of four equally legal systems through which land interests may be acquired and sustained.[6] In Tanzania, the Land Act (1999) deems an occupancy right issued by the state and a customary right issued at community level as of equal legal value and requires both to be protected as private property.[7] Its sister Village Land Act (1999) under which customary tenure in Tanzania is now administered reiterates this.[8] In Ethiopia, where customary tenure was abolished in 1975, new federal land laws (1997, 2005) nonetheless provide for 'existing holding rights' to be fully recognized and protected, many of which in practice have origins in customary rights. Kenya's draft Constitution provides for an entirely new class of tenure – Community Land (Art. 234–5). This would cover the still very large areas of land vested in the state and managed by county councils on its behalf. The draft specifically describes these as including 'forests, water sources, grazing areas or shrines' (Art. 239).

It is not only in East Africa that customary rights are gaining new status; this is also the case in Mozambique, Mali, Niger and Namibia and is well advanced in policy in Malawi, Lesotho, Benin and Swaziland among others (Alden Wily 2003b).

Many of these laws go further by enabling these informal rights to be formally registered and titled 'as is,' retaining their customary attributes, albeit within the limits of natural justice.[9] This is the case for example in Uganda, Tanzania, Mozambique and Ethiopia. Previously, the ability to register customary rights was limited to Botswana and Ghana, and *excluded* common properties. Registration of customary rights in new land laws is generally made voluntary.[10] This is crucial for the many millions of rural occupants who do not have the means to have their rights recorded. To limit uncertainty, some laws (e.g. Tanzania and Mozambique) make it clear that even an unregistered customary right will be upheld in the courts, provided the community endorses its existence.

New status for communal property rights. For our subject here the most important aspect of this development is that legal recognition and potential registration of customary rights must logically include not only those held by individuals and families but also those held by groups and communities. In this way, shared

---

6 Constitution; Art. 237; Land Act 1998; s. 5–10.
7 Land Act 1999; s. 4.
8 Village Land Act 1999; s.18.
9 For example, in the protection of women's land rights. See Alden Wily 2003b.
10 A significant exception is Côte d'Ivoire, where the new law of 1998 stipulates that all properties that are not registered within ten years will be deemed state property and subject to reallocation (Art. 6).

property rights over many millions of hectares of forests, pasture and wildlife rangeland come into new focus as essentially private rights.

In this respect it is worth recalling that many of those forests which are now under national or state tenure as reserves or parks were in fact originally the common property of communities but were able to be appropriated by colonial and post-Independence governments with ease for the very reason that state law did not recognize *communal* tenure as having the status of private property. For the purposes of the state, such lands were advantageously considered un-owned or *terres sans maître*. Without the legal support needed to entrench group-based ownership in the face of rapidly changing conditions, open access tragedies did indeed materialise in many places, confirming for many administrators the belief that commons were un-owned (*res nullius*) (Alden Wily and Mbaya 2001).

Putting a brake on this development by providing for common property registration gives many threatened forest commons welcome respite. Sacred forests are among these. Usable constructs being provided are several, ranging from a simple delimitation procedure in Mozambique and Côte d'Ivoire to the complex creation of new legal entities in which group-owned property may be vested (Uganda, South Africa). The former collective land titles have the disadvantage of including not just common properties but individual properties owned by members, and are in practice less entitlement than confirmation of community jurisdiction.[11] The latter are also imperfect, in requiring considerable resources and enterprise in order for the institution in which ownership will be vested, to be put in place. The most straightforward mechanism devised so far has been to simply make blanket legal provision for land to be held 'by a person, a family unit or a group of persons recognised in the community as capable of being a landholder', and providing for these diverse tenures to be recorded as such. This is the avenue provided by the new land laws of Tanzania, Uganda and Ethiopia.[12] The Village Land Act 1999 of Tanzania goes so far as to disallow adjudication and entitlement of individual holdings until the community has identified and registered its common properties.[13] Because each property must also be accompanied by a community-devised management plan, this has greatly encouraged the declaration of village and group forest reserves as described later.

Botswana is the latest in a small but growing number of states to advocate titling community based property rights, in order to secure dwindling commons (NRS 2003). Even where land reform is not well advanced, such as in The Gambia, the need to embed local tenure over forests has become so pressing through community forestry developments that new tenure procedures for this are being developed (Bongartz *et al.* 2003). Those communities

---

[11] Mozambique's Land Law 1997 provides for groups or communities to hold a joint title, in a name they choose (Art. 7, 9 and 10). A land tenure certificate in Côte d'Ivoire may be drawn up in the name of an individual or a collective, the latter explicitly comprising a village, clan or family (Law Relating to Rural Land, 1998; Art. 10).

[12] Tanzania Village Land Act 1999 s.22; Uganda Land Act, 1998 s. 4; Amhara Land Proclamation, No. 46 of 2000, Art. 6.

[13] Village Land Act 1999, s. 13.

not yet afforded opportunities to secure these community forests as private group-owned property, such as in Cameroon, are beginning to ask why not (Adeleke 2003).

Devolving land administration to local levels. Both as a consequence of broader commitments to decentralization and as a logical corollary of recognizing customary tenure, many countries are taking steps to bring land administration nearer to landholders. After all, customary tenure regimes are by nature community-based systems, not easily operated from afar. Many states have delivered these powers right to the community level; this is the case in Tanzania, Côte d'Ivoire, Niger and Burkina Faso and proposed in Lesotho, Malawi and Swaziland. In Tanzania, for example, already existing elected village governments have been declared the legal administrators of all land within the village area.[14] Other states devolve autonomous authority to district levels (for example the district land boards of Botswana, Namibia and Uganda and the commune land commissions of Senegal and Niger). The extent to which chiefs retain traditional powers of allocation varies but with a trend of tempering their powers with legal requirements for more consultative decision-making, often through obligatory elected land committees – the case in Namibia and Mozambique and proposed in Malawi. Constitutional proposals in Kenya to devolve administration do reach the community level in the form of location councils but this does not empower them to govern or regulate, only advise.

Devolution of control over land dispute resolution from formal courts to community based institutions is also appearing in new land laws. Almost everywhere save Eritrea, village level bodies using customary law are being formally recognized as 'courts' of first instance (Alden Wily 2003b). Such developments promise local communities a much higher role in defining and securing their land rights, including those they hold as groups or communities such as over sacred groves.

New limits on the appropriation of commons. Finally, the upgraded status of customary rights in many African states is also constraining willful appropriation of such lands by the state. As formally declared private property, it is less easy in practice than in the past for governments to help themselves to local lands. A particular disincentive is the obligation to pay compensation at the same rates as for other private properties such as land under freehold or leasehold tenure. Improved compensation at compulsory acquisition tends to be initially laid out in new constitutions.[15] The mechanisms are written into new land laws and have been taken to a fine art in South Africa and Tanzania. Tanzanian law for example imposes deliberately laborious procedures upon administrations seeking to arrogate village lands including the approval of the community itself.[16] Nor is compensation limited to payment for the value of lost crops or houses. The full open market value of the land, houses and improvements to the land

---

[14] Village Land Act 1999, s. 8.
[15] For example, in the Constitutions of Lesotho, South Africa, Eritrea and Mozambique.
[16] Village Land Act 1999 s. 4.

is to be calculated and paid along with transport and disturbance allowances.[17] It goes without saying that knowledge of land rights as laid down in new law is essential for rural people to benefit.

Crucially, common properties such as forests and pasture are treated in the same manner as those held individually. As the Tanzanian Forestry Division has already found to its cost in attempting to take over unoccupied village land to make way for an expanded National Forest Reserve, it is a good deal cheaper to drop such plans and instead persuade and assist communities to conserve the forest area themselves as their own property.[18] The Forest Act 2002 now firmly advises ministers seeking to bring more forests under reserved status to consider carefully if the area might not be as well protected under community juris- diction and tenure.[19] Such realities helped prompt legal provision for an entirely new class of non-government forest reserves as described shortly.

Do new forest laws support community interests?

Improving the process of reserve creation. The links between new land and forest policies will be clear. One of the immediate effects of new land legislation in Africa has been to necessitate a fairer process towards national reserve creation in corollary new forest laws. In Senegal, for example, participatory regional commissions have been established to investigate proposals through con- sultative means, lesser versions of which are also provided for in Congo, Benin and Togo.[20] Support from local communities for new government reserves is virtually obligatory under the new forest laws in South Africa, Namibia, Ethiopia and Tanzania.[21]

There is similar new restriction upon the random disposal of forests by governments, a matter of particular concern in Kenya where so many thou- sands of hectares of National Forests have been lost to private purposes (Alden Wily and Mbaya 2001:170–7). De-gazettement of state forests will now require Parliamentary approval and will be disallowed if *inter alia* it jeopardizes cultural site protection.[22] Many new forest laws additionally require compen- sation to be paid for loss of the customary forest use rights that existed if and when a forest reserve is declassified.[23]

Enabling communities to retrieve forests. A more radical provision enables certain national forests to be transferred to local government or community tenure.

---

[17] Village Land Act Regulations 2001; Part III.
[18] Reference is made here to the Derema Forest and Wildlife Corridor to be created out of 800 hectares of village land separating Amani Nature Reserve and Kambai Forest Reserve in Tanga Region. The compensation costs proved prohibitive resulting in the four villages instead being encouraged to create their own Village Forest Reserves (Widagri 2001).
[19] Forest Act 2002; s. 24–25.
[20] Senegal Forest Law 1998 (Art. 43), Congo Forest Bill 2000 (Art. 25), Togo Forest Bill 2000 (Art 16), Benin Forest Law 1993 (Art. 14).
[21] South Africa National Forests Act 1998, s. 9 and 49; Namibia Forest Act 2001, s. 13; Ethiopia Forest Proclamation 1994, Art.4.
[22] Kenya Forests Bill 2004 s. 27.
[23] For example, Namibia Forest Act 2002 s. 18.

This is the case under the land restitution policies of Namibia and South Africa. In Namibia, three very large areas which were scheduled to become new state forests are now in the process of being gazetted as community forests (Alden Wily and Mbaya 2001:60–1). In South Africa, seven National Forests are being restored to community tenure (Grundy *et al.* 2004). Elsewhere such opportunities are more limited, although many clarify the powers of governments as trustee managers, not owners, of reserves and parks.[24] In line with the new devolutionary imperative, forestry departments are increasingly advised by the law to transfer control to more local levels; the case for example in Lesotho and Tanzania.[25] Rural Tanzanians and Ugandans may themselves demand a review of the status of government forests with a view to their reclassification as local level reserves.[26]

Enabling communities to declare their own forest reserves. The structure of opportunity described above hinges directly upon the capacity of local communities to secure local forests as definitively their own property and to have these recognized and supported by new forestry law. It is provision for this which most distinguishes new from old forest enactments opening up a whole new class of non-government forest reserves. Over half of new forest enactments provide directly for variously-named community forests. The details are most developed in the laws of Tanzania, Uganda, Lesotho, Malawi, Namibia, The Gambia, Cameroon, Senegal and Guinea (Alden Wily and Mbaya 2001, Alden Wily 2003a). In practice, most are established only permissively, through formal agreement with state agencies and on the basis of an agreed management plan[27] or other limitations.[28] Sometimes formal survey and mapping of the forest is required, significantly delaying finalization (e.g. The Gambia) or raising costs for the community (e.g. Cameroon, Bongartz *et al.* 2003). A main exception is Tanzania where the law provides for formalization and registration of village and community forest reserves at the district level.[29]

The main arena for the declaration of community forests is off-reserve, within already customarily-held lands. It is within this context that the improving legal status of customary rights is so important for local forest holders. Where customary rights have not been significantly upgraded as private property rights, a community forest may not be recognized as fully locally owned (the case, for example, in Cameroon, Zimbabwe, Eritrea and Rwanda). Early drafts of Kenya's Forests Bill made provision for community forests but removed this in later drafts. Should the draft Constitution 2004 enter law, then many of the forests which the current Forest Bill refers to as local authority forests would, however, have to be reclassified as community-owned forests

---

[24] For example in the Madagascan forest law of 2001.

[25] Lesotho Forestry Act 1999, s. 11 (3), Tanzania Forest Act 2002, section 29 (1).

[26] Tanzania Forest Act 2002, s. 39, Uganda Forests and Tree Planting Act 2003, s. 16.

[27] For example Malawi Forestry Act 1997, s.31; South Africa National Forests Act 1998, s. 29–31.

[28] In Cameroon, for example, Community Forests may be established only in unclassified forest and are restricted to 5,000 hectares and ten-year agreement periods (MINEF 1998).

[29] Forest Act 2002, s. 34.

and, as noted above, these definitively include all those of cultural significance to the community.

Sacred groves as community forest reserves. As examined earlier, the degree to which community forests are shaped around socio-cultural attributes is relatively slight, although it is surely within their context that sacred forests are already being secured and may be formalized. Perhaps most consideration to socio-cultural factors is given by the Tanzanian Forest Act 2002 which provides not only for communities to create and declare community-owned forests out of local land areas, but for sub-groups of the community to do so as well. Whilst the former are to be registered as Village Land Forest Reserves, the latter may be registered as Community Forestry Reserves. These may be established by groups within the community 'which have strong traditional ties to the forest' (s. 42), and which have been 'formed in accordance with customary law' (s. 43). The law allows these groups to 'exercise existing rights to enter, occupy, use and harvest the products of the forest' although 'in a sustainable manner and in accordance with any by-laws, rules, or agreements made with the village council' (s. 47). More than 500 Village Forest Reserves have already been declared and registered, bringing more than half a million hectares of threatened forest under protected status (Alden Wily 2003a).

Engaging communities as forest managers. Virtually all new forest enactments provide directly for community participation in the management of forests, by contract or otherwise. The extent of participation varies widely. Sometimes this is little more than a legal obligation to consult with forest-adjacent communities (e.g. Côte d'Ivoire, Ghana, and Rwanda, Alden Wily 2003a).

The ability to determine how a forest may be accessed and used in the first place, including the right to define and exclude outsiders, remains elusive for many community managers.[30] Nor have more than a handful of country cases made it yet definitively possible for communities to regulate access and management in ways which courts are obliged to uphold should these rules be challenged. A prominent exception is Tanzania where communities have for some time been able to pass village by-laws under the aegis of their elected local governments (Village Councils). The achievement by communities of regulatory and policing powers is proving an important ambition and challenge in many cases. For in practice – and there is a great deal of implementation of new forest management paradigms – the concretization inherent in the declaration of a community forest does seem to establish a platform for the community to seek and root stronger local roles and powers. This is being seen clearly in Cameroon, Senegal, Nigeria, Madagascar, Ethiopia, Malawi and Namibia.[31]

Legal provision for the transfer of full management authority over national

[30] Most notably the case in Zambia, Rwanda and Ethiopia (Alden Wily 2003a).

[31] For example in the endowment of stronger rights for communities to regulate forest use themselves (Nigeria, Ethiopia, Namibia, Malawi), the relaxation of Government veto powers over the content of community designed management plans (Cameroon) or the extension of contracts for longer periods (Madagascar, Senegal).

forests to communities is technically availed in the forest laws of South Africa, Lesotho, Namibia, Burkina Faso, Uganda and potentially Kenya, but most fully developed and applied in The Gambia and Tanzania. The latter encourage communities to apply to manage state forests and provide new classifications to encompass these areas; Community Controlled State Forests in The Gambia and Village Forest Management Areas in Tanzania (to distinguish these from community owned and managed Village and Community Forest Reserves).[32] Tanzania is also possibly the only state where community participation is obligatory in all forest classes, and through which communities may act to secure socio-cultural forest access.[33]

Permitting communities and groups to apply traditional principles to management. Finally, there remains the question as to how far local actors may apply traditional approaches to forest management, a crucial consideration where the primary purpose of legally securing tenurial or managerial rights over the forest is socio-ritual. Direct provision for this is scarce. It is not the Forest Bill, for example, in Kenya which allows for this but the proposed new constitution which declares that communities shall have the right to apply traditional principles to management of community lands (Art. 239). Traditional procedures are also protected in respect of Mozambique's areas of historical and cultural value.[34] Elsewhere, this right must be assumed, even for such obviously traditional forests as the Laredo of Lesotho and the Dedicated Forests of Ghana. It may be assumed that where community forest is declared on the basis of social rather than economic values, customary modes will acceptably be applied. A contrary trend, however, limits powers which chiefs, headmen or other leaders or interest groups may have garnered at the expense of community-wide interests. There are also social justice concerns such as relating to the rights of women. Therefore whilst customary practice is accepted, a number of laws proscribe this. Thus, groups managing community forests in Tanzania are cautioned to review the customs, practices and rights of group members with a view to amending those which could jeopardize sound and fair management.[35]

Conclusion

In summary, several broad conclusions emerge. First, it seems that direct legal support for sacred groves is limited. Only two countries reviewed have made specific legal provision for this: Lesotho and Mozambique, with (less clear) provision forthcoming in Kenya. Legal arrangements for owner-managers of sacred forests to practice customary norms are provided unevenly or in uncertain ways. Socio-cultural factors in general are given a low profile overall, with more dominant emphasis upon the economic values of forests to communities.

[32] The Gambia Forest Act 1998, s. 73; Tanzania Forest Act 2002, s. 30–1.
[33] Forest Act 2002, s. 11 and 13.
[34] Forest and Wildlife Act 1999 Art.13.
[35] Forest Act 2002, s. 46–7.

Second, a range of significant new opportunities nonetheless exist through which social groups may secure sacred groves. This is occurring mainly through the new legal construct of community forests. There is little to no restriction against such areas being established for socio-cultural reasons. In practice (and practice has not been covered in this paper), the majority are being declared for a mix of social, economic and environmental reasons.

Third, it has been shown how changing land tenure policies and, in particular, the acceptance of customary land rights as statutorily protected, are dramatically improving the capacity of communities to legally hold on to their shared resources, sacred groves included. The right to hold land in common is itself being slowly but surely assured. Nor is it as easy as in the past for governments to appropriate these commons to themselves, either for alternative public use or for protection. This goes hand in hand with the very rapid evolution since 1990 of communities as the recognised front-line conservators.

With so much progress in place, the need for promotional action for sacred groves seems slight. In reality, however, inattention to socio-cultural values represents an enormous gap in the still-evolving paradigms and one that takes little advantage of the role socio-cultural objectives have in inspiring and sustaining forest protection at community level. This is to the loss of forest conservation, particularly where communities find that the much-promoted economic values of forests do not yield the returns anticipated, or do so in ways which divide rather than bind the community. Awareness-raising among policy-makers and practitioners to balance emphasis upon the returns to livelihood with the returns of socio-cultural values, seems in order.

References

Adeleke, W., 2003, 'Collaborative forest management in West Africa'. Paper presented to AFLEG Ministers Conference in Yaoundé, Cameroon, 12–16 October 2003. Washington, DC: World Bank.

Alden Wily, L., 2003a, 'Community forest management in Africa: Progress and challenges in the 21st Century'. In FAO, *Proceedings of the Second International Workshop on Participatory Forestry in Africa*. Rome: FAO.

—— 2003b, *Governance and Land Relations. A Review of Decentralization of Land Administration and Management in Africa*. London: International Institute for Environment and Development.

Alden Wily, L. and S. Mbaya, 2001, *Land, People and Forests in Eastern and Southern Africa at the Beginning of the 21st Century. The Impact of Land Relations on the Role of Communities in Forest Future*. Nairobi: The World Conservation Union (IUCN).

Augustinus, C., 2003, *Comparative Analysis of Land Administration Systems: African Review*. Washington, DC: World Bank.

Bongartz, U., A. Cham and C. Schade, 2003, 'Communities as forest managers and owners: Community forestry in The Gambia'. Paper presented to the World Forestry Congress, Quebec, Canada, September 2003.

Bruce, J. and S. Migot-Adholla, eds, 1994, *Searching for Land Tenure Security in Africa*. Dubuque, IA: Kendall/Hunt Pub. Co.

FAO, 2001, *State of the World's Forests 2001*. Rome: FAO.

—— 2002, 'Law and sustainable development since Rio. Legal trends in agriculture and natural resource management'. *FAO Legislative Study*, 73. Rome: FAO.

—— 2003, *Proceedings of the Second International Workshop on Participatory Forestry in Africa*. Rome: FAO.

Golan, E., 1994, 'Land tenure reform in the peanut basin of Senegal'. In *Searching for Land Tenure Security in Africa*, J. Bruce and S. Migot-Adholla, eds, pp. 231–49. Dubuque, IA: Kendall/Hunt Pub. Co.

Grundy, I., B. Campbell, R. White, R. Prabhu, S. Jensen and T. Ngamile, 2004, 'Participatory forest management in conservation areas: The case of Cwebe, South Africa'. *Forests, Trees and Livelihoods* 14:149–65.

Kohler, V., 2001, *Africa: A General Analysis of Forest Laws and Aspects of Implementation in Selected Countries South of the Sahara*. Eschborn, Germany: GWB.

Ministry of Environment and Forests, Government of Cameroon (MINEF), 1998, *Manual of the Procedures for the Attribution and Norms for the Management of Community Forests*. Yaoundé: Government of Cameroon.

Natural Resources Services (NRS), 2003, *Final Report: Botswana National Land Policy Review*. Gaborone: Government of Botswana.

Palmer, R., 2000, 'Land policy in Africa: Lessons from recent policy and implementation processes'. In *Evolving Land Rights, Policy and Tenure in Africa*. C. Toulmin and J. Quan, eds, pp. 267–88. London: DFID/NRI/IIED.

Ribot, J., 1999, 'Decentralisation, participation and accountability in Sahelian Forestry: Legal instruments of political-administrative control'. *Africa* 69(1):23–64.

Toulmin, C., and J. Quan, eds, 2000, *Evolving Land Rights, Policy and Tenure in Africa*. London: DFID/NRI/IIED.

Widagri Consultants Ltd., 2001, *Mid-Term Review of the East Usamabara Conservation Area Management Programme, Tanzania*. Helsinki: Wigdari Consultants Ltd.

Index

Congo 12, 215
Congo-Brazzaville 23
Congo River 66
Connell, J. 17
conservation 1-4 *passim*, 6, 7, 9, 10, 12, 13, 15-
  17, 25-30 *passim*, 42-61, 69, 84, 87, 88, 97-
  100, 103; 117-32, 164-6, 175-6, 193, 197-8,
  203, 205, 207, 219; costs of 198;
  International - and Development Programs
  203
Constitutions 210, 212 *see also* under individual
  countries
consultation, spiritual 197
Conteh, J.S. 57
Cooke, John A. 2, 62-86
Cooper, C. 137, 138
Copans, J. 143
coral 84
Corlett, R.T. 43, 54
coronations 4, 136-8 *passim*, 140, 141
corruption 64
cosmology 9, 105, 112, 115, 130
Côte d'Ivoire 5, 149-63, 173n12, 211-14 *passim*,
  217; Beng forest 5, 149-63
cotton 166-7, 170-2 *passim*, 174
courts 4, 185, 214
Couty, Ph. 143
creation, of sacred groves 6, 179, 180, 187-90,
  193, 196-8
Crumley, Carole 17
Culmsee, Heike 3, 87-102
cults 186
culture 9, 10, 12, 20, 29, 44-7, 57, 62, 70-1, 77,
  87-92, 115, 131, 134, 164-5, 197, 202, 210

Dahomey 168, 169
Daily, G.C. 43
Dalziel, J.M. 136
Darlington, Susan 11
Davies, G. 58
Davies, O. 179
debt 111
decentralization 12, 13, 28, 106, 133, 203, 209,
  214
Decher, J. 47
decolonization 20
De Corse, C.R. 57
defense, of forests 46, 83, 168-9, 173, 174
deforestation 9, 10, 12, 17, 42, 55, 114, 117,
  123, 160, 207
de-gazettement 215
degradation 2-4 *passim*, 6, 17, 64, 77, 79, 97,
  110, 111, 119, 132, 195, 196, 198, 201, 202,
  205
Deighton, F.C. 47
Deil, Ulrich 3, 87-102
deities/gods 5-6, 105-7 *passim*, 109, 114, 162,
  167-76, 188-92 *passim*
De Jong, Ferdinand 24
Demanet, Abbé 139

De Marees, Peter 191, 192
dendrochronology 84, 136
Denianké kings 138
desertification 17
destruction, forest 2, 5, 55, 56, 64, 84, 106,
  113-14, 186-7 *see also* deforestation
development, sustainable 9, 15
devolution 214, 216
Dia, Amadi 140
Diallo, Cheikh Oumy Mbacké 134
Diaw, Dame 141
Dieye, Ch. A. 143
Diop, D. 143
Diouf, B. 139, 142
Diouf, Hadi 141
Diouf, M. 140
diseases 42, 190
dispute settlement 139, 214
disturbance 2, 43, 46, 51, 54, 80, 97, 98, 196,
  201 *see also* human agency
diversity, biological 1, 2, 7, 9, 12, 27, 29, 43,
  57, 87, 117 *see also* biodiversity;
  cultural/social 1, 9, 12, 27, 29, 202; ethnic
  202
diviners 152, 154, 155, 158
Doneux, L. 140
Doornbos, Martin 28
Dorm-Adzobu, C. 10, 47
Douglas, Mary 25-6, 146
Dramé, Fodé Heraba 137
drought 67, 73, 197
Dublin, H.T. 65
Dudley, Nigel 9
Dunbar, R.J. 65
Durkheim, Emile 13
Dury, S. 22, 87
Dutch 178, 183, 184

East Africa 12, 65, 67 *see also* individual entries
earthworks 46, 57
Eco, Umberto 146
ecology 1, 5, 7, 9, 10, 12, 13, 15-20, 29, 84, 87,
  100, 103-7 *passim*, 115, 179, 196, 200-1
education 44, 62
Egerton, F.N. 16
Ehrich, P.R. 43
elders 5, 43, 64, 68, 70, 74-8 *passim*, 83, 170,
  171, 185, 188, 196, 197
elephants 55, 64, 65, 69
elites 23, 104, 106, 115, 179, 186, 192, 193
Ellenberg, H. 47
Ellis, Stephen, 24, 27
Elton, C. 17
Elwert, Georg 166, 174
Emberger, L. 92
endemism 62
environment 9, 11, 16, 17, 84
equilibrium 15-17 *passim*, 28, 29
Eritrea 214, 216
erosion, soil 113